Reputation Capital

Joachim Klewes · Robert Wreschniok

Editors

Reputation Capital

Building and Maintaining Trust
in the 21st Century

 Springer

Editors

Prof. Dr. Joachim Klewes
Pleon GmbH
Bahnstr. 2
40212 Düsseldorf
Germany
joachim.klewes@pleon.com

Robert Wreschniok
Pleon GmbH
Theresienhöhe 12
80339 München
Germany
robert.wreschniok@pleon.com

ISBN 978-3-642-01629-5   e-ISBN 978-3-642-01630-1
DOI 10.1007/978-3-642-01630-1
Springer Heidelberg Dordrecht London New York

Library of Congress Control Number: 2009933415

Cover design: WMXDesign GmbH, Heidelberg

Printed on acid-free paper

Springer is part of Springer Science+Business Media (www.springer.com)

Contents

Part II: The business case for reputation

Part III: The 21st century of reputation crisis

Part IV: New perspectives for reputation management in the 21st century

Part V: Reputation strategies for the 21st century

Part VI: Appendix

Reputation capital
Building and maintaining trust in the 21st century

Introduction

About reputation capital

Given the speed and diversity of the information on offer in today's global media society, the saturation of markets with high-quality, yet almost indistinguishable products, and a global shortage of qualified specialists, it is no longer self-evident that companies can retain employees and suppliers, keep their customers' loyalty, or convince investors to hold on to their shares for the long term. A growing tension is emerging between the emancipation of consumers and employees on the one hand, and their disorientation in a sea of information and goods on the other. Here, reputation is becoming more important as an intangible corporate asset and a means of orientation in society. This is because, for a long time now, product and price strategies have no longer been the only decisive factors for competition. Instead, the focus has increasingly turned to the competence, integrity and the attractiveness of a company in the battle for stakeholder trust. As Alan Greenspan already noted in 2001: "Over time, and particularly during the last decade or two, reputation has become the most important corporate value." As we approach the end of the first decade of the 21st century, Greenspan will probably be aware just how right he was. For we are now witnessing the outbreak of the biggest crisis in finance, the economy and confidence in more than 50 years. The massive write-downs in reputation capital resulting from this global crisis of confidence have meant that many now must do without this valuable asset, which had previously helped ...

J. Klewes, R. Wreschniok (eds.), *Reputation Capital*, DOI 10.1007/978-3-642-01630-1_1,
© Springer-Verlag Berlin Heidelberg 2009

- … release reputation bearers from the burden of being constantly monitored and reduce the likelihood of government or public supervision and control.

- … strengthen client trust, ease the recruitment and retention of capable employees and improve access to capital markets or attract investors.

- … legitimate positions of power and build up reserves of trust which allowed companies and politicians – but also researchers and journalists – to put their issues on the public agenda, present them credibly and mould them in their own interests.

But a fear of loss is not the only reason for the steadily increasing importance of reputation in corporate management today (or more especially, in the minds of top management). Rather, the main reason is that corporate reputation has shifted from being an unquantifiable 'soft' factor to a measurable indicator in the sense of management control. And it is a variable that is obviously relevant to a company's performance: recent studies by the European Centre for Reputation Studies and the Ludwig-Maximilians-Universität of Munich compared the stock market performance of a portfolio of the top 25% of reputation leaders (based on regular reputation measurements in the wider public) with that of the German DAX 30 stock market index. The results show that a portfolio consisting of reputation leaders outperformed the stock market index by up to 45% – and with less risk.[1]

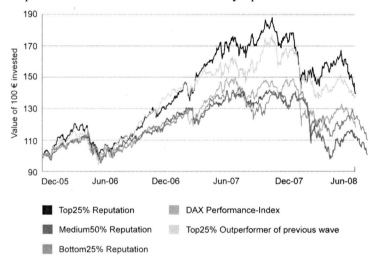

Fig. 1. Performance of 'reputation portfolios' vs. the DAX index
Source: LMU München, IMM

---

[1] See the article by Schwaiger (pp. 39-55) in this volume.

Building and maintaining trust in the 21st century

How can reputation capital be accumulated and managed, especially in the context of global markets and information streams? How can this fragile asset be secured and preserved in hard times as well? How does reputation impact on the behaviour of various stakeholders across the world, and which specific opportunities and challenges does globalisation present for successful reputation management? These questions are answered by an international team of authors in theory and practice in this book, "Reputation capital – Building and maintaining trust in the 21st century". Experts from various disciplines present concrete solutions for implementing reputation management in a world of global markets and issues, and shed light on the concept of reputation from a number of angles.

In our view, the term 'reputation' can best be understood as the sum of the expectations that the public places on the future behaviour of an agent or institution – based on the public's direct or indirect experiences (for example, via the media). Expectations, if fulfilled, produce the transitory asset of trust. Over time, this can crystallise into reputational capital. Reputation management, then, is in many respects also a question of managing expectations. Yet one should draw certain distinctions among stakeholder expectations: for example, a company must not only fulfil expectations regarding its functional competence (economic reputation), but also those regarding its integrity (social reputation). In addition, a positive reputation also requires maintaining an unmistakable and emotionally appealing identity (expressive reputation). Reputation management is therefore always subject to a tension between adaptation (expectation management) and delimitation (identity management).[2] If this balance can be struck, a positive reputation will secure a company or organisation long-term competitive advantages.

Yet the difficulty of striking this balance is clearly demonstrated from the very first part of this volume: "Reputation in the 21st century – Good or evil?" It contains two articles that, despite their different perspectives, agree on the central importance of communication in establishing reputation: "Trust and reputation in the age of globalisation" by Mark Eisenegger, who heads the Research Institute for the Public Sphere and Society (Forschungsbereich Öffentlichkeit und Gesellschaft, fög) at the University of Zurich, and "Reputation or: How I learned to stop worrying and love the market", by Jonathan Silberstein-Loeb of the Oxford University Centre for

---

[2] See the article by Eisenegger (pp. 11-22) in this volume.

Corporate Reputation. Both these articles open up a controversial debate on the meaning of reputation in the 21st century.

In the second part, "The business case for reputation", the authors explore the significance of reputation in detail. Manfred Schwaiger, who heads the Institut für Marktorientierte Unternehmensführung (Institute for Market-Based Management) at the Ludwig-Maximilians-Universität in Munich, demonstrates in his article "Recognition or rejection: How a company's reputation influences stakeholder behaviour" how reputation measurably affects not only stakeholder behaviour, but even a company's fortunes on the stock market. The following article, "What's measurable gets done – Communication controlling as a prerequisite for successful reputation management", is by Reimer Stobbe of Münchner Rück, who also heads the task force for communication controlling at the International Controller Association. He argues that it is necessary to view reputation factors from a controlling perspective so that they can be integrated into management processes. Kelvin Thompson, who locates and helps to place top executives worldwide, concentrates in "The role of corporate and personal reputations in the global war for talent" on reputation's role in employee branding, and examines which management factors really matter in the current crisis. This is followed by "The CSR myth: true beauty comes from within", a joint article by the Swiss reputation researcher Matthias Vonwil and Robert Wreschniok, who is responsible for reputation management issues on the consultancy side. They explain, using recent studies, why communicating corporate social responsibility can achieve a lot, but is of limited benefit when it comes to sustainably improving corporate reputation. The final article in the chapter, "The Brussels reputation story – the interplay of public affairs and reputation" by Brussels public affairs expert Peter Lochbihler, shows that there is a limit to what conventional communications can achieve in political lobbying, too – and even more so in Brussels when dealing with the European Union.

Risk is the focus of the third part in this volume: "The 21st century of reputation crisis". First, a completely new approach in the controversial debate about enterprise and reputational risk management is presented by an Anglo-French team headed by Jean-Paul Louisot, who teaches risk management at the Sorbonne in Paris, and Alex Hindson, Head of Enterprise Risk Management at AON Global Risk Consulting, in their trilogy on the management of reputational risk: "Managing reputational risk – A cindynic approach", "Managing reputational risk – Case studies" and "Managing reputational risk – From theory to practice". We are especially pleased that, with these articles, we can venture beyond the Anglo-American perspective, which tends to dominate current debates. Meanwhile, Hans Caspar von der Crone, a Zurich lawyer and law professor, opens up the field even further with his article "Regulation failure – The greatest threat to reputation", which questions the role of market and state regulators. Frank Herkenhoff, who heads media relations at Deutsche Börse AG, provides a conceptual framework for the approaches put forward in "Measuring risks to reputation". This article will be especially useful to those in charge of communications within companies who wish to identify and evaluate corporate reputational risks even more precisely. Ansgar Thießen of the University of Freiburg then adds another exciting aspect to the publicity risks explored by Herkenhoff: namely, the question of whether crisis communications is not itself becoming a new risk for corporate reputation ("Crisis management in the media society – Communicative integrity as the key to safeguarding reputation in a crisis"). The third chapter closes with two articles that draw on practical experience. One is by Jeremy Cohen, formerly responsible for branding at Shell, who explores the subject of 'greenwash' in his succinct article "Getting the stain out of sustainable brands". The other is by Dirk Popp, who heads the Crisis Management Practice at Pleon. In quite concrete terms, he shows which instruments will and won't work for crisis communications today in "Our reputation is at stake – Corporate communications in the light of the global economic downturn".

This sets the stage for the fourth part of the book, "New perspectives for reputation management in the 21st century". The chapter begins – how else? – with Barack Obama in an article by community branding expert Joachim Kuss: "Community reputation communicates change to the world". And it is a world that could change significantly for Turkey, depending on whether or not it succeeds in joining the European Union. The interview "EU accession: Turkey's reputation on its journey towards EU membership" sees Julia Schankin, an expert for country reputation management at the European Centre for Reputation Studies, in conversation with Arzuhan Doğan Yalçındağ, head of the Turkish Industrialists' and Businessmen's Association (TUSIAD). They discuss Turkey's opportunities, hurdles and reputation management activities. Joachim Klewes forges a link to the corporate world in his article "Consistency: a proven reputation strategy – How companies can optimise their message", which shows how complex addressing target groups has become for companies. And their messages, as Robert Wreschniok shows in "The Agora of the 21st century: On the invention of many-to-one communication", are increasingly reverberating in the marketplaces and opinion forums of the new social media. An interim summary is then made by the British reputation researchers Gary Davies and Rosa Chun, who point to "The leader's role in managing reputation" – regardless of whether one is managing the reputation of a community, a nation or a company. The chapter is rounded off with three case studies on reputation management from various industries: first, beverages in "Watching reputation grow – Reputation management by Coca-Cola Hellenic" by Jens Rupp, the Coca-Cola Hellenic Sustainability Manager since 2005, then luxury goods in "Never underestimate the importance of details" by Tomaso Galli, the long-standing head of communications at Prada, and finally the pharmaceutical industry, with an article by the former German Federal Health Minister, Andrea Fischer ("Is there no prescription? Reputation in the pharmaceutical industry").

In the final chapter, "Reputation strategies for the 21st century", editors Joachim Klewes and Robert Wreschniok present an outlook, describing four concrete reputation strategies that can help to accumulate and utilise valuable reputation capital in the 21st century – and safeguard it against loss. In doing so, the authors pose a question that is not all that easy to answer: who will be the first reputation millionaire of the 21st century? So, what would your response be?

Acknowledgements

First, you fashion the book according to yourself, and then yourself according to the book.

Jean Paul (1763–1825)

In all frankness: from the beginning, we had very clear ideas about the topics that had to be included in a volume on reputation management in the 21st century. In our work for international companies and organisations, not a day goes by without us dealing with the issue. We have felt challenged personally as consultants in reputation matters by the crisis of confidence that, during our work on this book, has assumed ever greater dimensions. And it was clear to us from the start that we would have to approach this topic not from a European, American or Asian perspective, but from a global perspective – that is, with an international team of authors. And, with just as much frankness: owing to this international perspective and the collective work on the articles, which has lasted over a year from conception to publication, a book has emerged that has exposed us as editors to new facets and interrelationships. For this, we would like first of all to thank all the authors, whose excellent articles and unconventional, new perspectives on reputation management have made **Reputation Capital: Reputation Capital. Building and Maintaining Trust in the 21st Century** a book capable of providing both theoretical insights and practical guidance. Further thanks go to the colleagues at Pleon, especially Ralf Langen, Frank Behrendt and Timo Sieg, and the entire international team at the European Centre for Reputation Studies. We also would like to thank Dr. Niels Peter Thomas of Springer Verlag for his patient and very helpful support.

Particular thanks are due to Julia Schankin, who not only has managed the entire project untiringly and reliably, keeping her good humour throughout, but also has contributed her expertise in the area of country reputation management in one of the most exciting articles in this volume. Further, we would like to thank Thomas Fischer, Sarah Jüttner, Saskia Schirmann, Susann Hoffmann, Mariya Mihaylova, Jürgen Langhanns and the Reputation Management Team in Munich for their continuous support and their helpful advice.

And especially because – as many readers will know – it is a real challenge to combine everyday work with work on a book, we would like to thank our families for their understanding and support. So, a huge thank you to Lisa, Paulina, Titus, Christina, David, Julian, Sarah and Geraldine. And last but not least, this book would not have been published had it not been for the skills and commitment of our translators Rowan Payton and Miles Staveley. A warm thank you to both of them.

As the editors of this volume, we of course remain solely responsible for any remaining shortcomings. We therefore welcome your comments, critical or supportive: please send us an e-mail to

joachim.klewes@pleon.com and robert.wreschniok@pleon.com.

Düsseldorf/Munich,   *Joachim Klewes*
July 2009   *Robert Wreschniok*

Part I: Reputation in the 21st century −
   Good or evil?

*Character is like a tree and reputation like its shadow. The shadow is what
we think of it; the tree is the real thing.*

Abraham Lincoln (1809-1865)

Trust and reputation in the age of globalisation

Mark Eisenegger

It will be shown in this paper that the reputation of all agents in our society invariably consists of three components. Firstly, their own competence and associated successes must be continuously demonstrated (functional reputation). Secondly, agents must adhere to social norms and values in a responsible way (social reputation). And thirdly, every agent relies on an emotionally attractive profile to separate him sharply from his competitors (expressive reputation). On the basis of this three-dimensional reputation approach, it is examined how the logic of reputation constitution has changed in the age of globalisation. Among other things, it becomes evident that the greatest reputation risks lurk in the sector of social reputation. In today's global communications society, significantly more attention is generated by denouncing moral misconduct than by honouring socially responsible behaviour. In particular, companies that boast in their external communications of having a clean vest carry a high risk of falling into the "moral trap". One of the rules of successful reputation management described in this paper is consequently: credible social commitment builds on actions and not on words. This rule applies all the more strongly at times like the current crisis of the financial markets. The concluding focus of this paper is directed to this crisis and its consequences for the reputation dynamics in the economy and society.

Trust and reputation – Fundamental and indispensable

It is trust – not power, wealth, or even love – that is the most important operational resource in our society. Why? Without trust, we would simply be unable to act. If we were not able to trust third parties to act as we expect them to act, we would do anything to avoid getting ourselves involved with them. For example, we would never think of entrusting our money to a bank in the crisis zone of Iraq. We would like to have faith that our bank

J. Klewes, R. Wreschniok (eds.), *Reputation Capital*, DOI 10.1007/978-3-642-01630-1_2,
© Springer-Verlag Berlin Heidelberg 2009

will comply with social standards, that we are not being duped or even cheated. And we want to be confident that the bank will handle our money competently and in our interest. The more we have learned to trust an agent (for example, a company), the more comfortable we are likely to be relying on that agent in the long term. For, trust is based on the experience that an agent has fulfilled our expectations in the past. And trust creates confidence that that agent will also fulfil our expectations in the future. For this reason, trust cements existing relations and at the same time acts as a magnet for future relations. Obviously, this applies not only in business. The same law holds in politics and other areas, even in our everyday lives and personal relationships.

However, it is only in rare cases that we can base our trust in those with whom we interact on our own experience. And this is where reputation comes in. For, whenever we are unable to rely on our own experience, we must fall back on the recommendations and judgements of others. Such recommendations, however, are nothing else but reputation judgements, which we then use to guide us – among other reasons, because it saves time and money. Whether we are deciding on a lawyer, a banking partner, a school for our children or which politician we should vote for, reputation judgements play a role that is central – and, in most cases, even decisive. Much more often than is commonly suspected, trust in those with whom we interact is based on the judgements of others, which influence us through direct or indirect communication (such as the media).

The true, the good and the beautiful – Three-dimensional reputation

But what is reputation? Or: what are the elements that constitute a reputation? Irrespective of which agent we consider, be it a company, a politician, or even an academic, an agent's reputation always consists of precisely three reputation dimensions.

The idea that agents must continually prove themselves in three respects is an extremely important theorem in the social sciences. Even the ancient Greek philosophers Plato and Aristotle distinguished the worlds of the good, the beautiful and the true (Wilber 1999: 50ff.). On this idea, the enduring respect of the ancient community would only be accorded those citizens who served the world of truth in their activities, showed themselves to be virtuous citizens in the world of good and also demonstrated the requisite inner and outward grace in the world of the beautiful. The same trio appears in Kant's famous three critiques in the form of objective, ethical and aesthetic judgements (Kant 2004a-c). We also see these three forms of judgement in Sir Karl Popper's distinction between an objective, a subjective and a social world (Popper/Eccles 1982). And, last but not least, these three dimensions make up the core of Jürgen Habermas's theory of communicative action, with his three validity claims (Geltungsansprüche): propositional truth, normative rightness and subjective truthfulness (Habermas 1984).

These three relationships to the world form the basis of our three-pronged approach to reputation, which can be applied to any chosen reputation bearer and which consists of three reputation dimensions: the functional, the social and the expressive (Eisenegger 2005; Eisenegger/Imhof 2008: 125ff.).

First, agents must, in the world of the true, prove their competence and demonstrate the required success. This functional reputation is proven in relation to the performance goals of the various functional systems (politics, the economy etc.). In the economic system, for example, it is measured by a company's profits. This reputation dimension follows a strictly fact-based logic: functional success or failure is measured by figures that can be objectively verified.

Second, reputation bearers must prove themselves in the social world of the good. This gives rise to the concept of social reputation. The central question here is to what extent actors are 'good citizens': that is, whether they simply trample on others in pursuit of success, or whether they act responsibly, in line with social norms and values. Having an intact social reputation requires following codified and non-codified social norms.

Further, losses of reputation in the social world weigh more heavily than losses of reputation in the objective world. Doubts about functional competence can be dispelled by demonstrating fresh success. Perceived moral deficiencies, on the other hand, have a longer-lasting effect on reputation, and can usually only be remedied with radical measures – such as publicly admitting fault.

Third, agents also possess an expressive reputation. Whereas judgements are fact-based for the functional reputation dimension and ethically based for the social reputation dimension, it is judgements of taste that dominate in the world of the beautiful (Kant 2004c). Reputation bearers are judged according to the emotional attractiveness of their individual character and according to how unique they appear. Agents with a positive expressive reputation appear fascinating, sympathetic and unique (see the summary in Table 1).

Table 1. Functional, social and expressive reputation

	Functional reputation	Social reputation	Expressive reputation
Reputation reference	Objective world of the true	Social world of the good	Subjective world of beautiful
	Performance tagets of function systems	Ethical standards	Individual character and identity
Reputation indicators	Competence; sucess	Integrity; responsibilty	Attractiveness; uniqueness
Appraisal style	Cognitive-rational	Ethical	Emotional
Reputation intermediaries	Agents with a cognitive world reference, i.e. expert, scientists,analysts, expert media etc.	Agents with an ethical world reference, i.e. political agents, NGO, intellectuals, mass media etc.	Agents with an aesthetic world reference, i.e. communications and style advisors, artists; designers, mass media etc.

Source: Eisenegger/Imhof 2008 p. 130

Thus it is always these three dimensions – the functional, the social and the expressive reputation dimensions – that interact to form the reputation of an agent. And this is true regardless of the domain in which the agent operates.

Our personal reputation, too, is always constituted at these three levels. Thus, we cultivate our functional reputation by showing ourselves to be successful and competent in our business lives. Second, we nurture our social reputation, clearly signaling that we are people of integrity – partners, buddies, friends, who act responsibly. And third – the match-winner – we do everything to be noticed and found fascinating. To avoid being seen as a bore or as a run-of-the-mill person: this is the goal of personal, expressive reputation management.

We are now in a position to describe the secret of positive reputation. Agents with an intact reputation successfully advance the aims of their organisation (functional reputation), they act responsibly (social reputation) and they have a profile that clearly delimits them from the competition (expressive reputation).

All in all, the secret of positive reputation centres around striking the difficult balance between adaptation to functional and socio-moral expectations and successful expressive delimitation (see Figure 1). It is important to emphasize this aspect of delimitation: successful reputation management requires occasionally not bowing to a social trend in order to remain true to one's self-image. To return to the example of banks used in the introduction: the ability of some banks to withstand the pressure of the derivatives industry in past years – that is, by staying focused on longer-term and more sustainable goals – has yielded dividends, at least, in the current financial crisis.

Functional reputation:	Fulfilling functional performance expectations	Adaptation
Social reputation:	Fulfilling socio-ethical expectations	
Expressive reputation:	Nurturing an emotional attractive identity	Delimitation

The secret of a positive reputation depends on a delicate balance between adaptation (expectation management) and delimitation (identity management)!

Fig. 1. Reputation management in tension between adaptation and delimitation
Source: Eisenegger/Imhof 2008 p. 131

Why is reputation important?

Reputation, then, creates confidence in functionally appropriate and morally correct behaviour and increases the expressive conspicuousness of its bearer. This points to the functions that reputation as a factor can fulfil.

There is considerable research already on the commercial utility of reputation. An intact reputation makes it easier to create customer bonds and attract competent personnel. It increases access to capital and reduces credit-related costs. Generally, a superior reputation erects for companies a barrier that forestalls customer loss, and keeps market predators at bay (Schwaiger 2004). Yet, merely listing such economic functions – however central they may be – by no means does justice to the importance of reputation. For, in our society at large, reputation performs a fundamental steering function.

One elementary function of reputation, from a global social perspective, is to legitimate disparities in power. Power vested in those above must be recognised by those below to be regarded as legitimate. Power that cannot be secured by means of violence or repression has to be earned by an adequate reputation. For this reason, positions of power sooner or later become fragile once reputations sustain significant damage. Not coincidentally, we almost daily learn of high-ranking politicians or CEOs forced from office because their tattered reputation means their position is no longer tenable. And because the modern mass media is skilled in critically examining the reputation of those with status, it plays an increasingly important role in deciding who among the 'top brass' can stay, and who must go.

Additionally, an intact reputation minimises social control. A good name removes the need to continually monitor the actions of reputation bearers. An intact reputation thus gives agents more freedom to act. By contrast, the more besieged the reputation of an institution, organisation or executive board, the greater the pressure to control and regulate them. In such cases, formalised rules (including the possibility of sanctions) compensate for the lack of reputation. It is therefore unsurprising that all substantial regulatory changes in the past have been triggered by reputation crises. The Sarbanes-Oxley Act and the surge in regulation of corporate governance can only be explained against the background of the huge accounting scandals and management excesses around the turn of the millennium. And one does not have to be a prophet to foresee that the current financial crisis and the associated loss of trust in the free-market economy will prompt a plethora of new regulations.

Regularities

Professional reputation management relies on knowing the most important factors that decide whether a good reputation is won or lost.

The following discussion outlines several important findings and how the logical constitution of reputation has changed in the age of globalisation. These findings are based on a study of the reputation history of seven global players in international media from 1965 to 2005.[1]

- Finding 1: Corporate social responsibility issues have become much more important

---

[1] The following companies were analysed: UBS (previously SBG / SBV), Credit Suisse, ABB (previously BBC), Holcim; Novartis (previously Ciba and Sandoz), Roche and Nestlé. The basis for the reputation analysis was the following group of quality newspapers: Neue Zürcher Zeitung, New York Times and Frankfurter Allgemeine Zeitung.

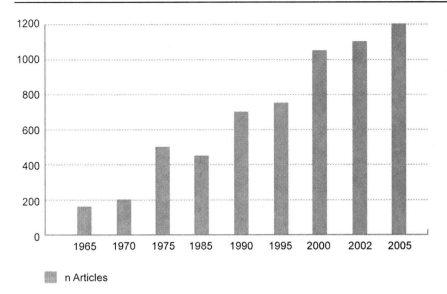

n Articles

Fig. 2. Development of reporting on corporate social responsibility in international news media

In the global age, corporate social responsibility, or social reputation, has become significantly more important. Figure 2 shows that reporting on corporate social responsibility topics increased continually from 1965 with respect to the global players analyzed. How can this be explained? On the one hand, it is important to note that ethical questions have assumed central news value in the international media arena. Questions about 'good' and 'bad' have become core ratings generators in modern journalism. On the other hand, politics has – crucially – not been able to keep up with the globalisation of the economy. Because politics, which for the most part operates at nation-state level, is unable to ensure social well-being on a global scale, pressure has increased on multinationals to assume social responsibility.

• Finding 2: Social reputation is a minefield

Managing one's social reputation has therefore become much more important in the age of globalisation. However, far greater risks attach to social reputation than functional reputation. This is illustrated in Figures 3 and 4.

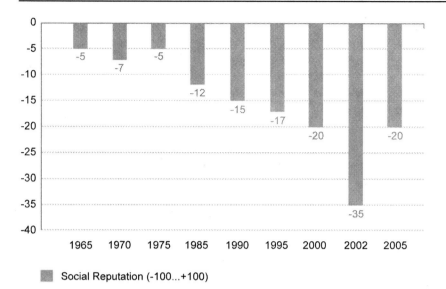

Social Reputation (-100...+100)

Fig. 3. Development of social reputation of analysed global players[2]

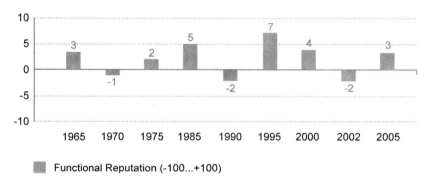

Functional Reputation (-100...+100)

Fig. 4. Development of functional reputation of analysed global players

What is immediately striking is that the values for social reputation (Figure 3) are always lower than those for functional reputation, based on the economic performance of the major corporations analysed (Figure 4). One can summarise this as follows: the world of social reputation is a minefield for global players. For the reputation management of global players this means: functional reputation offers the best opportunities for

---

[2] The reputation index here measures the reputation of the companies analyzed as conveyed by the media. For this, all media reports for a certain time period were coded. The index ranges from +100 to -100. A (hypothetical) value of +100 means that only positive reports on the company were published in the relevant time period. Conversely, a value of -100 means that reports on the company over the time period were exclusively negative.

profiling the corporation. By contrast, as far as social reputation is concerned, a defensive strategy is called for: the aim is not to garner applause, but instead to avoid attracting negative headlines.

Especially those companies that are somewhat too bold in presenting themselves as snow-white in external communications risk stumbling into a ethical trap. This was exactly the mistake made by IT company Google, for example. It wanted to profile itself with the motto "Don't be evil". It then became publicly known that the company was censoring internet sites under pressure from the Chinese regime. Google was accused of violating its own ethical principles. One can learn from this: credible social responsibility is about action, not words. In the social world, companies should quietly comply with social standards without continually broadcasting their commitment. Managing social reputation by public relations alone is perilous.

However, one should draw some distinctions here: the biggest risks in the social world are born by the Goliaths of the economy, that is, the global players. Barely a single large corporation has so far managed to score sustainable points in the social reputation dimension. On the other hand, the Davids – that is, companies that operate locally and regionally – are significantly more successful in the social world. The bigger and more powerful the global player, then, the greater the pressure of expectations and the more critically the actions of these market giants are monitored. It therefore is not surprising that McDonald's (as Number 1 in the market), and not Burger King, is the principal target of the anti-globalisation movement, or that Microsoft, and not Apple, is the preferred target for young hackers. As the size of a company increases, so too does the need to professionalise reputation management.

• Finding 3: Personality cults are harmful

Not only the rash cultivation of social reputation is dangerous, but also an exaggerated personality cult. The more strongly the reputation of a company is fixed to an entrepreneur or CEO, the more vulnerable it is. It is hard to attribute fault for wrongdoing to an abstract entity like an entire company. A famous person, by contrast, can be superbly pilloried. Also, if a company is perceived too exclusively in terms of its top management, it must rebuild its reputation each time management changes. This is expensive. Many companies have underestimated this in the past: they have encouraged a star cult, thus inhibiting the establishment of a sustainable reputation.

In conclusion: The financial market crisis and its consequences

We are now witnessing the biggest financial and economic crisis in 80 years. How will this impact on the dynamics of reputation in the economy and in society? First, we should observe that we are underrating the current financial crisis if we choose to describe it only in terms of hard economic figures. This crisis is not only about nose-diving share prices, the collapse of once-reputable banks and automobile companies, the bankruptcy of entire national economies or the danger of a global recession. This crisis is much more than that. It is a gigantic crisis of trust and reputation for the entire economic system. What began about one and a half years ago with the failure of a small number of mortgage banks, going on to engulf Wall Street and major international banks and now to reach the real economy, has swollen into a genuine crisis of confidence in the entire free market economy. Joseph Stiglitz, the famous Nobel Prize laureate in economics, is probably right in speaking of an end to the economic ideology that has long prevailed: namely, that free, deregulated markets always work better than those supervised by the state.

And so, we are now seeing a new arrangement emerge between the economy, the state and society. The free market economy, in the context of this crisis, is losing reputation, while politics and the state are gaining reputation. There are renewed calls for the state as shareholder and owner, the state as an active player in the economic process. State backing now creates a competitive advantage for the companies taking advantage of this state aid. For a long time the state was seen, especially by these agents, as a hindrance to the market economy. There is, however, the danger that confidence in companies that receive state guarantees will increase, while companies that have no need for such assistance – that is, those that have been circumspect in the past – will lose reputation.

In general, there are good grounds for supposing that the neo-liberal era is at an end. This has not, however, been caused solely by a rediscovery of the state. What matters here is the combination of a social and functional loss of reputation among the ruling, global business elite. This can be seen especially clearly in the development of the 'swindler' (Abzocker) debate about the permissible amount of management remuneration. Up until summer 2008, this issue was debated only at an ethical level. People regarded the often exorbitant salaries of management as perhaps immoral, but not as a threat to the overall system. The debate first began to make an impact when it became linked to the system as a whole: in other words, with the insight that compensation for the business elite and its consequences was not only a manifestation of market principles, but was also complicit in the demise of the free market economy in its neo-liberal form – both in real terms and ideologically. Shareholder value, short-term return targets, irrationally high equity returns, excessive management remuneration and bonuses are today seen as central causes for the irresponsible assumption of risks that have driven the economic system to the brink.

The neo-liberal principles of success, then, have run aground. The result: companies that can credibly combine economic success with social responsibility and that have always been oriented towards guaranteeing sustainable yields are experiencing a boost in confidence through the crisis. Unsurprisingly, there is a revival in reputation for regionally active business and local jobs, while financial market capitalism and the ideology of shareholder value are now massively on the defensive.

Crises of confidence as gigantic as the current one have the power to fundamentally reshape society. Things are sure to remain exciting for some time yet!

References

Eisenegger M (2005) Reputation in der Mediengesellschaft - Konstitution, Issues Monitoring, Issues Management. VS Verlag für Sozialwissenschaften, Wiesbaden

Eisenegger M, Imhof K (2008) The True, The Good and the Beautiful: Reputation Management in the Media Society. In: Zerfass A, Ruler vB, Sriramesh K (eds.) Public Relations Research. European and International Perspectives and Innovations. VS Verlag für Sozialwissenschaften, Wiesbaden:, pp 125-146

Habermas J (1984) The Theory of Communicative Action. Reason and the Rationalization of Society, Volume 1, Beacon Press, Boston

Kant I (2004a) Kritik der reinen Vernunft. Suhrkamp, Frankfurt

Kant I (2004b) Kritik der praktischen Vernunft. Suhrkamp, Frankfurt

Kant I (2004c) Kritik der Urteilskraft. Suhrkamp, Frankfurt

Popper Karl R., Eccles, John C (1997) The Self and Its Brain – An Argument for Interactionism. Piper, München

Schwaiger M (2004) Components and Parameters of Corporate Reputation – an Empirical Study. In: Schmalenbach Business Review, Vol 56 No 1 pp 46-71

Wilber K (1999) Das Wahre, Schöne, Gute. Geist und Kultur im 3. Jahrtausend. Fischer, Frankfurt

Reputation or: How I learned to stop worrying and love the market

Jonathan Silberstein-Loeb

Contrary to popular belief, reputation does not always remedy market imperfections, but may exacerbate them. This is obvious once it is made clear that as a form of belief corporate reputation is akin to testimony. As such, reputation may subsist on unreliable beliefs. Reputation neither holds market actors to account nor is it a panacea for problems associated with tacit, or incomplete, contracts. Once it is clear that reputation may distort the market, it follows that the way in which firms may profit from reputation is by employing it to maximise the advantages of there being scarce, and imperfect, information in the market. A series of propositions for the strategic deployment of reputation follows from this observation. The critical question facing any corporation that would profit by its reputation is the extent to which it can foster an unjustified reputation before the market catches up with it.

Studies concerning corporate reputation often begin with an epigram – typically from Shakespeare – intended, presumably, to indicate the timeless importance of reputation to human relationships. Although Cassio's childish lamentation in Othello about his loss of reputation is oft quoted in this context, noticeably overlooked is Iago's more mercenary reply. Iago advises Cassio not to fret about his loss of reputation. 'Reputation', says Iago, 'is an idle and most false imposition…' (2.3.268-69). Though Iago was a back-stabbing cheat, there is truth in his words, at least more than scholars of corporate reputation typically concede. Critical though its role in economic transactions may be, reputation and the market are at odds. This is because reputation may be unreliable. The interaction of a variety of different forms of information in the market reveals whether a reputation is reliable or not. When other forms of information do not move effectively in the market, an unreliable reputation may persist. It is for this reason that reputation may distort the market. Reputation neither holds market actors to account nor is it a panacea for problems associated with tacit, or incomplete, contracts. If it is a form of social capital, it exhibits some odd

J. Klewes, R. Wreschniok (eds.), *Reputation Capital*, DOI 10.1007/978-3-642-01630-1_3,

characteristics, as it is often a liability and may stymie innovation. The way in which firms may profit from reputation is by employing it opportunistically; which is to say, by using reputation to maximise the advantages of there being scarce, and incomplete, information. A series of propositions for the strategic deployment of reputation follow from this observation, which suggest that the critical question facing any corporation that seeks to profit by its reputation is the extent to which corporations can foster an unreliable reputation before the market catches up.

Reputation and testimony

As a form of information, reputation is similar to testimony. According to one standard definition, corporate reputation is the 'overall estimation in which a company is held by its constituents' (Fombrun 1996, p. 37). In other words, the beliefs or opinions of the community in question determine a company's reputation. This definition is unsatisfactory because it leaves unspecified the nature of the belief involved in reputation. The beliefs that are involved in determining reputation are typically acquired through testimony. In both the case of testimony and reputation, we are interested in the beliefs conveyed by other human agents (as opposed to the acquisition of belief via our senses, or via scientific instruments, or some other form of perception). Although a great number of beliefs arise through testimony, and the inferences drawn from it, accepting or believing such assertions on the word of the speaker may not seem satisfactory. At question is whether the speaker is reliable, but what constitutes a reliable source is not immediately clear, and some background about the source may be critical to such determinations (Bohnet and Huck 2004). In the case of online transactions, such as the purchase of comic books on eBay, reputation must be supplemented by knowledge about the seller. Even then, certification is believed to be more transparent, and so has a greater impact on prices, than reputation (Dewall and Ederington 2006). Reputation is largely gossip, the accepted whisperings of the haut monde, the received wisdom. This is well known in the social sphere and it is for this reason that while our reputations may precede us, we are enjoined not to judge books by their covers.

Corporate reputation may in fact be built on the absence of truth and reliability. Imagine the case of a dishonest, but nevertheless highly regarded, PR firm that issues false statements about a company. Here, through the work of the PR firm, the company has a reputation in the community, even though the beliefs about the company (and the PR firm) are unreliably held and false. This shows that neither reliability nor truth are necessary conditions for reputation. A reputation may be founded on falsely held beliefs, but, having said this, the beliefs that constitute a company's reputation are not necessarily unreliable or false. For example, beliefs about the reputation of a company are reliable if its PR firm delivers statements that are true more often than not (i.e. if the firm is a reliable provider of information). Determining whether or not the PR firm is reliable may require background information. At the same time, just as many beliefs acquired through testimony may fail the test of reliability, many beliefs about the reputation of a company may fail to pass the test as well. Accordingly, it may be said that 1) the reputation of a company is determined by testimonial belief, and 2) the beliefs that determine the reputation of a company may be either true or false. These characteristics determine the uses of corporate reputation.

In a market in which everyone has access to all the information that is potentially available about any company there would be no need for the nebulous and inexact element of communication known as reputation. Information about goods and services would move so effectively that it would be apparent if the beliefs held about a particular company were true or false. Reputation would not precede purchase, for other forms of information would forestall it. In many markets, however, information is scarce. It does not move smoothly and is often distributed unevenly, so that certain parties possess more information than others, which they exploit to gain advantages. This is all common sense and widely observed. Of course markets are imperfect. What is less appreciated, although no less commonsensical, is that reputation may not remedy imperfections but exacerbate them. It is for this reason that reputation is so critical to corporations, for reputation may be strategically deployed to take advantage of information asymmetries and to swell profits.

Reputation may distort markets because it is often a red herring. This is neither to deny that reputation plays an important role in determining what products people purchase, what companies they work for, and which companies they invest in (Fombrun 1996, p. 5), nor is it to contradict assertions that reputation may provide firms with a sustainable competitive advantage (Barney 1991), but given the nature of reputation as a form of belief, it is rather surprising that it should at times be so influential in colouring peoples' opinions. People believe in reputation, true or false, presumably because the costs of corroboration are too high, yet reputation is often forged of untrustworthy stuff. The extent to which reputation and other forms of testimony are reliable depends on the source, and some sources are more reliable than others, but ascertaining which sources are reliable is not so easy. There is also the difficulty that reliability does not necessarily ensure truth: a person who tells the truth more often than not is said to be reliable, but they may still lie on occasion. Indeed, the element of time and the frequency of observation exacerbate the problems associated with reputational beliefs. In addition, it is not readily apparent how one might set about testing the reliability of a particular reputation or ascertaining to what extent reputation is a determining factor, especially because of the multidimensional character of reputation (Dollinger et al. 1997). Yet, often models which appear to support claims that reputation reduces ex ante uncertainty, particularly those pertaining to investment bank and auditor reputation, assume that reputation is reliable (e.g. Balvers et al. 1988; Chemmanur and Fulghieri 1994; Banerjee and Duflo 2000). Models that assert reputation is causal may rely on proxies for reputation, such as firm size or compensation (e.g. Beatty 1989), which artificially constrains reputation and the externalities it exhibits.

Reputation and the market

As such, reputation has no rightful place in the market, where reliable information is the gold standard and anything less is base metal. So it is vexing that reputation nonetheless remains an intractable element of economic relationships. It is little wonder that reputation is so important in service-based industries, such as consulting, because the goods these industries provide are 'bought on faith' (Fombrun 1996, p. 7), but surely this observation is cause more for concern than reassurance! Reputation exists in the market in lieu of complete information. It has been imported from the social sphere in which all economic transactions are embedded (Granovetter 1985). Reputation is an inexact measure to be sure, but in the social sphere it is of paramount importance. For few are willing – who can? – to probe, prod, and inspect acquaintances, friends, and life-partners to ascertain if they make the grade. We cannot transform these relationships into measurable commodities, which is truly just as well, and reputation is much of all we have to go on when determining whom to befriend, avoid, or engage. Given the opacity of reputation, it is little wonder that the conducting of social relationships is a complex and inexact science, yet we would be foolhardy to wish it any other way because it would no less than transform interpersonal communication into commercial transactions.

Reputation occupies a place in market relationships because the market cannot be extracted from society without consuming it (Polanyi 2001). In the market, however, we do (we must!) prod, probe, and inspect the grade of our beef (and other commodities) because reputation alone is hardly an effective mechanism for avoiding Bovine Spongiform Encephalopathy. If anything, reputation impedes the necessary process of corroboration and certification because unless some system of inspection is imposed by statute, farmers with a good reputation may avoid scrutiny and infect the populace with impunity. Consider, for example, the recent case of Peanut Corporation of America, whose principal product was found to be contaminated with salmonella. The company was clearly unconcerned with its reputation, having been sued on several prior occasions for toxic contamination of its peanuts (Chapman and Newkirk 2009). The company flouted health codes, perhaps even on the wings of an unreliable, but good reputation, and it did so to the great financial gain of its principal owners because other forms of information did not move quickly and effectively through the market.

Other forms of reliable information are transmitted through, and generated by, the market, and as this information accumulates, it supplants reputation. The relationship between unreliable information and the market is dialectical. Reputation, reliable or not, may precede corroborating information. Further information may indicate that a reputational belief is reliable; alternatively, it may reveal it to be unreliable. In turn, a new reputation emerges and the process begins again. The extent to which the market functions as an effective conduit for information determines the remit of reputation. Consider, for example, the reputation of Bernard Madoff, the great scam-artist. Madoff's reputation as a suave investor was secure, and so were his falsified earnings, until reliable information about his actions caught up with him. This information slowly seeped through the market. As we now know, true beliefs moved all too slowly, and reputation, employed opportunistically, was allowed to hold sway over the thoughts of many. Madoff did not so much squander his reputation as much as he used it to great effect. He made effective use of reputation to exploit information asymmetries in the market. For all intents and purposes, the market failed and it was only after the authorities were roused to action that the ruse was revealed. Only now have investors realized how unreliable their belief in Madoff's reputation actually was. In short, the market is frequently an ineffective regulatory mechanism, and reputation may hinder its operation.

It is, however, sometimes claimed that reputation holds economic actors to account and that it fills the interstices between regulatory regimes without imposing upon the market the straightjacket of government intervention. According to this argument, corporations or individuals fear damage to their reputation and this fear obliges them to behave properly. Reputation is, of course, very much a part of the market, and so the central pillar of this thesis rests on claims that the market is self-regulating or at least self-enforcing. There are many instances to suggest that this is plainly not the case. Ever since the modern joint stock firm emerged in the middle of the nineteenth century, the state has been obliged to intervene in the affairs of corporations to prevent behaviour offensive to society (Foreman-Peck 1995). Since then, it has been obvious that reputation is not up to the job of playing taskmaster to corporations. Upton Sinclair understood this when he visited the jungle-like meatpacking warehouses of Chicago (Sinclair 1906), and it has been reaffirmed by the recent case of Peanut Corporation of America, which is but one more example in a long list of corporations that said one thing but did another.

The strength of the argument that reputation holds companies to account lies in the assumption that reputation aids the self-enforcing mechanism of the market but this is also contestable. Reputation may be too ambiguous and easily perverted to hold companies to account, for even when a firm is caught behaving badly, its reputation may emerge unscathed, as the Madoff saga exemplifies (Applebaum et al. 2008). It is certainly the case that social and cultural norms may, in the absence of statutory regulation, hold economic actors to account, but it is imperative not to confuse such norms with reputation. Adherence to social norms may facilitate the establishment of a good reputation, but this does not mean that fear of losing reputation will prevent actors from ignoring these norms. Whether these norms may hold agents to account depends upon their strength in a given society, and the extent to which they factor in to any risk-reward analysis. Punishment to cheaters, through lost future trade, may encourage cooperation between contract parties (Kreps 1990), but this enforcement mechanism requires that the cheater be apprehended, which is another way of saying that reputation enforcement is effective only when information about cheating is good and frequent (Allen and Lueck 1992, p. 369). If a firm calculates that the profits to be obtained from behaving poorly outweigh the risk of being caught, it is likely to behave poorly. If there is no fear of being caught, firms behave with impunity. Moreover, in certain circumstances, reputation may permit of illicit behaviour. An unreliable, but widely held good reputation, provides a suitable smokescreen from behind which firms may behave badly (Dejong et al. 1985). So far as economic actors are afraid of reputation it may be because it is an unknown quantity. It is, as Iago put it, 'oft got without merit, and lost without deserving' (2.3.269-70).

It is likewise confusion between social norms and reputation that leads some scholars to claim that corporate reputation is of significance for the maintenance of incomplete or tacit contracts because it underwrites promises. According to such arguments, reputation acts as an adhesive that binds parties together, and limits opportunistic behaviour, in circumstances when contracts are either infeasible or otherwise incapable of covering all potentialities. This is clearly the case, although little more that common sense, for in situations that cannot be reduced to economic or legal terms, society must hold sway. Tacit contracts are predicated foremost on social, and not economic, bonds, although they may be made for commercial reasons (vide Allen and Lueck 1992). As noted above, reputation is perforce a mechanism used to conduct social relationships, but it may still not be a suitable proxy. Instances of simplistic contracts, ill-defined products, divergent legal systems, and cross-boundary disputes (Banerjee and Duflo 2000) may be a product of poor lawyering, which reputation only occasionally and unpredictably remedies. A solution to such difficulties that adheres to the rule of law, as opposed to the caprice of social relationships, may be preferable. This is because reputation may be opportunistically employed in contracting. In certain circumstances a contracting party may favour entering a legally unenforceable, discretionary financial contract on the basis of its reputation so that when the party refuses to honour the contract, only its reputation is liquefied and its financial capital remains intact (Boot et al. 1993). Reputation may also be an unsatisfactory proxy for formal contract because there is just as much reason to believe that reputation may increase the costs of tacit contracts as much as there is reason to believe that it decreases them. The problem is that the actual effects of reputation in tacit contracts are not clear, and being uncertain this poses a risk. Anecdotal observations about social relationships suggest that reputation is ephemeral and not sufficiently binding to constitute a solid basis for long-term contracts. In social relationships that last and function well, more significant than reputation are other mechanisms of social interaction, such as love, reciprocity, respect, and trust.

Unlike respect and trust, reputation is not an obvious form of social capital, indeed it may be a source of considerable liability. Reputation and social capital are clearly linked, and though this relationship requires further exploration (Bohnet and Huck 2004), perhaps reputation may be said to act as a catalyst in the creation or diminution of social capital. A bad reputation, reliable or not, is clearly something to be avoided, in part because it may adversely impact the value of social capital. A bad reputation may not reflect current performance, but may follow a firm even after it has amended its ways (Tirole 1996). Call this the Scarlet Letter Syndrome after Hawthorne's Hester Prynne, who repented but was forever considered an adulteress. It is a sign of the fickleness and inadequacy of reputation as a form of information that even a good reputation may prove debilitating. Consider a firm that possesses a good reputation among a particular clientele. As soon as it attempts to attract wider patronage it may be seen as 'selling out'. Similarly, the distorting effect reputation has on public perception may prevent the implementation of effective government policy (Backus and Driffill 1985). Concerns about reputation, whether reliable or not, may also inhibit banks from accepting recapitalisation rescue packages in times of crisis, although prudent strategy suggests they do otherwise (Corbett and Mitchell 2000). As a reputation forms over time, and because it is predicated on networks of opinion and testimony, it may prove path dependent and, in this way, limit innovation and inhibit diversification just as in the social sphere reputation in a small town may constrain behaviour in stultifying ways.

In sum, reputation may harm market relationships. None of this is to contest the pivotal role that reputation plays in market relationships, but simply to call attention to what it is. There is no denying that reputation affects corporate profits and a firm's licence to operate, but to understand why this is the case, it must first be understood that reputation often distorts the market, takes advantage of information asymmetries, and exploits others' lack of information. It is not for some reason of 'enlightened self-interest' (Fombrun 1996) that firms should be interested in reputation. Rather, it is precisely because reputation effectively distorts the market that corporations should acknowledge it as a prime vehicle for exacting profits.

Propositions

From a corporation's point of view there are, broadly speaking, two kinds of reputation: good and bad. Good and bad reputations come in two varieties: reliable and unreliable. From the foregoing observations, we derive the following propositions:

1. To avoid a bad reliable reputation, don't do anything bad. If bad behaviour pays, pursue a good unreliable reputation.

If a company's reputation for delivering goods behind schedule is reliable, then it must deliver goods behind schedule. The market knows what the company is doing and dislikes it. There are two ways to overcome this problem: either a) deliver goods on time, or b) attempt to distort the market by generating an unreliable good reputation through some form of marketing. See proposition 4.

2. To overcome an unreliable bad reputation, continue to behave well, facilitate the flow of market information, and amplify this information with marketing.

If a company's reputation for delivering goods behind schedule is unreliable, then it must deliver goods on schedule. The market does not know what the company is up to, but thinks what it is doing is bad. To overcome this problem, increase the amount of information available in the market about the company and facilitate recognition of the company's good behaviour through marketing.

3. To establish a good reliable reputation, do what you say and say what you do.

If a company's reputation for delivering goods on schedule is reliable, then it must in fact deliver goods on schedule. In a well-functioning market, good behaviour will be rewarded with a good reputation. This is widely held to be the most sustainable approach to managing reputation effectively, but other authors typically arrive at this conclusion based on some argument about 'enlightened self interest' (e.g. Fombrun 1996). Here, this proposition follows from the relationship between reputation and the market explained above.

4. Maximise the benefits of a good unreliable reputation, but beware the market.

If a company's reputation for making quality products is unreliable, but nevertheless widely believed, the company may, for example, safely fabricate its products cheaply, sell them at an inflated price, and profit thereby. This is a risky strategy because the market may act as a strong corrective mechanism, but it is also potentially the most profitable. Whether or not the potential reward outweighs the risk must depend upon the extent to which the market distributes information effectively and the ability of the firm to keep such information concealed.

Markets, information, and reputation

Seen this way, the most important question facing any company that seeks to profit by its reputation is: how imperfect is the market? If the market is highly imperfect, and information moves slowly or ineffectively, then a company may safely profit from an unreliable good reputation. If the market is an effective source of information, however, then firms should be wary about pursuing such strategies. Future scholarship on the subject of corporate reputation might usefully address questions concerning how market arrangements affect a company's ability to profit by its reputation.

These questions should be directed toward determining the nature of the institutional environment in which the corporation in question operates and how this affects the flow of information. Recent work in socioeconomics may aid the study of the relationship between market environment and corporate reputation. Firms are embedded in social relations (Granovetter 1985), and whether a firm transacts more in a market or a network will affect its transaction costs and its performance (Uzzi 1996). Work on the importance of status in market relationships may also be useful (Podolny 1992). The strength and nature of the relationships in which a firm operates will affect the flow of information (Baker et al 1998) and as information becomes increasingly important to economic transactions, institutional forms may change (Adler 2001).

Relationships within markets, and the uses of reputation, may change depending upon the evolutionary state of a particular market. A market may be nascent, in which case relationships are uncertain. It may be established, so that relationships are more distinctly hierarchical. Alternatively, a market may be in a state of crisis, so that relationships are in flux (Fligstein 2001; 1996). Further research is required to ascertain whether, and if so how, the limits of corporate reputation change according to the classification of markets. A taxonomy of these arrangements is required based on the way in which each arrangement affects the distribution of information and the remit of reputation. Literature on inter-firm cooperation may help with this endeavour (Fear 2008). Similarly, further research is required to understand how the internalisation of inter-firm relationships affects the flow of information and the limits of corporate reputation (Blois 1972).

In assessing the setting in which firms operate, it is of particular importance to analyse the institutions that directly affect a firm's ability to distort the market by means of an unreliable reputation. The legal system, and especially the laws pertaining to contract, corporate defamation, and compliance, may be of importance. The perceived role of the media, among businesses, journalists, and the public, is also critical. So too is the perceived function of government regulators. Further study of the relationship between the news media and reputation should attempt to ascertain the extent to which the media aim to hold corporations to account and if this prevents corporations from profiting by their reputation. In assessing the role of regulators, students of reputation may be well served by investigating how the rules and oversight established by government affect the flow of market information. In addition, the different mechanisms by which information moves in labour markets should also be investigated.

Each of these market and institutional arrangements may differently affect the many facets of corporate reputation. Corporate reputation comes in many forms. It exists among businesses, within businesses, and between businesses and non-corporate actors. These categories may be further divided to include the various elements of the supply or production chain, labour relations, and consumers. The actors in these categories may in turn be classified according to function, such as banks, consumer groups, manufacturers, mid-level workers, and so on. For example, an individual's incentive to maintain a reputation may change depending upon the reputation of the group to which the individual belongs (Tirol 1996). At each level in this taxonomy of market relationships, the determining characteristic should be the extent to which different arrangements affect a firm's ability to manipulate its reputation to its advantage.

Once it has been observed how information moves through different market arrangements, this taxonomy may be linked with the study of corporate reputation. Presumably different forms of information will move more effectively through different arrangements. We may hypothesize that in markets where information moves quickly and is evenly distributed, firms will find it difficult to maintain unreliable reputations. In such scenarios, the most effective strategy vis-à-vis reputation will be for a corporation to do what it says and to say what it does. In circumstances in which information does not move effectively, or is asymmetrically distributed, it may be possible to develop and profit by an unreliable good reputation. We would also expect that in information-poor environments unreliable bad reputations would also increase and be more 'sticky' than in information-rich environments. In sum, though we may be loath to trust the testimony of a disreputable character, it appears that Iago's thoughts on reputation may help to develop a strategic role for reputation in different markets.

References

Adler P.S. (2001) Market, hierarchy, and trust: the knowledge economy and the future of capitalism. Organization Science, Vol 12 pp 215-234

Allen DW, Lueck D (1992) The "back forty" on a handshake: specific assets, reputation, and the structure of farmland contracts. Journal of Law, Economics, & Organization, Vol 8 pp 366-376

Applebaum B, et al. (13 Dec. 2008) All just one big lie. The Washington Post

Baker WE, Faulkner RR, Fisher GA (1998) Hazards of the market: the continuity and dissolution of interorganizational market relationships. American Sociological Review, Vol 63 pp 147-77

Backus D, Driffill J (1985) Inflation and reputation. The American Economic Review, Vol 75 pp 530-8

Balvers RJ, McDonald B, Miller RE (1988) Underpricing of new issues and the choice of auditor as a signal of investment banker reputation. The Accounting Review, Vol 63 pp 605-22

Banerjee AV, Duflo E (2000) Reputation effects and the limits of contracting: a study of the Indian software industry. The Quarterly Journal of Economics, Vol 115 pp 989-1017

Barney J (1991) Firm resources and sustained competitive advantage. Journal of Management, Vol 17 pp 99-120

Beatty RP (1989) Auditor reputation and the pricing of initial public offerings. The Accounting Review, Vol 64 pp 693-709

Blois KJ (1972) Vertical quasi-integration. The Journal of Industrial Economics, Vol 20 pp 253-72

Bohnet I, Huck S (2004) Repetition and reputation: implications for trust and trustworthiness when institutions change. The American Economic Review, Vol 94 pp 362-66

Boot AWA, Greenbaum SI, Thakor AV (1993) Reputation and discretion in financial contracting. The American Economic Review, Vol 83 pp 1165-83

Chapman D, Newkirk M (8 Feb. 2009) Blakely plant part of firm with humble start. Atlanta Journal-Constitution

Chemmanur TJ, Fulghieri P (1994) Investment bank reputation, information production, and financial intermediation. The Journal of Finance, Vol 49 pp 57-79

Corbett J, Mitchell J (2000) Banking crises and bank rescues: the effect of reputation. Journal of Money, Credit and Banking, Vol 32 pp 474-512

Dejong DV, Forsythe R, Lundholm RJ (1985) Ripoffs, lemons, and reputation formation in agency relationships: a laboratory market study. The Journal of Finance, Vol 40 pp 809-820

Dewall M, Ederington L (2006) Reputation, certification, warranties, and information as remedies for seller-buyer information asymmetries: lessons from the online comic book market. Journal of Business, Vol 79 pp 693-729

Dollinger MJ, Golden PA, Saxton T (1997) The effect of reputation on the decision to joint venture. Strategic Management Journal, Vol 18 pp 127-40

Fear J (2008). Cartels. In: Jones G, Zeitlin J (eds) The Oxford Handbook of Business History. Oxford University Press, Oxford

Fligstein N (1996) Markets as politics: a political-cultural approach to market institutions. American Sociological Review, Vol 61 pp 656-673

Fligstein N (2001) The Architecture of Markets: An Economic Sociology of Twenty-First-Century Capitalist Societies. Princeton University Press, Princeton

Fombrun CJ (1996) Reputation: realizing value from the corporate image. Harvard Business School Press, Boston

Foreman-Peck J (1995) Sleaze and the Victorian businessman. History Today, Vol 45 pp 5-8

Granovetter M (1985) Economic action and social structure: the problem of embeddedness. The American Journal of Sociology, Vol 91 pp 481-510

Kreps DM (1990) Corporate culture and economic theory. In: Alt J, Shepsle K (eds) Perspectives on positive political economy. Cambridge University Press, Cambridge

Podolny JM (1992) A status-based model of market competition. The American Journal of Sociology, Vol 98 pp 829-872

Polanyi K (2001) [1944] The great transformation: the political and economic origins of our time. Beacon, Boston

Sinclair U (1985) [1906] The Jungle. Penguin, New York

Tirole J (1996) A theory of collective reputations (with applications to the persistence of corruption and firm quality). The Review of Economic Studies, Vol 63 pp 1-22

Uzzi B (1996) The sources and consequences of embeddedness for the economic performance of organizations: the network effect. American Sociological Review, Vol 61 pp 674-98

Part II: The business case for reputation

The two most important things in any company do not appear in its balance sheet: its reputation and its people.

Henry Ford (1863-1947)

Recognition or rejection – How a company's reputation influences stakeholder behaviour

Manfred Schwaiger, Sascha Raithel and Matthias Schloderer

Even in times of financial crisis a large percentage of a company's market value is determined by intangible assets, among which corporate reputation is frequently quoted as the most important one. While some research has been done lately on the correlation between reputation and customer behaviour, we focus on the effects of a good reputation on financial performance and on the willingness to apply it surveyed in the recruiting market. The main findings cover the facts that reputation leaders substantially outperform the corresponding stock market index at lower risk and that there is a high correlation between reputation and willingness to apply as well as salary demand.

Reputation as a management objective

Looking at the market to book ratio of S&P 500 companies between 1980 and 2002 reveals that the proportion of tangible assets has climbed from 25% of the market value in 1980 to about 75% in 2002 – during the peak of the dotcom bubble this share has reached no less than 85% (Lev 2001, 2003; Ballow et al. 2004). We obtain a pretty similar picture when looking at the HDAX companies in Germany.

J. Klewes, R. Wreschniok (eds.), *Reputation Capital*, DOI 10.1007/978-3-642-01630-1_4,
© Springer-Verlag Berlin Heidelberg 2009

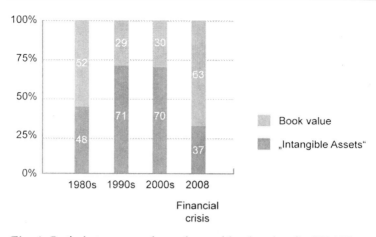

Fig. 1. Ratio between market value and book value for HDAX companies (1980-2008)[1]

Figure 1 provides strong evidence that, with the exception of the financial crisis in 2008/2009, more than two thirds of the companies' market value were based on intangible assets. Reputation is arguably the single most valued organisational asset (e.g. Gibson et al. 2006; Pharoah 2003), without doubt it is a construct of growing importance in management research.

Reputation is mostly described as a general evaluation of a company by its various stakeholders (Gotsi and Wilson 2001, pp. 27f.). According to Schwaiger (2004: pp. 49f.) reputation is best seen as an attitudinal construct combining an affective and a cognitive dimension we will call likeability (affective) and competence (cognitive) later on. As opposed to other conceptualisations we do not only allow for (objective) knowledge, but also for more subjective perceptions as well. In line with Dozier (1993: p. 230) we state that reputation may be based on direct experiences as well as on processed communication messages. Notwithstanding that reputation is based on a corporation's facts (like products and services, strategy, quality of management and employees, market position and many others), corporate communications play an important role in the reputation management process as not the real facts but how they are perceived by the stakeholders is decisive for the reputation of a company.

---

[1] HDAX contains stocks of 110 largest, publicly listed corporations in Germany (DAX, MDAX, TecDAX), 2008 excluded in column 2000s

Companies build competitive advantages and increase their market value by fostering reputation as research has given evidence of the strong link between a fine reputation and common management goals.

- A good reputation not only increases customers' confidence in products and services and advertising claims, but also lowers cognitive dissonance as reputation acts as surrogate for information (Eberl 2006; Fombrun and van Riel 1998; Goldberg and Hartwick 1990; Lafferty and Goldsmith 1999). Via better customer retention (Caminiti 1992; Preece et al. 1995) firms can achieve price premiums and higher purchase rates (Klein and Leffler 1981; Milgrom and Roberts 1986).

- Companies showing strong reputation have better access to capital markets, which decreases capital costs (Beatty and Ritter 1986) and lowers procurement rates (Schwalbach 2000). Moreover, for private investors a higher reputation of a company leads to a stronger weighting of the company's stocks (Schütz and Schwaiger 2007). This effect is intensified by unexpected negative price developments in the stock market (see chapter 3).

- Several studies (e.g. Turban and Cable 2003; Caminiti 1992; Dowling 1986; Eidson and Master 2000; Preece et al. 1995; Nakra 2000) report higher recruiting and employee retention rates among companies with stronger reputations, thus helping a company to win the war for talents (see chapter 4).

- A good reputation pays off in terms of general advantages in conducting negotiations with stakeholders (Brown 1997; Cordeiro and Sambharya 1997; Deephouse 1997; Fombrun 1996; McMillan and Joshi 1997; Roberts and Dowling 1997; Srivastava et al. 1997).

Given the impact of reputation on performance-relevant outcomes it is obvious that a company's market value ceteris paribus should grow with a better reputation. Eberl and Schwaiger (2005) as well as Roberts and Dowling (2002) show that corporate reputation supports the persistence of above-average profits and has a positive impact on net profit. Summarising, in accordance with both the scientific community and the majority of practitioners we may consider corporate reputation as an intangible asset that is scarce, valuable, sustainable, and difficult for a competitor to imitate. Therefore, reputation is an appropriate tool to achieve strategic competitive advantages, even if Haywood's (2002) and Sherman's (1999) statement that corporate reputation is now 'the ultimate determinant of competitiveness' (Haywood, 2002: ix) is still in need of scientific proofs.

Before we may start to discuss the impact of reputation on financial performance (see chapter 3) and in the recruiting market (see chapter 4) we need to explain our approach to measure and explain corporate reputation.

Our approach to corporate reputation management

There is no lack of reputation measurement and management concepts (see Chun 2005 and Schwaiger 2004 for an overview); however, existing concepts exhibit substantial deficits:

- Most concepts rely on expert interviews (e.g. Fortune's annual "America's" or "Global Most Admired Companies" [AMAC, GMAC] and German manager magazin's so called "Imageprofile" (Eidson and Master 2000, Hutton 1986)). Apart from the fact that inside and outside directors are not a stakeholder group of major relevance, experts may hardly be influenced by corporate communications and therefore do – if at all – reveal knowledge about the companies under evaluation, which may be congruent with stakeholder perceptions only incidentally.

- Some concepts suffer from flaws in operationalisation: The Harris-Fombrun-Reputation Quotient® (e.g. Fombrun et al. 2000) for example mixes aspects like good products & services, which is a driver of reputation and aspects like admiration of a company, which is a consequence of reputation. Averaging values obtained for a mix of driver and outcome indicators yields results that are hardly interpretable.

- Emotional aspects are taken into consideration in Fombrun's model solely, but only 3 out of 20 indicators represent a potential affective dimension of reputation. Thus we may state that emotional aspects are undervalued in most approaches.

- Finally, most rankings provide a reputation score only, not allowing an analysis of key performance indicators and therefore preventing the user from explaining the ranking position achieved. From a managerial perspective these ranking lists may be criticised as no tactical opportunities can be derived from such results.

Answering the deficiencies of prior concepts, we developed a reputation measurement and explanation model (Schwaiger 2004) based on multinational data which has been adopted by many blue chip companies, among them eleven DAX companies.

We consider professional reputation management as a closed loop system as shown in Figure 2.

Fig. 2. The Reputation Management Circle

As a good reputation is not a goal in itself, the reputation manager has to decide which outcomes should be focused. This may be loyalty or preference in the customer market, employees' commitment, willingness to apply in the recruiting market or willingness to buy and hold stocks in the financial community and so on.

Step 1: Reputation measurement

Once the outcomes are determined, we start measuring reputation and outcomes within the strategic group of a company in order to locate the company's position compared to benchmarks. We need the six indicators given in Table 1 to be surveyed on a Likert scale with a range from 1 (strong disagreement) to 7 (full agreement).

Table 1. Items to measure reputation

	[the company] is a company that I can better identify with than with other companies.
Likeability	[the company] is a company that I would more regret not having if it no longer existed than I would other companies.
	I regard [the company] as a likeable company.
	[the company] is a top competitor in its market.
Competence	As far as I know, [the company] is recognized world-wide.
	I believe that [the company] performs at a premium level.

The first three indicators are driven by the affective reputation component we call likeability; the last three indicators reflect the cognitive dimension called competence. We can prove that this two-dimensional structure based on principle component analysis is valid over time, industry sectors and cultural boundaries (Schwaiger 2004, Zhang and Schwaiger 2009).

Step 2: Driver analysis

As soon as we have learned about the level of reputation, we enter the second phase and perform a driver analysis in order to find out which aspects are responsible for the company's reputation. We start with four driver constructs that address the most important stakeholder groups: quality (customer market), performance (financial market), corporate social responsibility (opinion leader market) and attractiveness (employees and recruiting market). Each construct has to be operationalised with formative indicators, a task that has to be completed in accordance with the company's department of marketing, HR, strategic development etc. in order to make sure all potential aspects are covered. As always, omitting relevant indicators leads to biased results in the case of formative constructs (Bollen 1989). Measurement and driver indicators are then surveyed among the corresponding stakeholder groups including benchmark companies; in most cases companies adjust existing studies in the respective stakeholder group in order to save market research costs and unleash synergies. The analysis is done via Partial Least Squares (PLS) structural equation modelling to make sure all potential drivers are evaluated in cohesion with the defined outcomes. Evaluating them one by one in context with the outcome leads to an overestimation of significant drivers, as correlations between the various indicators are neglected in that case. Exemplary results are illustrated in Table 2.

Table 2. Exemplary results of a driver analysis

Rank (Impact on loyalty)	Position comp. to benchmark	Driver	Factor
1 (20.12%)	++	Rather innovator than imitator	Quality
2 (16.74%)	-	Well managed	Performance
3 (12.70%)	0	Customer centricity	Quality
4 (6.68%)	+	Physical appearance	Attractiveness
5 (6.22%)	--	Forthright information	CSR
6 ...		...	...

In that fictitious example the perceived degree of innovativeness accounts for more than 20% of the impact on the outcome customer loyalty via reputation. As we can see from column three the exemplary company is perceived to be much better than the benchmark (indicated by ++). On the other hand, the company is perceived to trail behind the benchmarks in providing forthright information to the public. However, raising the perceived forthrightness of information by one scale point will have only one third of the impact than raising the perceived innovativeness by the same degree, as forthright information only explains 6.22% of the total impact on loyalty.

As opposed to the measurement concept, the driver analysis is dependent on time, markets and cultural context and has to be adapted to the specific needs of a company.

Step 3: Develop guidelines and implement them creatively

Based on the results of the driver analysis the next task is to feed the drivers that have been identified to exert significant impact. As mentioned above, corporate communications may only serve as a moderator on the way from facts to perception. Exemplary actions may include programmes to improve product quality, the setup of a suitable CSR strategy and so on. Once the facts are created corporate communications may serve to drive perception. This step includes some qualitative work as well, for example a comprehensive analysis of reputation risks. Most executives keep an eye on avoiding bad performance, but board member deviance, legal issues, product flops, environmental scandals and communication disasters may harm their reputation no less.

Step 4: Control results

Check the implementation first and have a look at the media response as far as corporate communications activities are concerned. While this may be regarded as a production control, one shouldn't forget to check whether single measures have improved the corporate reputation (effectiveness and efficiency as expected?) and whether in general reputation has reached a higher level, at least in relation to the changes in benchmarks' reputation. This is where the loop closes and we have arrived at the measurement step again.

Reputation and capital market performance

Given the remarks in section 1, one may expect a significant financial out-performance of companies with a high reputation over companies that have a lack of reputation. Using regression analysis or other statistical methods to examine the impact of reputation on capital market perform-ance shows a severe drawback: As there is an investment effect (compa-nies investing in reputation show better performance) as well as a perform-ance effect (companies with a better financial performance obtain higher reputation values) reported in literature (see Eberl and Schwaiger 2005; Schwalbach 2000; Hildebrandt and Schwalbach 2000) the causality be-tween reputation and stock market performance remains unclear.

Our approach (see Raithel 2009 for a detailed analysis) was to create a portfolio with equal weighted investments in stocks of reputation champi-ons and compare the portfolio's performance to that of the corresponding stock market index. As we have comparable reputation data based on the perception of the general public for about 60 companies (including the DAX companies) since December 2005, we started setting up the portfolio at that date. Reputation measurement at the Institute for Market-based Management (IMM) is done every six months: TNS Infratest surveys ap-proximately 2,000 respondents which are asked to evaluate four companies each by means of the six items given in Table 1.

Based on the answers we calculate scores for likeability, competence and reputation ranging between 0 and 100%. The portfolio is updated at the end of June and December of every year in order to make sure the 25% of the DAX companies showing the highest reputation scores are con-tained in the "Top 25% Reputation" portfolio. Analogously we built a "Medium 50% Reputation" portfolio and a "Bottom 25% Reputation" portfolio. Financial data were added from the DATASTREAM database.

In order to tackle challenge of unclear causality we observed a portfolio of the Top 25% shares that have shown the best financial performance in the last six months. The performances of all four portfolios including the DAX as benchmark are displayed in Figure 3.

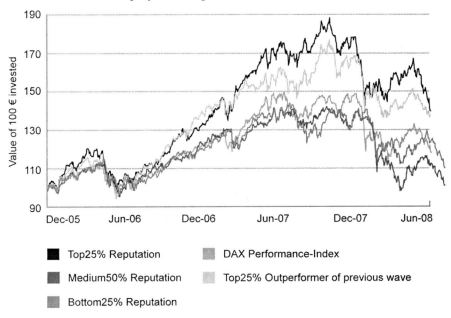

Fig. 3. Performance of 'reputation portfolios' vs. the DAX index

Results in Table 3 show that the Top 25% Reputation portfolio's value has achieved an increase of 39.6% compared to 18.7% of the DAX index value. Remarkably, this portfolio's value was at no point in time below the DAX index value. However, the most notable fact is that the risk – as expressed by the Beta factor – of the Top 25% Reputation portfolio is considerably lower than the market risk. But the financial outperformance of this portfolio is not only valid for the whole sample period; it is valid for four out of the five waves and for 63% of the months. In addition, the Top 25% Reputation portfolio outperformed the Bottom 25% Reputation portfolio in all five waves and 70% of the months.

Table 3. Results of the performance analysis

Portfolio vs. DAX 30	Last price 30-Jun-08 [Base: 100 on 30-Dec-05]	Max. delta [% points]	Min. delta [% points]	Avg. delta [% points]	Beta [calc. on a daily basis]
Top25% Reputation	139.6	39.8	0.0	17.5	0.78
Middle50% Reputation	111.5	3.7	-11.4	-2.5	0.98
Bottom25% Reputation	102.0	3.8	-19.3	-4.8	0.83
Top25% prev. Outperformer	138.6	29.4	-3.4	12.5	0.73
DAX	118.7				1.00

Summarising the results we may state that reputation champions out-perform the DAX significantly at lower risk. Moreover, we checked if the best advice is to stick to the reputation evaluation based on the perception of the general public. As we started in October 2007 to survey specific stakeholder groups (analysts, journalists, scientists, top executives, politicians, and representatives of NGOs and NPOs) we compared results for this wave between different stakeholder groups. Table 4 provides strong evidence that there is something like wisdom of the crowd. This means, if one would like to rely on the recommendation to invest in reputation champions the best advice is to stick to the reputation evaluations based on the general public.

Table 4. Comparison of Top 25% 'reputation portfolios' based on different stakeholders' perceptions

Top25% Reputation portfolio vs. Dax	Last price 30-Jun-08 [Base: 100 on 30-Dec-05]	Max. delta [% points]	Min. delta [% points]	Avg. delta [% points]	Beta [calc. on a daily basis]
General Public	157.1	60.3	-0.2	24.1	0.90
Opinion leaders	147.2	37.6	-1.0	12.2	0.81
Analysts	138.6	32.0	-0.5	10.2	0.77
Executives	147.2	37.6	-1.0	12.2	0.81
Scientists	108.0	0.8	-13.4	-5.5	0.89
Journalists	147.2	37.6	-1.0	12.2	0.81
NGO, NPO	148.6	39.8	-2.9	14.2	0.86
Politicians	146.3	37.6	-3.2	13.0	0.84
Average	142.5	35.4	-2.9	11.6	0.84
Dax	118.7				

Referring to competence or likeability instead of the overarching reputation scores does not yield any better results. However, even removing the halo effect of past financial performance and splitting the reputation dimensions competence and likeability into a predictable part from past performance and an idiosyncratic part as well as controlling for typical financial market risk factors (market size, book-to-market ratio, and momentum

effect), both dimensions have a significant impact on financial performance (Raithel 2009). Hence, we may not only conclude that, corresponding
to Porter's five forces, companies increase loyalty, build barriers and
strengthen their strategic position in their competitive environment by fostering their reputation, we may also state that building up reputation leads
to an increased shareholder value.

Reputation and the war for talents

Many studies about employer attractiveness draw the conclusion that
monetary aspects are not automatically the most important drivers of one's
willingness to apply for a job at a company (e.g. Lewandowski and Liebig
2004; Ernst & Young 2008). Surveys among high potentials proof that
reputation counts as well (Grobe 2003). One of our study's main goals (see
Schloderer 2009 for detailed analysis) was to find out the strength of the
link between reputation of a company on the one hand and valuable outcomes as willingness to apply and salary demands on the other hand.

In May 2008, 421 students in business administration, economics and
business education at LMU Munich were surveyed; every student had to
evaluate 12 randomly selected companies out of a list of 60 (selection of
DAX and other companies) regarding reputation and the intention to apply.
Reputation assessment again was done using the indicators shown in Table
1, the intention to apply was measured by the aspects "attractive employer" and "want to apply after studies".

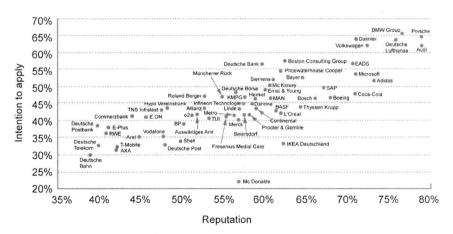

Fig. 4. Reputation and willingness to apply among LMU students

Figure 4 illustrates the strong correlation (r = .77) between perceived reputation and willingness to apply. Obviously, a fine reputation makes it easier for companies to win the war for talents.

Analogous to the concept of price premium in the area of consumer goods (Aaker 1996: p. 320; Crimmins 1992: p. 16; Park and Srinivasan 1994: p. 284), one can assume that good reputation results in a negative salary premium. Besides indirect approaches like conjoint analysis (Riediger et al. 2008), premiums can be measured by direct query (Aaker 1996: pp. 320f.). Therefore, we asked the respondents the following question: "Please suppose that your preferred company would offer you for the scope of activities of your choice at your preferred location a salary of €50,000 per annum. How much salary per annum would [company] have to offer you for the same scope of activities at the same location for that you would choose [company] instead?"

As a result of the study we observe a higher salary demand of +4.49% for the Top 3 reputation leaders in comparison to the desired company, which we consider to be a biased result as we could learn from reality that most people accept lower compensation when working for a well renowned company at least during the first year(s) of their professional career. However, we may assume that this bias (or say, this exaggeration) is applied to any company under evaluation without substantial difference. Hence, we may compare the distance between the reputation champions and the reputation laggards (Table 5), which reveals a salary premium of 18.65% that has to be paid on average by the laggards compared to the champions. Even if our sample is not a representative one, we have obtained strong empirical evidence that the higher the reputation, the higher the salary deduction is.

Table 5. Reputation ranking and salary demands among LMU students

If your position at the reputation ranking is at place ...	...Than there is a higher salary claim, compared to your preferred company, of about ...
Top 3	+4,49%
4-10	+10,12%
11-20	+13,99%
21-30	+14,61%
31-40	+15,63%
41-50	+17,56%
51-57	+18,17%
Bottom 3	+23,14%

From a scientific point of view, this study may fulfil exploratory purposes only, but results let us derive a few hypotheses we have to test on a representative sample in the future, using the indirect approach of choice-based conjoined analysis of detecting salary premiums which grants a even higher validity than the direct approaches.

Conclusion

The results presented in this article may be seen as further pieces of a puzzle representing the effect of a good corporate reputation in all relevant stakeholder groups of a company. We were not willing to rely on published articles so far, as the conceptualisation and operationalisation of the reputation construct has been flawed in many cases, e.g. when referring to Fortune or Harris-Fombrun reputation data. From a scientific perspective reputation has to be split into an affective and a cognitive component, what accounted for in IMM's) reputation measurement approach. Using this well grounded approach to measure reputation in all relevant stakeholder groups instead of letting a jury decide, we discovered a significant impact of reputation on willingness to apply and salary demand. Adding this to results obtained from empirical research in the consumer market (Eberl 2006) and in the private investors' field (Schütz and Schwaiger 2007) it is not surprising that reputation leaders do better than their competitors in terms of financial performance as well.

References

Aaker DA (1996) Building strong brands. Free Press, New York

Ballow J, Burgman R, Roos G, Molnar M (2004) A New Paradigm for Managing Shareholder Value. Accenture Institute for High Performance Business, Wellesley

Beatty RP, Ritter JR (1986) Investment Banking, Reputation, and Underpricing of Initial Public Offerings. Journal of Financial Economics, Vol 15 pp 213-232

Bollen KA (1989) Structural Equations with Latent Variables. New York et al.

Brown B (1997) Stock Market Valuation of Reputation for Corporate Social Performance. Corporate Reputation Review, Vol 1 pp 76-80

Caminiti S (1992) The Payoff from a Good Reputation. Fortune, Vol 125 pp 49-53

Chun R (2005) Corporate reputation: meaning and measurement. International Journal of Management Review, Vol 7 pp 91-109

Cordeiro JJ, Sambharya R (1997) Do Corporate Reputations Influence Security Analyst Earnings Forecasts. Corporate Reputation Review, Vol 1 pp 94-98

Crimmins JC (1992) Better Measurement and Management of Brand Value. Journal of Advertising Research July/August pp 11-19

Deephouse D (1997) The Effects of Financial and Media Reputations on Performance. Corporate Reputation Review, Vol 1 pp 68-72

Dowling GR (1986) Managing Your Corporate Images. Industrial Marketing Management Vol 15 pp 109-115

Dozier DM (1993) Image, Reputation and Mass Communication Effects. In: Armbrecht W, Avenarius H, Zabel U (eds) Image und PR – Kann Image Gegenstand einer Public Relations-Wissenschaft sein? Opladen, pp. 227-250

Eberl M (2006) Reputation und Kundenverhalten. Deutscher Universitäts-Verlag, München

Eberl M, Schwaiger M (2005) Corporate Reputation: Disentangling the Effects on Financial Performance. European Journal of Marketing Vol 39 pp 7-8 and 838-854

Eidson C, Master M (2000) Top Ten ... Most Admired ... Most Respected: Who Makes the Call? Across the Board, Vol 37 pp 16-22

Ernst & Young (2008) Studenten 2008, URL: <http://www.ey.com/Global/asets.nsf/Germany/Studie_Studenten_2008/$file/Studie_Studenten_20 08.pdf> [10 November 2008]

Fombrun CJ (1996) Reputation: Realizing Value from the Corporate Image. Harvard Business School Press, Boston

Fombrun CJ, van Riel C (1998) The Reputational Landscape. Corporate Reputation Review, Vol 1 pp 5-14

Fombrun CJ, Gardberg NA, Sever JM (2000) The Reputation QuotientSM: A Multi-Stakeholder Measure of Corporate Reputation. Journal of Brand Management Vol 7 No 4 pp 241-255

Gibson D, Gonzales JL, Castanon J (2006) The Importance of Reputation and the Role of Public Relations. Public Relations Quarterly Vol 51 No 3 pp 15–18

Goldberg ME, Hartwick J (1990) The Effects of Advertiser Reputation and Extremity of Advertising Claim on Advertising Effectiveness. Journal of Consumer Research Vol 17 pp 172-179

Gotsi M, Wilson AM (2001) Corporate Reputation: Seeking a Definition. Corporate Communications, Vol 6 pp 24-30

Grobe E (2003) Corporate Attractiveness: Eine Analyse der Wahrnehmung von Unternehmensmarken aus der Sicht von High Potentials. HHL-Arbeitspapier 50, Leipzig

Haywood R (2002) Manage Your Reputation. Kogan Page, London

Hildebrandt L, Schwalbach J (2000) Financial Performance Halo in German Reputation. Data Forschungsbericht. Institut für Management der Humboldt-Universität zu Berlin

Hutton C (1986) America's Most Admired Companies. Fortune Jan Vol 6 pp 16-22

Klein B, Leffler KB (1981) The Role of Market Forces in Assuring Contractual Performance. Journal of Political Economy, Vol 89 pp 615-641

Lafferty BA, Goldsmith RE (1999) Corporate Credibility's Role in Consumers' Attitudes and Purchase Intentions When a High versus a Low Credibility Endorser is Used in the Ad. Journal of Business Research, Vol 44 No 2 pp 109-116

Lev B (2001) Intangibles: Management Measurement and Reporting. Brookings Institution Press, Washington

Lev B (2003) Remarks on the Measurement Valuation and Reporting of Intangible Assets. Economic Policy Review September 2003

Lewandowski A, Liebig C (2004) Determinanten der Arbeitgeberwahl und Relevanz des Personalimages für die Bewerbungsabsicht. Mannheimer Beiträge zur Wirtschafts- und Organisationspsychologie, Vol 19 No 1 pp 15-28

McMillan GS, Joshi MP (1997) Sustainable Competitive Advantage and Firm Performance. Corporate Reputation Review, Vol 1 pp 81-86

Milgrom P, Roberts J (1986) Price and Advertising Signals of Product Quality. Journal of Political Economy, Vol 94 pp 796-821

Nakra P (2000) Corporate Reputation Management: „CRM" with a Strategic Twist. Public Relations Quarterly, Vol 45 No 2 pp 35-42

Park CS, Srinivasan V (1994) A Survey-based Method for Measuring and Under-standing Brand Equity and its Extendibility. Journal of Marketing Reseach, Vol 31 pp 271-288

Pharoah A (2003) Corporate reputation: the boardroom challenge. Corporate Governance, Vol 3 No 4 pp 46-51

Preece SB, Fleisher C, Toccacelli J (1995) Building a Reputation Along the Value Chain at Levi Strauss. Long Range Planning, Vol 28 No 6 pp 88-98

Raithel S (2009) The Value of Corporate Reputation for Shareholders: Evidence from Germany for DAX Companies, forthcoming

Riediger C, Sattler H, Völckner F (2008) The Impact of Brand Extension Success Drivers on Brand Extension Price Premium. Proceedings of the 37th Annual Conference of the European Marketing Academy, forthcoming

Roberts PW, Dowling GR (1997) The Value of a Firm's Corporate Reputation: How Reputation Helps Attain and Sustain Superior Profitability? Corporate Reputation Review, Vol 1 No 1 and 2 pp 72-76

Roberts PW, Dowling GR (2002) Corporate Reputation and Sustained Superior Financial Performance. Strategic Management Journal, Vol 23 pp 1077-1093

Schloderer MP (2009) Reputation in the Recruiting Market, forthcoming

Schütz T, Schwaiger M (2007) Der Einfluss der Unternehmensreputation auf Entscheidungen privater Anleger. Kredit und Kapital, Vol 40 No 2 pp 189-223

Schwaiger M (2004) Components and Parameters of Corporate Reputation – an Empirical Study. Schmalenbach Business Review 56 of zfbf 1, January pp 46-71

Schwalbach J (2000) Image, Reputation und Unternehmenswert. In: Baerns B, Raupp J (eds) Information und Kommunikation in Europa. Forschung und Praxis. Transnational Communication in Europe. Research and Practice, pp 287-297

Sherman ML (1999) Making the Most of Your Reputation. In: Institute of Directors (ed) Reputation Management: Strategies for Protecting Companies, Their Brands and Their Directors. AIG Europe, London

Srivastava RK, McInish TH, Wood RA, Capraro AJ (1997) The Value of Corporate Reputations: Evidence from the Equity Markets. Corporate Reputation Review, Vol 1 pp 62-67

Turban DB, Cable DM (2003) Firm reputation and applicant pool characteristics. Journal of Organizational Behavior, Vol 24 pp 733-752

Zhang Y, Schwaiger M (2009) An Empirical Research of Corporate Reputation in China. Proceedings of the American Academy of Advertising 2009 Asian-Pacific Conference. forthcoming

What's measurable gets done – Communication controlling as a prerequisite for a successful reputation management

Reimer Stobbe

Communication controlling represents a holistic view of communication management for companies, and for controlling corporate communication. Adopting managerial methods from controlling, a model for modern communication controlling is defined that is intended as a standard and a benchmark in both areas: controlling and communication. Reputation also plays a role in this holistic model of communication management. Methods for managing reputation often use a different language and different images, but are compatible with the management model of communication controlling in terms of the questions they address and their approach. Essentially, the model answers two questions:

1. How can one prove communication's contribution to a company's value creation?

2. How can communication and reputation be managed so that they make an optimal contribution to a company's value creation?

The basic model of communication controlling

At present, there is little connection between reputation management and communication controlling. But a glance at the general definitions in both disciplines shows this does not have to be so.

Reputation management?

Reputation management is here defined as the management of the expectations of all stakeholder groups and of their cognitive and emotional **attitudes** towards the company. That includes the identification of the reputation drivers and the assessment of its value creation.

J. Klewes, R. Wreschniok (eds.), *Reputation Capital*, DOI 10.1007/978-3-642-01630-1_5,
© Springer-Verlag Berlin Heidelberg 2009

Communication controlling?

Communication controlling means not only checking budgets and costs, but **management** as a whole. It establishes professional management for corporate communications with methods to measure its value creation.

The common goal is, then, proving the value created by soft factors.

What is meant exactly by management or controlling in the context of communication controlling?

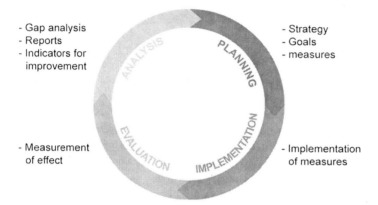

- Gap analysis
- Reports
- Indicators for improvement

- Strategy
- Goals
- measures

- Measurement of effect

- Implementation of measures

Fig. 1. Communication controlling includes the whole management cycle.

The management cycle is the foundation for an holistic model of controlling and thus for the management of corporate communications. Often, however, there are gaps in the cycle and thus deficiencies in management. In practice, corporate communication focuses too much on measures. There is often too little emphasis on strategies and goals at all levels – the measurement of success and evaluation take place haphazardly and are linked only to specific measures (most recently, see Nix/Schnöring/Siegert 2009). The motto here would appear to be "Do everything that's possible" or "The measure was successful, but why did we actually do it?"

Quite fundamentally, one must realise that nothing can be measured except the achievement of a goal. Key performance indicators (KPIs) only make sense when they are linked to a specific goal. In a sense, goals always formulate a question, to which the KPI provides an answer. To keep with the language of success measurement: for each KPI, a key performance question (KPQ) is needed. Among communicators, the methods of strategy development and goal planning are not endemic. They can benefit here from adopting management methods from controlling. To this end, various forms of goal scorecards have already been used in communication management to meet the important requirement of goal planning. One consequence, or benefit, of cleanly deriving goals from strategy is that you only have to measure what has been defined as a goal and thus as relevant. The numerous possibilities for evaluation and the wide range of potential indicators suddenly acquire focus. The 'yardstick' is defined by the goals. Measurements and indicators that are not linked to such a yardstick are pointless. For example, there is no need to conduct an expensive survey (or anything similar) of a group of people that is not defined as a target group in the sense of the goals. For this reason, one should not shirk the effort required to plan goals and define measurement criteria. Using the yardstick to guide decisions about which measurement methods and evaluation processes should be purchased or applied can save a great deal of internal effort and money. But the last step in the management cycle is indispensable as well – though to be precise, the last step in the figure above consists of two parts. The first, the gap analysis (where the actual situation is compared to the potential or desired situation), is the most conventional instrument in a controller's toolkit. Where the plan is not being met, reasons for the shortfall must be found, providing a starting point for identifying potential improvements. The results of the analysis are collated in reports so that they can be used in the next planning phase to correct and focus the strategy, goals and measures. In this way, insights resulting from measuring success can be incorporated into an executive report, to improve the strategy and to plan goals. Without defining and measuring the achievement of goals at a strategic and operational level, it is impossible to prove value creation or to control communications!

The management cycle forms the basis of the model used by the task force for communication controlling at the International Controller Association (http://www.controlling-online.eu/). The task force was founded in October 2006 and comprises about 25 members from corporate communication, controlling, agencies, academia and research. The members meet three times a year and for additional group work. The goal is to integrate communication controlling, with its methods and KPIs, into corporate management – that is, to integrate communications into the company as a strategic factor. As a result of this work, a 'controller statement' is due to be published in 2010, as part of the ICA's publication series, as a standard method.

The communications industry has been discussing methods for communication controlling for many years now. What sets this task force apart is that it builds a bridge between communicators and controllers. Connecting both communities and agreeing on a common language (and ultimately, on common methods) are necessary for integrating communications into strategic corporate management.

Apart from the management cycle, a fundamental requirement of the ICA's basic model for communication management is to produce a stringent relationship

1. between the company's value drivers and the strategic value drivers in communication, as well as between the goals of both levels, and

2. between the goals and the measures. Here, verifiable causal relationships define the link between the strategic level in the goal hierarchy of corporate communications, the goals at the subordinate level of communications departments and teams, as well as the operative level with all the measures, and finally, the goals of individual employees.

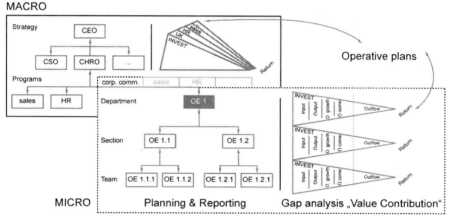

Fig. 2.

Relationship between a company's value drivers and communications

This relationship makes it possible to prove the value created by communications. Often, the link is missing from communication to the corporate strategy, or to the indicators used for corporate management (see, most recently, Nix/Schnöring/Siegert 2009). It makes sense to have value drivers that are defined over the long term as well as goals that relate to annual planning, because it is easier to align continuous measurement and a system of indicators to these long-term value drivers. The value drivers defined and agreed on for a company, together with the corresponding indicators, make it possible to define goals for annual planning more quickly and easily, and to match these goals to the indicators, which are being continuously monitored.

The numerous options for measuring the effect of corporate communication must therefore be critically examined to see whether they enable conclusions to be drawn about the value created and whether they make controlling easier.

Reputation measurement, too, is pointless if it is not linked to strategy development and goal planning, or if it fails to identifies operative drivers or is not embedded in the management cycle.

In a 2006 article, Money and Hillebrand summarise the major approaches to reputation measurement in relation to this point. They define a trio of "Antecedents – Corporate Reputation – Consequences" (Money & Hillebrand 2006) as a cause-effect relationship. At the strategic level, these antecedents are all "asset generating activities" – or, in the context of communication controlling, the measures in corporate communication's value driver tree. The consequences are the effects of reputation on the company's value creation. The authors regard reputation itself as an intangible asset. The chart is an attempt to map the main approaches towards reputation measurement onto this value creation chain, or cause-effect relationship. It can be seen that some approaches do not make these connections. They are focused on examining reputation itself. Neither of the two central questions in the communication controlling model is addressed here: if no link is made to the asset generating activities, the management of reputation by subordinate drivers is not transparent, and, consequently, no options for managing reputation result. In the model of communication controlling, the consequences are the contribution to value creation. Thus, if the consequences cannot be proven, there is also no way to prove the benefit of reputation to a company.

Table 1.

Antecedents ⇒ **Corporate Reputation** ⇒ **Consequences**

Strategic level	Asset Generating Activities		Intangible Assets *		Market Assets / Performance	
Fombrun (1996) Reputation Quotient (RQ)			Vision & Leadership Financial Performance Social Responsibility Products & Services Workplace Environment	Emotional Appeal		
Davies (2003) Corporate Personality Scale			Judgement of the personality of an organisation	(link to measures of satisfaction)	(link to measures of commitment)	
Berens & Van Riel (2004) Streams of Thought in Reputation Literature		Activities associated with the development of trust (implied)	Judgements in terms of social expectations Personality Metaphor	Trust		
Walsh & Wiedmann (2004) Extension of the RQ in Germany		Suggested the development of scales to measure stakeholder experience and involvement	Suggested the development of scales to measure sympathy, transparency, fairness and perceived customer orientation in addition RQ concepts	Suggested the development of scales to measure trust and satisfaction	Suggested the development of scales to measure loyalty and word of mouth	
MacMillan et al. (2004) SPIRIT	Outside Influences (What the media and pressure groups say)	Communication, Service Benefits, Non-Material Benefits, Material Benefits, Shared Values, Keeping Commitments, Coercion and Termination Costs		Trust Emotional Commitment Level of positive and negative emotions	Advocacy Co-operation Extension Retention Subversion	
Personal level	Observation	Experience	Beliefs	Attitudes	Intentions	Behaviours

Source: Money / Hillenbrand (2006): Figure 7, p. 6

A study that appeared in November 2008, the European Communication Monitor, confirms the vital importance of this view and its implementation in communication management (Zerfaß et al. 2008: 33-37). The study is a Europe-wide survey on trends in communication management and public relations, and analyses responses from more than 1500 professionals in 37 countries. The results reveal a demand for proving the value created by communication, in particular by linking corporate strategy and corporate communication strategy. The study confirms the need for standards that can be applied in practice. In addition, evaluation procedures seem now to be viewed more critically:

"Communication controlling is the most important and enduring issue for the profession. Strategic aspects of value creation (linking business strategy and communication) are seen as a challenge by 45% of the respondents, like last year. The operational level has been improved: only 16% (last year: 31%) still think that the development of new evaluation methods is a major issue.

This might be an effect of the ongoing debate in theory and practice: PR professionals have learned that there is already a wealth of reliable instruments for assessing communication activities, but there is no easy way to integrate them into concepts for managing public relations and demonstrating the bottom line." (Zerfaß et al. 2008: 37)

Those in charge of corporate communication cannot simply define, of their own accord, their contribution to corporate strategy and thus to the company's value creation. In the strategy development phase of the management cycle, an agreement should be reached with company management about the relationship between the corporate strategy and the corporate communication strategy so that communication is given an explicit task derived from the general strategy. Here, the task force for communication controlling at the ICA, together with other associations such as the Deutsche PR Gesellschaft (German Public Relations Association; DPRG), is seeking to set standards and provide orientation for both sides: company management and communication. Standards and agreements take the place of proofs, which cannot be provided for these relationships and for value creation.

The DPRG has had a working group dedicated to the topic of value creation through communications since 2004. White papers that present the results and provide a basis for discussion have been published on the internet in German and English (www.communicationcontrolling.de). These results are being discussed by other European PR associations as well. The methodological foundation for all the papers is to situate communications on a company's generic strategy map. This accords with the approach already outlined, which defines the fundamental contributions by communication to corporate success as success factors or value drivers. It is a question of the target contribution – that is, its effectiveness. The necessary causal relationship between communications and corporate success is represented as a value driver chain (value chain with value links) or as a value driver tree. To be suitable for controlling communication, an indicator must be sufficiently capable of being influenced by communication. For external communication, the DPRG) paper on the subject singles out reputation as the most important KPI still to be primarily influenced by communication (Fig. 2: The example of external communication). The drivers above this, by contrast, can no longer be clearly influenced by communication.

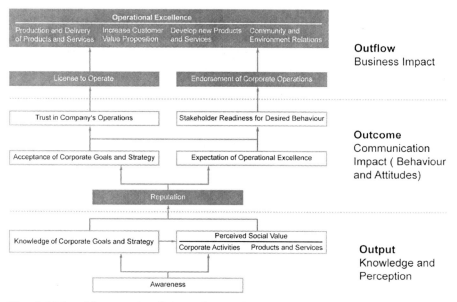

Fig. 3. Value drivers, value links and KPIs for external communication
Source: DPRG – External Communication – www.communicationcontrolling.de

As a strategic value driver, reputation is, according to this logic, a hinge between the value driver tree of corporate communication and the value driver tree of the entire company. For the company, reputation is therefore a significant soft success factor in the value creation chain. By using reputation as a value link – that is, as a link to the level of value creation within the company – corporate communication can relate the associated communicative activities and measures to value creation. Only in this way do they become value drivers, or levers for increasing value. For reputation management, this makes the consequences (in terms of Money and Hillenbrand above) visible.

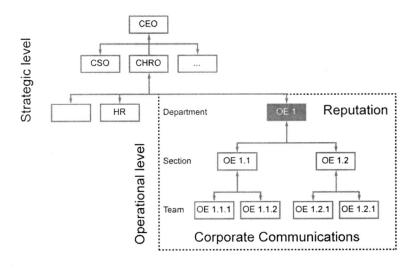

Reputation could be the value link between the company and corporate communications.

Fig. 4. Strategic and operational level

The DPRG's discussion paper on internal communication makes very clear how helpful for goal planning it can be to have a basic structure of value drivers as a foundation. The table 2, from the DPRG paper, shows how typical corporate goals can be matched to suitable success factors/value drivers in internal communication. These are measured by KPIs. (The column heading on the right, however, equates value drivers with KPIs.)

Markus Will (2007) has established a link between communication and value creation by expanding the definition of intellectual capital in a crucial respect. He first distinguishes two views. In the 'capital view', he adds a separate quantity, 'communication capital' (which has to do with opinions), next to conventional target group categories such as human or customer capital. More importantly, however, Will integrates relationship and reputation variables by using a new 'relations view'. All in all, he takes a 'communication view' and lays the theoretical foundation for integrating the company's capacity to communicate into external reporting. For him, too, reputation is the difference between the book value and the total value of the company.

Table 2.

Typical communication-relevant corporate targets in the learning and growth perspective (according to Kaplan/Norton)	Proposed KPIs for internal communication (measured via index variables)
• „Build up leadership personalities" • „Establish communication as a basic leadership task" • „Share knowledge"	(1) Information and communication behavior of leaders
• „Align human resources to strategy" • „Internalize vision, mission and key values"	(2) Strategic awareness of employees
• „Create readiness for change" • „Foster a culture of change and facilitation" • „Enhance creativity and innovation" • „Develop strategic employee ability"	(3) Employees' readiness for change
• „Focus employees on the customer" • „Nuture customer-focused behavior"	(4) Employees' customer focus
• „Communicate openly" • „Enhance employee motivation" • „Improve employee communication"	(5) Satisfaction with information and communication (as an assignable portion of employee commitment)
• „Attract and retain excellent employees"	(6) Fluctuation rate among qualified employees

Source: DPRG – Internal Communication – www.communicationcontrolling.de

In addition to what has already been said, reputation management is also about the management of the expectations of a company's stakeholders. There are two main guide rails for strategy development and goal planning for corporate communications: on the one hand, the high-level goals and requirements of a company; on the other hand, the expectations of stakeholders, which are incorporated into the planning phase of the management cycle through reputation measurements. As per the cycle, the effect of the measures on stakeholder attitudes towards the company is ultimately determined by the next reputation measurement. Of course, this requires that measurements are performed regularly. It is therefore vital that indicators are linked not to short-term goals but to value drivers. As far as controlling is concerned, a benefit exists only when the outcomes of the measurements change visibly over time as a result of the measures taken.

Relationship between strategic and operative levels

A central requirement of systematic communication controlling and the ICA model is that value drivers and goals in the hierarchy are connected, through defined relationships, with the measures and processes.

One practical example for creating a consistent relationship between strategic reputation management and the operative level of communicative measures was presented by HypoVereinsbank (UniCredit Group) at the Kommunikationskongress in Berlin in 2008 (Gfrerer 2008). On the one hand, there is communication performance management, which uses all aspects of the management cycle, making integrated controlling possible. On the other hand, there is reputation management, which provides content guidelines for stakeholder management. The HypoVereinsbank model integrates all levels with all goals, measures, variables and indicators. Further, issues management forms part of the system. The complexity that necessarily arises is handled with special software. This enables continuous reporting at all levels of the corporate hierarchy, from management to employees. A positive side effect is that all people integrated into the system benefit from it. This ensures, on the one hand, that the data entered are valid, and on the other hand, the commitment of management.

Measures within a company positively influence two main factors: on the one hand, the goals developed in the planning phase, and on the other hand, the strategically relevant issues and messages. Thus, the goals are just one dimension. After all, one role of communication is to reach target groups via the available communication channels and so to convince them about the issues the company would like to position itself on – of course, all in accordance with the goals defined. In relation to issues management, too, the steps in the management cycle can assist professionalisation and the monitoring of success.

Consistently linking the comprehensive operative level to the strategic level increases the complexity of the controlling system and its controllability. Clear rules, criteria and organising principles must be defined. These have to be carefully observed by all employees involved, so that there is no chance of a controlling error. To meet this challenge, it is important to map the system and rules using a special IT tool. This also increases efficiency and makes reporting easier. The attractiveness and benefits increase for all those involved, not only for management. Experience suggests this is the only way to ensure the quality of the input. Those who enter data into the tool are naturally more motivated to ensure it is of high quality if they can see it will ultimately be of benefit to them in their work.

It is certainly helpful to construct such a system in a modular way so as to quickly provide a 'proof of concept' and to ensure people can soon see the benefits.

Reputation in the impact level model of communication controlling

Ultimately, expanding and standardising the impact level model and the indicator categories is an important element of the management model proposed by the task force for communication controlling at the ICA in co-operation with the DPRG. The website is also in English (communication-controlling.de), so the impact level model is also available internationally.

The model assumes, first of all, that costs and effort will be invested into communication (input) that lead to the generation of communication activities. The output is the offering for contacting stakeholders, in other words the entire communications offering, including its content. At this level, the accessibility and usability of the offer are also important criteria. The communication offering is directly controlled by the company. Once one moves on to the impact of the communication on stakeholders (outcome), the complexity increases, because there is no longer an internal view, and because the company no longer has direct influence. Here, measurement methods from the social sciences are required. In the hierarchy of impact levels in the model, which build on each other, the direct impact – the perception and knowledge of the stakeholders – precedes the indirect impact. The indirect impact looks at attitudes towards the company, behavioural dispositions and, ultimately, the behaviour of the target group. When this behaviour impacts on the goals and value creation of the company, the final level, the outflow of the communication, is reached.

In the overall context of the impact levels, the variables and indicators for reputation clearly are situated at the outcome level; in particular, they attach to the indirect impact of communication. Reputation management can, in terms of this impact level model, be made verifiable and controllable, as the fulfilment of stakeholder expectations positively influences their attitude towards the company, motivates a positive reputation and thus creates trust.

The ICA model provides for the appropriate variables and indicators for all impact levels of the model at every level of the cascade, from the strategic to the operative level. It thus is possible to aggregate indicators upwardly multiple times over many levels, or at least to view them in the context of a defined cause-effect relationship. The European Communication Monitor mentioned above shows that, in practice, measuring the success of communication often is still restricted to the output level: media response analyses and online usage statistics are often used, in isolation, to manage communication (Zerfaß et al. 2008: 38-46). But if not all impact levels are transparent, no controlling and no proof of value creation are possible. The input level, too, is often neglected, although it is not possible without this level to prove the cost-benefit relationship – no matter how good the proof of effect is.

Conclusion and implementation

Reputation management can substantially support communication controlling with its conclusions about the indirect impact of communication. At the uppermost strategic level of communication, measuring reputation enables a link to be formed between the performance of corporate communication and a company's value creation. Reputation management can make transparent the relationships to the company's stakeholders. This is all the more important, given that it is no longer information and knowledge, but rather relationships and dialogue, that are at the heart of modern corporate communication.

On the other hand, communication controlling provides a clear management framework for the various approaches towards measuring reputation. Reputation is situated within the logic of value driver relationships and thus becomes controllable.

There is no contradiction between the methods of communication controlling and those of reputation management. On the contrary, the insights they provide complement each other, and together they enable professional management. Both approaches aim to prove the value created by soft factors.

The ICA's basic model allows a strategic decision by management to improve reputation to be implemented operationally in corporate communication. It does so by linking the strategic level in several stages with control levers at the operational level.

When implementing controlling of this kind within a company, a stage-by-stage approach is sometimes wise. For those in charge of PR especially, it can mean a confrontation with a new, managerial way of thinking –

which, in turn, means all the challenges of typical change processes. The first step needs to be putting in place strategy development and goal planning for communication in the way described. The first measurement of reputation incorporates the stakeholder perspective. Repeated measurements ensure the effect is monitored.

Only in the second phase can the full range of measures be linked to the target level in the way described. For this, the target system should already have proven its worth and management should have given their binding commitment to regular planning.

References

Deyhle A, Radinger G (2008) Controller Handbuch, 5. Vol, 6. edit.

DPRG white papers on communication indicators: The portal about value creation and evaluating communication. An initiative of Leipzig University and the "Value Creation through Communication" working group of the German Public Relations Association (Deutsche Public Relations Gesellschaft, DPRG): <http://www.communicationcontrolling.de/en/dprg-white-papers-on-communication-indicators.html>

Gfrerer A (2008): Communication Performance Management in der HVB. Presentation at Kommunikationskongress Berlin, 10 October 2008

Internationaler Controller Verein (International Controller Association <http://www.controlling-online.eu>

Nix P, Schnöring S, Siegert G (2009) Den guten Ruf professionell managen. Harvard Business Manager 1/2009, pp 8-11

Money K, Hillenbrand C (2006) Using reputation measurement to create value: An analysis and integration of existing measures. Journal of General Management, Vol 32 No1 pp 1-12

Pfannenberg J, Zerfaß A (ed.) (2005) Wertschöpfung durch Kommunikation. Wie Unternehmen den Erfolg ihrer Kommunikation steuern und bilanzieren. Frankfurt

Piwinger M, Porák V (ed.) (2005) Kommunikations-Controlling. Wiesbaden

Piwinger M, Zerfaß A (ed.) (2007) Handbuch Unternehmenskommunikation. Wiesbaden

Will M (2007) Wertorientiertes Kommunikationsmanagement. Stuttgart

Zerfass A., Moreno A., Tench R, Verčič D, Verhoeven P (2008) European Communication Monitor 2008. Trends in Communication Management and Public Relations – Results and Implications. Brussels, Leipzig: Euprera / University of Leipzig <http://www.communication-monitor.eu>

The role of corporate and personal reputations in the global war for talent

Kelvin Thompson

with contributions from Jodi Kaelle

And yet the war for leadership talent rages on

The war cry continues despite the volatile economic cycle. Leadership will make or break you – this is not new news. And yet it is clear that so many firms struggle to gain any ground because they are unaware of their leader's negative reputation for attracting talent, preparedness for battle or worse, both. And so often when all looks lost the solution is to hire an executive search firm that will revitalise your chances and bring you the choice of leadership you need. Does this sound familiar and was the end result, even if you did identify a "best athlete" to be CEO, the loss of more ground? Well as it's not all the headhunters' fault.

The reputation of a firm's CEO is a key contributor to the reputation the company has in the talent marketplace as well as being key to re-cruiting and motivating the right team to move the company forward.

People care about what others think. They care about what a com-pany's reputation is in the blogosphere, what they hear from friends, former colleagues and from other third party sources. For a "C-suite" candidate, the reputation of a leader is instrumental in the executives' decisions to join the executive team. If you believe in the trickle down theory, you know that poor leadership at the top drives all aspects of an organisation. Given the social networking and Web 2.0 world we have today, bad leadership is not kept a secret for long, and you will have a challenge in recruiting the right people at every level around the globe.

This chapter discusses these issues and how to meet the challenges presented.

J. Klewes, R. Wreschniok (eds.), *Reputation Capital*, DOI 10.1007/978-3-642-01630-1_6,
© Springer-Verlag Berlin Heidelberg 2009

Talent and the science of assessment

Ed Michael's renowned study for McKinsey on the Global War for Talent laid out the blueprint for what has become one of the most discussed but least understood battlegrounds. It is a theme that has joined the lexicon of every personnel consulting firm and executive search business painting a doomsday scenario to agitate clients into action.[1]

In parallel with this study, the term "human capital" has become a generally accepted term to describe the roles and efforts of strategic personnel management. In some cases these are distinct and separate functions in organisations.[2]

John Boudreau's excellent article on "Talentship" is one of the most striking perspectives on the subject. He highlights the need for human resources executives to better understand strategic decisions behind hiring and retaining talent resources. Boudreau goes further to describe that the bifurcation of the strategy and execution in many functions has been late to the party. Though it has been accepted and recognised that human capital is one of the cornerstones of any business, its acquisition and management is still viewed often very much as an art form. The lack of strategic management of human capital in an organisation leaves people disconnected to the larger mission. This leads to failure either to acquire the right human capital or to retain it and manage it to its maximum potential.

Symptomatic of this is the often quoted statistic that 40% of executive hires (external candidates) are unsuccessful. The executive search industry continues to use the same methodology that has generated such dismal performance for over 50 years. The industry has most recently offered an innovative way to address improving the odds of a placement's "stickiness" – namely, to give clients the chance to pay additional fees for the science of assessment! Shouldn't a full assessment of any executive be an imperative part of the process when hiring your next CEO or leadership team – not an add-on? We think so. It is no wonder that Brad and then Geoff Smart in the groundbreaking book "Topgrading" is so disdainful of the executive search industry.

The current economic recession has clearly affected the executive search business. Leaders are put to the test when the market applies downward pressure on stock prices, valuations and capital raising efforts.

---

[1] www.heidrick.com, www.spencerstuart.com, www.egonzehnder.com, www.boyden.com
[2] E.g. Goldman Sachs and GE

In addition, executives are much more likely to stay put and ride out a storm rather than take chances at a new company, whether or not they are happy in their current positions.

But despite the current economic turmoil, the executive search industry will continue to thrive because in all our years in search we have found one truth: in an up market you need a strong leadership team, and in a down market you need a strong leadership team. The competencies and experiences needed to be strong leaders can differ in each paradigm. In a volatile market strong teams excel in cost management, expectation management, ensuring the company remains profitable with a good reputation, and, if need be, serving as a calming influence. In a down market companies need leaders who can inspire employees, the board and shareholders despite revenue declines. In an up market, leaders need to focus on growth, examining all possible transactions, while being creative, cutting edge and transparent.

Of course we all know this and also that critical to success for leadership in any market is integrity and value creation. But this current market tests the authenticity of the mission and purpose of the firm – if the knee-jerk reaction to flagging financial results in tough economic times is to fire 15% of the staff or, as they say, implement a "Reduction In Force" (RIF) it leaves one to question that overused line on the company's mission statement that proclaims "people are our greatest asset". It is even more troubling for services businesses when customer service professionals are part of a RIF. That makes us all question the company's commitment and passion for the clients. If shareholders are the only primary stakeholders then loyalty to other stakeholders – such as clients and employees – is severely compromised. Furthermore, knee-jerk RIFs make it difficult to attract and retain top talent. The justification that is bandied around in defense is that one has to cut out mediocrity to keep room and resources for the top talent. That is a wonderful concept until you ask who hired and kept that talent in the first place, who put it on the important client teams and who paid it a performance bonus last year. If there is anything that sends a message of weak leadership it is the "RIF lemmings".

Reputation matters more than ever

However, regardless of the status of the economy, one of the most critical issues to highlight when recruiting leadership is the reputation of corporations and individuals. Why? Because it is one of the key factors in attracting A players and retaining them. There is no point going to battle if you can't attract the troops to work for you, and even worse if you can't keep them once the battle starts.

For at least two decades companies have been preaching to employees to manage their own career, giving flexible benefits packages and portable pensions/401(k) plans. The loyalty that historically characterised "lifers" versus "salary men" has disappeared. Add to those reasons the volatile global economy, rampant RIFs and quite bluntly, mass firing[3], we can see why loyal employees are far and few between. People are simply taking care of themselves because they have been forced to do so. One has to question the authenticity of the leaders who use mission statements that proclaim one thing while the firm acts in the opposite way "as it has a responsibility as a public firm". Here is a typical example:

"XXX is a multinational corporation engaged in socially responsible operations worldwide. It is dedicated to provide products and services of such quality that our customers will receive superior value while our employees and business partners will share in our success and our stockholders will receive a sustained superior return on their investment."

So with this background in mind what attracts top employees to the firm of today? What reputation does the firm need to espouse to attract the stars of the workforce? And what is the reputation of today's corporate leaders that makes them successful as talent magnets?

It is important to state up front that there is no catch-all solution for finding great executive leadership. Take John Doerr's (Kleiner Perkins) well-known division of leaders into two distinct groups: missionaries and mercenaries. Though his comments are targeted on the entrepreneurial community they can certainly be applied to companies in general and to leaders-at-large. After interviewing hundreds of executives around the world we have found that companies and leaders tend to fall into one of Doerr's two categories. But to place a mercenary in a missionary business or vice versa is akin to mixing oil and water – it doesn't work or, if it does, it is short-lived with more often than not a disastrous conclusion.

There are numerous examples quoted in the "Are leaders portable?" white paper from HBR studying the various levels of success for GE alumni. It is crucial to recognize what your corporate DNA is, and therefore who will be able to function effectively in a leadership position. Changing DNA is a long slow process and a painful one – changing lead-

---

[3] GM, Yahoo!, Google, Heidrick & Struggles, Microsoft and Merck are just a few from an ever-growing list.

ers when done successfully is quite the opposite. So what is your DNA? Once you have answered that question make sure you attract and hire leadership that will thrive with the body that you have, not one you wish you had.

For too long the excuse that recruiting is an art not a science has been used as an excuse for sloppy hiring and to paper over cronyism. There will always be some art to the process but the science of assessment is now tried and tested and when properly executed can dramatically increase the chances of a successful hire. In addition detailed referencing on executives is much easier today and less covert as the spread of citizen journalism and demands for transparency provide much content to reference beyond character referencing.

It is clear that we are near the end of the era when executives who have clearly not performed, many would suggest have put us in this economic mess, are rewarded with another top jobs and excessive compensation.[4] Given the media and the public's better understanding of what these companies were doing that bordered on criminal activity, those leaders will not be rewarded with another career move and they will be lucky to get another paycheck. This goes against the "good old boys' network" of yesteryear. The current public outcry has actually been a good exercise in understanding "what good looks like" in a company's leader, and it is now time to right the wayward ship and identify leaders who want long-term strategic growth and success for the global economy. These leaders are out there, and they will ultimately be rewarded with appropriate compensation and further career highlights if they tie their personal satisfaction and achievement to the success of their companies in the long term.

It is now time to find the next generation of leaders whose reputations show that they place the company success ahead of their own personal ambitions.

The search begins

A reputation for the mismanagement of human capital or ignorance of such mismanagement is one of the crucial reasons why firms are unsuccessful at hiring the talent they need to achieve their goals.

---

[4] Stan O'Neal of Merrill Lynch, Bernie Madoff, Frank Raines of Fannie Mae, or Angelo Mozilo of Countrywide.

My mentors told me early in my career that many searches fail before they start. This is not just because of obvious reasons such as the lack of job specifications or disunity in the hiring team. More often it is simply because companies and their chosen executive search partners fail either to accurately or comprehensively assess external marketplace factors before embarking on an expensive and time consuming search.

Before an executive search begins, questions you should ask include:

- What is our reputation in the marketplace?

- What hurdles will we have to overcome?

- What misconceptions exist in the market that we must address before this search begins to ensure that we won't have our lead candidate turn down our final offer?

Increasingly, potential candidates have new tools at their disposal through the rise of social networking websites such as Linked In and Facebook. And there are numerous blogs through which top executives will test the market themselves to try and understand the reputation and reality of a potential employer[5]. These media outlets give individuals direct one-to-one conversations with current and ex-employees, giving them something of an upper hand in the hiring process. The requirement on executives' contracts prohibiting them from disparaging former employers/employees is no longer as meaningful because opinions can now be shared easily and anonymously via cyberspace.

Of course you cannot change the past (though many have tried with wonderfully written mission and vision statements), but you can understand what the market is saying about you and how credible your company is before attempting to snare a prize fish. This preparation to better understand what you honestly have to offer is key and it will ensure that the messages you give to potential executives are viewed with authenticity, which increases your chances of success.

Your reputation is on the line as soon as a search begins. Whenever conducting a thorough executive search, internally or externally, you will have approximately 120 to 150 conversations with potential candidates or with sources for them. The image and perception of your firm will be influenced or even formed by that interaction. In addition to being potential candidates these executives may also be competitors, business partners and/or clients of your services/products. Over time, all companies will

---

[5] See www.glassdoor.com and www.vanno.com

conduct numerous executive hiring exercises with many different executive search partners. The number of executives who are approached will grow to a significantly and that exposure – more precisely, what occurs during the interaction – will be key to defining your reputation and brand in the executive marketplace. Do you put as much thought into this as you do when you conduct a marketing campaign? For example one recent project for a major European financial services institution seeking to replace the Asia Pacific management team with locals after a decade of expats in the roles identified that we would be speaking to approximately 1,200 senior executives during the course of the 12 months as potential candidates and sources – all of whom were also customers or potential customers. How do you ensure that your search partners are delivering the appropriate messages in a manner that supports your brand and reputation?

And how do you keep your star executives motivated when you have them? Do you understand who your top competitors for talent really are? What are those competitors doing to attempt to attract them?

Beyond the broader corporate reputation, how does the role of the CEO/Chairman affect brand/reputation in winning the war for talent? It is no surprise that the most famous CEOs – for instance Jack Welch when he was at the helm at GE and Hank Paulson at Goldman Sachs – are "hands on" with all senior hiring and also with potential departures needing to be convinced to remain. Though it is commonly accepted that the executive team, rather than an individual, truly runs the business, it has been proven time and time again that the reputation and brand of the company's leader is a critical factor influencing why people join an organisation. And in these days of transparency, citizen journalism, and public disclosure of compensation, it is crucial that the leaders of today's businesses are authentic and open. They also must communicate with great clarity what they stand for, what their objectives are, and where they are seeking to drive their business. Without such a stance it will be extremely to attract the right A players on to their executive team and to keep them as a team to drive the business forward.

Finally, the need to understand the importance of inclusivity and its effect on reputation are key. Provincialism is a thing of the past – we live in and work in a global marketplace. Companies that seek to win the war for talent must be attractive, productive and rewarding for all genders, races and religions. At a basic level, if you consider that a company has a reputation for sexist attitudes and behaviour, that company essentially is cutting itself off from employing 50% of the available workforce. Our firm is taking that theory one step further and we are currently conducting a study with an investment boutique to understand the truth in the hypothesis that firms who have had senior women in management positions over long periods of time should have a premium in their market value. So far the research supports that. It is becoming quite clear that in today's world, embracing diversity is an issue that will play an increasingly important role. Those that have a brand and reputation for inclusivity will undoubtedly have a competitive advantage in the war for talent.

But let's look at this in the simplest way possible: as headhunters the great reputations of a company and a CEO make it easier to do our job. Brand matters. And the partners you choose to work with will either enhance your brand or damage it. Executive search players stretch across the whole spectrum from missionary to mercenary – It only makes sense to be as careful with choosing your search partner as you would with a new hire – after all they are the ambassadors for your brand in the executive talent battlefield.

As we see more layoffs occur regularly these days, this resonates loudly in the talent pool. Companies are often pressured to let go of their employees when economic conditions require it but such cost-cutting measures come with a high cost in terms of both morale and long-term growth prospects. At the same time, it is key to reward and retain the employees you have identified as high potentials so that you can hold on to them when the market goes up. Employee loyalty is often built and strengthened during a down cycle rather than a growth cycle when there are many other job options to consider. Investment in employees should not stop when there is a recession and, in fact, it should be a time to solidify their loyalty.

Why executive search can help

Many would say that a company is only as good as its current and past leadership, but the executive team behind that leader is just as important. The right executive search professionals can help you tie all of this together, regardless of the marketplace ups and downs. A company with an inspiring mission and purpose will always attract the right talent. It is key, however, to remember that good talent is sacred and worth an investment in good times and in bad, if you want the reputation of a good employer in the marketplace. Understanding what your reputation is and managing it authentically is key to your ability to win in the war for talent.

References

Michaels E, Handfield-Jones H (2001) The War for Talent. Beth Axelrod, Harvard Business School Press

Boudreau JW, Ramstad PM (2006) Talentship and HR measurement and analysis: from ROI to strategic organizational change. Human Resource Planning, Thomson Gale Publishing

Smart BD, Smart G (1999) Topgrading: How Leading Companies Win by Hiring, Coaching and Keeping the Best People. Prentice Hall Press

Doerr J (2005) Mercenaries and Missionaries. Kleiner Perkins, Caufield & Byers<http://ecorner.stanford.edu/authorMaterialInfo.html?mid=1274>

Groysberg B, McLean AN, Nohria N (2006) Are Leaders Portable. Harvard Business Review OnPoint Article

The CSR myth: true beauty comes from within

Matthias Vonwil and Robert Wreschniok

The rapid spiralling of the property and financial crisis in the USA into an international economic crisis has been mirrored by an equally rapid increase in talk of a global crisis of confidence that is throwing into doubt trust in the entire economic system, companies and many of their managers (Schranz 2008). But which mechanisms are responsible for this growing loss of faith? This article argues that the reputation of persons, companies or even institutions is always part of a network of tensions between functional, social and expressive reputation. The authors examine the measures with which the economy attempts to regain lost confidence. They ask whether established corporate social responsibility (CSR) measures are in a position to improve a company's social reputation. Does the desired effect justify the financial expense and manpower in this area? Is it right for many CSR strategies to focus their communication on measures that mainly highlight social commitment or should the focus be more on solving problems in-house?

When companies with a good and intact reputation are examined, it becomes apparent that public perception of these businesses is primarily shaped by sober corporate and business communication (see also Eisenegger 2005). Companies with an excellent reputation have managed – as market leaders, hidden champions or niche specialists with a clear, unique position – to build up a strong functional reputation and a clearly mapped out expressive reputation. The social reputation of these enterprises, on the other hand, plays a more subordinate role in the general evaluation of their overall reputation.[1]

---

[1] Economic reputation, social reputation and expressive reputation are the three fundamental constants of reputation configurations in the modern media society. These constants determine general perception and judgement of people in the public eye and of companies: (1) Functional or economic reputation: this requires functional role requirements to be fulfilled competently (expertise); (2) Normative or social reputation: this requires compliance with socio-moral demands (integrity); (3) Expressive reputation: this represents the individual and emotionally engaging aspects (identity).

J. Klewes, R. Wreschniok (eds.), *Reputation Capital*, DOI 10.1007/978-3-642-01630-1_7,
© Springer-Verlag Berlin Heidelberg 2009

The issue becomes interesting when we closely examine companies that have to compete on the market with a less distinguished or even poor reputation. Instead of concentrating on improving their functional reputation or elaborating their expressive reputation, many enterprises have a knee-jerk recourse to CSR measures to improve their social reputation. And they often employ not inconsiderable effort: a study by the Bertelsmann Stiftung[2] foundation back in 2005 confirmed that 57% of the companies[3] studied have a dedicated budget for CSR averaging about €800,000. The Boston Consulting Group estimates that in 2008, the world's leading listed companies invest one to two per cent of their EBITDA (earnings before interest, taxes, depreciation and amortisation) in corporate social responsibility[4] measures.

The question now facing us is: Is this investment – putting to one side purely philanthropic motives – justified if the company is dedicated to a lasting improvement to its reputation in the market among its stakeholder groups?

To answer this question, we shall look into the following:

- What do enterprises understand by the term CSR and are the prevalent definitions compatible with efficient reputation management for companies?

- What value proposition do CSR measures achieve as one of many functions in an intact corporate social reputation?

- How accurately is the social reputation of companies perceived in the general populace and what share of the public's overall evaluation does it contribute to?

- Does actively cultivating social reputation by means of CSR measures hold more opportunities or risks for a company's reputation?

- Last but not least: What conclusions should be drawn for the strategic alignment of the CSR engagement and the tactical implementation of the measures?

---

[2] Gewinn und Verantwortung – study by the Bertelsmann Stiftung on CSR (2005)

[3] The Bertelsmann Stiftung commissioned the survey in May and June of 2005. The managers surveyed head companies that had at least 200 employees or a turnover of €20 million in 2004. More than 60% of the companies are in the manufacturing and service sectors, a quarter are active in the financial services sector and in retail, just under seven percent are in the primary sector.

[4] Lecture by BCG in summer 2008 in the Ludwig-Maximilian-Universität of Munich

Corporate social responsibility – an approximation

A multiplicity of concepts, ideas and notions has grown up around the wide field of CSR. Academic discourse alone has produced a range of different approaches to the subject. Since the 1990s, at the latest, the debate has moved beyond the academic arena and has been increasingly discussed in public (Eisenegger and Vonwil 2004). This development has led to existing terms and concepts becoming less focussed and more arbitrary, which have in part become replaced by new terms that are often not really any more precise (Schranz 2007)[5].

By far the most widespread and accepted approach is Carroll's definition of CSR, which represents the levels of a company's social responsibility in the form of a CSR pyramid (Carroll 1991).

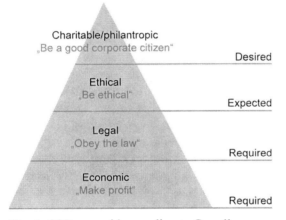

Fig. 1. CSR pyramid according to Carroll.
Source: Carroll 1991, p. 42

It is this comprehensive perspective that we shall follow here, which, in addition to the economic level, also recognises legal, ethical and philanthropical levels. The European Commission also ties into Carroll's view by defining the social responsibility of companies as follows: CSR is a "concept whereby companies integrate social and environmental concerns in their business operations and in their interaction with their stakeholders on

---

[5] Schranz (2007) provides a very good overview.

a voluntary basis.[6] Amongst other things, this definition helps to emphasise that:

- CSR covers social and environmental issues in spite of the English term corporate social responsibility;

- CSR is not or should not be separate from business strategy and operations: it is about integrating social and environmental concerns into business strategy and operations;

- CSR is a voluntary concept;

an important aspect of CSR is how enterprises interact with their internal and external stakeholders (employees, customers, neighbours, nongovernmental organisations, public authorities, etc.)"[7]

In addition to this, it is important to emphasise that, besides the various definitions, companies need to take account of the constantly changing ideas of social responsibility. What is considered socially responsible changes over time and also depends in no small part on the specific arrangement and organisation of politics and the economy, as well as media publicity (Donsbach and Gattwinkel 1998; Eisenegger and Vonwil 2004; Imhof 2006; Schranz 2008). As such, social responsibility today includes not only social and economic components, but above all an ecological component as well. Whereas social and economic responsibility have been discussed since the beginnings of the modern era, which saw the specialisation and differentiation of the economic system, ecological responsibility only began to establish itself from the 1970s onward. Today, in the context of the debate on global warming, it has become firmly anchored as the third pillar of a company's social responsibility. This point is all the more relevant for business in practice because as a person responsible for CSR, it is not possible to fall back on static definitions; instead, you have to commit to meeting the times. This is no easy task, as is shown by a recent study from the communications consultancy Pleon (2008), which surveyed stakeholders from the world of politics, science and NGOs about their current expectations of companies' CSR commitments. The result: First and foremost, companies should design their core business activities responsibly. Instead of, for example, sponsoring major sporting events or improving playgrounds, they would be better advised to comply with industrial safety provisions or environmental standards. "Seen from the outside, companies show the most serious deficits in areas such as 'humane pro-

---

[6] Green Paper Promoting a European Framework for Corporate Social Responsibility, 2001, KOM (2001) 366 final.
[7] http://ec.europa.eu/enterprise/csr/index_en.htm

duction abroad', 'the environment' and 'role as a taxpayer'. This is where we find the widest gap between what the stakeholders expect and the degree of compliance" (Pleon 2008). Other important aspects that shape the public's expectations of a company's social reputation are labour protection, sustainable production, further training or maintaining production sites in the home country. In this ranking, support for international educational and social projects fall far behind. In the overall evaluation, aspects that are directly linked to the company's business are a third more important than other aspects. The study concludes: Companies are worst in the areas in which society expects most of them, that is, their expertise at solving problems in-house. The results suggest that companies improve their social reputation by means of CSR measures that have a measurable effect on internal social and environmental processes.

CSR as a function of social reputation

CSR as social, economic and ecological sustainability can be classified within an overarching reputation model that reinforces the good reputation of an organisation or a person in line with social theory (Eisenegger 2005). The reputation model here is a conceptual prerequisite for clarifying how assessments of reputation are formed in society.

Eisenegger developed this type of model by conceiving reputation as "the public standing that a person, institution, organisation or, more generally, a (collective) subject enjoys in the mid- to long-term and which results from the diffusion of prestige information to unknown third parties out from beyond the ambit of personal social networks. (Eisenegger 2005)". Unlike pre-modern honour, reputation is not linked to notions of origin, but can be acquired by anyone. In exchange, it is subject to the need for constant legitimation, it must be produced communicatively and must be safeguarded by constant reproduction. Understood in this way, reputation is recognition accorded to actors (persons, organisations, institutions) who manage to adapt themselves enduringly to the expectations of important reference groups.

A definition backed up in this way by communication theory means that we can always evaluate a company's reputation in terms of three views of the world (Habermas 1999[3]).[8] According to this, an organisation or person can be assessed to the extent to which it acts correctly, well or truthfully.

---

[8] In accordance with Habermas' (1999[3]) three world views. See also: Eisenegger and Imhof (2007).

"Correct" refers accordingly to the rational, "good" to the normative and "true" to the expressive reputation. Reputation (Habermas 1999[3]) is subdivided into:

- Functional reputation: this requires the competent fulfilment of functional role requirements (expertise). In the economic context, this can also be referred to as the economic reputation.

- Normative reputation: this requires compliance with socio-moral requirements (integrity). The normative or social reputation corresponds to the demands of corporate social responsibility. In other words, a party that acts sustainably in social, economic and ecological terms has a good normative reputation.

- Expressive reputation: this represents the individual and emotionally engaging aspects (identity).

The challenge to reputation management consists of the difficult balance between managing expectations in the dimensions of functional and social reputation, and differentiation and uniqueness in the face of the competition in the dimension of expressive reputation.

Social reputation in the public's perception

Our introductory remark, that when evaluating an intact company reputation, the expectations of the company's stakeholders are focussed between 70 and 90 percent on economic and not social affairs (Schranz 2007)[9] plays a large role in answering the question of whether CSR measures help to improve a company's reputation on the market. The reason for this is that it suggests how a company's social reputation is perceived at all by the general public. Current data concerning this is provided by the Business-Reflectors from GfK Switzerland in an investigation in 2008. In a representative online survey (3400 participants), the reputation of the most important Swiss companies (115 companies from 19 sectors) was examined.[10]

---

[9] As well as unpublished benchmarking studies in consulting projects from Pleon, ECRS and fög from 1999 to 2008.

[10] fög's theoretical model was used here to measure reputation, and the three types of reputation (functional, social and expressive reputation) were recorded by means of three questions each. Accordingly, the results can be compared to regularities in fög's reputation research. For more about the reputation types, see: Eisenegger and Imhof (2007).

In principle, it was established that social reputation has a lesser effect on the overall company reputation than the functional reputation does.[11] Furthermore, the companies' social reputation was evaluated significantly worse than their functional reputation. In a reputation index of 0 to 100, social reputation was at least five index points lower than the functional reputation for more than 60 percent of the enterprises in 2008. For 40%, it was even ten index points lower.

If the assumption that a good social reputation is beneficial to the overall reputation were true, the companies at the top of the reputation ranking would also have a good social reputation. However, this is not backed up by the evidence. The 20 top-ranked best known Swiss companies[12] (see Figure 2) include only three companies with a social reputation that is better than their functional reputation (Migros in forth place, Coop in ninth and Migrosbank in eighteenth).

For the three most respected companies, the difference between the social and functional reputation was more than 18 index points. For more than half the enterprises, the difference was at least eight index points. In other words: an excellent overall reputation is down to a firm functional reputation. Social reputation should not be evaluated poorly here, but it often trails behind by comparison.

A look at the last ten places confirms this view (see Figure 3).

The difference between the functional and social reputation here is much smaller. Three of the companies have a better social reputation, but that does not help them much at the bottom of the ladder. The functional reputation in the last places is never more than eight index points better than the social reputation. This means that these companies are missing the positive impetus of economic efficiency and performance. In other words: the companies with the worst reputation values do not score poorly due to their social reputation but rather due to a lack of positive evaluation of their economic capability.

---

[11] In 2008, social reputation accounted for 28% of the overall reputation, whereas the economic reputation accounted for 30%. At 42%, the expressive appraisal played the largest role. GfK BusinessReflector 2008.

[12] Only companies with a prompted level of recognition of at least 90% were selected.

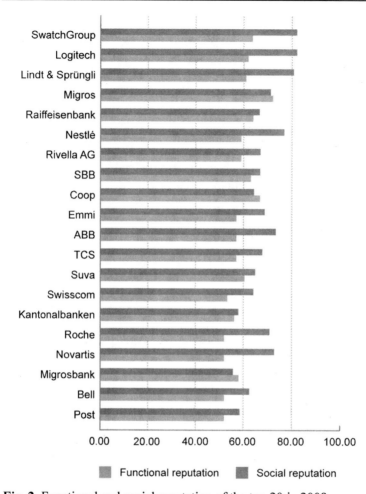

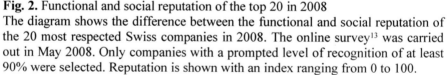

Fig. 2. Functional and social reputation of the top 20 in 2008
The diagram shows the difference between the functional and social reputation of the 20 most respected Swiss companies in 2008. The online survey[13] was carried out in May 2008. Only companies with a prompted level of recognition of at least 90% were selected. Reputation is shown with an index ranging from 0 to 100.

---

[13] Information at: http://www.gfk.ch/methods/cr_methoden_01/002648/index.de.html

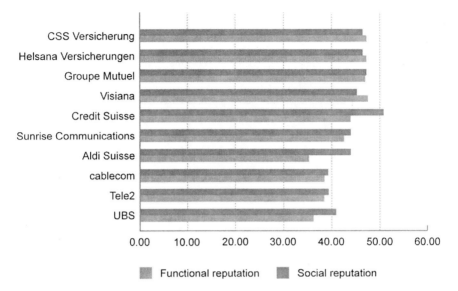

Fig. 3. Functional and social reputation of the bottom 10 places in 2008. The diagram shows the difference between the functional and social reputation of the ten Swiss companies with the lowest reputation values in 2008. The survey was carried out in May 2008. Only companies with a prompted level of recognition of at least 90% were selected. Reputation is shown with an index ranging from 0 to 100.

But are there also companies that successfully manage the balancing act between functional and social reputation? In the top 20 places, there are 5 companies in which the difference between the reputation types is no more than 3.5 index points. Migros (forth place), Raiffeisenbank (fifth), Schweizerische Bundesbahnen SBB (eighth), Coop (ninth) and the Cantonal Banks (fifteenth). These companies have two main things in common; two aspects that Schranz also points out in his examination of public communication (Schranz 2007). One aspect is that, with the exception of SBB and the cantonal banks, these are all cooperatively organised companies. Unlike incorporated companies, the main aim of the cooperative is not to maximise profit for the benefit of the shareholders, but to promote the interests of its members. Furthermore, the cooperative belongs to its members (not individual shareholders) and is managed according to democratic principles. Social responsibility is therefore an integral part of the business policy of cooperatively organised companies, which gives them corresponding legitimation. The other aspect is that all five companies are markedly oriented towards the domestic market; that is, the organisations are highly or exclusively focussed on Switzerland. Their corporate cultures have strong national, regional and local roots and direct their activities in many areas according to generally accepted economic, social and cultural values and norms, bringing them closer, so to speak, to the population than the global players are. Although this data was gathered before the world-wide upheavals on the financial markets, we can assume that this situation has been aggravated, if anything, by the global economic crisis and ensuing crisis in confidence.

Actively cultivating social reputation as a reputation risk

The GfK BusinessReflector survey showed that social reputation generates systematically lower values than the functional reputation among the general public. In the following, we will demonstrate that actively cultivating social reputation in media reporting has some surprising results.[14]

Cultivating corporate social responsibility to maintain a good reputation is today seen as an integral part of good corporate governance. The move towards a more morally responsible corporate culture, triggered by the growing influence of the media over the economy, forces companies to justify the expectations of a critical public. There are numerous different views and concepts concerning how this can be done. However, the aim is always the same: strengthening your reputation in order to use the benefits that come with a good reputation to further economic success.

Whereas the concept of a functional reputation that is used here is viewed as objectively as possible, social reputation, with its demand for overall societal integrity, refers beyond the role "into the realm of motivation, character and also morals" (Voswinkel 2001). Added to this, as pointed out before, is the fact that reputation in a media society can no longer merely be seen as fulfilling obligations, but rather must be constantly reproduced in communication. And this is precisely why it constantly risks the suspicion of being staged. Ignoring this logic brings the danger of systematically underestimating the risk of actively cultivating social reputation. For as soon as communicative measures in favour of social reputation are exposed as nothing more than marketing actions, they

---

[14] It is not our intention to draw a causal link between media reporting and public opinion. There have not yet been any studies in the scientific community of agenda-setting effects regarding the reputation of companies. A systematic comparison of media reporting and public opinion in Switzerland is currently being carried out in a long-term research project by GfK Switzerland and the Research Institute for the Public and Society (fög) at the University of Zurich. However, not enough time has passed to make any valid statements.

lose their credibility and the organisation loses its authenticity. This is why it is dangerous to see cultivating social reputation as advertising and delegating the task to the Marketing or PR departments. Analyses of public communication at the Research Institute for the Public and Society (fög) at the University of Zurich have demonstrated clear findings in this area.

For example, various empirical studies by the fög have uncovered the basic rules that govern social reputation in the media society (Eisenegger and Vonwil 2004). First of all, there is a clear verdict on concentrating the issue on social reputation. If we examine all the reports that have a measurable influence on the overall reputation of a company – due to their centrality, lasting character and diffusion across various major media outlets – and if we then extract the portion of the reporting on social reputation (that is, the part of reporting to which the company draws attention in the context of social evaluation criteria), we find an average value of between 10% and 30% (Schranz 2007). The share is therefore markedly smaller than the share that addresses economic performance; that is, a company's functional reputation. In other words, "contrary to statements by many management consultants, the principal focus on a company continues to remain on 'hard figures'"(Schranz 2007) and is far less concerned with how the company treats its employees or the ecological effects of its actions.

If we now examine the value judgements applied to companies in reporting, we can see that social reputation tends to be a negative factor, leading to the generation of negative effects on reputation. These findings argue against profiling the company's reputation by working on social reputation "because, firstly, this subject area is not particularly highly regarded and, secondly, reporting in this area tends to be more negative than in other areas" (Schranz 2007). In most cases in which the integrity of a company is addressed in the media, the issue at hand involves making a scandal out of corporate misconduct and not praising corporate commitment. On the contrary: the attempt to actively cultivate a corporate social reputation in the media by means of CSR measures leads to additional risks to reputation, which – perversely – primarily have a massively negative effect on the functional reputation in the public's perception. For if scandal relating to social reputation takes on such a central role in editorial reporting in times of crisis, the stabilising effects that a functional reputation give to a company are overshadowed. This can be seen clearly in a whole series of prominent examples, such as the culmination of the Siemens corruption affair or the Mannesmann trial of Josef Ackermann. In both cases, the issue of social reputation – that is, the question of morally correct behaviour on the part of the companies in question and their top managers – took up far more than 70% of the overall evaluation in the public media.[15] The consequences are clear to see: The affected company no longer manages to get across to the public information that would be relevant to the constitution of the fundamental functional reputation. By necessity, crisis communication circles around questions of morals and integrity; aspects of social reputation, that is. However, defensive crisis communication also ensures that the weighting between functional and social reputation remains misbalanced, thereby aggravating existing reputational damage.

But is it at all possible to positively influence media reporting in the area of social reputation? Will the media and journalists allow themselves to be instrumentalised in this type of reputation management? Cultivating social reputation by means of active communication, such as press releases, press conferences or interviews has hardly any effect, according to Schranz's research. 26% of all articles centring on the subject of a company's social reputation can be traced back to active PR measures on the part of enterprises. Projected against the entire set of reports about a company, this brings us to an effect of 2.6% to 7.8% of reporting on social reputation that is influenced to a greater or lesser degree by the company itself. Having said that, these measures have a positive effect on reputation, albeit only a slight one.

True beauty comes from within

In summary, we can conclude that successful management of a company's reputation requires strategies that foreground questions and answers about the company's economic development. Communicating social commitment brings more risks to reputation than opportunities.

This suggests two conclusions: Firstly, it is necessary to introduce to considerations of reputation every suitable internal step and measure that entails a high degree of moral integrity in corporate policy and in the management, in order to counteract any later public scandal.

Secondly, the question of what the added value of suitably communicating the company's CSR behaviour is has not yet been satisfactorily answered.

---

[15] Media reaction analyses from ECRS, Pleon, fög 2005, 2006, 2007, 2008 (unpublished).

This is due to cultural, communicational and strategic misunderstandings or shortcomings that lead to many companies' CSR commitment being misdirected:

The cultural dilemma: Unlike the more utilitarian basic approach of Anglo-Saxon and North American society, which sees the social benefit aspect of social commitment as the basis for its moral evaluation of a company, a widely-spread Continental European understanding of ethical behaviour is strongly influenced by Kantian ethics, which bases its evaluation of social obligation on moral noble-mindedness. In the European cultural area, it is not the outcome of a CSR commitment that is evaluated, but the motivation behind that commitment. Accordingly, "fig-leaf rhetoric" and presenting CSR management as a (bad) exercise in salving the company's conscience takes up a relatively large part of the, generally critical, reporting.

The communication trap: Frequently, communicating your own commitment, such as in CSR or sustainability reports geared towards the company's reputation, develops little staying power of its own. One major reason for this is certainly that decisive points of criticism and grievances concerning the company's actions are very often left out of these reports. In addition to this, the fact that the social and environmental standards to which companies commit themselves in reports frequently represent nothing more than the minimum legal standards does not do much to encourage confidence in the integrity of the business world. Also, many areas of social marketing, from the (in)famous "drink beer for the rain forest" campaign to the "with special thanks to" financed, corporate design-compliant donation appeals tend to leave more of an insipid aftertaste among the European public than public statements of solidarity and thanks for corporate social work carried out.

The strategy focus: Finally, the strategic focus of prevalent CSR measures seems to be misplaced. Even if there is now a consensus that CSR should be constructed alongside a business case and this business case is substantially different from company to company, the challenge of defining an individual CSR approach for an enterprise has not become any easier. This is generally due to the fact that questions are often asked in this context that attempt to measure the value contributed to the company balance by what are generally very diverse CSR commitments. Instead, enterprises should ask the fundamental question of whether the form of the commitment currently undertaken is at all compatible with the business case.

Beyond CSR: towards a new approach to corporate social responsibility

The search for business case compatibility has led us to a very pragmatic initial question in day-to-day consulting: "Which in-house and societal problems can the planned CSR commitment help to solve?" The starting point of our considerations is therefore not the question "Where can we usefully become involved?"; rather it is "What societal and in-house problems are there in the context of our company that could be effectively tackled by the use of CSR measures?" Where can we assume our corporate responsibility by achieving genuine corporate social impact?"

This article shows, for example, that CSR is not necessarily the best method for solving the problem of a poor reputation. In fact, by examining the stakeholders' expectations of a meaningful CSR commitment on the part of the company, we have suggested that this is primarily concerned with perhaps the most important of the company's relationships, i.e. its relationship with its employees. Obviously, CSR is aimed at internal effects (confident action) and external effects (reputation). However, the key lever is held by the company's employees themselves. This is why we consider CSR measures to be on the right track if they have a lasting impact on both the mindset and the behaviour of internal and external target groups. Only if this is the case is it possible to provide solid proof that there has been a contribution towards solving in-house and social problems. An approach that also helps companies to clearly measure the success of their commitment, that is to say, the contribution made towards the defined solution.

There is now a whole range of excellent CSR measures available that are able to satisfy this requirement, such as the Earthwatch Program from KPMG, which invites employees to take part in a competition of ideas about how KPMG can improve its environmental and community performance around the world. Or the "Human Element Programme" from Dow Chemical that begins with employees but is explicitly designed to improve the company's reputation, as well as the "Towers of Waste" that allowed Hiram Walker & Sons Limited to substantially reduce operating waste in cooperation with its employees in recent years. In the "Together" programme from the Metro Group, approaches were developed together with employees to make Metro more attractive to customers of immigrant origin. In this way, the retail group has become actively engaged in the diversity discussion. Or Deutsche Telekom, whose *direktzu René Obermann* [direct line to René Obermann] campaign starting in early 2009 has opened up a direct line of communication between the CEO and each and every employee, thereby sending a signal that Deutsche Telekom listens to its staff as competent, committed and entrepreneurial individuals, eye to eye.

Summary: Questioning CSR

There can be no doubt that, in the future, companies – complex, social entities with multiple and frequently contradictory interests and a very heterogeneous group of managers and employees (especially as enterprises become larger) – will continue to have difficulty in defining a CSR commitment that is, in fact, considered genuine by the public and that is perceived as based on a moral noble-mindedness in the Kantian sense. According to our observations, consistent compliance with this type of *ethos* is most likely to be seen in smaller and medium-sized family companies and public institutions, church institutions and private foundations. Interestingly, the latter is also true of foundations with close links to companies. This is most likely due to the fact that foundations are designed with a large degree of autonomy, thanks to their dedicated endowment funds, and are not committed to short-term corporate goals, focussing instead on the long-term objectives to which the foundation was originally dedicated.[16] As an example, the generic medication manufacturer betapharm was able to achieve genuine social impact within its sphere by making permanent its social commitment to Bunter Kreis (an organisation for chronically ill children) by setting up a dedicated betapharm company foundation.

However, the question of what the right CSR strategy is does not hinge on selecting the right means but on the particular company itself, its history, its self-image, its production processes and how it interacts with its own employees. You should always start with the right questions:

1. Which structures and processes in my company result in which patterns of perception and judgement in the stakeholder groups that are most important to the future of my company?

2. What type of culture do we live out, cultivate, reward and sanction in our company and how does this specifically affect the behaviour of our employees and managers in practice?

---

[16] Corporate foundations are often linked to the aim of strengthening close ties between the company and society: It is surely no accident that there has been an exponential growth in the setting up of foundations in recent years. In Switzerland, for example, more than 50% of the foundations active today – frequently referred to in academic discussions as seismographs of societal trends – were founded after 1993. Significantly, the majority of endowment funds are used in the "social" sphere.

3. How do we have to alter these structures to make it possible to actually give life to the moral ethos that made our company great and to which our employees and managers feel bound?

4. What means do we have at our disposal to tackle the problems for which our company is justifiably responsible?

If you can answer these questions for you and your company, you have taken the first step towards lasting reputation management.

References

Carroll AB (1991): The Pyramid of Corporate Social Responsibility. Toward the Moral Management of Organizational Stakeholders. In: Business Horizons, pp 39-48

Donsbach W, Gattwinkel D (1998): Öl ins Feuer. Die publizistische Inszenierung des Skandals um die Rolle der Ölkonzerne in Nigeria. University Press. Dresden

Eisenegger M, Imhof K (2007): The True, the Good and the Beautiful: Reputation Management in the Media Society. fög discussion paper 2007-0001

Eisenegger M (2005) Reputation in der Mediengesellschaft, Konstitution – Issues Monitoring – Issues Management. VS Verlag für Sozialwissenschaften, Wiesbaden

Eisenegger M, Künstle D (2003) Reputation und Wirtschaft im Medienzeitalter. In: Die Volkswirtschaft, Vol 11 pp 58-62

Eisenegger M, Vonwil M (2004) Die Wirtschaft im Bann der Öffentlichkeit. Ursachen und empirische Evidenzen für die erhöhte öffentliche Exponiertheit ökonomischer Organisationen seit den 90er Jahren. In: Medienwissenschaft Schweiz 2/2004 pp 80-89

Habermas J (1993) Theorie des kommunikativen Handelns. Suhrkamp: Frankfurt am Main

Imhof K (2006) Die Rache der Moral. Die moralische Regulation löst die Deregulation ab. fög discussion paper OK-2006-0002

Schranz M (2007) Wirtschaft zwischen Profit und Moral. Die gesell-schaftliche Verantwortung von Unternehmen im Rahmen der öf-fentlichen Kommunikation. VS Verlag für Sozialwissenschaften, Wiesbaden

Schranz M (2008) Die Finanzmarktkrise – Reputationswandel in Krisen-zeiten. fög research paper 2008-2009 | November 2008

Voswinkel S (2001) Anerkennung und Reputation. UVK-Verlag, Konstanz Norman Mailer 1999 (correspondence: Copyright 2008, The Norman Mailer Estate, All Rights Reserved, reproduced in Spiegel 44, 27 October 2008)

The Brussels reputation story – the interplay of public affairs and reputation

Peter Lochbihler

For companies, reputation is becoming increasingly important while at the same time, reputation is also a fundamental issue for any politician. At the European level especially, it is clear that the EU is paying attention to its reputation among citizens. Reputation has an influence on the share price of companies just as it determines a politician's success or defeat. But what is the significance of reputation at the intersection of business and politics – where, in the context of public affairs, there is direct dialogue between the representatives of various interests on the one hand and politicians or civil servants on the other? What are the characteristics of a good reputation that matter in context of political lobbying? How should an organisation present itself to EU institutions in Brussels in order to earn their trust?

We address these questions by looking at the practice of public affairs in Brussels. After an introductory explanation of the concept of public affairs, we go on to distinguish the dimensions of reputation that are especially relevant for particular target groups (or subgroups). As will become clear, it is not possible to achieve a uniform reputation among the various target groups in the EU bodies – owing to the importance of cultural and national backgrounds, personal convictions and personal networks.

Concrete examples are given in support of the thesis that even though a positive reputation generally helps public affairs in Brussels, it can never guarantee lobbying success. One can intelligently utilise an organisation's good reputation for successful lobbying in Brussels, but it must be maintained, expanded and developed by local representatives – based on fundamental values such as honesty, credibility, reliability, responsibility and continuity.

J. Klewes, R. Wreschniok (eds.), *Reputation Capital*, DOI 10.1007/978-3-642-01630-1_8,
© Springer-Verlag Berlin Heidelberg 2009

Reputation and the European Union

When the European Commission took office under President José Manuel Barroso in 2004, one of its priorities was to improve both the understanding of the EU and its reputation among the wider public. For years, there has been too much distance between EU decision makers in Brussels and the citizens of the EU. There has been a great gap, too, between the well intentioned (or even actually beneficial) political initiatives from Brussels and the public's perception of it as a bureaucratic behemoth that is out of touch with citizens. The anti-globalisation movement also branded the EU as an advocate of global free trade. This contributed, among younger voters especially, to the demise of the EU constitution after failed referendums in France and the Netherlands in 2005. Certainly, by the time the Irish had delivered their not-so-surprising No to the Lisbon Treaty in 2008, alarm bells were sounding in the Commission's Berlaymont building.

According to Eurobarometer surveys regularly commissioned by the European Commission, two-thirds of the Irish population regard their country's membership of the EU as positive, and three-quarters are convinced that Ireland, on balance, benefits from being an EU member. On average across the EU, 53% consider their country's membership a good thing. The mood is especially good in the Netherlands, where this figure is 80%. Almost half those surveyed trust EU institutions. With regard to the image of the EU, 45% of those surveyed felt positive (Eurobarometer 70, Dec 2008)[1].

Yet, analyses of the referendum results in France, the Netherlands and Ireland show that an often diffuse scepticism towards the EU still prevails among citizens. A glance at the outcome of the referendum in Ireland suggests that voter confidence in the EU is not in a good way. There, scaremongering about the EU succeeded in cancelling out for Irish voters the enormous economic progress the country has been able to make since its accession to the EU in 1973 – progress due to the intelligent use of massive EU aid. The failure of the referendum in Ireland also suggests that the Commission's communications and information campaigns in the lead-up to the poll, like those of the Irish government, missed their target.

Since then, the Commission's political initiatives have targeted obvious issues that affect citizens and consumers. It has pushed for popular causes, such as consumer or environmental protection. Reduced roaming costs for

---

[1] European Commission, Eurobarometer 70 – Public Opinion in the European Union, December 2008 <http://ec.europa.eu/public_opinion/archives/eb/eb70/eb70_en.htm>

mobile communications, ambitious targets for climate protection, a ban on incandescent light bulbs, stricter product approval for pesticides – measures like these typically guarantee positive headlines in national media. When EU institutions themselves are paying a great deal of attention to their reputation, it is worth asking to what extent political decision makers and civil servants are aware of the importance of reputation when in contact with lobbyists. Or, to put it another way: do companies, associations or NGOs with a good reputation have an advantage when working together with the Commission or the European Parliament? What characteristics of a good reputation are especially important in Brussels? How does an organisation have to present itself in Brussels to enjoy the trust of EU institutions?

Reputation and public affairs

As early as in 1766, Adam Smith laid what could be regarded as the foundation stone for reputation management. He noted – with reference to the trade of goods – that fraud does not pay because, if it becomes public, a single instance of fraud does more harm in the mid and long term than it generates profit in the short term. A similar principle holds in public affairs and can be understood as actively shaping dialogue with politics and society on behalf of an organisation: honesty, trustworthiness, credibility, reliability, responsibility and continuity are crucial elements for successful public affairs work. The connection between reputation and public affairs, then, is clear. But is public affairs a building block for reputation management? Or is it the other way around?

First of all, we must clarify the concept of public affairs. Public affairs work in Brussels aims at learning about the Commission's legislative and regulatory proposals as early as possible and at actively helping to shape – or even influence – them as early as possible. But when lobbying external organisations, one must have a foundation of thorough groundwork to build upon. The first step for public affairs professionals is to define the issues and political areas that affect a company and to evaluate potential consequences – positive and negative. Systematic monitoring makes it possible to stay up to date and ready to act at all times on a specific issue. In political monitoring, not only is the media evaluated, but political decision-making processes are actively followed – for example, by attending meetings of parliamentary select committees and stakeholder hearings or by having background talks with politicians and civil servants. Such analyses and recommendations for action are a core part of political monitoring, which also acts as an early warning system when new trends or political initiatives emerge. For each topic, stakeholder maps are created, which list the relevant agents in a political procedure and evaluate them according to their importance – from the working level through to the highest relevant political level. Here, it is not only the politicians and civil servants in the institutions who matter, but also associations, organisations and media in the political environment. It is essential to establish and maintain a network with these agents. This means making contact, organising conversations, comparing positions and possibly arranging alliances. Well structured, concise briefing documents and position papers with clear messages supported by fact are a fundamental requirement for lobbying talks. Only then, and after thorough preparation, can one begin with the actual lobbying work and issues management – in other words, actively shaping how issues develop and moving them forward. In this part of the public affairs spectrum, media relations plays an important role, since politicians often orient their behaviour around opinions published in the media. Successful public relations calls for integrating the widely different aspects of a problem, a focus on solutions and creativity in implementation.

Fig. 1. Public affairs services

How does an organisation's reputation have an impact on public affairs activities with EU institutions?

Having clarified what public relations is about, we now deal with the question of how reputation impacts actual public affairs work in Brussels. The European Union is a complex political system, and bears little resemblance to the structures of a traditional national democracy. The interplay between the Commission, the Council and the Parliament is partly similar to political processes at national level between the government and parliament, governing coalition and opposition – but only partly. Politicians' allegiances in the Parliament and in the Commission are a mixture of national origin, party politics and personal conviction. But most importantly, every institution – at political and administrative level – has representatives from 27 member states, each with differing cultural, historical and political backgrounds. In all, the EU recognises 23 official languages. Not every working document is translated into all the official languages, and not every session is interpreted into 23 languages, but the number of languages alone expresses something of the diversity and complexity in the political systems of the EU.

The factors that influence the thinking and actions of political decision makers are thus extremely diverse.

Given its role as 'guardian of the treaties', with the European Commission it is European interests that generally prevail. The Commission's role is to develop draft legislation for the entire EU, to ensure rules are adhered to, while ensuring all member states are treated equally. But, of course, commissioners and civil servants do not simply put their nationality to one side once they join the Commission. Commissioners and top civil servants are usually regarded in their home countries as having privileged access to the Commission, so that (at least unofficially) a certain balance is strived for when filling the higher posts. Apart from nationality, areas of responsibility and personal convictions naturally decide the extent to which the reputation of an organisation can help or hinder the pursuit of interests. On the topic of climate protection, a Greek environmental NGO will presumably get a better reception from the Greek Environment Commissioner Dimas, while a German car manufacturer dealing with the same topic might prefer to approach the German Industry Commissioner Verheugen.

An organisation's reputation often evolves within a specific national context, and is accordingly perceived differently by different target individuals. Just as crucial as the national context are content and ideology: while the directorates-general for the internal market and enterprises champion the competitiveness of European industry and sales opportunities on the internal market, the directorates-general for the environment and consumer protection are bound to pursue initiatives for the environment and the protection of consumers. In this sense, there is no uniform perception of stakeholders within the Commission. Rather, reputation diverges enormously from one office to the next, from one commissioner to the next, and from one desk officer to the next.

Unlike in the European Commission, national interests are officially in focus in the Council. Indeed, the governments of member states have a basic responsibility to represent their national interests there. However, one can see how difficult it is even to find a national position in the numerous disputes between national ministries – when it comes to balancing environmental and industrial politics, for example. It is not unusual for the environment minister of a given country to maintain a position in the Environment Council that is contrary to the position adopted in the Competitiveness Council by his or her cabinet colleague with the economic portfolio. Almost without exception, however, the Council and thus national governments will listen to arguments that relate to the location of industries, i. e. to jobs in their countries. Unlike with the Commission, the national reputation of an organisation can be used here with national governments for public affairs. National champions such as utilities, banks or auto manufacturers can use their often good domestic reputations in their home country to ensure their arguments are heard by their national government.

In the European Parliament, the situation is particularly complex: select committee membership, personal political focus, caucus membership, nationality, public interest and the political relevance of an issue for one's own electorate – these are the factors that influence the thinking and actions of the more than 700 MEPs. In the European Parliament, there are no traditional dividing lines between a governing coalition and an opposition. Caucus discipline is much weaker than in national parliaments. When voting, members sometimes follow the caucus line, sometimes their national delegation, or quite often, simply their own personal conviction. As a result, there are always shifting majorities that, depending on the issue at hand, can often be hard to predict.

A stakeholder's reputation is even less likely to reliably secure a position in the European Parliament than is the case with other EU bodies. Generally, the socialist, communist and Green MEPs value input from NGOs on issues related to the environment, consumer protection or human rights. Economic or industrial interests are probably better placed with conservative or economically liberal members. More than in any other EU institution, it is necessary to distinguish a range of target groups when dealing the Parliament. A software company's reputation might be good in an industry select committee, but can also be the very emblem of consumer rights violations in the select committee responsible for data security. The reputation of an organisation, then, has a clear impact on public affairs in the European Parliament, but not in the sense that 'one reputation fits all'. A professional public affairs strategy takes precise account of these distinctions and uses reputation with various target groups to construct majorities. Thus, the core messages presented to an industry select committee will have a different emphasis to those presented in the select committee for civil liberties. In one case, the focus might be on research budgets, innovation, and jobs, and in the second, on cooperation by the software manufacturer with data-security initiatives.

In sum, one can say that a reputational strategy that confines itself to national borders will only help public affairs at a European level to a very limited extent. A good reputation across broad sections of society helps lobbying in Brussels, but is nothing like a guarantee for success. It can assist public affairs measures, but for successful public affairs, reputation must be established and maintained with the political target groups there in a direct and nuanced way. A generally poor reputation (for example, the tobacco industry) certainly makes it more difficult to successfully implement public affairs measures. A strategic public affairs concept takes account of the diversity of EU institutions and essentially answers the question: which people in which organisation should we contact at which time on which topic?

A glance at public affairs in practice

The political debate about REACH, the reform of rules for registering, evaluating and authorising chemicals, suggests that the negative reputation of a whole industry affects political decision-making processes. The reputation of the chemical industry in broader society could hardly be worse. Chemical companies are associated with toxic residues, polluted rivers, air emissions and cancer.

From 2001 to 2006, the EU developed new rules for chemicals through protracted political negotiations between the Commission, the Council and the Parliament. The industry, in one of the most intensive and drawn-out lobbying battles in Brussels in recent decades, tabled countless studies about the potential harm for innovation and competitiveness caused by stricter regulations and indefatigably pointed out how vitally important chemicals are for almost every area of everyday life. Yet it was the studies advanced primarily by environmental NGOs about chemical residues in blood samples from European citizens that clearly captured the imagination of politicians. The then Environment Commissioner, Margot Wallström, attracted much media attention by offering to have her blood tested for chemical residues, and headlines ahead of the vote in the European Parliament were a sure bet. The chemical industry's essentially negative reputation and the attendant lack of trust among politicians meant the industry's typically scientific or technical arguments, which tried to distinguish the 'risk' from the 'danger' of chemical products, could get no purchase.

Much the same situation held for the regulation of pesticides. Here, too, the agricultural industry was on the defensive from the outset. An experienced parliamentary employee summed it up: "The reputation of pesticide producers hovers somewhere between that of al-Qaida and seal killers." Major producers such as Syngenta, BASF and Bayer have not succeeded enough in counterbalancing with objective arguments the emotional headlines generated by environmental NGOs about 'poison cocktails' in our food. As the political debate unfolded, global prices for corn, soy and wheat climbed to such dizzying heights that the United Nations had difficulty financing its World Food Programme – the perfect lead-in, really, for the argument that pesticides protect and increase harvests. And yet, the argument that pesticides make a significant contribution to feeding the world's growing population made little headway in the political debate. For, environmental groups are skilled at emotionalising political issues, as they did here. Testing fruit and vegetables sold at the supermarket in the European Parliament for pesticide residue ensures journalists' attention just as much a study on pesticides in wines. That the residues found were almost without exception below the statutory threshold, and thus harmless, was only mentioned in the details.

The industry had some success in the protection of intellectual property and in the fight against illegal imports. But it was not possible to prevent stricter approval criteria for pesticides. It seems to be the case, then, that politicians believed in producers' capacity for innovation and wanted to guarantee and provide incentives for this. But when it came to ensuring the safety of pesticides for consumers and the environment, there was more belief in the NGOs' arguments than trust in the producers' awareness of their responsibilities.

Take the example of the software patents directive. The European Parliament, after a long and heated debate, rejected with an overwhelming majority the Commission and Council's proposal for the patentability of "computer-implemented inventions", even though an impressive lineup of global IT players, from Microsoft and IBM through to Intel, SAP and Nokia, had lobbied intensively for the software patents directive. In the end, however, the open source movement won – in this case by profiting from a conflict between EU institutions. The Parliament had felt ignored by member states and the Commission after important amendments proposed by MEPs were not adopted. Although the global software alliance boasted enormous economic clout, mistrust reigned among MEPs about the true state of affairs. Many politicians felt 'over-lobbied' and pressured from both sides. In the end, the reputation of the IT industry, by all means positive due to its strong capacity to innovate, was not enough to ensure a majority for software patents in the European Parliament. Despite its rather modest financial means, compared to the IT industry's million-dollar communications budgets, victory went to the open source movement, whose grassroots activities saw supporters from across Europe gather to demonstrate in front of EU buildings in Brussels and Strasbourg.

What characteristics of a good reputation matter especially in Brussels, and how must an organisation present itself there to enjoy the trust of EU institutions?

Competition for the attention of decision makers in Brussels is enormous. Each day, between 15,000 and 20,000 lobbyists fight for the interest of MEPs and officials at the Commission. Each day, there are countless conferences, workshops, press interviews, round table meetings and stakeholder hearings. EU institutions see a constant stream of heads of government, CEOs and Nobel laureates. How can an organisation stand out in this tough opinion market?

Let us begin with the fundamental distinction, as it relates to companies, between economic reputation and social reputation: both the economic reputation (that is, expectations towards and judgements about a company as an economic agent) and the social reputation (that is, moral or ethical expectations and judgements) are relevant for EU public affairs. Depending on the stakeholder category and target group, however, these two dimensions can be weighted quite differently.

One can describe public affairs in Brussels with an image from ice skating, where there is both a 'compulsory programme' and a 'freestyle section'. The 'compulsory programme' is about fulfilling the expectations that political institutions now place on every stakeholder who wishes to be heard. Stakeholders must actively observe and accompany legislative and regulatory decision-making processes. They must also present fact-based, solution-oriented positions that support decision makers by providing additional and useful information. For companies, economic reputation is especially important in this respect. In the political sphere, companies are expected to contribute in a solution-oriented way on relevant matters.

If a company has in the past met the expectations of a defined target group – in this case, the political sphere – the representatives of this target group will be more open to the company's concerns. For companies and other organisations, the opportunity lies in fulfilling expectations. The resulting trust will impact on the future.

The 'freestyle section' provides an opportunity to fulfil ethical or moral expectations above and beyond the 'compulsory programme'. Only here can a stakeholder actually set itself apart from the competition as a responsible agent who thinks about the long term and about wider issues than simply those that affect core business. When positioning itself in this way, a company's corporate social responsibility (CSR) activities can help it improve its reputation both among politicians and with society at large. Given the ongoing battle against climate change, for example, it certainly helps to have a reputation for acting sustainably as a 'protector of the environment'; implementing the appropriate CSR activities can bolster reputation and assist public affairs in Brussels. But a study by Pleon shows that CSR activities need to be closely linked to a company's core economic competence – that is, near a company's core business – in order to make a credible impression on the target audience. Concepts such as human dignity in overseas production, employment protection, environmentally-friendly and sustainable production, industry training, co-determination and childcare services are valued much more highly by those in politics, science and society than a company's sponsorship of charity or culture.

An organisation's reputation will only have a long-lasting impact on its lobbying in Brussels if it has a European dimension. This means, on the one hand, that a reputation that exists solely at national level will only impact a small subset of EU bodies. On the other hand, the core activities of an organisation must be clearly relevant for the EU and its member states.

Certainly, non-European companies such as Microsoft, Pfizer or Gazprom have significant influence on EU politics. They thus set aside sizeable budgets for communications and political advisors, because they are massively affected by EU decisions. But what does 'non-European' even mean in the age of a global economy? What matters to decision makers is, on the one hand, the importance of a company for Europe in terms of jobs in Europe, investment in research and innovation, and on the other hand, their specialist expertise, which can help politicians to make informed decisions.

Apart from the European dimension, it is crucial to note that a good reputation with certain target groups will not automatically rub off on EU decision makers. EU institutions are much too complex and diverse for that. A good reputation, or at least being well known, can help open doors. Persuasion, on the other hand, only succeeds through personal contact and well prepared arguments underscored with data, facts and figures. Personal networks, alumni associations, discussion groups, think tanks, high-level rounds of talks, national networks (for example, the network of elite French universities) are highly significant for public affairs professionals in Brussels. Such personal networks are probably more decisive than the reputation of an organisation in the population as a whole. The reputation of representatives in Brussels, which is based on personal experience, is more readily projected onto the organisations they represent than the other way around; that is, the rather abstract reputation of a company is less often projected onto its representatives in Brussels.

Finally, and this completes the arc from reputation to public affairs, an organisation must present itself to EU institutions in a way that is honest, trustworthy, credible, reliable, responsible and continuous. Adhering to these fundamental values, combined with a consistent 'compulsory programme' of public affairs and an ambitious, innovative 'freestyle section' builds the foundation for gaining trust and reputation among decision makers in EU institutions.

Part III: The 21st century of reputation crisis

One can survive everything, nowadays, except death, and live down everything except a good reputation.

Oscar Wilde (1854-1900)

Managing reputational risk – A cindynic approach

Sophie Gaultier-Gaillard, Jean-Paul Louisot and Jenny Rayner

Reputation is the main asset of any organisation and managing reputation is therefore one of the major tasks of executives and board members. Future uncertainties may be both threats and opportunities depending on how decisions are made and stakeholders involved in an information consultation process to develop their trust in the future of the organisation, and their understanding of its contribution to the sustainable development of the society so that the organisation establishes and reinforces its "social licence to operate."

Although it is still relatively new, the management of a reputation can learn from a theoretical approach to learn from experience armed with a conceptual and epistemological framework.

Although it has mainly started as a practical, hands on wheel, discipline, reputation risk management would benefit from a more conceptual approach to improve the learning process from experience and equip decision makers with a framework in which to organize their thinking process. Cindynics was developed twenty years ago and offers precisely a theoretical and practical model to explain the root causes of potential ruptures in complex systems where the human factors are a key to explaining the situation. The model is here applied to the specifics of reputation management.

The essential triangle: the organisation, its message and its partners' expectations

For any organisation, reputation is both one of its resources and the ultimate "melting pot" where all its resources combine to create the organisation's value. Therefore, it derives its level from the quality of the synergies

J. Klewes, R. Wreschniok (eds.), *Reputation Capital*, DOI 10.1007/978-3-642-01630-1_9,
© Springer-Verlag Berlin Heidelberg 2009

linking all the internal resources of the organisation and depends on the efficient use of all its assets.

The organisation as a dynamic combination of resources

Any organisation is a complex combination of tangible and intangible assets or resources as illustrated in Table 1.

Table 1. Physical and intangible assets or resources

Physical & Intangible Assets or Resources	
Human	
Technical	• Patents, licenses, copyrights
Informational	• Brands
Partnerial	• Know-how
Financial	• Innovation capacity
Free (exchanges with environment)	• Advertising

As an illustration of this complex combination, the stock exchange should take into account all of these elements to assign a value to an organisation: the physical as well as the assessable intangible assets play a role but the major issue is the trust investors place in the quality of its governance and the capacity of its leadership to drive it through a potentially rocky future.

Patent and trademark registrations are a security for the future. In fact the synergies between the portfolios of tangible and intangible assets are the best security for the future of the organisation and are therefore at the core of its reputation. But how can this synergy be measured? In reality the cement of the whole construct is the trust of stakeholders, investors being at the forefront, and this justifies assessing the reputation as the difference between the market capitalisation and the total valuation of its assets.

The message through the ontological space

If investors are at the forefront of reputation valuation, there is increasing pressure on all organisations to take into account other stakeholders, which means that optimising the economic efficiency of resources is not enough. General public and specific pressure groups as well as regulatory bodies request transparency in the decision process and communication/consultation on the impact of risks. This implies that the organisation must state clearly its values, its internal rules and its ultimate goals and it will strive to uphold them in its daily operations. In the words of a contributor to the Harvard Business Review (Nov 2007)" it must not only outperform its competitors but also 'outbehave' them."

No organisation can afford to ignore the demands of the general public, consumers, investors and state institutions. This corporate banner that Bourdieu called its symbolic capital is embodied in the corporate project upheld by the directors and executives. But is it so far from what has become usual to call "economic capital" for financial institutions? Clearly, the financial market meltdown and looming economic crisis we are experiencing illustrate the strong correlation between "symbolic" and "economic" capital.

This message was anticipated in what Georges-Yves Kervern[1] describes as the ontological space of the organisation. In this context "ontological" could be translated as ethics in action.

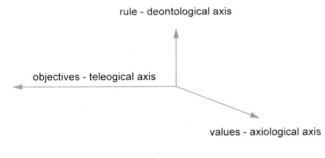

business plan (or symbolical capital according to Bourdieu)

Fig. 1. Organisations are complex system combining.

The ontological space illustrated above in Figure 1 is composed of three dimensions:

- The laws and regulations – imposed from its environment –,

- The values – chosen by the organisation and embedded in its culture –, and

- The missions and objectives it assigns to itself.

If the operational framework within which the organisation operates together with the confidence in its future is the structural foundation of its reputation, the ontological space embeds the message and image that it

---

[1] Latest Advances in Cindynics; Georges-Yves Kervern; Economica Paris 1994

wishes to convey to society. Therefore the organisation's management must ensure that its project is realistic, not only in relation to its present and future resources, but also in the light of its partners' expectations.

Heterogeneous partners' expectations

The transmitter (the organisation) wishes to communicate its message embedded in the ontological space to a public that is diversified, i.e. composed of various segments whose expectations are both heterogeneous and contradictory. Each actor or stakeholder has his own expectations from the organisations and the main groups are stockholders, the general public, institutions, pressure groups, consumers, the media, etc.

The image of the organisation perceived by each stakeholder is formed on the information available (Annual report, specialised and professional magazines, Internet, etc.) processed through the prism of their own value system, i.e. the confrontation of the organisation's projected ontological space and their own. Therefore, one difficulty for the organisation is to capture its partners' expectations, meaning understanding their current status as well as anticipating their evolution. Another challenge is to identify the actors or actors' networks and priorities to determine which should be targeted and satisfied, in which priority. However, nowadays, any organisation has to communicate with all of its stakeholders, the challenge there is to satisfy their individual hunger for information while ensuring full coherence between the different messages: any contradiction could ruin the trust and confidence of all as it is likely that the different "targets", seen as separate from the perspective of the organisation, interact at other levels.

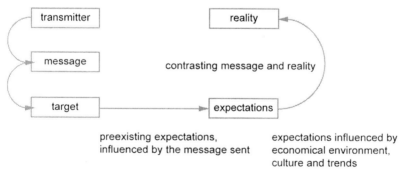

Fig. 2. Reputation founded on coherence

An organisation's reputation is a complex construct as illustrated by the Figure 2. Furthermore, it also explains why it is so essential that it is totally coherent in its internal processes and set of values, the image it conveys and the expectations of all its internal and external partners. Let us stress again that different target groups require tailored communication but if each of them is addressed on its terms, the overall picture must provide a coherent image for the viewers. When the contradictions prove too extreme, the organisation may have to explain candidly to some why their expectations cannot be met.

The message emitted by the organisation towards each target is then perceived through the prism of their own biases and compared with the reality and information obtained through external channels, outside of the control of the organisation.

Should it be effective, which is the organisation's objective, the message sent by the organisation modifies its partners' expectations. By the same token, it raises the stakes and any discrepancy between expectations and delivery will give rise to a sense of betrayal so that trust may prove difficult and long to restore. This is why the organisation must manage cautiously its reputation triangle reality, message, expectations. To summarise, do not promise if you cannot deliver!

The mechanisms of reputation

Figure 3 illustrates the relationships between the organisation's business plan, the operational processes and the partner's expectations. The organisation promotes its business plan to justify its "social licence to operate." The diverse partners' expectations are illustrated here by the spatial dispersion of each ontological space.

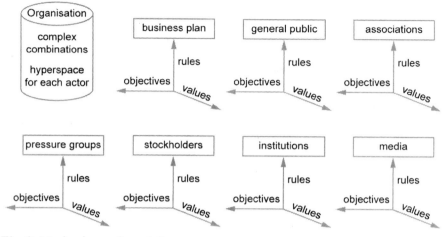

Fig. 3. Mechanisms of reputation

As mentioned earlier, the reputation of an organisation is a reality in "the eyes of the beholders". Therefore, for any organisation, reputation should be plural as it is based on every stakeholder's segment expectation. If we think of Total after the 1999 Erika pollution, whereas it maintained an excellent reputation with the investors, as the results and the dividend were maintained, the reputation with the "green" groups was far less shiny!

The aggregation of individual reputation generates the overall reputation and:

- The soundness of the construction (physical and financial assets), the development potential (patent, copyrights, etc.) and the team professionalism (competencies, know-how, etc.) must inspire trust.

- The business plan must satisfy the investors' financial objectives while promoting "societal expectations".

We have stressed how reputation is based on a triangle to be managed with caution. As a matter of fact, there are many perils that may upset the balance at any time. The drivers identified above in exhibit 3 can be used to structure the risk analysis around the three dimensions of the ontological space.

Objectives and missions

Financial performance and long-term investment value

Does your business have a solid track record of financial performance with no surprises? What are its future prospects? Will it prove a good investment in the longer term? Could something throw the business off track and lead to a profits warning? Which stakeholders are most interested in your financial performance? How do they rate you and what do they expect of you in the future? Do you furnish them with the information they need to maintain their trust?

The post-mortem into the \$38bn write-down at UBS due to the US subprime mortgage crisis blamed the huge losses on excessive risk-taking and poor controls at the once conservative Swiss bank. The 50-page report compiled by UBS for the Swiss federal banking commission revealed that senior executives had no idea of the bank's vast exposure to the complex mortgage-related derivatives that led to the losses. In April 2008 shareholders approved a SFr 15bn rights issue, the bank's second recapitalisation in two months. Their assessment of the bank's management and 'conservative' approach will no doubt also have been re-evaluated.

Rules – Laws and regulations

Corporate governance and leadership

Is an appropriate "tone at the top" set by a board and senior management team? Does the business have a compelling and realistic vision for the future? Does it have an appropriate supporting strategy and good quality management to deliver it? Does it display good corporate governance?

Hill and Knowlton's 2006 global survey of financial analysts[2] found that, other than financial performance, the perceived quality of management, particularly the CEO, is the single most crucial factor driving corporate reputation in a way that influences analysts' investment recommendations.

---

[2] Hill & Knowlton/MORI Return on Reputation – Corporate Reputation Watch 2006 – a global survey of the opinions of 282 buy and sell-side analysts on corporate reputation management

Today, more than ever before, business leaders are expected to embody their corporate brand and its espoused values. This can boost a business's reputation when things are going well, but a fallible leader can equally prove a liability and can tarnish the business's standing if they fail to live up to the exacting standards expected of them.

"Today, the environment in which power is exercised, whether by politicians or business leaders, is harsher. Standards of behaviour may well have improved, but so too has scrutiny, and the punishment for transgression is undoubtedly more severe. This has made managing reputation both more important and more difficult than ever"(Kellner 2008).

Remuneration and incentives for the board and senior staff must also be appropriate. Could your business's incentive scheme encourage managers to behave in ways not compatible with the business's ethos and values? When former Citigroup Chief Executive Charles Prince flew to Japan to apologise for the behaviour of senior executives in Citigroup's private banking operation who had violated Japanese banking regulations, he said that they had put "short-term profits ahead of the bank's long-term reputation". Personal greed combined with inadvertent perverse incentives can prove a lethal combination.

Corporate responsibility

Is the business a good corporate citizen? Does it strive to minimise the negative impacts and maximise the positive impacts of its activities on society and the environment? Does it act in the long-term interests of its stakeholders?

"In today's business environment, integrity, honesty, social responsibility and transparency are 'baked into' a company's reputation and have taken on an importance at least equal to that of a company's financial performance. In other words, a company is no longer judged on its financial performance – it is also judged on how it achieves that performance" (Stansfield 2006).

This driver covers a wide range of potential issues from environmental emissions, labour standards in the supply chain to supplier payment practices, bribery and corruption. The list of large corporations facing corruption probes has continued to grow. French engineering group Alstom is cooperating with Swiss and French authorities investigating suspected bribery to win foreign contracts in South America and Asia between 1995 and 2003. This follows ongoing investigations into Germany's Siemens and the UK's BAe Systems. Allegations of malpractice alone can lead to a loss of stakeholder confidence and a drop in share price even before legal action commences.

The Woolf Committee (2008), established to make recommendations on BAe Systems plc's ethical policies and practices following allegations of bribery and corruption relating to the award of defence equipment contracts, commented:

"High standards of ethical business conduct, and demonstrating such standards have been met, have become a requirement for companies in any sector wishing to succeed globally. In the global economy, reputation has become an essential part of an enterprise's value and the effective management of ethical and reputational risks has become a critical element of corporate governance."

Regulatory compliance

Is the business seen as law-abiding? Does it comply with the spirit – not just the letter of relevant laws and regulations? Does it comply with its own internal standards, policies and procedures?

A 2005 survey by the UK's Economist Intelligence Unit (2005) indicated that the biggest threat to reputation is from non-compliance with legal or regulatory obligations (66% ranked this as a major risk), followed by exposure of unethical practices (58%), security breaches (57% e.g. sensitive data leaks, hacking of customer financial data) and failure to deliver minimum standards of service and product quality to customers (47%).

Post-Enron, complying with the letter of the law is, in many countries, no longer a sufficient condition for maintaining stakeholder confidence. Businesses are now often expected to go beyond minimal compliance and act within the spirit of the law.

A French court filed preliminary charges in May 2008 against Noël Forgeard, former co-chief executive of EADS, for insider trading. It is alleged that Forgeard exercised stock options worth €2.5 million in March 2006, just before the company announced significant delays with its A380 super-jumbo jet. Seventeen other EADS top managers are also facing investigation. EADS' shares crashed by 26% in one day when the problems were made public in June 2006. The company is also likely to face lawsuits from investors who saw millions of euros wiped off the value of their shares. The alleged corruption charges have tarnished the reputation of the company.

Values or internal forces

Delivering customer promise

Does the business provide consistently good quality and fairly priced products and services? Does it innovate and successfully launch new products and services? Is its marketing responsible? Does it keep customer data secure? How good is its customer service? How well does it respond to customer feedback and complaints?

Today's customers are highly sophisticated – and have high expectations. If they feel they have been duped by misleading marketing claims they will punish the transgressor by voting with their feet. When Proctor & Gamble launched Sunny Delight in the UK in a blaze of publicity in 1998, consumers were soon to learn that this apparently fresh, fruity, child-friendly lunch-box alternative to 'pop' was actually a sugar and e-number laden concoction later condemned by health experts. When the truth emerged, sales of Sunny Delight plummeted as consumers lost confidence and deserted the brand. In 2004 P&G offloaded the controversial brand to a private group in the US for an undisclosed amount.

Workplace talent and culture

Is the business able to recruit, develop and retain high quality staff? How well does it treat its employees? Does the culture encourage employees to take pride in the business and give of their best?

A business's reputation is crucial if it is to succeed in recruiting good candidates. A 2008 Hill and Knowlton global study of MBA students (Hill and Knowlton 2008) demonstrated that three out of four respondents see corporate reputation playing an extremely or very important role when deciding where to work after completing their MBA. The students' prime focus was internal workplace policies, in particular the attention, remuneration and environment provided for employees. The quality of management and of employee talent was another key consideration. These were ranked above financial performance and quality of products and services.

Communications and crisis management

A business may manage its risks supremely well, but if it fails to communicate what it is doing to its major stakeholders a gap can emerge between reality and their perception. Does the business provide meaningful and transparent information which allows stakeholders to understand its values, goals, performance and future prospects? How good is it at handling crises?

The Hill and Knowlton (2006) analyst survey also highlighted the importance of transparent disclosure and clear and consistent communication with key stakeholders. Almost 80% of the analysts polled had given negative ratings in the past because of poor communication. A negative rating would a have direct impact on the company's valuation.

Effective communication is an integral part of reputation risk management. You must communicate continuously or others will move in to fill the void and may paint a picture of your business which is inaccurate or misleading. You must be proactive in telling your stakeholders what your business is and what it stands for. Communications should be honest, transparent and consistent and not over-hyped. You should be prepared to admit your failings, outline your plans to overcome them and apologise unreservedly when necessary.

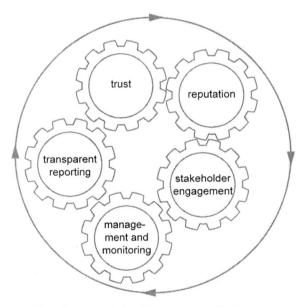

Fig. 4. The virtuous circle of transparent disclosure
Source: Rayner 2003

Many businesses now provide examples in their annual reports of how they have implemented and ensured compliance with their corporate policies. French cosmetic company L'Oreal's 2007 Sustainable Development

Report details amongst its key achievements the commissioning of 585 independent labour standard audits at suppliers', subcontractors' and traders' sites.

Establishing your stakeholders' concerns, monitoring and reporting on them can convey a powerful message of responsibility and transparency which bolsters stakeholder trust and enhances business reputation as illustrated in Figure 4.

The following points should also be taken into account:

- **Pillars of legitimacy**

Although risks to reputation can derive from any source, risks related to core values or fundamental licence to operate issues ("pillars of legitimacy") can cause the greatest damage to reputation. A financial institution that fails to keep customer data secure, a company marketing 'green' products that pollutes the environment, an external audit firm that is not perceived to be independent and objective may find their reputations irrevocably tarnished. For Andersen at the time of the Enron crisis it proved fatal. Considering the pillars of legitimacy for your business and identifying the risks to them can prove a useful focus.

- **Sector-induced reputational risk**

An entire sector can find itself under scrutiny because of the misdemeanors of one or two players. The 'rogue trader' debacle at Société Générale has raised the profile of internal controls throughout the banking sector globally and has caused regulators to revisit regulatory standards and their own monitoring regimes. The additional danger arising from this type of sector-wide fall-out is that the profile of the sector will be raised, although it was perhaps previously below the radar. This means that all companies in the sector will be more vulnerable to reputational scrutiny, not just from regulators but also from investors, clients and other stakeholders.

Potential dissonances impacting negatively reputation

As mentioned above, the risks to reputation are generated by dissonances between the three components of the triangle of reputation: reality, message and partners' expectations. These dissonances may appear at three levels:

- Differences between departments and individuals inside the organisation

- Discrepancies between the reality of the organisation and its message/business plan

- Divergence between the message and the partners' expectations.

Differences between departments and individuals inside the organisation

This is the principle of contradictory objectives which indicates that the different actors or departments within the organisation may have diverging objectives that may be in direct opposition to one another. In such a situation it is essential that the executives clearly lead the way and establish priorities for the organisation as a whole.

The internal operations of the organisation also form the backbone of its reputation. Dissonances between internal actors may have a direct impact on services and goods delivered to the partners, but may impact even more acutely its credibility as its environment is made aware of such dysfunctions.

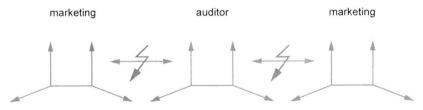

Fig. 5. Internal dissonances between departments

Discrepancies between the reality of the organisation and its message/business plan

The impact of media on the economic world, not to speak of regulations and supervisory bodies, is such today that no organisation can afford not to communicate transparently to both its stockholders and all its stakeholders on its financial objectives and the values it intends to uphold. Although strangely silent during the times of crisis, ethical funds may find reasons to rebound when the economy finds its new balance and then values will become a necessary banner under which trust is restored.

Dissonance may still occur when the organisation operates under the ambiguity principle: The ontological space is not clearly defined and dissonances may be revealed at any time when it is confronted with a difficult situation. The actions undertaken to "save the day" may be at odds with the business's values and create a gap with stakeholders. We have already stressed the importance of social responsibility that may be in conflict with short-term economic efficiency when lay-offs may seem the only way out.

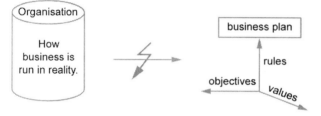

Fig. 6. Dissonances between business plan and its execution

Divergence between the message and the partners' expectations

To name but a few, dissonances between the organisation's strategy and the external stakeholders may be caused by the following:

- Discrepancies between the organisation's business plan or execution and the fundamental expectations of society,

- Discrepancies between the organisation's business plan or execution and the fundamental expectations of its key partners,

- Difficulties arising from paradoxical expectations,

- Systemic reputation slump for the industry in which the organisation operates.

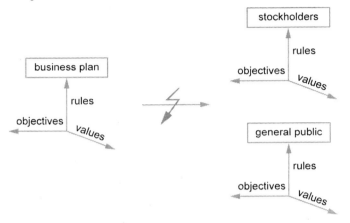

Fig. 7. Dissonances with general public

Discrepancies between the organisation's business plan or execution and the fundamental expectations of society

In professional settings, the image of an organisation refers to its perception by its stakeholders, i.e. the various social groups it interacts with. As we already mentioned earlier, their vision of its economic and social performance rests on the information available, and the objectives and values set and achieved processed through their own value systems. However, these systems are not set in stone and experience profound evolution according to times and circumstances.

For the last twenty years, the long-term trend was on environmental issues, transparency, and social responsibility. Therefore, these are areas of specific concern as inappropriate behaviour in their handling could result in permanent damage to reputation.

There remains to be seen how the present crisis modifies the grid through which stakeholders assess the organisation's behaviour. However, the trust and confidence in directors' and officers' probity and competencies will undoubtedly remain among the top five elements of investor appraisal. The tolerance for executives' impropriety or lack of oversight will be low. We can imagine the impact of uncovering impropriety or criminal activities like corruption or embezzling. Should such a circumstance be unveiled by the media, the stock price might tumble.

Based on the long-term trend however, global players like Danone or AREVA have long established communication strategies on ecology and fair trade. Such topics must be tackled with caution as disappointment might prove catastrophic.

As an illustration, the financial sector is going through systemic turmoil and may have to reinvent itself. For the last twenty years bankers, and to some extent insurers, have prided themselves on their capacity to manage market risks, and more recently operational risks. As more was expected of them, banks are seen by the general public as having betrayed them. The governments have no choice but to try to restore public confidence in the system through massive and concerted efforts.

Discrepancies between the organisation's business plan or execution and the fundamental expectations of its key partners

Conflicts of interest are part of life (in the nature of things) and the general public understands that. Petrochemical industries, nuclear power plant operators, tobacco companies need not masquerade to please stakeholders. Greenpeace does not expect AREVA to pause to end nuclear energy production, but it can still stress its involvement in renewable energies like solar and wind. Anti-tobacco groups do not expect British Tobacco to finance anti-smoking campaigns, but they demand the truth on the conclusion of studies conducted to assess the health impact of smoking. While targeting priority groups, any organisation must maintain communication even with antagonistic groups, if only to avoid major disturbances that would be contrary to priority constituencies' interests.

Systemic reputation slump for the industry in which the organisation operates

Although the organisation's own actions and messages are the core of its reputation; there is no escaping it being part of its environment. The professional context within which it operates impacts the perception of its stakeholders as already mentioned above. More specifically, the industry's reputation is a driver of each actor's individual reputation.

In early 2008, it was revealed that cash was exchanged between leaders of the Metallic and Metallurgy Industries Union (UIMM) and labour union elected officials. This led to a feud with bitter exchanges between the

UIMM and the MEDEF (French Manufacturers Association) that tainted the reputation of all involved.

A crisis in one organisation may impact the reputation of all its competitors. If the accident of Three Mile Island was rapidly contained, Chernobyl had an enduring effect on the nuclear industry worldwide, but especially in France, which relies on nuclear energy for nearly two-thirds of its energy needs. It even prompted some anti-nuclear activists to question safety in the French plants.

In the same way Paris suffered as a global financial (market) centre as a result of the "mad trader" episode in which Soc-Gen suffered a loss in excess of €5 billion. Of course ten months later and in the midst of a meltdown that may reach several trillion dollars this episode is replaced in perspective. However, the public has become much more sensitive and a somewhat limited similar incident, a loss of a "mere €600 million" prompted the resignation of the three main executives at the Caisses d'Epargne in France. The court of public opinion demanded it!

The reputation interdependency extends also to the supply chain as a number of actors learned it the hard way. It took Adidas several years to recover from the soccer World Cup balls incident: child labour employed by a sub-contractor of a sub-contractor to manufacture them. It took vigorous action and a new contract to address the issue and restore Adidas image. The supermarket chain Leclerc was very prompt to recall tainted products and deal openly with the problem. Although technically the Erika was not Total's vessel, nor was it directly contracted, nevertheless the pollution on the beaches tainted its reputation and did not help when the AZF explosion in Toulouse occurred nearly two years later.

Beyond the systemic dissonances listed above, there are some possible "fracture lines", accepted or accidental, that should be addressed, especially when they involve various partners whose objectives are not necessarily aligned with the organisation's own:

- **Endogenous and exogenous causes that reveal dissonances**

The revelation of a dissonance may involve a dysfunction or criminal act committed in an organisation and may be prompted by internal or external events or sources that escape the control of top management.

The inside source may be a whistleblower, for legitimate purposes or for revenge. This was the case of the Buffalo Grill crisis prompted by a leak to the press by a disgruntled former employee on the use of potentially mad cow disease infected meat imported from the UK at the time of the embargo.

The outside source or event may be seen as the tip of the iceberg, like in the case of the Exxon Valdez the leaks on a North American pipeline, or the explosion of a chemical plant in Bhopal.

All these situations, and many more, illustrate a fundamental principle of reputation risk management: as painful as it may prove, an organisation should come clean and public as soon as it learns of a situation that may generate public outrage.

- **Existing dissonances could be exacerbated**

A dissonance that may seem limited originally may receive undue public attention if it serves a potential stakeholder's interests.

A pressure group, a consumers' association, a lobby whose interests are contrary to the organisation's may be tempted to make sure that even minor incidents that could be helpful to boost their agenda are exploited to the fullest. It happens often with minor leaks on nuclear power points that antinuclear elements try to present as potentially "lethal".

Professional as well as public media, can find a "good story" or an audience building story out of an incident that the organisation would have liked to see soon forgotten. An illustration is the story of the military speed boats sold to Taiwan.

Keeping at all times an interactive communication with major media and a consultation channel with antagonistic pressure groups will prove useful when they come to you first before acting publicly on their (limited or biased) information.

- **Some partners may have a vested interest in spreading rumours of dissonances**

Some stakeholders may be competitors or organisations preparing to market substitutes to the goods and services of an organisation. One of the most famous cases is probably the saga of Perrier in the United States. Perrier was commanding a quasi monopoly on high end bottled sparkling waters. A story surfaced from nowhere stating that "Perrier was contaminated with traces of benzene". Although this "pollution" did not constitute a health hazard, it made Perrier less than "perfect", its long-standing advertising slogan. It is now believed that frustrated competitors may have been behind the attack: whom does the crime benefit?

A similar story affected salmon farms that were said to carry bacteria potentially harmful to human health. This gave a boost to the sales of wild salmon.

Monitoring information emanating from stakeholders whose interests are antagonistic is essential; that may include open source economic intelligence if the stakes warrant it.

- **Impact by association**

The partnerships a business forms can also affect its reputation. If an adviser or a customer's reputation is tarnished, it can impact the reputation of the business itself. Bankers and external auditors to Italian dairy company Parmalat found themselves embroiled in lengthy investigations when the company collapsed in the wake of a massive fraud in 2003. How could they have failed to spot the solvency problems and mounting debt of the company that was dubbed "Europe's Enron"?

Five years on, as the fraud trial commenced in March 2008, Parmalat's new management was still pursuing Citigroup, Bank of America, UBS, Deutsche Bank and Credit Suisse through the courts, having already won €1.2 billion in settlements. €420 million was from Italy's second largest bank, Intesa Sanpaolo which, while denying wrongdoing, stated it had reached a settlement to "avoid a long-lasting and very complex litigation" that would no doubt have proved even more damaging to its reputation.

Having an impressive list of highly respected and responsible clients and suppliers can enhance reputation.

"Association with reputable organisations can add value. Their presence on a list of suppliers or clients adds prestige and may help to attract other key clients and talent."

Department of Trade and Industry[3]

- **Portfolio change risks**

Another fertile area is reputational risk arising from cultural and ethical differences post acquisitions and mergers. A mismatch between the acquiring and acquired companies' values, ethos and standards may prove problematic.

UK medical devices group Smith and Nephew announced in May 2008 that it was considering clawing back some of the $889 million it paid to acquire the Swiss company Plus Orthopaedics 14 months earlier as inte-

---

[3] Creating Value from your Intangibles, Department of Trade and Industry, London (2001)

gration had "uncovered sales practices in parts of Europe which are unacceptable."[4] The group estimated that it would lose $100 million in annual sales after putting a stop to Plus commercial tactics. Although not confirmed by the company, these were believed to include paying kick-backs to surgeons who used their products, particularly in Greece. Due diligence prior to the take-over had failed to uncover these dubious practices. Shares in Smith and Nephew fell by 13% after this was made public.

Acquisitions may also provide a source of competitive advantage and a potential opportunity to enhance reputation. If the acquired business enjoys a better reputation than the parent company the challenge will be to learn from – and not destroy – the subsidiary's ethos while integrating it.

Whatever the source of the revelation or the amplification of a dissonance, the effect will be all the more damaging if it affects stakeholders' fundamental expectations, like the essential qualities of a product or services for the customers, or if it taints a core value posted by the organisation in its corporate communication. This is why an on-going monitoring must be implemented.

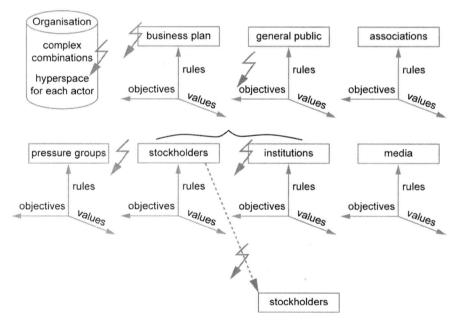

Fig. 8. General summary of potential dissonances

---

[4] Statement made by Smith and Nephew Chief Executive David Illingworth in May 2008.

As illustrated in Figure 8 above, there is a real probability of a widening gap between the reality of the organisation, the message sent and the expectations of the market and/or the stakeholders. The gap may widen across space, as the organisation going "global" has operations further and further away from its founding place and its comfort zone: cultural issues may become a major source of dissonance. The gap may widen also across time as groups' expectations change, sometimes dramatically. This is why a strategic vigilance is an important building block in managing risks to reputation, threats as well as opportunities. Its pertinence relies heavily on a precise analysis of the acceptability of the risks generated by the organisation by each stakeholder group identified, specifically those impacting the main reputation drivers. This study will enlighten the decision makers on the rules that they will apply to balance threats and opportunities generated by the organisation and grant it their trust, a gage of long term sustainability.

Consciously or unconsciously, individuals and societies tend to establish boundaries when it comes to "acceptable" risks. They may take the form of taxes, norms, thresholds that should not be crossed. However, these boundaries are essentially mobile and hard to quantify at any point in time. The nuclear industry with its heavy emphasis on safety has defined the ALARA system (as low as reasonably acceptable). As it matured, the nuclear safety research moved from acceptability to tolerance.

When a risk lends itself to further reduction, it might be acceptable and yet not tolerable. For any exposure, each individual balances the risk he perceives and the benefit he may personally experience. Therefore, the level of acceptability may be raised depending on surrounding conditions (firm's budget, ethical conscience, etc.) and the firm's objectives (profitability, etc.). Thus the "frame of mind" of the individual is based on nine elements identified by B. Fischoff and his colleagues:

- the risk is chosen (voluntarily) or assumed (involuntarily);

- the impact of risk is immediate or differed;

- the level of scientific knowledge is established;

- the benefit is low whereas the level of risk is high, and the reverse, high benefit and low risk level;

- the level of control the individual may have on the risk;
- the risk is emerging (new) or familiar;
- the risk is recurrent or exceptional and of catastrophic proportions;
- individuals are accustomed to live with the risk or fear it;
- the level of consequences (is there an identified risk of death).

An approach to stakeholder groups using these nine dimensions will help understand how they are likely to prioritise the risks they are confronted with and hence will facilitate the monitoring of stakeholder expectations mentioned earlier.

Reputational risk management – A vital approach within the ERM framework

The international exports gathered in Davos in early 2009 for the World Economic Forum seem to have come up with a new concept, if they are to be believed. "The financial crisis has demonstrated that risk management is not enough; it is imperative now to develop risk governance." And John Drzik, the CEO of Oliver Wyman even adds: "For risk management to be efficient, it must be approached in a strategic prospective, not a mere compliance exercise". The need for such a stance clearly shows the damages caused by the rush to compliance, be it called Sarbanes Oxley, Coso 2 or any other name. Every time brainstorming is replaced by box ticking there is a minefield ahead!

These high personalities, and no doubt many of them sit on several boards worldwide, and may be even risk and audit committees, have even produced the solution: "Risk governance is about asking the right questions to the right persons so that it can be assured that the risks taken are within the boundaries of the organisation's risk appetite." Sounds familiar? Well the Davos delegates had to take the measure of the economic turmoil of the world to reinvent in 2009 the global and integrated management of risks that the professional have developed for over a decade and ERM (Enterprise-wide Risk Management). No doubt they will need another year at least to reinvent Business Intelligence Systems to provide the "reasonable assurance" that the information received, transformed and released to all parties is of the highest quality.

This is very important news as it is likely that non-executive board members will feel the need to gain the competencies to do a good job at monitoring risk management activities in their organisations – all the more since with the transposition of the European directive 3, 7 and 8 in national laws, as it was done in France in 2008, the responsibility for managing risks really rests on the board and the executives. At their level the issue is long-term sustainable growth and the key asset is reputation.

To be successful and sustainable, i.e. to achieve a sound level of resilience, any business needs to enjoy the trust and confidence of all its stakeholders and that can be achieved only when its actions are in harmony with its words. In practice, that requires integrating into the overall strategy the key elements of trust building: corporate governance, risk management, corporate social responsibility and reputation management. At a time when all practitioners, directors and officers have become aware of the need for a global corporate risk management strategy, there seems to be a mushrooming of new "silos" in risk management such as sustainable development risk management, procurement risk management, marketing risk management, etc. Therefore, reputation risk management may well prove to be the cornerstone of the desired integration, provided executives and board members keep in mind that a reputation must be built both "inside out" and "outside in." Furthermore, a corporate reputation serves as a reservoir of goodwill to draw upon when challenges and difficulties arise. More than ever in this time of crisis, triggered by a justified drop of confidence in the financial sector, executives must strive to build an authentic business: "A defining feature of an authentic business is that its profound and positive purpose shines through every aspect of what it does, whether paying invoices (claims), parting with a member of staff, or presenting at a conference" (Crofts, 2005)

Ethical conduct is the core ingredient of trust, hence of reputation. As the financial industry has experienced since the summer of 2007, individual lapses are always possible, but they may uncover systematic risks. Therefore, we must stress how important it is for any organisation to prepare for a disaster, should it strike. In a recently published book on corporate integrity the authors stress that: "As we found with hurricane Katrina, being unprepared can cause a disaster that is far greater than the damage caused by the underlying event. The ethical disaster risks facing organisations today are significant and the reputational damage caused can be far greater for those companies that find themselves unprepared... Although we can't predict an ethical disaster, we can and must prepare for one" (Brewer et al. 2006).

The final word we borrow from Madeleine Albright, former US Secretary of State. While addressing the subject of risks of war, terrorism and deadly pandemics and reflecting on her work during the Clinton administration at a Marsh breakfast during the RIMS convention in Honolulu on April 25, 2006, she gave this essential piece of advice to risk management and business leaders: "Decisions are only as good as the information you have… Although the crisis for which you prepare may never happen, one will happen… Being prepared for a crisis is never a waste of time."

References

Akerlof, G (1970) The Market for Lemons: Qualitative Uncertainty and the Market. In: Mechanisms Quarterly, Journal of Economics, Vol 84 pp 488-500

Anderson DR (2006) The critical Importance of Sustainability Risk Management. In: Risk Management Magazine, pp 66-74

Bauer RA (1960) Consumer behavior as Risk Taking, Dynamic Marketing for a Changing World, R.S. Hancok (ed.), American Marketing Association, pp 389-398

Brewer L, Chandler RC, Ferrell, OC (2006) Managing Risks for Corporate Integrity: How to Survive an Ethical Misconduct Disaster, Business/Business Ethics/Marketing, Thomson Corp.

Cagan P (2006) On finding linkages: corporate governance and operational risk. In: The John Liner Review, Vol 19 pp 4

Chemmanur TJ, Fulghieri P (1994). Reputation, renegotiation, and the Choice between Bank Loans and Publicly Traded Debt, Review of Financial Studies, Vol 7 No 3 pp 475-506

Crofts N, (2005) Authentic Business, Capstone Publishing Company

Diamond, DW (1991) Financial Intermediation and Delegated Monitoring, Review of Economic Studies, Vol 51 pp 393-414

Douglas, M., Widawsky, A, (1982) Risk & Culture. Gaultier-Gaillard, Louisot, 2006. Geneva Papers. Fischoff & all, p 78

Ducarroz C, Scarmure P, Sinigaglia S (2003) Tintin au pays des enchères: information sur la qualité et réputation des vendeurs. In: Actes du XXème Congrès AFM, Vol. 6&7 May 2004, St Malo (France)

Fagart MC, Kambia-Chopin B (2003) Aléa moral et Sélection Adverse sur le marché de l'Assurance, working paper CREST/THEMA

Fombrun C, Gardberg NA, Barnett ML (2000) Opportunity Platforms and Safety Nets: Corporate Citizenship and reputational risk. In: Business and Society Review, Vol 105 No 1 pp 85-106

Fombrun CJ (2005) A World of Reputation Research, Analysis and Thinking – Building Corporate Reputation Through CSR Initiatives: Evolving Standards <http://www.ingentaconnect.com/content/pal/crr/2005/00000008/00000001/art00001;jsessionid=1ajaykh8bli1c.victoria>. In: Corporate Reputation Review, Vol 8 No 1 pp 7-12

Gaultier-Gaillard S, Louisot JP (2004) Diagnostic des risques AFNOR (ed)

Graham P, Fearn H. (2005) Corporate Reputation: What Do Consumers Really Care About?. In: Journal of Advertising Research <http://journals.cambridge.org/action/displayAbstract?fromPage=online&aid=407477&fulltextType=RA&fileId=S0021849905050361##> Vol 45 pp 305-313

Hill, Knowlton (2008) Economist Intelligence Unit, Reputation and the War for Talent,. Corporate Reputation Watch 2008. The survey canvassed 434 MBA students at the 12 top ranked international business schools in the US, Europe and Asia.

Kellner P (2008) Face Value: Your Reputation as a Business Asset, Coutts and Co.

Kreps DM (1990) Game Theory and Economic Modelling. Oxford University Press

Kreps DM, (1990) Corporate Culture & Economic Theory. In: Perspectives on positive Economy, Alt JE & Kenneth (ed.), Cambridge University Press, pp 90-143

Larkin J (2003) Strategic Reputation Risk Management. Palgrave McMillan.

Louisot JP (2004) Managing Intangible Asset Risks: Reputation and Strategic Redeployment Planning. In: Risk Management: An International Journal, Vol 6 No 3 pp 35-50

Louisot JP (2005) 100 questions pour comprendre la gestion des risques, AFNOR (ed)

McDonald C, Slawson V (2002) Reputation in Internet Auction Market. In: Economic Inquiry, Vol 40 pp 633-650

Menilk M, Alm J (2002) Does a Seller'E-Commerce Reputation Matter? Evidence from e-Bay Auctions. In: Journal of Industrial Economics, Vol 1 pp 337-349

Nelson A, Etue D (2006) Reducing the Risk of Information Leakage. In: The John Liner Review, Vol 20 p 1

Rayner, J. (2003) Managing Reputational Risk: Curbing Threats, Leveraging Opportunities, Wiley (ed.)

Reputation (2005) Risk of risks. Economist Intelligence Unit

Resnick, P, Zeckhauser R (2002) rust Among Strangers in Internet Transactions: Empirical Analysis of e-Bay's reputation system. In: Bay M. (ed.), The Economics of the Internet and the e-Commerce, Elsevier, pp 127-157

Rotschild, M. Stiglitz. J.E. (1976) Equilibrium in Competitive Insurance Markets: an Essay on the Economics of Imperfect Information. In: Quartely Journal of Economics, Vol 90 pp 629-650

Sami, H (2004) Firm's Financial Distress and Reputational Concerns, Working paper.

Schelling TC (1960) The Strategy of Conflict, Oxford University Press

Selva KF (2005) How it's difficult to ruin a good name: An analysis of reputational risk, CISSP, 19 Sept 2005

Simon, HA (1951) A Formal Theory of the Employment Contract, In: Econometrica, Vol 19 pp 293-305

Standifird S (2001) Reputation and E-commerce: e-Bay's Auctions and the Asymetrical Impact of Positive and Negative Rating. In: Journal of Management, Vol 27 pp 279-285

Standifird S (2002) Online Auctions and the Importance of Reputation Type. In: Electronic Markets, Vol 12 p 1

Stansfield G (2006) Some thoughts on reputation and challenges for global financial institutions. In: The Geneva Papers, Vol 31 pp 470-149

Tirole J (1993) A theory of Collective Reputations. mimeo

Woolf Committee, Business ethics, global companies and the defense industry: Ethical business conduct in BAE Systems plc – the way forward (May 2008)

Managing reputational risk – Case studies

Alex Hindson and Jean-Paul Louisot

Reputation is the main asset of any organisation and managing reputation is therefore one of the major tasks of executives and board members. However, it is still relatively new and the management of a reputation can learn from past experience and benchmarking and case studies are a key to going forward.

Enterprise-wide risk management is based upon creating a learning organisation where management and staff actively share the outcomes of risk management situations. The aim is to capture successful risk-taking events and learn from situations where risks were not effectively managed. Similarly, much can be gained from understanding how other organisations have been faced with reputational risk challenges. Everyone will eventually learn from their mistakes, but 'Risk Intelligence' requires the ability to also anticipate challenges based on understanding the successes and failures of others. Case studies in managing reputational risk are therefore in this context an invaluable resource.

A survey conducted by AON in 2007[1] rated damage to reputation as the number one global business risk, although half of the survey's respondents said they were not prepared for it. Whereas the management of reputational risk is a relatively young and rapidly developing area, good practices are still being developed. Much can be learnt by comparing case studies of incidents and how different organisations have responded when challenged by a major crisis incident. This is indeed the basis of Knight and Pretty's (1997) important study. At the same time we will aim to draw out these key lessons and make conclusions regarding the current state of development of reputational risk management.

---

[1] Aon's Global Risk Management Survey 2007 was based on responses from 320 organisations in 29 countries.

J. Klewes, R. Wreschniok (eds.), *Reputation Capital*, DOI 10.1007/978-3-642-01630-1_10,
© Springer-Verlag Berlin Heidelberg 2009

Case study 1 – Tylenol product recall – Treating contamination?

Johnson & Johnson: a global consumer health company providing a wide range of medical devices, diagnostics, biologics and pharmaceuticals. The organisation has 250 operating companies in 57 countries employing 119,400 people. Worldwide headquarters are in New Brunswick, New Jersey, USA.

The business is driven by a credo set of values defined by the founding Chairman, Robert Wood Johnson. "Our credo challenges us to put the needs and well-being of the people we serve first. We believe it's a recipe for business success. The fact that Johnson & Johnson is one of only a handful of companies that have flourished through more than a century of change is proof of that."

The incident

Johnson & Johnson (J&J) is perhaps best known for its advancement of crisis management regarding the cyanide contamination its blockbuster Tylenol® painkiller. In September 1982, seven Chicago-area individuals died after taking cyanide-laced Extra-Strength Tylenol® capsules (bayer 2002). Representing 7% of all of J&J sales and 17% of its profits, Tylenol® was a brand that the corporation could not afford to lose.

The Extra-Strength Tylenol® capsules in question were each found to contain 65 milligrams of cyanide. The amount of cyanide necessary to kill a human is five to seven micrograms, which means that the person who tampered with the pills, used 10,000 times more poison than was needed. The publicity about the cyanide laced capsules immediately caused a nationwide panic. A hospital in Chicago received 700 telephone calls about Tylenol® in one day. People in cities across the country were admitted to hospitals on suspicion of poisoning by cyanide.

Along with a nationwide scare, the poisoned capsules brought with them copycats, who attempted to simulate the tampering in Chicago. In the first month after the Tylenol® related deaths, the Food and Drug Administration counted 270 incidents of suspected product tampering. The FDA estimated that only about 36 of the cases were "true tampering", the remainder being an over-reaction to events.

The decision

Lawrence Foster (Kaplan 1982), Corporate Vice President of Johnson & Johnson, at the time of the Tylenol® poisonings, explains that Johnson & Johnson simply turned to their corporate business philosophy, which they call "Our Credo", when determining how to handle the Tylenol® situation.

Foster indicates that although, at the time of the crisis, corporate planning groups were had crisis management plans, no plan would have been appropriate to tackle the Tylenol® poisonings. This is because no management could ever be prepared for a tragedy of this scale. So, Johnson & Johnson turned to their credo for help. The credo was written in the mid-1940s by Robert Wood Johnson, the company's leader for 50 years. Johnson outlined his company's responsibilities, "We believe our first responsibility is to doctors, nurses and patients, to mothers and fathers and all others who use our products and services". Johnson believed that if his company stayed true to these responsibilities, his business would flourish in the long run.

The reaction

J&J chose to take a very proactive approach to the crisis. It eventually re-called 31 million bottles worth over $100 million from retail stores, in addition to offering to exchange tablets for capsules for all customers at no charge. It pioneered the tamper-proof, triple-sealed packaging that is the industry standard today.

The news of this incident travelled quickly and was the cause of a massive, nationwide panic. These poisonings made it necessary for Johnson & Johnson to launch a public relations program immediately, in order to save the integrity of both their product and their corporation as a whole.

Phase One of Johnson & Johnson's public relations campaign was executed immediately following the discovery that the deaths in Chicago were caused by Extra- Strength Tylenol® capsules. As the plan was constructed, Johnson & Johnson's top management put customer safety first, before they worried about their company's profit. The company immediately alerted consumers across the nation, via the media, not to consume any type of Tylenol® product. They told consumers not to resume using the product until the extent of the tampering could be determined. Johnson & Johnson, along with stopping the production and advertising of Tylenol®, recalled all Tylenol® capsules from the market. The recall included approximately 31 million bottles of Tylenol®, with a retail value of more than $100 million. This was unusual for a large corporation facing a crisis, particularly in 1982 when recognising the reputational impact of such incidents was still quite a new concept. In many other similar cases, companies had put themselves first, and ended up doing more damage to their reputations than if they had immediately taken responsibility for the crisis.

The outcome

In an article Jerry Knight stated "Johnson & Johnson has effectively demonstrated how a major business ought to handle a disaster" (Washington Post 1982). Hey applauded Johnson & Johnson for being honest with the public. The Washington Post article stressed that it must have been difficult for the company to withstand the temptation to disclaim any possible link between Tylenol® and the seven sudden deaths in the Chicago area. According to the article, "what Johnson & Johnson executives have done is communicate the message that the company is candid, contrite, and compassionate, committed to solving the murders and protecting the public."

Immediately after the crisis, the drug's market share dropped from 37% of the pain relief market to 7%. The company's share price dropped 33% in the 200 days following the crisis. However, by May of 1983, its market share returned to 35%. Tylenol® had become the number one alternative to aspirin, in the nation. The product had 37% of the market for over-the-counter painkillers.

Because Tylenol® was such a huge money-maker for Johnson & Johnson, the company unleashed an extensive marketing and promotional program to bring Tylenol® back to its position as the number one over-the-counter analgesic in the United States. Chairman of the board, James E. Burke said, in regard to the comeback, "It will take time, it will take money, and it will be very difficult; but we consider it a moral imperative, as well as good business, to restore Tylenol® to its pre-eminent position." Tylenol® capsules were reintroduced in November 1982 with bearing a new triple-seal tamper-resistant packaging. J&J spent time developing a new tamper-resistant packaging design. The Tylenol® comeback was a great success and the tamper-resistant packaging became an overnight industry leading concept and in many ways now an industry standard for the pharmaceutical industry.

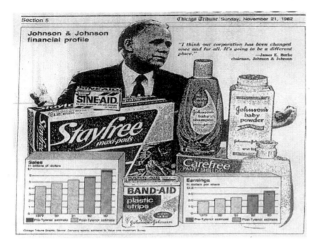

Fig. 1. Media impact
Source: Chicago Tribune (1982)

Learning points

Why did Johnson & Johnson act as they did?

Johnson & Johnson management had a difficult decision to make with limited information. They had a clear process for decision making and certain guiding business principles that determined how they should act under these circumstances.

Is it always appropriate to be open with the public in sharing information?

Generally the answer is 'Yes'. Overcoming public mistrust in risk communication needs to focus on improving the credibility of information being provided and those individuals delivering it. Leading thinking on risk communication, Vincent Covello (1992) believed that three key issues need to be understood:

- Perception is reality' for the general public

- The primary goal of communication is to establish trust and credibility. Conveying facts is very much a secondary objective during a crisis situation.

- Public trust and organisational credibility start low, and has to be earned.

According to Covello credibility is related to how the public perceive the following attributes of communicators:

- Empathy and caring

- Competence and expertise

- Openness and honesty

- Dedication and commitment

These have been found to be the factors that the public evaluate in assessing communication on risk or during a crisis. To the extent that these factors are addressed, crisis communication will be successful. This evaluation is made very quickly and is extremely challenging to reverse.

What can be learnt from this approach?

It is possible to turn a near-terminal crisis affecting a core issue within a business, such as product safety and integrity in the pharmaceutical industry into a business opportunity. Not only where J&J placed in a strong position of moral authority by the stance they took in proactively managing their recall, but they managed to develop an industry leading and clearly differentiated product packaging that placed their product at a premium in terms of product safety and tampering.

What is the importance of corporate culture in managing reputational incidents?

As we can see from this situation Johnson & Johnson had a 'credo' that guided their senior management in difficult times. This was no mere mission statement adorning the shelves of management offices. This credo fundamentally defined how the business operated and help to guide the business in its strategic planning and corporate planning. Managers at all levels recognised and responded to the issue in a consistent manner.

Case study 2 – Coca-Cola product contamination – Leaving a bad taste.

The Coca-Cola Company is a global branded drinks and refreshment sales and distribution organisation. Established in 1886, The Coca-Cola Company operates in more than 200 countries and markets more than 2,800 beverage products. These products include sparkling and still beverages, such as waters, juices and juice drinks, teas, coffees, sports drinks and energy drinks. The company owns four of the world's top five non-alcoholic sparkling beverage brands: Coca-Cola, Diet Coke, Sprite and Fanta.

The incident

Over 120 people, including adolescents from five schools in northern Belgium, became sick after drinking Coca-Cola products between 8 and 14 June 1999. It should be noted that the Coca-Cola Company does not manufacture finished sparkling products in Western Europe. Finished product in most of Western Europe is manufactured by Coca-Cola Enterprises, an independent bottler of which The Coca-Cola Company has an equity ownership interest.

In four other schools in western Belgium a total of 72 children became ill. The potential cause identified by Coca-Cola Enterprises was that the illnesses were caused by cresols, which contaminated the product. These cresols used in wood fungicides may have reacted with chlorinated disinfectants inside coca cola vending machines to form methyl-cresol, which penetrated the cans. This has not been verified.

The initial explanation was however the poor quality carbon dioxide had been used at their Antwerp factory to carbonate the drinks. The incident revealed that carbon dioxide for carbonation was primarily sourced as a by-product of the manufacture of ammonia, a precursor of nitrogen-based fertilisers. This information was used by the media to heighten concerns amongst the public as to the nature of the contamination.

The decision

The Atlanta headquarters of The Coca-Cola Company (BBC 1999a) took charge of communications. Their initial reaction was to deny it was a serious issue. No senior managers visited Europe and the issue was managed from the United States. The official line being that it was "merely a bad odour, no risk to public health". However severe damage was done to this approach when European Union officials dismissed their explanations as "highly unlikely". Coca-Cola Enterprises eventually withdrew 17 million cans and bottles of soft drinks from European markets after consumers reported suffering from headaches, nausea, abdominal pains, vomiting and diarrhoea.

"For 113 years our success has been based on the trust that consumers have in that quality. That trust is sacred to us", CEO Ivester said (BBC 1999b). His statement came after four European countries – Belgium, France, the Netherlands and Luxembourg – started taking Coca-Cola soft drinks off their shelves on Monday and Tuesday.

The reaction

The European Union also criticised the French and Belgian governments for overconfidence in the company's risk assessment of the situation (BBC 1999c). A French regulation requiring the withdrawal of certain batches of Coca-Cola did not work and Belgian efforts were concluded to be inadequate.

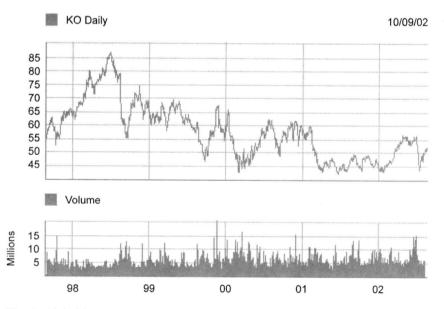

Fig. 2. Global impact on Coca-Cola Corporation share price

The outcome

By 16 June The Coca-Cola Company had changed direction with CEO Douglas Ivester stating that Coca-Cola regretted recent problems experienced by its European customers, and pledged to take "all necessary steps" to guarantee the safety of its products. "For 113 years our success has been based on the trust that consumers have in that quality. That trust is sacred to us." His statement came after widespread product withdrawals in France, Belgium and the Netherlands through 14 and 15 June 1999.

The Belgian authorities and public were particularly sensitive to public health scares because of dioxin having been found earlier that year in meat and eggs. This caused a major government scandal. "According to the Belgian authorities, the contaminated drinks triggered a blood disorder that causes the destruction of red blood cells" (BBC 1999d).

Actually the impact may not have been as severe as first thought. "The recent illnesses associated with Coca-Cola in Belgium may have been caused by fears over contamination rather than any impurities in the soft drink, members of the Belgian health council have said. They said that the actual levels of contamination found in the soft drink were not high enough to cause the illnesses reported" (BBC 1999e). This demonstrates that reputations are dependent more on perceptions of how issues are managed than on the reality of the situation being faced.

This incident has been cited by many commentators as a key factor in the surprise early retirement of CEO Doug Ivester in December 1999.

Learning points

What could the organisation have done differently?

The organisation should have reacted more quickly to the incident. The response is however typical of a large multinational company where head office retains control of crisis management activities and there is a lack of clarity regarding the respective role of local and corporate management.

Did Coca-Cola understand the European context of this event?

Local management within Coca-Cola Enterprises in Belgium and France may well have understood the implications of the incident within a European context, but clearly this perspective was not communicated clearly to the head office of The Coca-Cola Company in Atlanta. Recognising that a crisis is happening is often the first step in developing a successful response.

Ultimately what impact did this have on the organisation?

In many ways this was a 'Road to Damascus' for the organisation. Since 1999, The Coca-Cola Company has invested heavily in developing emergency planning and crisis management arrangements. These plans have focused particularly on the training of local management and on ensuring that managers at each level in the organisation are clear on their respective roles. The Coca-Cola Company has invested significant resources in undertaking a range of exercises to simulate the events associated with product recall and other types of crisis.

As mentioned earlier, in a strategic move in 1986, the organisation had already separated its bottling organisations in Western Europe into a separate legal entity with the spin-off and creation of Coca-Cola Enterprises. However, after the incident, The Coca-Cola Company requested that their bottling subsidiaries give added focus to the management of product quality and supply chains.

Case study 3 – Mattel recall – Playing with safety?

Mattel Corporation is the largest toy company in the world, a publicly traded organisation with a market capitalization of over $6.5 billion, employing approximately 36,000 people worldwide in 42 countries whose products are sold in 150 nations.   .

The incident

In the summer of 2007 Mattel suffered a major product recall incident. The first recall was as a result of vendor failure in China where traces of lead paint were discovered on 83 different products on August 2nd 2007. This led to a recall of 1.5 million items worldwide. The products contained levels of lead paint that failed the product specification. The US media reaction was limited, possibly because this was the day a bridge collapsed in Minneapolis.

A second wave of recalls was triggered on August 14th 2008 (Wearden 2007). This was as a result of an investigation launched following the first incident. A larger number of products were voluntarily recalled because of fault with magnets. There was a concern that magnets could be released from toys and hence swallowed. A solution had been identified and applied to new products.

The recall was large because Mattel took a principled stance that all products with the defect back to 2002 should be recalled also. This was an unprecedented decision to apply the recall retrospectively. Over 17 million items were eventually recalled as a result because the magnet did not meet 2007 Mattel standards.

The decision

Firstly Mattel accepted that despite its high standards, there were failings in its controls over quality of products manufactured within its Chinese supply chain. Control over supply chains in China has become a growing concern, with significant evidence that sub-contracting is a major challenge in ensuring product quality.

There were design flaws associated with products containing magnets that could come loose under certain conditions. Mattel had a global crisis management and communication that it implemented. However the important facet was that of leadership. CEO Robert Eckert took personal control of the issue. "We will do the right thing" he told his management team (Bush 2007).

Lisa Marie Bongiovanni, VP Corporate Communications, was quoted as saying: "The main strategy has been to be open and transparent. I hope we are not judged on the issues, but on how we responded to them."

The reaction

Based on corporate decision to be open and to provide as much information as possible to worried parents, a proactive communication strategy was essential. This involved multiple teams from public affairs and brand communication. Media interest grew exponentially on 14 August. Mattel proactively approached multiple media outlets to offer news releases, teleconference calls and scheduled TV appearances. The message was Mattel takes responsibility for its actions and will commit to appropriate remedial actions as well as continuing to report on progress.

This was far from easy. In the first day, the CEO delivered 20 TV interviews and calls with individual reports. This leads to hundreds of media inquiries in the first week. In fact there were over 1 billion news items and impressions created including Internet-based media.

This was part of an overall proactive and sustained communication exercise seeking to reach both parents and opinion formers. Mattel recognised the power of the Internet and new media. The Internet clearly could spread bad news very quickly. However Mattel used these modern methods to 'get the word out'. The company used bold red ads on high traffic sites such as Yahoo.com to find owners of their products and draw them to a Mattel website with the information they needed. They aimed to empower consumers to find the information they needed quickly rather than wait on consumer care telephone lines or worse at their retail outlets. Their own recall websites (Mattel.com) were recognised by many as being extremely clear and helpful in providing the information required in a timely manner. Information was provided in 20 separate languages for global consumers. This process dealt with over 6 million consumer queries.

This was supplemented by a series of personal video messages from the CEO providing updates. Ross (2008) reports that "Eckert featured in a personal video on Mattel's website, made sincere apologies to parents and gave numerous interviews how the company was addressing the problem. He also candidly admitted: "We are by no means perfect.""

This does not mean the process was easy and certainly 'alternative news media' such as satirical press and television programmes were a significant challenge to manage.

Importantly the overall communication package also recognised the need to communicate with their staff. Information was provided through newsletter, E-mails and website alerts so that staff could continue to act as ambassadors for the organisation.

The outcome

In some ways, writing in late 2008 it is too early to tell the long-term impact on Mattel as an organisation. It has however been widely recognised that its CEO took personal responsibility for the incident and took control of the recovery. The CEO speaking directly was recognised by

Lewis (2007) as giving a halo effect. There was no attempt to blame others or hide behind their suppliers.

The direct costs of the recall have been estimated at $30 million, although the impact on brand and reputation is potentially much larger. Mattel focused on getting the word out to parents and customers. Bongiovanni reports that, "it was a difficult time, but when you are doing the right thing it makes it easier."

Welford (2007) reports that: "the attention given to just one company is hiding some bigger issues. The US toy maker is widely considered to be one of the most scrupulous and socially responsible operators in the toy sector in China." The LA Times and other news organisations reported that Mattel did everything they could to get our message out, earning high marks from consumers and retailers. The Harvard Business Review described Mattel as an example of how to responsibly conduct a recall.

Since the recall, Mattel has consolidated its position by formalising its Corporate Responsibility Division with 500 staff worldwide dedicated to ensuring its ethical standards are in place. A new Senior Vice President reporting to the CEO has been appointed to ensure the division delivers its role. There approach to supplier management is now "Trust but Verify"(Waldmeir 2008).

Learning points

What drove Mattel's response?

Mattel had a highly structured approach to corporate responsibility as evidenced by its 2007 Global Citizenship Report (Mattel 2007). Mattel establish Global Manufacturing Principles (GMP) as early as 1997 in terms of defining the standards they aspire to. The GMP standards recognise wage and working hours, age requirements, forced labour, discrimination, freedom of association, living conditions, workplace safety, health, emergency planning and environmental protection. These are supported by internal and independent auditing.

This initiative is personally led by the Chief Executive Officer and is closely aligned to its brand and market positioning. 'Playing fair' is a core value of the business. The business has made a significant commitment to these values and culturally had to respond in a manner consistent to these values.

According to Quelsh (2007), "The CEO has taken personal charge of the situation. He has apologized publicly and taken immediate steps to tighten quality assurance requirements on Mattel's suppliers. There has been no effort to duck behind blaming suppliers and distributors or, even worse, consumers – as Audi attempted to do in the famous unintended acceleration recall of the late 1980s."

What are the implications for other organisations with Chinese supply chains?

Welford reports that 80% of all toys sold in the United States are manufactured in China. A supply chain may involve over 3,000 factories in China. The task of quality control and auditing is a significant challenge.

Mattel is recognised as having some of the most stringent standards in the industry. If it can happen to them then it means that the challenge in controlling Chinese supply chains is significant. Mattel uses a large number of plants in China and has done so since the 1960s.

This is a challenge for 'Brand China'. The government needs to recognise that 'Made in China' may come a warning signal for global consumers and strategically China may lose inward investment compared to other South East Asian markets.

Are supply chain audits an effective means of controlling product quality and hence corporate reputations?

Welford questions the value of audits. "The reality is that many factories have got very good at passing audits and appearing compliant, without actually being compliant... Any auditing or inspection system is vulnerable because it is always open to falsification of records, ineffective sampling and testing, poor enforcement of regulations or sometimes the rampant bribery that allows products to pass safety checks."

"Many factory owners and managers openly complain that they are being asked by the big brands to do more on CSR but that the brands are often not willing to pay for it".

What was the impact on the Chinese manufacturers?

Zhang Shuhong, the owner of the manufacturing company Lee Der Industrial in Foshan, reportedly committed suicide shortly after the recall was instigated. Lee Der was one of Mattel's most trusted suppliers, having been reliable for 15 years. It is reported that Lee Der Industrial in turn was let down by a local paint supplier. The paint was provided by an uncertified and unauthorized supplier. A number of Chinese contractors and subcontractors have had their contracts terminated by Mattel since the incident.

Summary of the lessons learned from the cases

Any case study is only valid to the extend that it allows to draw out these key lessons and the three case studies described here above highlight some key themes in terms of what differentiates a positive reputational risk response.

Recognition

Firstly the organisation needs to recognise there is a major issue occurring and perceive that this is more than a technical or localised issue. The organisation needs to have a risk aware culture where potential impact on brand and reputation and understood quickly.

Decision

The organisation needs to move quickly. In a crisis time is of the essence. The immediate reaction within first day may influence how the organisation is perceived over the weeks and months that follow. This means that roles need to be clearly defined and managers capable of taking decisions with the best advice but in some cases very limited information.

Leadership and culture

Critical to all these examples is the issue of leadership. Successful management of reputation, particularly in a crisis requires a clear direction from the top, invariably the Chief Executive Officer. This requires a culture of responsibility and risk awareness where bad news is dealt with. If there is a blame culture where bad news is 'buried' then it is highly likely that the outcome of a major reputational incident will be negative. Good organisations respond well to major challenges. They draw on their common values to understand the expectations of their stakeholders. Their management show leadership and 'stay with the issue' until it is resolved positively. In a number of circumstances the organisation emerges from the crisis strengthened, both internally and in the eyes of its key stakeholders.

Enterprise risk management

Enterprise Risk Management (ERM) (Hindson 2008) is a strategic process that considers the threats and opportunities across all functions of an organisation that could materially impact its objectives. By weighing up the implications of key decisions, appropriate actions can be agreed and delivered to support the chosen strategy. It has to be a top-down process seeking to support executive management in their decisions regarding how to balance risk with reward in strategy making.

Enterprise Risk Management (ERM) enables an organisation to create the culture and processes to ensure that managers are risk aware. It creates an internal framework whereby key aspects of managing reputational risk can be defined. Defining clear accountabilities and processes area first enabling step in ensuring an organisation is 'risk intelligent'. Hence ERM is really about how managers make good decisions in managing their key asset, their organisation's reputation. Ultimately ERM is more a state of mind than a technique or process. Maybe that is why it can be at the same time so challenging yet so simple and effective.

'Learning organisation'

The ability to learn from risk events, should they occur within or outside an organisation, is a key factor in ensuring the risk management thinking is embedded in an organisation. As we have seen this requires an organisational culture that is supportive of effective communication on risk. It is then within the grasp of management to understand and respond appropriately to specific reputational risk challenges. In this context case studies are invaluable in making the case for this being a board-level issue for most organisations.

References

Bayer RC (2002) Ethical Reasoning in Business How to Make Ethical Decisions: <http://www.fiveoclockclub.com/articles/2002/2-02-ethics.htm>

BBC (1999a) Coke's contamination story 'highly unlikely': <http://news.bbc.co.uk/1/hi/business/the_company_file/423056.htm>

BBC (1999b) Coca-Cola 'regrets; contamination, <http://news.bbc.co.uk/1/hi/world/europe/371300.stm>

BBC (1999c) Business: The Company File, Belgium bans Coca-Cola <http://news.bbc.co.uk/1/hi/world/europe/369089.stm>

BBC (1999d) World: Europe, Belgium considers lifting Coke ban, <http://news.bbc.co.uk/1/hi/world/europe/370681.stm>

BBC (1999e) Health Coke scare blamed on mass hysteria. <http://news.bbc.co.uk/1/hi/health/383337.stm>

Bush, M (2007) Mattel takes crisis efforts global for second round of toy recalls, <http://www/prweekus.com/Mattel-takes-crisis-efforts-global-for-second-round-of-toy-recalls.html>

Chicago Tribune, 21 November 1982

Covello V (1992), Risk communication, trust and credibility – in Health and Environmental Digest, Vol 6 No 1 April 1992 pp 1-4

Hindson, A (2008), Enterprise Risk Management – fact or fiction? European Business Review , September 2008

Kaplan T (1982) The Tylenol® Crisis: How Effective Public Relations Saved Johnson & Johnson. <http://www.personal.psu.edu/users/w/x/wxk116/Tylenol/crisis.html>

Knight R, Pretty D (1997) The Impact of Catastrophes on Shareholder Value, Oxford Executive Research Briefings, Templeton College, University of Oxford

Lewis T (2007) Mattel tackles crisis with solid comms. PR Week, 12 November 2007, p 25

Mattel (2007) Play Fair. Play with Passion. Play to Grow. Play together. 2007 Global Citizen Report 2007

Quelch J (2007) How to Run a Recall <http://discussionleader.hbsp.com/quelch/2007/08/how_to_run_a_recall.html>

Ross LG (2008) Communicate until your tonsils bleed. In: Ethical Corporation, March 2008, p 39

The Washington Post, 11 October 1982

Waldmeir P (2008) The lesson is, don't trust, verify. In: Financial Times, 3 October 2008, p 9

Wearden, G. (2007) Mattel recalls toys over magnet fears, The Guardian, <http://www.guardian.co.uk/business/2007/aug/14/china.usnews1>

Welford R (2007) The stories behind the Mattel recall, CSR Asia Weekly, Vol 3 Week 32 pp 1-3

Managing reputational risk – From theory to practice

Sophie Gaultier-Gaillard, Jean-Paul Louisot and Jenny Rayner

Reputation is the main asset of any organisation and managing reputation is therefore one of the major tasks of executives and board members. Future uncertainties may be both threats and opportunities depending on how decisions are made and stakeholders involved in an information consultation process to develop their trust in the future of the organisation and their understanding of its contribution to the sustainable development of the society so that the organisation establishes and reinforces its "social licence to operate".

Although it is still relatively new, the management of a reputation can learn from past experience and benchmarking and the main elements of an efficient process are now well established.

Warren Buffett (Chairman and CEO, Berkshire Hathaway) once said: "It takes 20 years to build a reputation and five minutes to ruin it. If you think about that you'll do things differently." The teachings to draw from this quote are manifold. Firstly, it demonstrates that risk is a social construct (Douglas and Wildawsky 1982). Secondly, it shows that people tend to perceive it as a threat and totally miss the dual aspect of risk. Thirdly, it implies that people should react and learn from past errors and improve their behaviour.

But is this what happens in real life? At the beginning of the 21st century managing reputational risk has become a major preoccupation for businesses in the private, public and not-for-profit sectors. A survey conducted by AON in 2007[1] rated damage to reputation as the number one global business risk, although half of the survey's respondents said they were not prepared for it.

---

[1] Aon's Global Risk Management Survey 2007 was based on responses from 320 organisations in 29 countries.

J. Klewes, R. Wreschniok (eds.), *Reputation Capital*, DOI 10.1007/978-3-642-01630-1_11,
© Springer-Verlag Berlin Heidelberg 2009

In the aftermath of the Enron, WorldCom, Parmalat and other corporate catastrophes, more stringent corporate governance and regulatory compliance requirements, strengthened regulator powers, the growing influence of pressure groups and rising stakeholder expectations have sharpened the focus on business reputation. Added to this, the advent of real-time global telecommunications and 24/7 media scrutiny can result in an apparently minor incident in a far-flung part of a company's operations hitting the international headlines and provoking a major crisis.

Enjoying a good reputation yields many rewards: not least the continuing trust and confidence of customers, investors, suppliers, regulators, employees and other stakeholders, the ability to differentiate the business and create competitive advantage. A bad reputation, conversely, can result in a loss of customers, unmotivated employees, shareholder dissatisfaction and ultimately the demise of the business itself.

The challenge of managing reputation and its associated risks is well illustrated by the Warren Buffett quote at the start of this chapter. Hard-earned reputations can be surprisingly fragile and can be tarnished or irrevocably damaged as a result of a moment's lapse of judgment or an inadvertent remark. That is why it is so vital to manage risks to reputation as rigorously as more tangible and quantifiable risks to the business.

What is reputation?

According to the Compact Oxford English Dictionary, reputation is "the beliefs or opinions that are generally held about someone or something". Depending on the field studied, reputation may have different meanings (Gaultier-Gaillard and Louisot 2006) but always constitutes an intangible asset. The main question should then be to determine what makes a good reputation. The theory is simple: an organisation enjoys a good reputation when it consistently meets or exceeds the expectations of its stakeholders. A bad reputation results when the organisation's words or deeds fall short of stakeholder expectations. This concept is expressed in the reputation equation in Figure 1.

Reputation = experience - expectations
Oonagh Mary Harpur

Fig. 1. The reputation equation
Source: Harpur 2002

Stakeholder expectations are shaped by their beliefs about what a business is and what it does. These beliefs are influenced by what the business says about itself and by what others say about it. Stakeholders then measure their actual experience of how the business acts against their expectations.

A good reputation is achieved when there is congruence between a business's purpose, its goals and values (what it professes to be), its conduct and actions (what it does it practice) and the experience and expectations of its stakeholders.

Maintaining a good reputation therefore requires continuing identification and management of emerging gaps between experience and expectations and between claims and reality using a risk-oriented approach.

Why is reputation valuable?

A business's reputation is valuable on two counts: first, its intrinsic current value as an intangible asset and secondly, its ability to create – or destroy – future value.

Reputation will not appear as a separate item on a business's balance sheet but generally represents a significant proportion of the difference between market value and book value (minus any quantifiable intangibles such as trademarks and licences). As total intangibles now often account for some 75% or more of market value, reputation is, for many businesses, their single greatest asset.

A good reputation not only underpins a business's continuing licence to operate, but provides it with a licence to expand and generate new partnerships and income streams e.g. by helping to secure preferred partner status on future projects or by enabling premium pricing for products and services. Reputation is often not only a business's single greatest current asset but also a potential source of competitive advantage and a key determinant of future business success (see exhibit 1 below).

Reputation is also a critical business differentiator. As Alan Greenspan, former US Federal Reserve Chairman, has observed: "In today's world, where ideas are increasingly displacing the physical in the production of economic value, competition for reputation becomes a significant driving force propelling our economy forward. Manufactured goods often can be evaluated before the completion of a transaction. Service providers, on the other hand, usually can offer only their reputations." This is particularly true of service industries where the end product is invisible, as the present crisis illustrates clearly and gives an ironical twist to Greenspan's assertion. Insurers, for example, are in the business of promising to pay out on a claim at an unspecified date in the future. The policyholder cannot assess the insurer's willingness and ability to fulfil the promise at the time of purchase and may have insufficient grasp of the finer detail of a complex policy. His purchase decision can therefore only be made based on the business's reputation and the level of trust and confidence it engenders. If the business's reputation is eroded, and stakeholder trust and confidence diminish as a result, the insurer may find that policyholders rush to surrender their policies.

The queues of customers desperate to withdraw savings outside Northern Rock's branches in August 2007, jammed telephone lines and a website crash are a graphic example of how quickly stakeholder trust can evaporate and a corporate reputation can crumble amidst rumours of financial difficulties. British government assurances did little to restore public confidence and this first run on a British bank since Victorian times led ultimately to the temporary nationalisation of Northern Rock and attacks on the reputations of the Bank of England and the Financial Services Authority, the company's regulator.

Perhaps the greatest benefit of a 'good' reputation is its capacity to provide a reserve of goodwill (often called 'reputational capital' or 'reputational equity') that can help the business withstand future shocks and crises. Such reputational capital, which underpins stakeholder trust and confidence, can act as a buffer at times of crisis and persuade stakeholders to give a business the benefit of the doubt and a second chance. In the case of Northern Rock, the shock was too severe, should have been predicted and had too immediate an effect on customers for the bank to weather the storm.

Reputation may impact
• Stockholders' decisions to hold onto their shares
• Customers' desire to buy products and services
• Suppliers' desire to establish partnerships
• Competitors' eagerness to enter the market
• Media coverage
• Pressure groups/NGO activity
• Control and regulatory authority attitudes
• Cost of capital
• Recruitment of high potential individuals
• Motivation of current workforce
• Inclination of stakeholders to grant the benefit of the doubt when a crisis emerges.

Fig. 2. Reputation impact on stakeholders behaviour

The stakeholder perspective: who counts?

As the key to a good reputation is meeting stakeholder expectations, it is vital to establish who your most significant stakeholders are, what expectations they have of you and how they currently perceive you. Only then can you pinpoint any gaps and start to correct them. You might start by listing and then prioritising your business's stakeholders – both internal (employers) and external (shareholders, investors, suppliers, customers, regulators, analysts, insurers, regulators, government, etc.). The relative importance of stakeholders will vary between sectors. For example, in heavily regulated sectors such as financial services the regulator is likely to be a key stakeholder. It also is vital to consider a sufficiently broad range of stakeholders to ensure that no major interest group is neglected, as the sole omission may prove to be the source of an unidentified killer risk. Their expectations depend on the sum of their perceptions and their representations. As reputational risk is a social construct, their expectations on reputational risk are also a social construct.

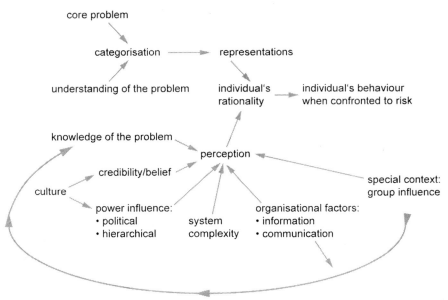

Fig. 3. Risks and perception

Once you have identified the main characteristics of the context where your stakeholders are, your prime focus should be on key players: those critical stakeholders with whom it is vital to maintain an active two-way dialogue so you can continuously track what they are thinking and saying about your business and what they expect of you, both now and in the future. Only in this way can a business truly identify not only its vulnerabilities but also opportunities to create competitive advantage.

Reputational risk: Risk or impact? Threat or opportunity?

There is no such thing as reputational risk – only risks to reputation. The term 'reputational risk' is a convenient catch-all for all those risks, from whichever source, that can impact reputation. The source could be legal non-compliance, a data security lapse, an unexpected profit warning or unethical behaviour in the boardroom.

This broad interpretation of reputational risk has a growing following compared with the school of thought that classifies reputational risk as a discrete class of risk in itself that should be isolated and managed. It requires a business to assess all risks for potential reputational impact and ensures that risks to reputation are fully integrated into the core business risk management framework, are reported alongside other business risks and receive attention from the right person at the right level. Reputational risks are not simply parcelled up and handed to the public relations department for action, although PR can play an important supporting role.

When discussing reputational risk, many organisations consider only the downside threats that could damage corporate reputation. However, uncertainty can also have positive outcomes and can present business opportunities which, if exploited, can create competitive advantage and added value for a business. Climate change is a potential business threat but many firms have spotted and exploited the flip-side opportunity to create a competitive edge by developing green technologies and promoting themselves as environmental leaders in their sector.

Reputational risk can be defined as:

Any action, event or situation that could adversely or beneficially impact an organisation's reputation.

Key sources of reputational risk

The most crucial step in managing reputational risk is the initial identification of those factors that could impact reputation, either positively or negatively. But there remains the question of finding a starting point. You may wish to consider the key drivers of reputation as defined by several well-respected reputation surveys around the world[2] as they are likely to be the most fertile sources of reputational risk. These are distilled into seven drivers of reputation and sources of reputational risk in Figure 4 below.

Fig. 4. Reputation drivers and source of risk
Source: Rayner 2003

A useful question to tease out risks to reputation is: what newspaper headline would you least like to see about your business? And what event or situation could trigger it?

With increasingly complex supply chains and partnership arrangements and a wide range of customers in different sectors and territories, today's businesses need to consider all risks within the extended enterprise. Risks to reputation cannot be outsourced and should be borne and managed actively by the business itself. If a supplier's sub-contractor is found to be using child labour or a toll manufacturer slips a cheap toxic ingredient into a supposedly 'green' product formulation the reputation of the company marketing the product will be tarnished, as companies including Nike and Mattel have learned to their cost.

A good starting point is to consider each of the seven drivers of reputation in the light of the stakeholder group(s) which have an interest in it. This can be mapped on a reputation risk driver/stakeholder matrix (illustrated by Table 1 below) to produce a 'heat map' highlighting potential reputational hot spots which warrant further attention.

---

[2] These include: Fortune magazine's annual Most Admired Companies survey; the Financial Times World's Most Respected Companies survey; and the Reputation Institute's Global Pulse study on the World's Most Respected Companies. No French companies were ranked as 'Excellent/Top tier' (required score above 80/100) in the 2008 Global Pulse Survey. L'Oreal achieved the top score in France (75.68), with Société Générale scoring the lowest (37.82).

Table 1. Stakeholders/reputation drivers

	Financial Performance and long-term value of investments	Governance & leadership	Corporate Social responsibility	Workforce Competencies & culture	Delivering customer promise	Legal & Regulatory Compliance	Communication & crisis management
Employees							
Customers							
Suppliers							
Community							
Investors							
Supervisory bodies							
Pressure Groups/NGOs							

Source: Rayner 2002

Each of the seven drivers of reputation must be examined in more detail, so as to understand better the interactions between them and to identify potential dissonances (See article on a cindynic approach).

Implementing risk management for the risks to reputation

As the cindynic framework[3] indicates and the cases illustrate the risk management for risks to reputation is based on a few simple principles and trust of others is at the heart of any strategy. However, if the strategy seems relatively easy to develop, risk management for reputation is above all an art of execution and therefore some key elements to ensure success, or at least avoid abysmal failure can be summarised here.

---

[3] See Gaultier-Gaillard et al. pp. 115-141

Evaluating and prioritizing reputational risks

"While reputation is 'intangible', damage to an institution's reputation (and the resulting loss of consumer trust and confidence) can have very tangible consequences – a stock price decline, a run on the bank, a ratings downgrade, an evaporation of available credit, regulatory investigations, shareholder litigation, etc." (Stransfield 2006).

What makes risks to reputation particularly difficult to evaluate is the random nature of a strike. Often, an issue deemed minor by a business can cause severe reputational damage, whereas an apparently major issue can pass without comment. Geography can also play a part. A minor event at a distant manufacturing site in a developing country may attract little or no media or stakeholder interest, whereas that same event in the business's heartland can provoke a reputational storm.

An assessment of reputational impact also needs to take into account the resilience of corporate reputation. This will depend on the amount of 're-putational capital' built with stakeholders and the nature and extent of the issue or risk. Was this a predictable and preventable incident, such as anti-competitive activity, bribery condoned by senior management or an acci-dent resulting from blatant disregard for human safety? If so, stakeholders are unlikely to be forgiving. Or was it an unforeseeable occurrence which could not have been avoided, such as 9/11 or a natural disaster where stakeholders will be sympathetic?

Even after such catastrophic events stakeholders expect businesses to learn and adapt. So, post 9/11 and Hurricane Katrina, investors, regulators and customers now require businesses to have risk management systems and business continuity plans in place to counter the effect of such risks.

Another challenge in assessing impacts on reputation is that the initial impact of a risk crystallising may be relatively small, perhaps a fine result-ing from a minor breach or regulations. However, this may chip away in-sidiously at stakeholder trust. A series of minor bad news stories can have a cumulative effect whereby a 'tipping point' is reached, after which stakeholders suddenly lose confidence, the business's share price plum-mets and current and all past misdemeanours are raked over in the ensuing media frenzy making it very difficult to recover.

Oil and gas company BP enjoyed a formidable reputation with investors and other stakeholders under the leadership of its much-admired former CEO Lord Browne. Its hard-won reputation allowed it to withstand a num-ber of crises in the early 2000s. However, the death of 15 workers and injury of 500 others when overfilled storage tanks exploded at BP's Texas City refinery in the US resulted in a massive loss of confidence in the company, a top-management shake-out and a new strategic approach.

Understanding precisely how stakeholders perceive your business at any point in time can help you judge whether you are approaching your reputational tipping point, where just one more bad news story could push you over the brink, and to evaluate reputational impact and respond accordingly.

It may be possible to place a monetary value on reputational risk e.g. via loss of future contracts/income; cost of loss of licence to operate; impact on Net Present Value (NPV); impact on share price; impact on brand value. However, these cannot be applied to all reputational risks. Many businesses therefore use a qualitative approach to initially assess reputational impact (see exhibit 6 below which uses a four level scale), alongside financial and other relevant impact criteria. Both the short-term and longer-term impacts of a risk on the business's reputation should be considered, including the effect on stakeholder behaviour and hence on the future value of the business.

Table 2. Assessing impact on reputation

Low	Moderate	High	Very High
• Local complaint/ recognition	• Local media coverage	• National media coverage	• International media coverage
• Minimal change in stakeholders' confidence	• Moderate change in stakeholder confidence	• Significant change in stakeholder confidence	• Dramatic change in stakeholder confidence
• Impact lasting less than one month	• Impact lasting between one and three months	• Impact lasting more than three months	• Impact lasting more than 12 months/irrecoverable
		• Attracts regulators' attention/comment	
			• Public censure/ accolade by regulators

Developing risk responses

The appropriate response to a risk impacting reputation will depend on its source (safety, project management, acquisition, IT security, and supply chain labour practices), whether it is a threat or an opportunity, its expected impact, the exposure relative to the business's risk appetite, whether the risk is treatable and the cost of treatment. The right response may be a zero tolerance accident regime, recruitment of a professional project manager, more rigorous due diligence covering ethical standards and commercial practices, enhanced security standards or independent third party audits of suppliers and sub-contractors. Suppliers and contractors themselves are now often required to abide by a business's code of conduct and core standards as part of their contractual relationship so they do not bring it into disrepute.

Risk responses should be designed to bridge gaps between reality and perception, between experience and expectations. They may therefore also include improving communications to certain stakeholder groups or helping to shape stakeholder expectations so they are more closely aligned with what the business can realistically deliver.

However good a business's risk management systems, there will always be an unforeseen crisis or risk that cannot be mitigated. Having an 'off the shelf' generic crisis plan which is proven, well rehearsed and can be quickly adapted and invoked to suit specific circumstances is an essential contingency measure to minimize reputational damage. The nature of the risk event needs to be carefully considered when mounting a response; a huge damage-limitation exercise in the case of a self-inflicted wound such as loss of data due to poor internal security will be ineffective.

Monitoring and reporting

Once risks to reputation have been identified and responses designed and implemented, the risk should be regularly monitored by management to ensure they are having the desired effect. The trick with risks to reputation is to build in early warning indicators that will provide advance warning of an impending crisis while there is still time to take corrective action. Systematic review of complaint trends may point to a product performance weakness which can be dealt with long before disgruntled customers resort to litigation. Data on safety near misses, if collected and analysed with the right mindset, may provide vital insights into an impending fatal accident.

In so many reputational disasters the early signs were missed, sidelined or ignored. If spotted early enough and dealt with promptly by involving relevant specialist personnel (legal department, safety advisers or public relations) at an early stage, a crisis can be averted or even turned to reputational advantage.

Risk information needs to reach the right people (both internally and externally) at the right time if it is to have the desired effect. Timely and accurate reporting of reputational risks is an important, and often neglected, aspect of the reputation risk management process.

Roles and responsibilities

Who should be the custodian of a business's reputation? Ultimately the CEO supported by the board of directors, but everyone working for an organisation bears some responsibility for safeguarding and enhancing the business's reputation. This includes suppliers, contractors and other partners.

All need to be made aware of the value of the business's reputation – and of the risks facing it – so each can play their part as reputational ambassadors.

The CEO and the Board should set an appropriate tone through a corporate vision, values and clearly articulated risk appetite which inform decision making and prescribe behaviours throughout the business and its supply chain. If awareness of reputational and other risks can be raised sufficiently the warning signs are more likely to be spotted and corrective action taken before a crisis strikes.

External non-executive and independent directors can play a particularly crucial role by using their broad experience to constructively challenge the business's risk profile. Have the right risks been identified? Have key stakeholders been consulted? Is anything missing? Has reputational impact been correctly assessed or is the business deluding itself?

Management's role is to continuously scan their area of operation for threats and opportunities that could impact business reputation; record and assess them; design, put in place and operate appropriate responses; monitor their effectiveness and hence the changing status of risks; and report to senior management and the board.

Risk management personnel can ensure that the risk management system is functioning well and that the data within it is updated regularly so timely and accurate reports can be generated to inform decision making.

An internal audit function can assist by providing independent assurance to the Board and management on the effectiveness of the risk management system and on whether individual key risks are being managed appropriately within the risk appetite set by the Board.

Public relations and communication staff can also play a critical role by monitoring and evaluating stakeholder perceptions and expectations to inform the risk management process, particularly in the evaluation of reputational impact and design of appropriate responses to mitigate threats and leverage opportunities. PR can help to design stakeholder engagement processes that not only help the business to keep in tune with the changing stakeholder mood, but also provide the opportunity to shape stakeholder opinion and minimize any perception/expectation gaps. The PR department should be involved sufficiently early in the process to make a difference; summoning PR at the eleventh hour when a crisis is about to erupt is not good risk management!

As suppliers and logistics personnel are often in the front line interacting daily with customers and communities, they too, if properly harnessed can become effective ambassadors for the business by working to enhance its reputation.

Overcoming the barriers to effective reputation risk management

So why, when risk to reputation is rated the number one risk to business today, do so many organisations struggle to manage it effectively? A full 62% of companies in the Economist Intelligence Unit Risk of Risks survey maintain that reputational risk is harder to manage than other type of risk (Stansfield 2006).

There are several reasons for this:

- Low awareness of the true value of reputation as a key intangible asset and driver of business success and the need to safeguard and enhance it;

- Lack of awareness of potential sources of a reputational risks so they can be identified and managed actively;

- Lack of clarity on ownership and consequently regarding reputational risk as a category of risk in itself which is the preserve of the PR department. Defining reputational risk as anything that could impact reputation, either positively or negatively, can help to ensure that risks affecting reputation are mainstreamed, actioned at source and attract attention at the right level.

- Underestimating the impact of risks to reputation by focusing exclusively on short-term financial impact. Thinking that if you can't quantify the impact precisely it's not worth managing. A guesstimate of reputational impact, involving the right people and based on sound management judgement can get you a long way.

- Having a defensive, downside focus on threats; neglecting the positive upsides of reputational risk and failing to capture and exploit opportunities to boost reputation.

Building resilience through sustainable reputation: the way forward

"You can't build a reputation on what you're going to do"
Henry Ford

Reputations are ever-shifting and potentially transient; they need to be painstakingly built and carefully nurtured. Businesses must be constantly vigilant; not only thinking about reputation when things go wrong, but managing risks to reputation actively all the time. Reputation risk management is both an 'inside out' and an 'outside in' challenge.

The starting point is setting out your stall 'inside out' by defining a clear vision and values, backed up by policies and procedures which will guide behaviours and inform decision making throughout the business and its supply chain. This will also enable your stakeholders to know what you stand for, what your goals are and how you plan to achieve it so they know what to expect.

The second part of the challenge is 'outside in': keeping in close touch with major stakeholders and systematically tracking their evolving perceptions and expectations so gaps are minimised, emerging trends are spotted early and opportunities to offer new products and services in new ways in new markets are exploited.

Stakeholder expectations of businesses and their reputations have never been so high; being authentic, being the real thing has never been so important. The concept is far from new, but the way it's handled by businesses is quite new. The corporate responsibility (CR) and sustainable development (SD) agendas have clearly modified the traditional economic role of firms and added aims to their strategies. Nowadays businesses must integrate all their stakeholders, not only shareholders. In this way, they try to create competitive advantage and improve their reputation by the addition of an ethics element. Reputation must always be adapted to the context if it is to be resilient and sustainable. It is all the more crucial that perceived reputation is taken into account, for perception is reality in the minds of stakeholders. It is not enough to be sure of one's actions but the organisation must also monitor carefully the image perceived by its stakeholders, even if it is subjective. This bias may be the source of many dissonances between the value put into reputation and the perceived value, which is the only "real" value at the end of the day.

References

Akerlof G (1970) The Market for Lemons: Qualitative Uncertainty and the Market. In: Mechanisms Quarterly, Journal of Economics, Vol 84 pp 488-500

Anderson DR (2006) The critical Importance of Sustainability Risk Management. In: Risk Management Magazine, pp 66 -74

Bauer RA (1960) Consumer behavior as Risk Taking, Dynamic Marketing for a Changing World, R.S. Hancok (ed.), American Marketing Association, pp 389-398

Brewer L, Chandler RC, Ferrell OC (2006) Managing Risks for Corporate Integrity: How to Survive an Ethical Misconduct Disaster, Business/Business Ethics/Marketing, Thomson Corp.

Cagan P (2006) On finding linkages: corporate governance and operational risk. In: The John Liner Review, Vol 19 pp 4

Chemmanur TJ, Fulghieri P (1994) Reputation, renegotiation, and the Choice between Bank Loans and Publicly Traded Debt, Review of Financial Studies, Vol 7 No 3 pp 475-506

Crofts N (2005) Authentic Business, Capstone Publishing Company

Diamond DW (1991) Financial Intermediation and Delegated Monitoring, Review of Economic Studies, Vol 51 pp 393-414

Douglas M., Widawsky A, (1982) Risk & Culture. Gaultier-Gaillard, Louisot, 2006. Geneva Papers. Fischoff & all, p 78

Ducarroz C, Scarmure P, Sinigaglia S (2003) Tintin au pays des enchères: information sur la qualité et réputation des vendeurs. In: Actes du XXème Congrès AFM, Vol 6&7 May 2004, St Malo (France)

Fagart, M.C., Kambia-Chopin B. (2003) Aléa moral et Sélection Adverse sur le marché de l'Assurance, working paper CREST/THEMA.

Fombrun C, Gardberg NA, Barnett ML (2000) Opportunity Platforms and Safety Nets: Corporate Citizenship and reputational risk. In: Business and Society Review, Vol 105 No 1 pp 85-106

Fombrun CJ (2005) A World of Reputation Research, Analysis and Thinking – Building Corporate Reputation Through CSR Initiatives: Evolving Standards <http://www.ingentaconnect.com/content/pal/crr/2005/00000008/00000001/art00001;jsessionid=1ajaykh8bli1c.victoria >. In: Corporate Reputation Review, Vol 8 No 1 pp 7-12

Gaultier-Gaillard S, Louisot JP (2004) Diagnostic des risques AFNOR (ed.)

Graham P, Fearn H. (2005) Corporate Reputation: What Do Consumers Really Care About? In: Journal of Advertising Research <http://journals.cambridge.org/action/displayAbstract?fromPage=online&aid=407477&fulltextType=RA&fileId=S0021849905050361##> Vol 45 pp 305-313

Harpur, Oonagh Mary (2002) Corporate Social Responsibility Monitor. London : Gee Publishing Chapter B 4

Kreps DM (1990) Game Theory and Economic Modelling. Oxford University Press

Kreps DM, (1990) Corporate Culture & Economic Theory. In: Perspectives on positive Economy, Alt JE & Kenneth (ed.), Cambridge University Press, pp 90-143

Larkin J (2003) Strategic Reputation Risk Management. Palgrave McMillan.

Louisot JP (2004) Managing Intangible Asset Risks: Reputation and Strategic Redeployment Planning. In: Risk Management: An International Journal, Vol 6 No 3 pp 35-50

Louisot JP (2005) 100 questions pour comprendre la gestion des risques, AFNOR (ed.)

McDonald C, Slawson V (2002) Reputation in Internet Auction Market. In: Economic Inquiry, Vol 40 pp 633-650

Menilk M, Alm J (2002) Does a Seller'E-Commerce Reputation Matter? Evidence from e-Bay Auctions. In: Journal of Industrial Economics, Vol 1 pp 337-349

Nelson A, Etue D (2006) Reducing the Risk of Information Leakage. In: The John Liner Review, Vol 20 pp 1

Rayner J (2003) Managing Reputational Risk: Curbing Threats, Leveraging Opportunities, Wiley (ed.)

Resnick P, Zeckhauser R (2002) rust Among Strangers in Internet Transactions: Empirical Analysis of e-Bay's reputation system. In: Bay M. (ed.), The Economics of the Internet and the e-Commerce, Elsevier, pp 127-157

Rotschild M, Stiglitz JE (1976) Equilibrium in Competitive Insurance Markets: an Essay on the Economics of Imperfect Information. In: Quartely Journal of Economics, Vol 90 pp 629-650

Sami H (2004) Firm's Financial Distress and Reputational Concerns, Working paper.

Schelling TC (1960) The Strategy of Conflict, Oxford University Press

Selva KF (2005) How it's difficult to ruin a good name: An analysis of reputational risk, CISSP, 19 September 2005

Simon HA (1951) A Formal Theory of the Employment Contract, In: Econometrica, Vol 19 pp 293-305

Standifird S (2001) Reputation and E-commerce: e-Bay's Auctions and the Asymetrical Impact of Positive and Negative Rating. In: Journal of Management, Vol 27 pp 279-285

Standifird S (2002) Online Auctions and the Importance of Reputation Type. In: Electronic Markets, Vol 12 pp 1

Stansfield G (2006) Some thoughts on reputation and challenges for global financial institutions. In: The Geneva Papers, Vol 31 pp 470-149

Tirole J (1993) A theory of Collective Reputations. mimeo

Woolf Committee, Business ethics, global companies and the defense industry: Ethical business conduct in BAE Systems plc – the way forward (May 2008)

Reputation and regulation

Hans Caspar von der Crone and Johannes Vetsch

Where information asymmetries are inherent in markets, reputation serves as an enforcement mechanism. Regulation takes the task of informing participants of their counterparties' standing by sending quality signals to support their reputation, thus allowing for efficient trade. Effective regulation creates expectations, which may force regulators to assume responsibility for the quality signals issued. The extent of both financial and reputational risk to which governments are exposed in financial markets requires strong regulation with clear rules for predictable intervention.

In discussions about the current financial crisis, two issues in particular seem to stand out: reputation and regulation. While the crisis has tainted the reputation of many financial institutions and audit companies, as well as regulating authorities, it has also increased the demand for stronger regulation as a means to solve the crisis. However, a closer look at the situation reveals a system of much more complex interdependencies between reputation and regulation. This essay aims to address questions regarding the mechanism of reputation in the context of regulation as well as challenges to regulation. The final section looks at the concept of regulation in the financial market.

The mechanism of reputation

Ideally, contracting parties have full access to all information necessary to define and assess the quality of the performance of the respective counterparty. Under such conditions of full and symmetrically distributed information, parties can write a complete contract specifying all details of their future interaction. Virtually no contract, however, is entirely complete, as some aspects of the performance relevant to the parties usually cannot be

J. Klewes, R. Wreschniok (eds.), *Reputation Capital*, DOI 10.1007/978-3-642-01630-1_12,
© Springer-Verlag Berlin Heidelberg 2009

defined in detail ex ante [5, 11, 15].[1] The resulting lack of specification reduces the ability of a court to assess and enforce the performance of a contract: when formal enforcement is not available, there is limited certainty regarding satisfactory performance.[2]

Knowing that important aspects of the performance cannot be formally enforced, parties will select their counterparties based on their reputation. When searching for the best physician or the best lawyer,[3] for example, people will enquire amongst their friends or business relations for experiences they have had with potential candidates. Physicians and lawyers, in turn, know about the importance of their reputation for their business perspectives. Keeping their long-term reputation in mind, they will refrain from opportunistically making short-term use of the incompleteness of their contracts [10, 15, 26, 27]. Reputation therefore is a key element in the governance of some of the most important standard contracts of a modern economy,[4] as the concern for one's own reputation serves as an alternative enforcement mechanism.

Mechanisms of reputation will only become effective on two conditions. First, there needs to be repeated interaction within a group of principals and agents: in a repeated play, parties know that cooperation will come to an end if performance does not meet expectations [20]. Reputation extends the mechanism of two-party repeated plays to multi-party interaction [15]. Second, since mechanisms of reputation infer from past to probable future behaviour, at least some aspects of past behaviour must be observable. Reputation, in this context, is an aggregate of the experiences other principals have had when dealing with the respective agent in the past, given that such information is at least partially available to other principals [1, 33].[5]

---

[1] A complete contract would lead to prohibitive costs both in drafting and enforcing the contract. Such a contract can only serve as a model.

[2] There are substantial variations in the degree of completeness of contracts: while contracts regarding standardised commodities usually are complete to a high level (because many such contracts are fulfilled in single transactions and thus are not subject to changes in circumstances), contracts for services show a much larger degree of incompleteness [15]. In Swiss law, the incompleteness and lack of formal enforceability of contracts for services is acknowledged with the option to terminate a mandate without notice (Art. 404 of the Swiss Code of Obligation) [32].

[3] Lawyers and physicians are two professions dealing with the issue of information asymmetry due to hidden information, i.e. information not available to the principal despite his ability to observe the agent's activities [11].

[4] Including all principal-agent relations, i.e. all relations in which a principal hires an agent to act on his behalf. On the principal-agent theory, see Jensen and Meckling [12].

[5] One modern way to communicate experiences with certain agents is online feedback systems: especially in dealing with anonymous counterparts (e.g. sellers in online auctions), where information is hidden and distributed asymmetrically, their reputation becomes a dominant factor in the selection. Online feedback systems allow participants to share experiences and, by so doing, maintain the market [41].

Emergence of regulation

Establishing the reputation of potential counterparties can be a time-consuming undertaking, especially for outsiders who are not regularly contracting for the respective goods or services. Buyers (principals) may therefore incur substantial search costs in trying to establish the reputation of different service providers (i.e. agents). They will thus be interested in quality signals that reduce their search costs.

Under certain circumstances, agents as well are interested in quality signals: in highly reputation-sensitive industries, the reputation of peers will to some extent become interlocked. A bad reputation for the sector as a whole will negatively affect individuals offering services of high quality. As demonstrated with the market for used cars,[6] high-quality providers in such markets will not easily succeed in proving that they offer superior quality, and thus, they will not be able to charge the correct price for their service. High quality providers can therefore be expected to act against low quality providers by establishing standards or labels and issuing quality signals to potential customers [11, 28]. Under such conditions, self-regulation can be expected to emerge. Examples are professional organisations of physicians or lawyers. If a sector is critical to the public interest, quality signals may be supported by specific laws, or the standard-setting function may be assumed entirely by the state.

Whether a quality signal actually leads to a reduction of search costs depends on its performance. The performance of a standard or the reliability of its setter is only partially measurable. Consequently, this issue is subject to information asymmetries as well and, therefore, to the mechanism of reputation. To some extent, the reputation of the individual service provider is complemented or replaced by the reputation of the standard or the standard setter.

---

[6] An example of the so-called "market for lemons". The term refers to a problem of information asymmetry: if there is a high level of information asymmetry in a market with potentially bad agents, the probability of getting a bad product (a "lemon") rises; therefore, consumers' willingness to pay high prices is reduced in general [1].

Regulation and moral hazard

Quality signals always have distorting effects. According to the "club theory", it is typically attractive to only minimally meet the standards [6]. Standards thus foster a tendency to favour form over substance.[7]

If market participants observe that merely formal compliance is sufficient, the regulator risks not being taken seriously any more. The regulator's reputation and its ability to issue a quality signal are compromised. Setting and enforcing standards resembles an arms race: the regulator will continuously be challenged by attempts to dodge its standards and, unless it accepts the risk of losing its reputation, the regulator will have to fight back with ever more sophisticated standards and enforcement procedures. Within such a cycle lies a risk of over-regulation, as the regulator is most likely to be challenged by the marginal – and not the average – market participant [13].

Regulation and risk awareness

Successful regulation gives market participants a sense of safety in dealing with a regulated counterparty. In selecting their counterparties, market participants become less attentive to the counterparty risk. In areas such as public transport electronic goods, or financial institutions, regulation replaces the natural risk awareness of consumers who thus tend to be less aware of the risks inherent in their contracting.[8] While at first sight this may seem to be just another case of moral hazard, replacing mistrust with trust can create important social benefits. Complex markets such as the financial market could not function on the basis of mistrust; rather, it requires a certain level of trust [4].[9] Such a "guarded trust" – a neither naive nor permanently suspicious attitude towards each other – relieves parties from burdensome search costs of individually establishing their counter-

---

[7] One can typically get away with substantive, but not with formal non-compliance. One means to counteract such tendencies could be to argue with the abuse of rights; a measure, however, that is usually bound to very strict conditions [40].

[8] Even if a cableway or a ski lift looks old, people will use it without further ado, trusting in proper maintenance prescribed and (hopefully) enforced by regulation. A study in Switzerland even showed that pedestrian crossings crosswalks tend to be the most dangerous place to cross a street, mainly due to the pedestrian's inattentiveness based on their trust in the crossing's safety [21].

[9] There are, of course, still many advocates of free markets, as the current controversial discussion regarding the financial market crisis shows [13].

parties' standing. In this way, regulation can provide for faster and more efficient contracting, and thus creates a more efficient market as a whole.

Regulator as guarantor

While this reduction of risk awareness allows for more efficient trading, it also creates certain expectations of market participants towards the regulator.[10] The effect of regulation on the behaviour of market participants is similar to the effects of an insurance contract: within a regulated market, participants will behave differently in screening, selecting and monitoring their counterparties. Under an insurance contract, though, the insured pays the insurer for the assumption of a specific risk, and receives, in return, a well-defined claim against the insurer upon the occurrence of the event insured. The regulator typically does not assume a formal liability for the quality of the regulatory signal, just as he is not specifically compensated for assuming the relevant responsibility. As a consequence, while market participants grow inattentive of inherent risks, they do not receive a legally enforceable claim for compensation against the regulator even if the regulatory signal was wrong. Regulation creates expectations without assuming responsibility.[11]

During testing times – such as natural disasters, plane crashes or the current financial crisis – this fact may come to the attention of market participants. In a singular occurrence, the regulator will try to sustain the validity of the regulatory signal, for example by explaining the incident with factors not related to the signal. If, however, the crisis turns out to run deeper, the reputation of the regulator is questioned, and the regulatory signal itself no longer considered trustworthy. There is a risk that mistrust might replace the "guarded trust" amongst market participants.[12]

---

[10] Expectations rise with a positive track record (i.e. a good reputation) of the regulator, since market participants become accustomed to a certain level of trust.

[11] The case is different if a regulator violates its own duty to supervise the implementation of regulatory standards. This could lead to a legal responsibility of the government based on a law regarding the liability of the state (Verantwortlichkeitsgesetz, SR 170.32). The conditions are strict, as demonstrated when a liability claim against the Swiss Federal Banking Commission (SFBC) was rejected in a 1990 decision of the Swiss Federal Supreme Court (BGE 116 Ib 193, 196); see also [39].

[12] This could be seen in the current financial crisis: while banks reacted to the loss of trust by refusing interbank credits, customers withdrew their savings from 'infected' banks.

Re-establishing the reputation

Deregulation

One radical answer to regulatory failure might be deregulation. What cannot be effectively regulated is better not regulated at all: no wrong signals are sent. Without "guarded trust" instilled by regulation, people will again become risk conscious. As attractive as such an approach may seem at first, it cannot work in complex markets for two reasons: first, regulatory signals are a prerequisite for efficient trading in complex markets. Replacing regulatory signals by market participants' individual caution would lead to astronomically high transactions costs, in effect strangling such markets. Second, market participants are accustomed to a certain degree of regulatory protection. Once the market has become used to trading based on a certain level of trust, the road back to Hobbes' state of general mistrust is blocked.

Assuming responsibility

Lacking the alternative of fundamental deregulation, regulators will therefore have to fight to re-establish their signalling capability. One strategy for reaching this goal is to assume the responsibility for the expectations created by the regulatory signal. In deciding whether to assume responsibility, the regulator will find itself in a precarious position. If the regulator does not act against market participants complying only formally with standards while neglecting its substance, the regulator's reputation will be affected. On the other hand, if the regulator does offer help to companies facing difficulties, it could face opportunistic behaviour from market participants who bet on and seek to profit from such an implicit government guarantee.[13] In general, assuming responsibility for past signalling can therefore only be an intermediary solution.

---

[13] This balancing act could be seen in the financial crisis in 2008, during which some banks were saved by financial support from regulators (to strengthen the system), and others were not (to set examples) [18].

Strengthening regulation

In the long run, the regulator has little choice other than strengthening regulation. There are different ways to do so: with a long-term perspective, the regulator may choose a new approach to regulation, i.e. restructuring market supervision as a whole. It may introduce changes in the regulation's concept, or new requirements. This, however, takes time, and is not an adequate short-term response to an imminent crisis. Another approach to strengthen regulation is to set up tougher rules, i.e. to eliminate flaws in the previous framework.[14] Finally, the focus may be shifted to the enforcement of existing rules. Because lawmakers tend to focus on rules and neglect their enforcement, many regulations are conceptually sound but insufficiently enforced.[15]

Regulation of financial markets

The financial sector – as one of the most important but also most complex markets of the economy – provides a good example for the interaction of reputation and regulation.

Financial markets: Need for reduction of complexity

The financial stability of a company is assessed based on its balance sheet, i.e. the assets and liabilities a company has. The relatively simple mathematics of the balance sheet may give the impression that the total worth of a company can be represented and its future performance assessed with plain and reliable numbers. The valuation of the individual assets and liabilities, however, reveal the complexity behind it.

---

[14] Although such action is certainly required, one cannot overlook the political dimension: usually, regulators ask for tough rules, which are scaled down in the course of the political decision-making process. By acknowledging the failure of the existing regulation and setting up new and tougher requirements, the regulator is able to openly criticize previous political decisions, and thus create momentum for future actions.

[15] Again, for political reasons, the approach of focusing changes on the enforcement of rules is very popular among regulatory authorities: it translates into further powers and higher budgets for regulators.

Balance sheet

The balance sheet of the Credit Suisse Group – one of the few big European banks that until now has managed to refinance itself without state support – may serve as an example for the developments in bank balance sheets within the last fifty years. Looking back to 1957, Credit Suisse was mainly a domestic bank. All markets in which it was active were heavily cartelised and, consequently, volatility was low. Back in 1957, the bank had assets with a book value (corrected for inflation) of CHF 4.5 bn and an equity ratio of 7.5% [24]. Today, Credit Suisse is a global player in highly competitive and highly volatile markets. The reported capitalisation by far exceeds regulatory requirements. In 2007 Credit Suisse had assets of CHF 1.415 bn. The equity ratio, however, has dropped to 3.17%. While the balance sheet of Credit Suisse is rather conservative compared to other banks, it has become more than twice as risky since 1957, notwithstanding the fact that the bank today is confronted with market risks which would have been inconceivable in 1957.

Valuation models and intangibles

A glance at the assets reveals important changes as well. In 1957, all assets had to be reported at historical value, reflecting the initial purchase price of an asset, minus depreciations. Historic accounting tends to understate asset values: in 1957, the bank's real estate, for example, was booked at roughly one-fifth of its fair value [25]. Such understatement creates latent reserves. Under today's IFRS rules,[16] assets have to be reported at fair value, i.e. at current prices. Conceptually, fair-value accounting is clearly superior to historic accounting: while the latter requires booking assets at the initial purchase price, fair-value accounting reflects the current value of the assets. The benefit of the conservative (historical) approach was its cushioning effect: companies could go through shorter restructurings without announcing them to the markets, and could thus protect their reputation. The paradigm shift has revolutionized accounting by making it much more accurate. But with the disappearance of latent reserves, companies' balance sheets became substantially more risky.

Fair-value accounting aims to reflect the current worth of the company in its balance sheet. Assets that are traded on liquid markets are booked at their market value (mark-to-market). Other assets are valued based on

---

[16] IFRS 7, IAS 39.

valuation models (mark-to-model). While such models may give a reasonable estimation of the value of an asset under the model's assumptions, the true value of the asset is difficult to determine [34]. Liabilities as well are valued according to the fair-value rule: the fair value of a liability depends on the creditworthiness of the debtor, and is either equivalent to its nominal value (if the company is in good financial standing) or lower. Consequently, the downgrading of a company results in a profit booked in the profit and loss statement.[17]

A further complexity stems from assets or liabilities that are nontangible. If in a takeover a premium is paid to the seller, that amount is booked as goodwill in the balance sheet.[18] Moreover, certain intangible assets such as patents, know-how or innovations are booked at estimated values [9].[19]

Self-regulation and government regulation

These difficulties in the valuation of assets and liabilities clearly show that accounting cannot resolve all information asymmetries between market participants. As a consequence, market participants cannot evaluate all risks inherent in financial transactions themselves.[20] They have to rely on signals regarding traded assets, counterparty risks as well as the stability of the market as a whole. To that effect, standards and rating procedures have been developed aimed at ensuring a certain quality of assessment. However, these measures of self-regulation do not fully eliminate information asymmetries, either. Financial reporting, for example, reduces information asymmetry by providing financial information in aggregate form. As shown, though, the reliance on valuation models leaves the market with few means for establishing the accuracy of this representation. This requires yet another quality signal: by giving formal audit clearance, the

---

[17] According to its third-quarter financial statement of 2008, Swiss bank UBS was able to book a profit of CHF 2.2 bn solely on valuation gains on its liabilities [31].

[18] According to IFRS rules, there are clear rules on how to book goodwill (see IFRS 3 and IAS 36.15), but companies may still 'hide' goodwill by assigning that amount in ways so as to compensate for losses.

[19] Such distortions of a company's balance sheet may create expectation gaps. Zurich Financial Services distinguishes between the IFRS balance sheet and the "Available Financial Resources", i.e. an economic view of financial resources to cover policyholders in the event of a worst-case loss. In such a calculation, among other adjustments, intangible assets are removed and intangible liabilities added to the shareholders' equity [42].

[20] As one bank manager put it: "The requirements for information [...] have gone beyond our abilities to gather it." [4].

auditor confirms that the financial reports are an accurate and adequate representation of the company's financial standing.[21] Similar mechanisms are in operation regarding the valuation of a company's risk exposure or the assessment and rating of complex financial instruments [4].

In the end, financial standards, rating agencies and auditors – all institutions in charge of providing the market with quality signals regarding certain aspects of the financial market – are subject to mechanisms of reputation themselves. Again, the determination of such reputation is difficult and time-consuming, and thus expensive. Given the important economic and social function of the financial sector,[22] governments cannot afford inefficiency in financial markets. Governments, therefore, are required to issue quality signals regarding the various aspects of the market: the state, through its regulator, supports quality signals regarding financial institutions, reporting standards, auditors or rating agencies, thereby assuring the soundness of the financial market as a whole.[23] By issuing such signals, the regulator creates a "guarded trust" among market participants, and thus provides for the possibility of efficient interaction.

The current financial market crisis

Moral hazard

Market participants rely on quality signals when selecting counterparties, traded assets or risks. In other words, they favour form over substance: transactions in complex financial instruments[24] as well as the assessment of counterparty risk[25] are based on ratings or regulatory approval. In effect, they are thus based on the reputation of the respective regulatory institu-

---

[21] "Accountants are the gatekeepers of our financial markets. Without accountants to ensure the quality and integrity of financial information, the markets for capital would be far less efficient, the cost of capital would be far higher [...]." [38]; see also [22].

[22] In Switzerland, the financial sector alone accounts for about 10% of GDP, generates up to 14% of value added, and contributes to around 10% of total tax revenues at all levels. Moreover, the financial sector employs more than 5% of the total workforce in Switzerland [30].

[23] The state could do so by introducing licences for banks, auditors or rating agencies. Also, it can support or prescribe the usage of certain reporting standards.

[24] Within the past decade, financial institutions have increasingly traded derivatives, although according to Frank Partnoy, University of San Diego expert on derivatives, "[n]o one, including regulators, could get an accurate picture of this market" [13; see also 4, 7].

[25] In June 2008, the Belgian bank Dexia, for example, reported a risk-weighted (Basel II) equity ratio of 11.4% and thus met regulatory requirements. But its core capital ratio (i.e. the ratio that determines long-term creditworthiness) at that time was only 1.6% [3].

tions [4, 17]. The reliance on quality signals creates an incentive to just minimally meet the respective requirements. Financial reporting and assessment procedures leave room for individual adjustments of substantive issues. A company's management could be tempted, in case of negative developments, to take a short-term view and cover up losses with assessment adjustments, hoping that things will straighten out before the day of reckoning.[26] The risk in such a procedure is well known. Yet knowing that governments would ultimately step in to save failing banks for systemic reasons, there is no incentive – either for a bank's managers or its owners – to stop speculating or to question the system of quality signals currently in place.

Failing regulatory signals

The concurrence of low capitalisation and a reliance on risk and valuation models have led to the current crisis in financial markets. Like most market participants, regulators did not have the mathematical knowledge for their own independent assessment of risk-control concepts. As a consequence, they restricted themselves to a rather distant review of the banks' internal risk-control and valuation models. By doing so, banking regulators sent a positive signal regarding the capitalization of the big international banks without fully understanding their balance sheets. During the summer of 2007, the markets started to realise that regulatory capital requirements were inadequate, notably in the case of banks that had many basically illiquid assets on their balance sheets.

Banks knew from their own balance sheets that complying with formal requirements did not mean that one was sufficiently capitalised to be creditworthy. Blind trust was thus replaced by realistic credit risk assessment; quality signals were no longer trustworthy, and market participants were no longer prepared to bank on these regulatory signals at more or less risk-free rates [2, 37].

The consequence was a breakdown of the regulatory signalling capacity. The current crisis in financial markets, therefore, is also a product of regulation. The megatrend towards much riskier balance sheets, combined with complex accounting standards, could not have happened without regulators

---

[26] When market prices fell dramatically during the current financial crisis, banks tried to convince regulators that the "true" value of their assets was not reflected by the mark-to-market rule, but rather by applying models (such as the discounted cash flow model) even to frequently traded (but undervalued) assets [19].

issuing approving signals which replaced the market's natural risk awareness with trust among participants.

Consequences for the regulator

Assuming responsibility

The fault, of course, cannot be solely assigned to the regulator. Yet it was an unavoidable consequence of the regulators' signalling that the state had to step in and assume responsibility to a certain extent. At first, the regulators sought to control the situation by helping a few banks while neglecting others, and explaining their failures with factors not related to regulatory issues. The crash of Lehman Brothers, though, proved that the bankruptcy of systemically important institutions is no reasonable option for financial markets. That incident led to a massive loss of trust and to the failure of the credit market in 2008. Although governments realised the importance of interventions their actions were unpredictable both in scope and aims [4] and thus further decreased the level of trust in the financial market.

In the financial sector, the implicit government guarantee [16] is a consequence of the constant and strong exposure of the government's regulatory signals and their inherent assurance regarding the market. What is lacking, though, is a clear set of rules for predictable and balanced intervention [4].

Strengthening of regulation

The state cannot refrain from strengthening the rules. The regulatory framework is constantly updated in line with the evolution of the financial market itself. Tougher rules and better enforcement procedures are being discussed [8, 29, 36].

The assumption of responsibility in certain cases can strengthen the regulatory signal. This concept of an implicit government guarantee, however, leaves the state in a precarious position: while companies will always bet on the government not letting down an important market, the government does not have enough influence to control its own risk exposure. The massive negative impacts of the failure of a bank (for example, Lehman

Brothers), has put an end to the idea that the assumption of responsibility would be the regulator's choice: in markets as complex and important as the financial sector, the government will always be a lender of last resort [16]. A long-term solution thus has to focus on the institutional setting.[27] Regulation can no longer be delegated to various state and non-state actors with uncoordinated powers. It has to be acknowledged that the regulation of the financial market is a core task of the government. Predictable state intervention requires a clear set of rules, including the assignment of responsibility to a central authority and the adjustment of risk exposure based on a state's financial strength.[28] An effective control of the government's regulatory signal can only be based on better access to information, and thus a stronger integration of the government in the financial market.[29]

Conclusion

In incomplete contracting, i.e. contracting based on asymmetric information, the reputation of parties is a key factor in selecting counterparties. Especially for repeated interactions within a group of players, reputation is often the only mechanism to enforce performance. In order to simplify the process of selecting counterparties, reputation signals are issued, usually by some standard-setting body or the state. If such a quality signal becomes strong, market participants will no longer test their counterparties' qualities themselves, but rather rely on the signal. However, a quality signal may not be based on a thorough analysis of the whole market, and, thus, its signal may fail. For regulators of complex markets, the answers to such regulatory failure are limited: while deregulation is not an option, the regulator will have to both assume some responsibility for the expectations created, and try to strengthen the regulation.

An economy's most fundamental sectors cannot be left unregulated. The financial market especially, where information is distributed highly asymmetrically, cannot function without regulatory signals. Regulation in these markets is to be viewed not as an interruption to market forces, but as a fa-

---

[27] The Group of Thirty, a think tank of economy leaders, in its 2008 "A Framework for Financial Stability", proposed steps aimed at "[r]eforming the structure of prudential regulation, including the role of central banks, the implications for the workings of 'lender-of-last-resort' facilities and other elements of the official 'safety net' [...]" [8].

[28] The financial power of a state may be assessed by its GDP. The problem has become apparent in Iceland, where the failed banks were almost too big to rescue [35].

[29] The economic and social importance of financial markets is comparable to that of national security, a public good that is ensured by classical state institutions. Many financial institutions have been (partially) nationalised in the course of the current crisis [23].

cilitator of efficient trade – and thus, regulation has to be viewed as a core task of government. In light of weaknesses of the signalling capacity due to the difficulty of accurately assessing many market risks, a regulator's signal is likely to overreach, or fail, at times. In such situations the regulator (i.e., in effect, the government) has to take responsibility for the expectations created, based on the mechanism of reputation. In order to provide for predictable circumstances of state intervention, a stronger regulatory framework requires a clear set of rules to that end.

References

[1] Akerlof G (1970) The Market for Lemons: Quality Uncertainty and the Market Mechanism. Quarterly Journal of Economics, Vol 84 No 3 pp 488-500

[2] Economist (2008) Banker's Trust. The Economist, 24 Apr. 2008

[3] Economist (2008) Mewling and puking. How damaged is the Basel 2 accord? The Economist, 23 October 2008

[4] Economist (2009) A special report on the future of finance. The Economist, 24 January 2009

[5] Fleischer H (2001) Informationsasymmetrie im Vertragsrecht. C. H. Beck, München

[6] Goodhart CAE (1998) Financial Regulation – why, how and where now? Routledge Chapman & Hall, London

[7] Gratwohl N (2009) Ergebnisse lösen Flucht aus. Handelszeitung, 21 January 2009

[8] The Group of Thirty (2009) Financial Reform – A Framework for Financial Stability. (Special Report by the Working Group on Financial Reform, Washington, DC)

[9] Harvey MG, Lusch RF (1999) Balancing the Intellectual Capital Books: Intangible Liabilities. European Management Journal, Vol 17 No 1 pp 85-92

[10] Herbig P, Milewicz J, Golden J (1994) A Model of Reputation Building and Destruction. Journal of Business Research, Vol 31 No 1 pp 23-31

[11] Hunziker S (2007) Das Prinzipal-Agent-Problem im schweizerischen Vertragsrecht. Thesis, University of Zurich

[12] Jensen MC, Meckling WH (1976) Theory of the Firm: Managerial Behavior, Agency Costs and Ownership Structure. Journal of Financial Economics, Vol 3 pp 305-360

[13] Lipton E, Labaton S (2008) A Deregulator Looks Back, Unswayed. The New York Times, 16 November 2008

[14] Mazumder S (2006) Finanzmarktregulierung im Spannungsfeld von Überregulierung und Deregulierung. Der Schweizer Treuhänder, Vol 8 pp 519-523

[15] Milgrom P, Roberts J (1992) Economics, Organization and Management. Prentice Hall, Englewood Cliffs

[16] Nobel P (1994) Die Nationalbank als Lender of Last Resort – ein leeres Versprechen oder Notrecht? In: Walder HU, Jaag T, Zobl D (eds) Aspekte des Wirtschaftsrechts, Festgabe zum Schweizerischen Juristentag. Schulthess, Zürich, pp 497-510

[17] Nuoy D (2008) Supervisory perspectives. Journal of Financial Stability, Vol 4 pp 346-350

[18] NZZ (2008) Bestrafter Hochmut. Neue Zürcher Zeitung, 18 September 2008

[19] NZZ (2008) Die Wallstreet traut dem Markt nicht mehr. Neue Zürcher Zeitung, 18 September 2008

[20] Pacheco JM, Traulsen A, Ohtsuki H, Nowak MA (2008) Repeated games and direct reciprocity under active linking. Journal of Theoretical Biology, Vol 250 pp 723-731

[21] Paganini R (2008) Das Auto steht im Zentrum, der Rest ist sekundär. TagesAnzeiger, 25 November 2008

[22] Raar J (2008) The new global accounting community: Rationale for dialogue to establish is accountability? Critical Perspectives on Accounting

[23] Sanger DE (2009) Nationalization Gets a New, Serious Look. The New York Times, 26 January 2009

[24] Schweizerische Nationalbank (2007) Die Banken in der Schweiz 2007 (Information made available by the Swiss National Bank, Bern)

[25] Schweizerische Kreditanstalt (1957) 101. Geschäftsbericht. Zürich

[26] Shapiro C (1983) Premiums for High Quality Products as Returns to Reputations, The Quarterly Journal of Economics, Vol 98 No 4 pp 659-680

[27] Smith A (1766) Lectures on Jurisprudence – Part II. Clarendon Press, Oxford

[28] Spence M (1973) Job Market Signaling. The Quarterly Journal of Economics, Vol 88 pp 355-374

[29] Swiss Federal Department of Finance (2008) Botschaft zu einem Mass-nahmenpaket zur Stärkung des schweizerischen Finanzsystems. Federal Finance Administration, Bern

[30] Swiss Federal Department of Finance (2006) Swiss financial centre and financial market policy. Federal Finance Administration, Bern

[31] UBS AG (2008) Financial Reporting, Third Quarter 2008

[32] vd Crone HC (1993) Rahmenverträge. Schulthess, Zürich

[33] vd Crone HC (2000) Verantwortlichkeit, Anreize und Reputation in der Corporate Governance der Publikumsgesellschaft. ZSR 119 (2000) II pp 239-275

[34] Wall Street Journal (2008) Behind AIG's Fall, Risk Models Failed to Pass Real-World Test. The Wall Street Journal, 31 October 2008

[35] Wall Street Journal (2008) The Isle that Rattled the World. The Wall Street Journal, 27 December 2008

[36] Wall Street Journal (2008) Unlocking Europe's Supervisory Borders. The Wall Street Journal, 28 October 2008

[37] Wall Street Journal (2009) Let's Write the Rating Agencies Out of Our Law. The Wall Street Journal, 2 January 2009

[38] Wallman SMH (1995) The future of accounting and disclosure in an evolving world; the need for dramatic change. Accounting Horizons, Vol 3 pp 81-91

[39] Weber RH, Kaufmann C (2008) Haftung für mangelnde staatliche Aufsicht im Finanzmarktbereich. HAVE 3/2008 pp 6-12

[40] Zeller E (1981) Treu und Glauben und Rechtsmissbrauchsverbot. Schulthess, Zürich

[41] Zhou M, Dresner M, Windle RJ (2008) Online reputation systems: Design and strategic practices. Decision Support Systems, Vol 44 pp 785-797

[42] Zurich Financial Services (2007) Capital Management. Presentation at Zurich Financial Services Investor's Day, 28 Mar. 2007. London

Measuring risks to reputation

Frank Herkenhoff

In recent years, we have seen subtle attempts to deconstruct "reputation" into measurable, and therefore manageable, figures. Some of these have been gathered together in this book. Objective figures are an important prerequisite to systematically planning and using reputation as a profitable resource. It is also an important prerequisite for communicating with top management, who are used to making decisions primarily on the basis of numerical parameters.

To make it possible for the intangible value of reputation to be integrated beyond this into company-wide risk management and to visibly "increase" it in the eyes of top management, we will now examine the main features of empirically measuring risks to reputation. It is only in empirical feasibility, after all, that the viability of concepts is proven. This is equally true for the catchphrase "reputation management". We must bear in mind here that the term "risk" in the context of modern risk management represents two sides of the same coin: on the one hand it is the danger of loss, but on the other it is also the opportunity to profit.

As the parameter "reputation" includes a means of approaching operational risk management, the requirement of the Control and Transparency in Business Act (KonTraG) that companies provide an annual risk report concerning the financial statement, is also satisfied for those who have to declare risks for a company to investors.

The location of reputation risks

In communication science, increasing attention is being paid to the role that Internet blogs and forums play in forming opinions in downstream processes (e.g. Zerfaß/Welker/Schmidt 2008). Practical consultancy has followed close behind and offers a range of scanning instruments for the relevant Internet sites. However, this cannot hide the fact that risks to repu-

J. Klewes, R. Wreschniok (eds.), *Reputation Capital*, DOI 10.1007/978-3-642-01630-1_13,
© Springer-Verlag Berlin Heidelberg 2009

tation only occur when traditional mass media (TV, print, radio) take up the matter. If this were not the case, people responsible for communications today would have to give up in the face of the sheer number of reputation-damaging events, comment, conjecture and attacks that can be found on the Internet at any given moment for any given company. The catalysing effect of traditional mass media should not be underestimated at this time.

The basic model of risk management

Two issues are significant for risk management; two issues that also represent the main variables: the probability that a risk will occur and its valency, that is, the (preferably monetary) assessment of the risk. It must therefore be possible to determine both for reputation risks.

Anyone reading the various different articles and books on reputation management might well become confused from time to time, considering that almost anything can be a source of risks to reputation. The list of suspects stretches from personal lapses on the part of management, though product faults, to natural disasters which those "responsible" mishandle, thereby damaging the reputation of a region, for example.

From an analytical viewpoint, the causes of reputation risks lie not in the events themselves, needless to say, but rather in the attentive structures of the mass media. These structures define what reaches the surface of public perception. Everything below this surface does not occur, for all intents and purposes, and does not initially present any risk to reputation. Given this situation, it makes sense to examine more closely the question of why certain circumstances make the news and others do not.

Theoretical basis: selection research

Among the different ways of viewing risk management, only theories that can be influenced – and therefore controlled – by the company's management are of interest here. The news value theory and the framing approach thus form the starting point for a risk management model. To examine this problem, we must understand theory in its widest sense: the issue at hand is not simply to describe and explain effects on reputation, but more importantly to forecast these effects.

News value theory

In Europe, the news value theory was primarily developed by Östgaard (cf. 1965), Galtung/Ruge (1965), Sande (1971) and Rosengren (1970) and was subsequently reconceptualised by Schulz (1976). Research since then has built on the work of these authors.

Using "common-sense perception psychology" as their basis, the Scandinavian researchers Galtung and Ruge proposed twelve factors to explain the selection of news items when reporting on foreign affairs (ibid. 1965 p. 66). Eight of these factors are true for all cultures, but four others are culture-dependent and only important in this form for Western Europe (ibid. p. 68). Galtung and Ruge define the following as culturally-independent: frequency, threshold, unambiguity, meaningfulness, consonance, unexpectedness, continuity and composition. The four culture-dependent factors are: reference to elite nations, reference to elite persons, reference to persons and reference to something negative (cf. ibid. p. 70f.).

Staab (cf. 1990) divides his research into an American and a European tradition. The American tradition is focussed on experimental design with fewer news factors investigated on average, while European researchers frequently conduct output analyses in the tradition of Galtung and Ruge against a background of democratic theory.

In his investigations, Staab ties in to Schulz's news factor catalogue, via four contentious issues (35-hour week, asylum seekers in Germany), and expands the catalogue to a total of 22 factors (negativism, surprise, involvement of celebrities, etc.). Like Schulz, Staab also identifies news factors using a four-tier scale of intensity. The investigation, designed as an output study, recorded reporting in the major national newspapers, selected regional papers, two newsstand papers, the evening news on five radio broadcasters and the main news programmes from German public-service television broadcasters ARD and ZDF. The fundamental predication: the more intensive the characteristic of the news factors, the larger the news value of a situation and the larger its coverage in the media.

Kepplinger reasons that "although news factors are a *conditio sine qua non* for positive selection decisions" (ibid. 1998 p. 22), the theory does not provide any explanation for editors' selections because there are also reports with the same characteristics that are not published. The decisive issue is that news value can change over time and therefore events with a large, verifiable concentration of news factors do not necessarily lead to publication. This links into a further aspect of the historicity of news factors: the theory does not differentiate between reporting in or about exceptional situations and routine coverage. It assumes that the selection process always takes place in the same way in the media. However, it can be demonstrated that in times of crisis or catastrophe, events with the same or even lower news value result in publication. This type of situation leads to waves of articles without any change in the frequency of the events on which the reports are based. It should also be observed that further, primarily thematically influenced and discourse-dependent selection patterns for choosing news need to be taken into account. These patterns go beyond any individual article and can be addressed using the framing approach.

Framing approach

Framing can be understood in general terms as the creation of a framework for interpretation, a method of conscious contextualisation for processing and passing on information. Almost every subject is delivered in (in the majority of cases) ready-made analysis frameworks. Abortion, neo-Nazi violence, managerial salaries, etc.

Brosius/Eps (cf. 1995 p. 170) identified core aspects that are important to the emergence of media frames:

- Frames format which incidents a journalist conceive of as an event;

- Frames format which aspects of an event are selected for reporting;

- Frames format the context in which an event is presented.

In theory, the discursive level in the media system would also be of interest. However, this would be difficult to research because it requires participation in the editing staff's formal and informal discussions. Furthermore, the investigations of Brosius and Eps (1993), Scheufele (2003), Scheufele/Brosius (1999) and Brosius and Scheufele (2002) suggest that there is not a permanent exchange by means of patterns of interpretation within the editorial department, but that this only exists in the orientation phases. Orientation phases should be distinguished from routine phases because messages are selected on the basis of established frames during routine stages. Three reasons are cited for this: the recurrent orientation of colleagues and efficient processing of information flows using frames, the relatively strong elaboration of journalistic frames, and their perpetuation due to follow-up stories, which continue to activate the same frames and thereby stabilise them. Orientation phases are characterised by a "struggle" for the prerogative of interpretation. This is demonstrated particularly keenly in the initial wave of reports concerning a (supposed) scandal. Within a few days, a media standard is developed that formats the frame of interpretation and which is drawn upon from then on (cf. Kepplinger 2001, p. 18ff). From a communication strategy perspective, orientation phases can be seen as valuable opportunities: first of all to replace established frames with new ones more favourable to the company. Secondly, orientation phases also make it possible to make subjects that would otherwise have been given no attention available to the media.

The degree of "fitting" is key to the activation of frames. Fitting refers to the degree of conformity between fixed schemata in the media, on the one hand, and the schemata information present in the particular case.

There is a whole range of findings from mass communication research that can be reinterpreted in the light of frame research. These findings primarily involve empirical studies that investigate the relationship between reality outside the media (extra-media reality) and media reality at various points in time. The results of these studies almost always establish that extra-media reality has hardly changed. The reported media reality, however, has. For an example of this, let us look at the investigations of Fishman (1978), which examined the waves of reports concerning crimes directed against older people in New York. In the context of news factor research, Fishman reasoned that we must assume an increased sensitivity between and within editorial departments in the event of catastrophes and crises. The frame approach explains this situation by means of the orientation phase and the changing of frames in transformation phases. For if we assume that these events have not occurred in clusters outside media reports, then these events are no more worthy of reporting after a key event, from a journalist's point of view, than they were before.

In the context of risk analysis, we can understand this type of reporting wave as a serial effect, with the criterion of the series being a media pattern of interpretation. After all, the events themselves are not logically connected (e.g. a "series" of accidents in nuclear power plants; cf. e.g. Brauner 1990 cited in: Kratzheller 1997, p. 100).

The modulation of frames described previously can also be examined for potential risk. Someone who serves established frames can expect a higher news value. In contrast, an entity that does not take existing frames into account in its communication takes the "risk that target audiences will perceive the communicator as lacking credibility – or will even fail to understand what the communicator is talking about" (Entman 1993 p. 55).

The structure of media frames

How are media frames structured? Harden (cf. 2002, p. 86ff.) postulates six elements in frames on the basis of a study of the literature: problem definition, causes, proposed solutions, evaluations, protagonists and dynamic. For Harden, the problem definition is the basis of the frame, its "inner point of reference". He sees the subject in terms of a headline. A problem definition is characterised here by a comparison between the current status and the desired status. Harden assumes that not every element necessarily occurs in an individual text but that the elements develop over the course of various articles.

Scheufele explains the composition of frames on the basis of his cognitive-discursive basal model (cf. ibid. 2003, p. 92f. and Figure 1). He constructs a model with various slots that can be filled with specific default values. These form the criteria that a journalist creates in a specific, applied case (e.g. dubious marketing policy).

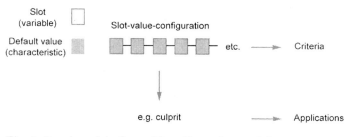

Fig. 1. Basal model of cognitive-discursive models
Source: Scheufele 2003, p. 92

Summary: Using theories concerning news values and media frames, which have previously only been used to describe and explain circumstances in the media, it is possible to design a model that empirically accounts for the probability of reporting. We will return to this later.

The process of risk management

Identifying risk

Risk identification represents the starting point for the entire risk management process. The decisive factor in this step is to balance the aim of recording risks as completely as possible against the enormous organisational and financial effort that this requires.

Literature concerning risk management provides a plethora of methods that would far exceed the scope of this account. However, when identifying media circumstances, special premises apply.

Premises for identifying risk

It is not necessary to know the original stage of any circumstances that may later be considered risky from the company's point of view, because there is no generally proven causal link between this initial state and later risks, either in business management or communication science literature. Furthermore, the original stage can also be ignored because an essentially undirected, unspecific search is highly uneconomical. The identification method must therefore – to put it in positive terms – be able to record and process complex information. For we can assume that as time progresses from the making of a decision at time T_e , more information will become available than at time T_{e-1}.

If we put ourselves in the position of an editorial team, we can also consider weak signals equally irrelevant. The object of potential editorial reporting is, after all, generally "stories", ignoring for the moment that there also straightforward information columns. Generally speaking, stories can be understood as sets of connotations that are coherent in themselves, and that assign presumed or actual causes to actors, roles and trajectories. Weischenberg, for example, stresses the importance of the arrangement of the content references and a recognisable connectivity of the information in a piece of news (cf. ibid. 1988, p. 98). Laroche advises journalists: "Tell the backstory" and "point out the connections" (1988, p. 102f).

Management also includes a control and checking component. In order to implement this component in strategies, it must, generally speaking, be possible to specify "rules" for the sequence of incidents for the particular field in which the management is to intervene. However, this should not be seen as strict cause-and-effect connections, but rather as recognisable patterns or regularities that can, in part, be influenced. The important issue is not whether the parties involved update this pattern entirely consciously, it is sufficient if only one of the involved sides does or can.

Summary: In order to identify the risks that are of interest to us here, the crucial period is the stage shortly before a potential decision by the editorial staff. In this stage, a journalist has knowledge of the core actors and problems that are linked to a situation, as well as speculation (at the least) regarding the causes of these problems. This is linked to a certain "thematic maturity" at which point a situation begins to appear interesting to the media; this is the point at which a journalistic story starts to take on an outline (cf. Hallahan 1999, p. 220f). Shifting back to the perspective of a company, we can, of course, conceive of a whole series of stories about a business that (could) affect its reputation (e.g. stories about marketing, price or investment policy). The company experiences an equivalent to the journalistic story in the form of a scenario. Depending on the sensitivity of the issues, scenarios are either developed internally or elaborated in moderated workshops with consultants. Scenarios projected in the near future are crucial to reputation risks because the mass media's publication cycles set the pace here.

Risk assessment – how great is the likelihood of selection?

The aim of assessment is to position each scenario in relation to others within the company. Relational positioning is pivotal and an absolute at the level of the overall media system because the methodology should provide the risk manager with orientation regarding communication risks that need to be handled first *within the company itself*, without giving an overview of all critical circumstances in the media agenda. Risk management is, after all, a control program induced on the part of the company, which therefore also only focuses on risks that the company can influence.

The entire procedure is based on two basic premises. Firstly, a scenario has a larger news value the more news factors with strong characteristics can be brought together in the particular circumstances and the more the scenario fits into established media frames. Secondly, a larger news value means there is a greater possibility that the situation depicted in the scenario will be selected.

The methodology for recording the probability of publication is arranged into four steps (for details, cf. Herkenhoff 2008):

1. News factor analysis of business scenarios

2. Analysis of frames at the level of the discourse product

3. Fitting analysis of the scenario and media frame

4. Risk scoring

News factor analysis of business scenarios

The news factor analysis makes use of an underlying situation in perception theory; that is, the fact that news factors have been understood as "common perception psychology" ever since Galtung/Ruge's first essay (ibid. 1965, p. 66). In other words, this does not involve a category specific to the field of journalism or an institutionalised programme of decision-making, but rather general factors governing the drawing of attention. For example, Eilders (cf. 1997) introduced a fundamental examination of this subject in her work and investigated the significance of news factors on public reception.

Considered together, these explanations suggest that news factors can also be used by anyone as criteria for selecting or assessing the relevancy of events, independently of the journalist as a person. Consequently, the first step consists of applying a news factor analysis to the scenarios documented.

Identifying the media frames

Journalists prefer information that is covered by their frames or schemas: "The more attributes [...] fit into the slots [of a corresponding] schema, the more likely that the journalist [...] will make a report" (Scheufele 2003, p. 102). This makes it possible to model a risk constellation from the perspective of risk management. To paraphrase, a risk exists if events or constellations in the company fulfil attributes that currently occur in existing media frames. Furthermore, assuming that information that does not fit into the schema is not (or far more rarely) used by journalists, we can also describe the risk situation as follows: if company-related scenarios do not fulfil slots in the media frames, the risk is low. The following step introduces this view as an investigation of the "structural fit", called a fitting analysis.

As frames can be imagined as slot-value configurations and events within the company fit the slots to varying degrees, it is possible to see the risk situation on a continuum. Matthes/Kohring (cf. 2004) describe various methods for analysing frames. A structurally grounded method such as the hierarchical cluster analysis promises the most success.

Fitting analysis

A fitting analysis cannot assume a dichotomous relationship of "fits" versus "does not fit". Instead, it is based more on a degree of fitting that can be diminished or intensified across various levels.

Essentially, media frames are regarded as a master frame in the fitting analysis, with the degree of structural fit being defined in alignment to the master frame. The reason for this is the fact that reputation risks originate in the media system – and not vice versa.

Mediaframes as Slot/Value-Configurations

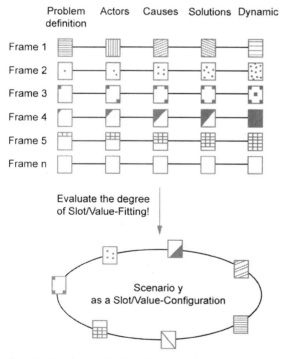

Fig. 2. Starting point for fitting analysis
Source: Author

The fitting analysis clarifies the degree of structural fit that the scenario's slot/value configurations have in terms of the various media frames. It goes without saying that not all scenarios can be compared to all media frames. There must be a rough thematic coherence. For example, it is only useful to investigate the fit of a marketing scenario to similarly positioned frames in the media.

Risk scoring

The results of the above analytical steps are now brought together by means of scoring. This scoring is oriented using the same models that are used in the country risk analysis. In general, the benefits of this type of procedure are the consistent assessment of complex circumstances, guaranteeing transparency of process even with a larger group of persons, making it possible to systematically compare different scenarios.

Scoring for news factors

Table 1. Scoring table for news factor analysis

Weighted and totalled scale rating	Risk scoring	Risk class	Description
100 >	DD	11	Publicity is extremely likely
90 - 99	DDD	10	
80 - 89	C	9	
70 - 79	CC	8	
60 - 69	CCC	7	
50 - 59	B	6	
40 - 49	BB	5	
30 - 39	BBB	4	
20 - 29	A	3	
10 - 19	AA	2	Publicity is extremely unlikely
0 - 9	AAA	1	

Source: Author

Depending on the characteristic of the news factors, each scenario "k" receives a risk score (SNFk = scoring news factors for scenario k) and is assigned to a risk class. There is no direct upper limit to the class. However, it can be determined mathematically by the number of news factors retrieved, multiplied by the largest scale rating. In the style of scoring models, the classes are also described using letters, in order to make it possible to differentiate between them at a glance. The same applies for the fitting scoring.

Scoring for frame fitting

The fitting scoring proceeds in a similar way to that of the news factors. Table 2 shows assigned (value = 1) and unassigned (value = 0) cause slots resulting from a frame analysis on the left-hand side, and cause slots from a scenario on the right.

Table 2. Example of an initial situation for a fitting analysis

Cause slots in a frame		Cause slots in a scenario
Description	Occurence	Absolute number
„Causes are in a marketing policy"	1	1
„Causes are in training measures"	1	0
„Causes are in top management"	1	1
„Causes are assigned to suppliers"	0	1
„Unspecific causes"	1	0

Source: Author

An initial overview of the proximity is provided by constructing a relative proximity index. Here, the number of slots in the scenario that fit slots in the frame is divided by the total number of slots that are actually addressed in the relevant media frame. The resulting coefficient can have any value between 0 and 1. A value of 1 would, in the above example, mean a complete match between the attributed causes in the scenario and those in the frame, which would be a maximum fit. The fitting is merged into an overall fitting (SF = scoring fitting) for each scenario. Table 3 shows a corresponding risk scoring.

Table 3. Risk scoring for fitting

Relative fitting coefficient (rF_j) at the scenario level	Risk scoring	Risk class	Description
1.0	DD	11	Publicity is
0.90 - 0.99	DDD	10	extremely likely
0.80 - 0.89	C	9	
0.70 - 0.79	CC	8	
0.60 - 0.69	CCC	7	
0.50 - 0.59	B	6	
0.40 - 0.49	BB	5	
0.30 - 0.39	BBB	4	
0.20 - 0.29	A	3	
0.10 - 0.19	AA	2	Publicity is
0.00 - 0.09	AAA	1	extremely unlikely

Source: Author

Overall scoring

The results of the individual scores can be compared by means of the risk classes. This assumes an interval scale with the same intervals between the class values. The overall score for a scenario k (OS_k) is made up of the total of $SNF_k + SF_k$.

Identifying damage/benefit per scenario

As reputation risks can generally be considered speculative risks, they need to be assessed both in terms of opportunities or profit, and loss or damage. Fundamentally, the assessment can take either a qualitative or quantitative form. The decisive factor here is what data is available. And so, the assessment process draws again on the judgement of experts, on the one hand, and on the plethora of information available in the company, on the other. Pragmatically and using risk assessments for risk constructs with similarly complex positioning (cf. e.g. Brühwiler 2001, p. 77ff.; Martin/Bär 2002, p. 99f.), a damage or opportunity classification is proposed here into which the particular scenario can be arranged.

Table 4. Risk assessment classes for the valency of media risk

Damage side	Assessment class	Profit side
Destructive	7	Excellent
Existence-threatening	6	Very advantageous
Fatal	5	Advantageous
Noticeable	4	Noticeable
Minor	3	Minor
Insignificant	2	Insignificant
Practically undetectable	1	Practically undetectable

Source: Author

Risk portfolio

The risks, assessed in terms of likelihood of occurring and damage/benefit, are arranged in a risk portfolio in order to determine how suited they are to risk management measures.

Risk management

In this process step, the various management strategies familiar from traditional risk management are applied: risk avoidance, risk reduction, risk diversification, risk transfer, risk provisioning, risk self-supporting and even risk intensification.

No matter which strategy is selected, the steps must, of course, be taken on the basis of the news factors and frame components that have been identified. In certain cases, for example, it is worth lowering the "fame" news factor by having the board stop commenting on a specific subject. Or increasing it in a targeted manner to raise the probability of publication. In other cases, it could be advisable to launch new causes for an established frame of interpretation. This is the starting point for strategy development.

References

Brauner C (1990) Das verdrängte Risiko. Können wir Katastrophen verhindern? Freiburg/Breisgau et al.: Herder

Brosius HB, Eps P (1993) Verändern Schlüsselereignisse journalistische Selektionskriterien? Framing am Beispiel der Berichterstattung über Anschläge gegen Ausländer und Asylanten. In: Rundfunk und Fernsehen, Vol 41 pp 512-530

Brosius HB, Eps P (1995) Framing auch beim Rezipienten? Der Einfluss der Berichterstattung über fremdenfeindliche Anschläge auf die Vorstellungen der Rezipienten. In: Medienpsychologie, Vol 7 pp 169-183

Brosius HB, Bertram S (2002) Eskalation in Krisen- und Normalphasen. Der Zusammenhang zwischen Medienberichterstattung und Fremdenfeindlichkeit in den neunziger Jahren. In: Esser F, Scheufele B, Brosius HB (ed.) (2002): Fremdenfeindliche Gewalt als Medienthema und Medienwirkung. Deutschland im internationalen Scheinwerferlicht. Opladen: Westdeutscher Verlag, pp 39-93

Brühwiler B (2001) Unternehmensweites Risk Management als Frühwarnsystem. Methoden und Prozesse für die Bewältigung von Geschäftsrisiken in integrierten Managementsystemen. Bern, Stuttgart, Vienna: Haupt

Eilders C (1997) Nachrichtenfaktoren und Rezeption. Eine empirische Analyse zur Auswahl und Verarbeitung politischer Informationen. Opladen: Westdeutscher Verlag

Entman RM. (1993) Framing: towards clarification of a fractured paradigm. In: Journal of Communication, Vol. 43 No 4 pp 51-58

Fishman M (1978) Crime waves as ideology. In: Social Problems, Vol 25 No 5 pp 531-543

Galtung J, Ruge MH (1965) The structure of foreign news. The presentation of the Congo, Cuba and Cyprus crisis in four foreign newspapers. In: Journal of Peace Research, Vol 2 No 1 pp 64-91

Kratzheller JB (1997) Risiko und Risk Management aus organisationswissenschaftlicher Perspektive. Wiesbaden: Dt. Universitätsverlag

Hallahan K (1999) Seven models of framing: implications for public relations. In: Journal of Public Relations Research, Vol 11 No 3 pp 205-242

Harden L (2002) Rahmen der Orientierung. Eine Längsschnittanalyse von Frames in der Philiosophieberichterstattung deutscher Qualitätsmedien. Wiesbaden: Dt. Universitätsverlag

Herkenhoff F (2008) Risikomanagement für Public Relations. Berlin: Helios Media

Martin T, Bär T (2002) Grundzüge des Risikomanagements nach KonTraG: Das Risikomanagementsystem zur Krisenfrüherkennung nach §91 Abs. 2 AktG. Munich, Vienna: Oldenbourg.

Matthes J, Kohring M (2004) Die empirische Erfassung von Medienframes. In: Medien & Kommunikationswissenschaft, Vol 52 No 1 pp 56-75

Kepplinger HM, Habermeier J (1996) The impact of key events on the presentation of reality. In: European Journal of Communication, Vol 10 No 3 pp 371-390

Kepplinger HM (1998) Der Nachrichtenwert der Nachrichtenfaktoren. In: Holtz-Bacha C, Scherer H, Waldmann N (ed.) (1998) Wie die Medien die Welt erschaffen und wie die Menschen darin leben. Opladen: Westdeutscher Verlag, pp 19-38

Kepplinger HM (2001) Die Kunst der Skandalierung und die Illusion der Wahrheit. Munich: Olzog.

Kratzheller JB (1997) Risiko und Risk Management aus organisationswissenschaftlicher Perspektive. Wiesbaden: Dt. Universitätsverlag.

Östgaard E (1965) Factors influencing the flow of news. In: Journal of Peace Research, Vol 2 No 1 pp 39-63

Rosengren KE (1970) International news: intra and extra media data. In: Acta Sociologica, Vol 13 No 2 pp 96-109

Rosengren KE (1974) International News: Methods, Data and Theory. In: Journal of Peace Research, Vol 11 No 2 pp 145-156

Sande Ø (1971) The perception of foreign news. In: Journal of Peace Research, Vol 8 No 3 and 4 pp 221-237

Scheufele B, Brosius HB (1999) The frame remains the same? Stabilität und Kontiniutät journalistischer Selektionskriterien am Beispiel der Berichterstattung über Anschläge auf Ausländer und Asylbewerber. In: Rundfunk und Fernsehen, Vol 47 No 3 pp 409-432

Scheufele B (2003) Frames – Framing – Framing-Effekte. Theoretische und methodische Grundlegung des Framing-Ansatzes sowie empirische Befunde zur Nachrichtenproduktion. Wiesbaden: Westdeutscher Verlag

Schulz W (1976) Die Konstruktion von Realität in den Nachrichtenmedien. Analyse der aktuellen Berichterstattung. Freiburg et al.: Alber

Schulz W (1989) Massenmedien und Realität. Die „ptolemäische" und „kopernikanische" Auffassung. In: Kaase, Max/Winfried Schulz (ed.): Massenkommunikation. Theorien, Befunde. Opladen: Westdeutscher Verlag, pp 135-149

Staab JF (1990) Nachrichtenwert-Theorie. Formale Struktur und empirischer Gehalt. Freiburg et al.: Alber

Weischenberg S (1988) Nachrichtenschreiben: journalistische Praxis zum Studium und Selbststudium. Opladen: Westdeutscher Verlag

Zerfaß A, Welker M, Schmidt J (eds.) (2008): Kommunikation, Partizipation und Wirkungen im Social Web. Cologne: Halem

Crisis management in the media society – Communicative integrity as the key to safeguarding reputation in a crisis

Ansgar Thießen

The value of reputation is unquestionable: an organisation with a good reputation attracts better people, is perceived as providing better value or even has more loyal customers or members respectively. Reputation is therefore to be protected carefully, since at times when value to a great extent comes from intangible assets such as goodwill or intellectual capital, a lost reputation may be the beginning of the end. During organisational crises, reputation may serve as a reservoir of goodwill on the one hand, but it also comes under attack on the other. In the age of the media society strategic crisis communications management therefore becomes a key instrument for protecting reputation sustainably. Once lost, rebuilding reputation is more like a marathon than a sprint, and it may take many years to recover. Although reputation is only conditionally manageable in times of crisis, two main drivers which help safeguard it from further harm: meeting the expectations arising from an organisation's reputation in the functional, social and emotional dimensions, and communicative integrity. Reputation can only be safeguarded if stakeholders remain trustful toward an organisation even if it does wrong.

The value of reputation for organisations

Regulators and industry groups as well as companies and consultants have developed sophisticated guidelines over the years for communicating during crisis situations (Löffelholz and Schwarz 2008, pp. 22 f.). However, crisis literature has so far largely ignored the question of how to define and measure threats to reputation (Eccles et al. 2007, p. 106). And although crisis management is "among the most important functions of reputation management" (Tucker and Melewar 2005, p. 378), its role has yet to be de-

J. Klewes, R. Wreschniok (eds.), *Reputation Capital*, DOI 10.1007/978-3-642-01630-1_14,
© Springer-Verlag Berlin Heidelberg 2009

fined. To demonstrate how to prevent reputation from long-term damage, the following article will focus on crisis situations as a severe threat to corporate reputation. The approach is therefore not one of risk management but of crisis management: how to reactively maintain reputation through organisational communication. The idea is to refrain from case-study approaches, because "the variables in any particular crisis situation are so numerous that no historic case is likely to be comparable to the point of providing an optimal response. Any paradigmatic approach to crisis management is, therefore, suspect" (Berg and Robb 1992, p. 180). According to the logic of a reputation management process, first a way to assess crisis situations will be developed. Second, this article shows why crises are a threat to reputation. The text regards reputation as primarily formed through public opinion. Hence communication that is the main vehicle for safeguarding reputation during times of crisis. But communication also poses a risk to reputation since dishonesty, inconsistency, dilatoriness or even deception will all cause great damage in the long run.

Reputation – Far more than a dazzling term

The term "reputation" is generally used in a great variety of contexts and now admits of a vast number of interpretations.[1] In the field of marketing, it is characterised as the result of a branding process, in the principal-agent theory as a signal of future behaviour, in accounting as a kind of goodwill, in organisation theory as the manifestation of corporate identity, and in the field of management as a potential market entry barrier (Schwaiger 2004, p. 48). It becomes an important criterion for differentiating between organisations, and since services, products or performance often largely resemble each other, a good reputation is a competitive factor too. A good reputation proves more resilient than a bad one (or no reputation whatsoever) and organisations with a good reputation are more likeable: research has shown that good reputation has an impact on the perception of the management style as well as on purchasing decisions. It attracts qualified staff, determines investor satisfaction and loyalty, and as relational capital it deepens relationships and even guides investors through investment decisions. As it is formed through the relationship between an organisation

---

[1] Reputation is interpreted in many different ways depending on the scientific background (Bromley, 2002 p. 35; Fombrun and van Riel 1997, p. 5 ff.). Fields of research are likeability and purchasing decisions (Lyon and Cameron 2004, p. 226; Schütze and Rennhak 2005, p. 11), loyalty (Helm 2007, pp. 33 f.), trust building (Ingenhoff 2007), relational capital (de Castro et al. 2006 p. 576; Fombrun and van Riel 2004) or the loss of reputation during crisis situations (Coombs 2006b, p. 124; Davies et al. 2003; Dowling 2002; Jones et al. 2000, pp. 27 f.).

and its key stakeholders, it may be favourable or unfavourable: positive interactions build favourable reputation and unpleasant interactions lead to unfavourable reputation.

Building a good reputation among stakeholders may therefore create a reservoir of goodwill and serve as a resource to draw on in bad times such as a crisis. Although the value of reputation has mainly been discussed and analysed for economic organisations, its positive impact may be transferred to non-economic organisations as well. Their reputation may often not be settled over time, but non-governmental organisations can both still build and utilise positive reputation (Eisenegger 2005, p. 57), for example to attract donors (Parks 2008, p. 217).

Reputation as a multidimensional construct

It is "difficult, both academically and practically, to discuss the management of corporate reputation without a distinct understanding as to the nature of the concept itself" (Tucker and Melewar 2005, p. 377). From the perspective of the stakeholders, it would be sufficient to argue that reputation is a general third-party perception of an organisation. But the construct goes beyond this interpretation, as it is an attitude that includes a stakeholder's beliefs or affects and that even influences behavioural intentions. This article also adopts a multidimensional understanding of the concept of reputation which integrates both cognitive and emotional components (Eberl and Schwaiger 2005; Nguyen and Leblanc 2001; Schwaiger 2004).

Reputation can be seen as "the net perception of a company's ability to meet the expectations of all its stakeholders" (Fombrun 1996, p. 37). It is a synthesis of individual attitudes towards an organisation's past behaviour and future prospects (Davies and Chun 2002; Post and Griffin, 1998). Accordingly, different stakeholder groups have diverse perceptions of an organisation's reputation (Caruana et al. 2006 pp. 430 f.). While there is no question about the two elements 'past behaviour' and 'future prospects', the determining factors of reputation are still being vigorously debated. To summarise the current literature, reputation unfolds in three dimensions (Eisenegger and Imhof 2007, pp. 3 ff.; Ingenhoff and Sommer 2007). First, the evaluation of competence and performance by an organisation gives rise to a functional reputation. The leading question for stakeholders is whether or not an organisation is capable of serving its original purpose and can allocate resources effectively. Functional reputation is constituted by the objectives of an organisation and may serve as an indicator for professional competence. But there is more to reputation than just its functional aspects. Organisations must legitimate their behaviour within the context of society. Therefore, second, social standards and values help form a social reputation. The leading question is whether or not an organisation is conforming with social values. Social reputation only remains intact as long as functional success corresponds to the moral standards that hold in society. Finally, there is an emotional dimension of reputation. An answer to the question whether or not an organisation is likeable/attractive/fascinating (or not) centres on an organisation's character: that is, its emotional reputation.

All three dimensions of reputation cannot be seen as separate. In fact, functional and social reputation are drivers for emotional reputation – sympathy towards an entity is often the result of an organisation's performance and moral standards. Moreover, emotional reputation serves as a mediating variable between functional and social reputation on the one hand, and constructs such as trust on the other (Ingenhoff 2007, pp. 56).

Crisis situations as a threat for reputation

As stated above, reputation is an important intangible asset for organisations of any kind. Hence, the analysis of risks to reputation has become an issue of growing importance and is increasingly being discussed in scientific and business literature (Csiszar and Heidrich 2006, p. 382; Neef 2005). Almost any concept unfolds its own idea of reputation and risk, which makes it difficult to compare research results. The reason for the variety of definitions of risk is that there is generally no such thing as 'objective risk'. Neither practical management nor science is therefore able to find generalised models (Baumgärtner 2005, p. 17). One common aspect of most risk definitions that helps its classification is its distinctness from danger. While danger is a threatening situation, risk holds the possibility that a situation may become threatening. Transferring this idea to the context of reputation, a risk to reputation consequently may or may not become a reputational threat. A general risk to reputation is not yet a threat to reputation – in contrast to crisis situations. Crises are no longer a situation of a possible risk to reputation but an actual and severe danger (Barton, 2001; Davies et al. 2003). And the reputation of organisations becomes most vulnerable when attacked in its core business (Gaultier-Gaillard and Louisot 2006, p. 443). In this article, we discuss crises as a threat to reputation rather than as risk and argue that the logic of media society predominantly determines the threats to reputation during a crisis.

Reputation is primarily built through public communications (Eisenegger 2005; Eisenegger and Imhof 2007; Herger 2006). It can be seen as the trustworthiness forged by the actions and attitudes of an organisation over time (Eisenegger 2005, p. 25). This trustworthiness builds either through personal experiences or through a third party's opinion (Yoon et al. 1993, p. 218). Since most stakeholders are not able to rely on direct experiences with an organisation, publicly transmitted information becomes the crucial source for building trust and reputation. In fact, without public opinion reputation cannot come into being (Herger 2006, p. 182) or will fade significantly (Eisenegger 2005, p. 45). This idea is in tune with the assumption that reputation is built not only at the level of personal experience but at a level of collective opinion formation (Bromley 2001, p. 317). The (mass) media are therefore important vehicles for building corporate reputation. They contribute to a large part of what stakeholders believe (or do not believe) about an organisation, because in today's modern society, "the most elevated degree of access is enjoyed by the mass media" (Forstmoser and Herger 2006, p. 409). Media publicity is vital in building corporate reputation, since reputational assets are valued highly by a large number of stakeholders. And managers have meanwhile largely adapted to the logic of media communication for building reputation (Eisenegger 2005, p. 58).

But this practice has negative consequences too. First, shaping reputational opportunities through the mass media becomes a major challenge. A large number of agents are competing within one public arena only, and all are seeking the same maximum amount of attention and legitimacy (Ronneberger 1977). Second, and most importantly, gaining and losing reputation is like two sides of the same coin. The main vehicle for building corporate reputation, the public sphere, also transports the negative issues that damage reputation to the same large number of stakeholders (Nolting and Thießen 2008, p. 10). Crises can bring organisations into "disrepute", which has an impact on profitability or even organisational survival (Lerbinger 1997, pp. 6 f.). Consequently, public scandals are a major threat to an organisation's reputation. Barely a day goes by without some organisation facing assaults to its reputation, and as research shows, reputational crises are on the rise (Gaines-Ross et al. 2007, p. 2): "It is not a question of if or whether an organisation will experience a crisis; it is only a matter of what type of crisis will occur, what form it will take, and how and when it will happen" (Mitroff et al. 1996, p. 40).

Communication itself may even become a threat to reputation. For example, it has been comprehensively demonstrated that simply disguising apparent problems in crises is not an appropriate communication strategy (D'Aveni and MacMillan 1990, p. 634; Ruth and York 2000, p. 19). And new technologies such as blogs, e-mail or websites help stakeholders to quickly form a network to attack an organisation's wrongdoings – worldwide (Coombs 2008, p. 275, see also the article by Wreschniok in this volume). If an organisation reacts too late or inappropriately with communications, stakeholders have an opportunity to fill the information gap. And once the organisation has lost the initiative, it is hard to regain (Seeger, Sellnow and Ulmer 2003, p. 128)[2] . In terms of communication, organisations may react in three ways during a crisis: denial and not communicating at all, communicating inaccurately or too late, or establishing communication channels and finding suitable responses. Unfortunately, the latter is still rarely to be found.

Although for economic organisations, for example, studies that discuss the financial impact of reputation have produced conflicting results, there is no question that poor reputation management can be disastrous (Cravens and Oliver 2006, p. 295). The majority of global business executives believe that it is harder to recover from reputation failure than it is to build or maintain reputation. Moreover, recovering from crises that hit reputation takes time – often many years, in fact, which is a long time to rebuild the trustworthiness one already had before (Milewicz and Herbig 1994, p. 44). Recovering from a crisis is consequently more of a marathon than a quick sprint, which underlines the necessity for sophisticated reputation management either long beforehand (issues management) or at the moment of threat (crisis and communication management).

Safeguarding corporate reputation through crisis communications

Safeguarding reputation in a crisis unfolds in two main steps: first, it is important to precisely assess the crisis situation. The better crisis managers know what situation they are dealing with, the better the communication strategies that can be developed. Second, these strategies must align with crisis and reputation management. Following this logic, I will first intro-

---

[2] In 1994, Deutsche Bank CEO Hilmar Kopper referred in a press conference to DM 5 million lost because of unpaid bills as "peanuts". Although he only meant to say that for Deutsche Bank, bills of such amounts are only a minor problem, the words he chose triggered public outrage. Many years later, Deutsche Bank is still recovering from his linguistic faux pas.

duce a way to assess crisis situations before discussing a way to safeguard reputation through integrity in crisis communications.

Victim, accidental and preventable crises

During a serious crisis, the crisis management process begins with an accurate assessment of the situation. It helps crisis managers, communications managers and reputation managers alike to choose or adapt an appropriate strategy. Crisis typologies help because "each crisis type produces a unique crisis management dynamic. As a result, each crisis type must be examined separately" (Coombs 1999, p. 138). The list of such typologies is long: from the perspective of management, scholars distinguish between the degree of danger to management activities (Krystek 2006, p. 51; Müller 1986, p. 25). From the perspective of communications, both content and intensity of news coverage is often used to categorise crisis situations (D'Aveni and MacMillan 1990; Eccles et al. 2007; Huang 2006). Such concepts are common since they benefit analytical research (e.g. to codify crisis situations afterwards). But they also lack practical relevance: neither management nor communications typologies are helpful for strategic decisions in crisis situations. This underlines the necessity for approaches that take content criteria into account (what the crisis is about) rather than judging its degree of danger or news coverage, both of which are high anyway.

One way to classify crises in terms of content criteria is to evaluate the responsibility attributed by central stakeholders. "Crisis responsibility, that is how much stakeholders attribute the cause of the crisis to the organisation, is a function of the crisis type and severity of the damage" (Coombs 2006a, p. 243). Depending on the degree of crisis attribution, three crisis clusters can be identified: a victim cluster, an accidental cluster and a preventable cluster, each of which has its own characteristics (see Table 1).

The relation between crises and reputation therefore is linked to the attribution of crisis responsibility: the stronger an attribution by key stakeholders, the more damage it will inflict on reputation (Coombs 2006a, pp. 243 f.; 2007, p. 169). Consequently, not all crises damage an organisation's reputation and not all crises demand reputation management.

Table 1. Crisis clusters

Cluster	Characteristic and attribution of crisis responsibility	Example
Victim	Organization is victim of the crisis (weak attributions)	e.g. natural disaster, false information, malevolence
Accidental	Organizational actions leading to crisis were unintentional (minimal attributions)	e.g. stakeholder claims, technical-error accidents or product harm
Preventable	Organization knowingly placed people at risk, took inappropriate actions or violated law (strong attributions)	e.g. human-error accidents, management misconduct, organizational misdeed with/without injuries

Source: Coombs 2007, p. 168

The three clusters have been developed from an economic organisation's point of view and rely on only a general concept of reputation. As mentioned above, reputation consists of functional, social and emotional dimensions. Also, crisis situations do not affect reputation in general but have a distinct impact on the three reputational dimensions. When, for example, an organisation in crisis does not meet certain moral expectations of society (e.g. by jeopardising labour standards), the threat is to social rather than to functional reputation. In order to choose an appropriate reputation management strategy, the organisation must analyse the situation as accurately as possible. Therefore, the existing classification of crises must be extended to take account of the three dimensions of reputation, which result in three different types of threats (see Table 2).

This matrix provides reputation managers with a tool for assessing both the degree and dimension of reputational threats (e.g. functional victim crisis). Unlike the matrix above, process and management models serve only as a vague guide for deriving adequate strategies at the moment of attack. Knowing, on the basis of content criteria, both the degree of the threat and which dimension of reputation is in danger helps in developing more precise management and communications strategies.

Table 2. Crises as a reputational threat

	Functional crisis	Social crisis	Emotional crisis	
Victim crisis				Mild reputational threat
Accidental crisis				Moderate reputational threat
Preventable crisis				Severe reputational threat

The role of communications in safeguarding reputation

While reputational risk may be assessed early and managed accordingly by means of issues management (Ingenhoff 2004, p. 270; Röttger and Preusse 2008, p. 159; see also the article by Gaultier-Gaillard et al. in this volume), reputational threats or crises are only conditionally manageable. And in terms of managing reputation, as independent observations by internal and external stakeholders, scholars seem right in assuming that it cannot be managed at all (Haywood 2002; Steward 2006). But this line of argumentation overlooks the fact that in times of crisis organisations have control over the way in which they communicate corporate behaviour.

"If managers can strongly influence reputational assessments by involving themselves in boundary-spanning activities [...] media accounts heavily condition their firm's reputation" (Fombrun and Shanley 1990, p. 253).

In today's media society, mediated communication becomes the predominant mechanism for constituting reputation (Eisenegger 2005, p. 69; Seemann 2008 pp. 79 ff.). Consequently, in situations where reputation is under fire, one aspect of crisis management assumes great importance: communication. Crisis situations are an attack on reputation, which may prove either to be a threat or an opportunity. Which of the two it is strongly depends on how an organisation's behaviour is perceived by major stakeholders (Gaultier-Gaillard and Louisot 2006 p. 426). In fact, external communications in a crisis can result in favourable public perception (Penrose 2000 p. 167). And since crises are observer-dependent (Kohring, Görke and Ruhrmann, 1996), the role of communications is more than simply to inform the public about the crisis but to influence the course of the crisis (Köhler 2006, p. 22).

Two aspects are vital in safeguarding reputation during a crisis through communications management: meeting the expectations arising from an organisation's reputation, and communicative integrity. First, as discussed above, reputation can be seen as the anticipation of trustworthiness towards an organisation. Reputation therefore is established through a continuous process of credibility transactions (Herbig et al. 1994), which means constantly signalling trustworthiness in the functional, social and emotional dimensions. When an organisation runs into a crisis, this signalling mechanism initially fails. The misconduct – whatever the form and extent – did not meet stakeholders' expectations (Coombs 2007, p. 166). As a result, they immediately begin to question the organisation's behaviour: does it match previous personal experiences or – if there are none – its perceived reputation? This is the moment when crisis communications needs to court trustworthiness as well as present facts and figures about what is going on (Bohnet and Huck 2004 pp. 362 f.).

On a more general level, in times of crisis a reputation-reality gap arises that comes from a discrepancy between the expected (reputation) and actual (reality) behaviour of an organisation. Reputation can only be safeguarded if this gap does not widen: a "perceived reputation lowers if it [...] fails to fulfill its stated intentions" (Herbig et al. 1994, p. 23). However, closing the gap is a fragile task for both management and communications. The main challenges are short-term adjustments:

"For example, reputation-reality gaps concerning financial performance often result in accounting fraud and (ultimately) restatements of results" (Eccles et al. 2007, p. 108).

Therefore, closing the reputation-reality gap must – despite the short-term danger in a crisis – always aim at building long-term reputation.

The second aspect, which goes hand in hand, is building trustworthiness through consistency, or even better: communicative integrity. Reputation building is a long-term process, which means that in a short-term situation such as a crisis, managers are only able to influence the core of reputation: that is, its trust-building character (see also Baumgärtner 2008, pp. 55 f.). Reputation is a central determinant of trust (Einwiller 2003, p. 204; Herger 2006, p. 49) as is trustworthiness for reputation (Klenk 2005, p. 99). So if an organisation fails to prove credibility and trustworthiness, reputation falters. Trustworthiness that is built through communications can be damaged in many ways. However, four central factors that negatively influence it are a discrepancy between behaviour and communication, a discrepancy between different actors within the same organisation, a discrepancy between messages at different points in time and a discrepancy between moral standards and actual behaviour (Bentele 1994, p. 148). These discrepancies consequently lead to three fundamental strategies for maintaining trust and, with it, safeguarding reputation.

- Integrity in communication and management

An organisation in a crisis must practise what it preaches. If communication does not reflect managerial behaviour, a huge amount of trustworthiness may be lost immediately. Generally speaking, if communications do not reflect an organisation's actions, it becomes a reputational threat itself (see the article by Cohen in this volume)[3].

- Integrity in messages (content, agent and time)

In crises, organisations must communicate clear messages, which have to be consistent among those who communicate and across time. The problem often is that organisations start by giving incorrect information, which they later need to revise. Or, one spokesperson relates certain details differently from another. Yet again, there is immense potential here for trust to be lost. Dealing with different groups of stakeholders becomes especially challenging: informing the media requires a different way of delivering information than presenting the crisis to employees, interest groups or casualties. But still, even though the language, form and level of detail may differ, the key message must stay the same (see also Stephens, Malone and Bailey 2005).

- Integrity in moral standards

Finally, the actual behaviour in crises has to meet moral standards – including the organisation's own code of conduct and general standards of social responsibility. Violating the latter especially is often the starting point for citizens' initiatives, which can lead to a communicative disaster[4].

---

[3] The German food supplier Humana was embroiled in a scandal in 2003. The company was accused of producing soy-based baby food with dangerously low levels of vitamin B1, resulting in the deaths of several young children in Israel. The strategy was not only telling the public the company was doing everything possible to solve the issue, but also doing it. Within a few hours, not only had the responsible employee been suspended, but also extra quality measures were implemented immediately and all Humana baby food was taken off the shelves in Israel. By doing this, credibility and trustworthiness was gained so that media coverage was unemotional and largely accepting of Humana's swift and proactive strategy.

[4] The telecommunications company Nokia follows – according to its own mission statement – an open communication policy. However in 2008, when closing the production plant in Bochum (Germany), its communications were cautious and enshrouded, which conflicted entirely with Nokia's overall

These three strategies form a framework for safeguarding reputation in crises. Integrity regarding an organisation's communications and behaviour, its messages by spokespersons, or its compliance with moral standards help prove its trustworthiness: the better an organisation is able to avoid discrepancies in each case, the less trust is ultimately lost and the more reputation is safeguarded. Referring again to the crisis clusters introduced above, all three aspects of reputation must be kept in mind when formulating the crisis communications strategy. Integrity in crisis communications means integrating functional, social and emotional answers into the process of finding a suitable strategy. Regardless of whether or not it is a victim crisis, an accidental crisis or a preventable crisis, focusing on functional aspects of reputational risk is by no means enough. As demonstrated, in crises reputation can be lost on the functional, social and emotional dimension. Among stakeholders crises may even be perceived differently, reputation is constituted by different factors depending on the stakeholder group (Caruana et al. 2006, p. 438). Especially interest groups (which often form spontaneously) broach the issue of moral standards[5]. Therefore it may be that for one group of stakeholders (for example, the members of an NGO) a crisis questions the social reputation, while for another (for example, the board of trustees) functional aspects are under attack. Since most crises affect an entire network of stakeholders, the strategic groups that are most affected must be identified (Wiedmann & Böcker, 2005 p. 1535) and addressed accordingly.

Conclusions and outlook

Research has identified two main sources for the constitution of reputation: experience and information. Safeguarding reputation during crisis situations therefore depends on both behavioural actions, on the one hand, and consistent communication, on the other. Crisis communications is a central but not the only element of sustainable reputation management in crisis situations.

---

communications policy. Besides the negative coverage of the layoffs themselves, Nokia lost trustworthiness for not adhering to their very own communication goals in a crisis.

[5] In 2008, Rick Wagoner (CEO General Motors), Alan Mullaly (CEO Ford) and Robert Nadelli (CEO Chrysler) went to a US Congressional hearing to plead for financial support. The automobile industry was at the time at the beginning of a collapse and millions of jobs were about to be cut. Ironically enough, all three managers arrived with their own private jets. In doing so, they immediately lost so much credibility and trustworthiness that none of the Congressmen present granted them any support. Moreover, the issue went on negatively through press and online media for weeks.

From the perspective of strategic management, reputation management must be seen as a holistic concept rather than a single activity. It is the notion of how to induce and maintain favourable assessments by key stakeholders (Fombrun 2001, p. 24) regardless of the use of issues management, crisis management, customer relations management or even quality management as a tool. Robust reputation management means coordinating many different management activities in order to establish a good reputation among key stakeholders.

Even if an organisation focuses on communications for safeguarding its reputation in a crisis, it must be seen in line with other reputation management activities as well. But regardless of reputation's long-term character, short-term crisis situations threaten it because within a single moment, they can do lasting damage. Accordingly, crises are fragile moments for both managers and those in charge of communications. As shown, closing the reputation-reality gap and integrity in communications are key issues in safeguarding reputation when under attack.

Scientific research on safeguarding or even building reputation in extreme situations such as crises is in the fledgling stages. Communications science and economic science need to address the lack of systematic corporate reputation management concepts, and ultimately help develop practical and sustainable guidelines for organisations of any kind. The major challenge is to overcome the many case-study and toolbox approaches as well as the corporate bias, in order to gain a deeper insight into reputation and crises at a more general level. It has been established that corporate crisis communications is a vital tool for safeguarding reputation from further harm (see also Fombrun 2001, p. 23; Lyon and Cameron 2004, p. 232; Rayner 2003, p. 14). However, transferring these insights to non-profit organisations or connecting them with other scientific areas are endeavours that have only just begun.

References

Barton L (2001) Crisis in organizations II (Vol. 2nd edition). Cincinnati: College Divisions South-Western

Baumgärtner N (2005) Risiko- und Krisenkommunikation – Rahmenbedingungen, Herausforderungen und Erfolgsfaktoren dargestellt am Beispiel der chemischen Industrie. Verlag Dr. Hut, München

Baumgärtner N (2008) Risiken kommunizieren – Grundlagen, Chancen und Grenzen. In: Nolting T, Thießen A (eds) Krisenmanagement in der Mediengesellschaft. Potenziale und Perspektiven der Krisenkommunikation. VS Verlag für Sozialwissenschaften, Wiesbaden

Bentele G (1994) Öffentliches Vertrauen – normative und soziale Grundlage für Public Relations. In: Armbrecht W, Zabel U (eds) Normative Aspekte der Public Relations. Grundlagen und Perspektiven. Eine Einführung. Wiesbaden: Westdeutscher Verlag, Wiesbaden, pp 131–158

Berg D, Robb S (1992) Crisis management and the "paradigm case". In: Toth E, Heath R (eds) Rhetorical and critical approaches to public relations. Lawrence Erlbaum Associates, Hillsdale

Bohnet I, Huck S (2004) Repetition and reputation: Implications for trust and trustworthiness when institutions change. The American Economic Review, Vol 94 No 2 pp 362–366

Bromley D (2001) Relationships between personal and corporate reputation. European journal of marketing, Vol 35 No 3and 4 pp 316–334

Bromley D (2002) Comparing corporate reputations. Leagute tables, quotients, benchmarks, or case studies? Corporate reputation review, Vol 5 No 1 pp 35–50

Caruana A, Cohen C, Krentler K (2006) Corporate reputation and shareholders' intentions: An attitudinal perspective. Journal of brand management, Vol 13 No 6 pp 429–440

Coombs T (1999) Information and compassion in crisis responses. A test of their effectiveness. Journal of public relations research, Vol 11 No 2 pp 125–142

Coombs T (2006a) The protective powers of crisis response strategies. Managing reputational assets during a crisis. Journal of Promotion Management, Vol 12 No 3 and 4 pp 241–260

Coombs T (2006b) Unpacking the halo effect: reputation and crisis management. Journal of Communication Management, Vol 10 No 2 pp 123–137

Coombs T (2007) Protecting organization reputations during a crisis. The development and application of Situational Communication Theory. Corporate Reputation Review, Vol 10 No 3 pp 163–176

Coombs T (2008) The future of crisis communication from an international perspective. In: Thießen A, Nolting T (eds) Krisenmanagement in der Mediengesellschaft. Potenziale und Perspektiven der Krisenkommunikation. VS Verlag für Sozialwissenschaften, Wiesbaden, pp 277–289

Cravens K, Oliver E (2006) Employees: The key link to corporate reputation management. Business Horizons, Vol 49 No 4 pp 293–302

Csiszar E, Heidrich G (2006) The question of reputational risk: Perspectives from an industry. The Geneva papers, Vol 31 No 3 pp 382–394

D'Aveni R, MacMillan I (1990) Crisis and the content of managerial communications: A study of the focus of attention of top managers in surviving and failing firms. Administrative Science Quarterly, Vol 35 No 4 pp 634–657

Davies G, Chun R (2002) Gaps between the internal and external perceptions of the corporate brand. Corporate Reputation Review, Vol 5 No 2 and 3 pp 143–156

Davies G, Chun R, da Silva RV, Roper S (2003) Corporate reputation and competitiveness. Routledge, London

de Castro GM, Navas López JE, López Saéz P (2006) Business and social reputation: Exploring the concept and main dimensions of corporate reputation. Journal of business ethics, Vol 63 No 4 pp 361–370

Dowling G (2002) Creating corporate reputations. Identity, image and performance. Oxford University Press, Oxford

Eberl M, Schwaiger M (2005) Corporate reputation. Disentangling the effects on financial performance. European journal of marketing, Vol 39 No 7 and 8 pp 838–854

Eccles R, Newquist S, Schatz R (2007) Reputation and its risks. Harvard Business Review pp 104–114

Einwiller S (2003) When reputation engenders trust: An empirical investigation in business-to-consumer electronic commerce. Electronic markets, Vol 13 No 3 pp 196–209

Eisenegger M (2005) Reputation in der Mediengesellschaft. Konstitution, Issues monitoring, Issues management. VS Verlag für Sozialwissenschaften, Wiesbaden

Eisenegger M, Imhof K (2007) Das Wahre, das Gute und das Schöne. Reputations-Management in der Mediengesellschaft. fög discussion paper, 2007 (0001) pp 1–23

Fombrun C (1996) Reputation. Realizing value from the corporate image. Harvard Business School Press, Boston

Fombrun C (2001) Corporate reputation. Its measurement and management. Thexis, Vol 4 pp 23–26

Fombrun C, Shanley M (1990) What's in a name? Reputation building and corporate strategy. Academy of management journal, Vol 33 No 2 pp 233–258

Fombrun C, van Riel C (1997) The Reputational landscape. Corporate reputation review, Vol 1 No 1 pp 6–13

Fombrun C, van Riel C (2004) Fame and fortune. How successful companies build winning reputations. Financial Times Prentice Hall, New York

Forstmoser P, Herger N (2006) Managing reputational risk. A reinsurer's view. The Geneva papers, Vol 31 No 3 pp 409–424

Gaines-Ross L, Diamond J, Polansky H et al. (2007) Safeguarding reputation. Weber Shandwick, Vol 1 No 2

Gaultier-Gaillard S, Louisot JP (2006) Risks to reputation. A global approach. The Geneva papers, Vol 31 No 3 pp 425–445

Haywood R (2002) Manage your reputation. Kogan Page, London

Helm S (2007) The role of corporate reputation in determining investor statisfaction and loyality. Corporate Reputation Review, Vol 10 No 1 pp 22–37

Herbig P, Milewicz J, Golden J (1994) A model of reputation building and destruction. Journal of Business Research, Vol 31 No 1 pp 23–31

Herger N (2006) Vertrauen und Organisationskommunikation. Identität – Marke – Image – Reputation. VS Verlag für Sozialwissenschaften, Wiesbaden

Huang YH (2006) Crisis situations, communication strategies, and media coverage. Communication research, Vol 33 No 3 pp 180–205

Ingenhoff D (2004) Corporate Issues Management in multinationalen Unternehmen. VS Verlag für Sozialwissenschaften, Wiesbaden

Ingenhoff D (2007) Integrated Reputation Management System (IReMS): Ein integriertes Analyseinstrument zur Messung und Steuerung von Werttreibern der Reputation. PR-Magazin, No 7

Ingenhoff D, Sommer K (2007) Does Ethical Behaviour Matter? How Corporate Social Responsibility Contributes to Organizational Trustworthiness. Paper presented at the 57th Annual Conference of the International Communication Association (ICA)

Jones G, Jones B, Little P (2000) Reputation as reservoir: Buffering against loss in times of economic crisis. Corporate Reputation Review, Vol 3 No 1 pp 21–29

Klenk V (2005) Der ignorierte Kontrollverlust der Corporate Communications. In: Köhler T S (ed) Public Relations – Perspektiven und Potenziale im 21. Jahrhundert. VS Verlag für Sozialwissenschaften, Wiesbaden, pp 99–108

Köhler T (2006) Krisen-PR im Internet. Nutzungsmöglichkeiten, Einflussfaktoren und Problemfelder. VS Verlag für Sozialwissenschaften, Wiesbaden

Kohring M, Görke A, Ruhrmann G (1996) Konflikte, Kriege, Katastrophen. Zur Funktion internationaler Krisenkommunikation. In: Meckel M, Kriener M (eds.) Internationale Kommunikation. Eine Einführung. Westdeutscher Verlag, Opladen

Krystek U (2006) Krisenarten und Krisenursachen. In: Hutzschenreuter T, Griess-Nega T (eds) Krisenmanagement. Grundlagen – Strategien – Instrumente. Gabler, Wiesbaden, pp 41–66

Lerbinger O (1997) The crisis manager. Facing risk and responsibility. Lawrence Erlbaum Associates, Mahwah

Löffelholz M, Schwarz A (2008) Die Krisenkommunikation von Organisationen. Ansätze, Ergebnisse und Perspektiven der Forschung. In: Thießen A, Nolting T (eds) Krisenmanagement in der Mediengesellschaft. Potenziale und Perspektiven der Krisenkommunikation. VS Verlag für Sozialwissenschaften, Wiesbaden, pp 23–37

Lyon L, Cameron G (2004) A relational approach examining the interplay of prior reputation and immediate response to a crisis. Journal of public relations re-search, Vol 16 No 3 pp 213–241

Milewicz J, Herbig P (1994) Evaluating the brand extension decision using a model of reputation building. Journal of Product & Brand Management, Vol 3 No 1 pp 39–47

Mitroff I, Pearson C, Harrington K (1996) The essential guide to managing corporate crises. A step-by-step handbook for surviving major catastrophes. Oxford University Press, New York

Müller R (1986) Krisenmanagement in der Unternehmung. Vorgehen, Maßnahmen und Organisation. Lang, Frankfurt a.M.

Neef D (2005) Managing Corporate Reputation and Risk. A Strategic Approach Using Knowledge Management. Butterworth-Heinemann, Oxford

Nguyen N, Leblanc G (2001) Image and reputation of higher education institutions in students' retention decisions. The International Journal of Educational Management, Vol 15 No 6 pp 303–311

Nolting T, Thießen A (2008) Krisenmanagement in der Mediengesellschaft. In: Nolting T, Thießen A (eds) Krisenmanagement in der Mediengesellschaft. Potenziale und Perspektiven der Krisenkommunikation VS Verlag für Sozialwissenschaften, Wiesbaden

Parks T (2008) The rise and fall of donor funding for the advocacy NGOs: under-standing the impact. Development in Practice, Vol 18 No 2 pp 213–222

Penrose J (2000) The role of perception in crisis planning. Public Relations Review, Vol 26 No 2 pp 155–171

Post J, Griffin J (1998) Corporate reputation and external affairs management, Vol 1 No 1 pp 165–171

Rayner J (2003) Managing reputational risk. Curbing threats, leveraging opportunities. John Wiley & Sons, West Sussex

Ronneberger F (1977) Legitimation durch Information. Econ, Düsseldorf

Röttger U, Preusse J (2008) Issues Management. In: Nolting T, Thießen A (eds) Krisenmanagement in der Mediengesellschaft. Potenziale und Perspektiven der Krisenkommunikation. VS Verlag für Sozialwissenschaften, Wiesbaden

Ruth J, York A (2000) Framing information to enhance corporate reputation: The impact of message source, information type, and reference point. Journal of Business Research, Vol 57 No 1 pp 14–20

Schütze T, Rennhak C (2005) Die Wirkung der Unternehmensreputation auf Anlageentscheidungen. Munich Business School Working Paper, 2005, Vol 15

Schwaiger M (2004) Components and parameters of corporate reputation – an empirical study. Schmalenbach business review, Vol 56 No 1 pp 46–71

Seeger M, Sellnow T, Ulmer R (2003) Communication and organizational crisis. Praeger Publishers, Westport

Seemann R (2008) Corporate reputation management durch corporate communications. Cuvillier Verlag, Göttingen

Stephens K, Malone P C, Bailey C (2005) Communicating with stakeholders during a crisis. Evaluating message strategies. Journal of business communication, Vol 42 No 4 pp 390–419

Steward G (2006) Can reputation be "managed"? The Geneva papers, Vol 31 No 3 pp 480–499

Tucker L, Melewar T (2005) Corporate reputation and crisis management. The threat and manageability of anti-corporatism. Corporate reputation review, Vol 7 No 4 pp 377–387

Wiedmann K P, Böcker C (2005) Corporate reputation in different service industries. Results of an empirical study in Germany. Services Systems and Services Management, Vol 2 No 1 pp 1528–1535

Yoon E, Guffey H, Kijewski V (1993) The effects of information and company reputation on intentions to buy a business service. Journal of Business Research, Vol 27 No 3 pp 215–228

Getting the stain out of "sustainable brands"

Jeremy Cohen

Having spent almost ten years in the UK media and then ten years help-ing manage the reputations of Fortune 100 companies (and Fortune 5 companies for that matter), I've been closer than I would have some-times liked to the stretch between words and action. The strain between saying and doing. The struggle between desired perception and reality.

Reputation management today is all about that stretch, and nowhere is this more evident than in the area of Sustainability or Green branding as I'll refer to it. I'll use "brands" as shorthand for "reputation" because of the heavy use of marketing in trying to establish a green reputation. In Sustainability, the gap between what organisations are saying and doing has never been bigger. Not necessarily because they are behaving worse than they have in the past – on the contrary, sustainability is a bigger priority in most companies than ever.

No, the stretch occurs because of the unprecedented scrutiny organi-sations are under, and the ease of availability of information to scruti-nize them with. Partly that scrutiny is by the media, but the push usually comes from elsewhere. It's not coming from governments or regulatory bodies – with them we get into a discussion on semantics. NGOs play a role, but they are starting to resemble the institutions they tackle. The real reputational pain is coming from regular people. Individuals – the so-called "man-on-the-street" – can look under a company's hood with a few clicks of a mouse, and they are largely in for a bad surprise when they do so. And when they're angry they draw in the other player – the NGOs, government organisations the media – and they bring change.

In this chapter we will together look at that reputation stretch – I'll call it the "brand stretch" and look at some companies sprinting blindly into the reputational abyss, and a few who are starting to "get it". Repu-tation Management needs to grab the new tools and technologies avail-able to us, and radically overhaul the skill sets of reputation manage-ment. Those who don't are in for a bumpy ride.

J. Klewes, R. Wreschniok (eds.), *Reputation Capital*, DOI 10.1007/978-3-642-01630-1_15,
© Springer-Verlag Berlin Heidelberg 2009

In PR terms – Green is red hot

Yes, the world economy is in crisis, and yes, ad spending is and will continue to fall in terms of overall growth. But when you look at decades of compound annual growth, there's no doubt that companies continue to throw bucket loads of cash at trying to shape brand perceptions through advertising. A few statistics:

- Global ad spend in 2007 was an estimated US$454 billion (ZenithOptimedia);

- 50% of that was in the US; China spend is growing at more than 20% per annum;

- Global ad spend is expected to grow at 6.4% in 2008, the highest growth for three years;

- The biggest industry spenders: automotive, mobile communications, entertainment, jewellery, fast food...then energy;

- The automotive industry is focusing on smaller and more fuel efficient vehicles – in the UK 52% of advertising is for smaller cars, and spend on more fuel-efficient cars has doubled to over 40%;

- "Green Marketing" spend – advertising with some reference to the environment – is estimated at approximately 5% and remains one of the fastest growing segments.

Don't believe it? Take the Time-Fortune-Economist Test

If you don't buy the above statistics – which would by the way imply that "Green Advertising" is worth a cool US$22.7 billion and growing (fast) – then do your own test.

As anyone who knows me well, or has seen me speak will attest, I'm a simple guy. I feel things in my gut and tend to follow that intuition. That being said, I do try and test out my theories in the least scientific way possible. So here's an unscientific test for all those other "gut-instinct" readers. Pick up a random sample of back-issues (pre-financial crisis) of the European editions of Time, Fortune, and The Economist. Now, go through each edition and count up all the ads, and then count up the environmental references in the ads.

If you get to the same place as me, this is what you will find:

- 12-15 full page advertisements per issue

- 25-33% reference the environment/sustainability

- Those "green advertisers" come from industries including energy, automotive, banking… to private jets

So we're seeing some of the "dirtiest" industries on the planet (or at least some of those responsible for the largest CO_2 emissions), investing huge amounts of capital in green advertising. What is it that they expect as a result of that investment, exactly?

Green branding – A new industry

It's not just ad spend. Green branding is effectively becoming an entire industry. To some extent it makes sense. The environment is towards the top of many people's priorities.

So Green is important, we get that. Companies get that too and so they invest millions in green branding. Some companies are even taking a step beyond advertising, and bringing out green products or even product ranges. A few examples: let's start with Green TV.

Al Gore TV

In 2007 NBC Universal launched Green Week. A week in which the famous "Peacock" logo was turned green, along with the scripts of a large part of the network's prime time programming. Shows as wide ranging as Scrubs, The Office, ER, and The Bionic Woman all turned out with green storylines. Some of the best was self-parody, such as the "green" episode of 30 Rock where the show continually poked fun at mother company GE for trying to go green whilst battling chemical dumping cases in the real world – the cameo by Al Gore was hilarious, and so the theme made sense. On the whole, however, audiences immediately felt the brand stretch. They saw exactly the 30 Rock joke – NBC is owned by GE and the GE is in the midst of a roster of environmental pollution litigation that they have been contesting for years. Popular TV blog, TVEnvy, summed it up best for me:

"Ok, I'm all for saving the world, cleaning up the air and preventing whatever horrible fate Al Gore has decided awaits us in the coming decades – but this NBC "Green Week" is absolutely awful... What did NBC deliver...? The guy from Windtalkers (later on Law & Order: SVU) telling me to recycle a pizza box before he almost gets blown up by the bomb inside."

"You've disappointed me NBC. You've insulted my intelligence and the intelligence of millions of Americans by thinking that a company owned by GE(!) could possibly persuade us to plant a tree. You've disappointed me by assuming that you could persuade a country full of TV-loving couch potatoes (me included) to recycle during primetime television, when all we wanna' do is watch Stabler and Benson [Law and Order SVU] arrest some pedophiles."

This is the problem with brand-stretch. A TV network owned by a company whose environmental credentials (in the US at least) are questionable in public perception, "greening" the network for a week with a green logo and some green storylines crowbarred-in. And then the question of whether or not it's a network's role to provide this public service message vs. regular entertainment. Not only does the public react sceptically, but it leaves many of them with a bad taste in the mouth.

So what did the network do as a follow-up on 2008's Green Week? Well, halfway through the week they fired the entire workforce of Forecast Earth, an environmental show airing on The Weather Channel (acquired by NBC Universal in September 2008), and cancelled the show. So the coverage of NBC Green Week in 2008, already not much better than 2007, nosedived on this news.

Green bleach

Other brands have fared somewhat better, but are still riding the thin line that is brand stretch. Clorox is one of the biggest chemicals and food manufacturers in the US. Before we even question the niceties of chemicals and food sitting under the same corporate roof, non-American readers should know that Clorox Bleach is the number one bleach product in the US and their related product lines are all chemical-heavy cleaners and disinfectants.

Seeing the green wave, Clorox launched "Green Works" in early 2008, a range of "natural" cleaning products. Now I think these are great products – great cleaning results, without all the chemicals. Clorox is thrilled with the (sales) performance of the product line and has since expanded it. The "stretch" appears when you look at the rest of the Clorox business.

Still overwhelmingly chemical-based, and responsible for massive amounts of polluted wastewater coming from millions of homes in the USA. At best this water will have to be processed, cleaned, and recycled. At worst it will find its way back into the environment as pollution.

This stretch has led to complaints about advertising claims being upheld by the Better Business Bureau, and protests from parts of the US environmental NGO The Sierra Club, which has endorsed the product line. Can a bleach and chemical company claim a sustainable reputation on the back of just one, albeit very profitable, product line, or is it a stretch too far?

Green guzzlers

This is precisely the issue the automotive manufacturers are running into. The Chevrolet Tahoe – previously the evil poster child of the gas-guzzling consumer – will shortly be coming out with an option of a Hybrid engine. And whilst this configuration will deliver a much-improved environmental performance, can a three-ton, five-seat 4x4 which will rarely, if ever, leave the road for the average driver, ever be a sustainable vehicle? The stretch for car manufacturers is not a result of them manufacturing better-for-the-environment vehicles. The stretch comes from the fact that they are putting these vehicles front and centre, whilst still producing 95-99% standard-for-the-environment (i.e. bad) vehicles.

The car company that best exemplifies this stretch, and the risk that the entire industry is running, is Toyota. Firstly, Toyota deserves much credit. They went against the industry grain by developing and bringing to market the Toyota Prius. First on sale in Japan in 1997, the Prius was the world's first mass-produced hybrid. Much of its success outside Japan was based on the Prius' brand and reputation, most significantly helped by celebrity endorsees who made it a great example of "geek chic".

Helped by both soaring petrol prices and the green wave, the Prius has become the iconic green statement for environmentally-conscious drivers. Toyota was already on the way to becoming the world's largest carmaker, and one of the most profitable, and the Prius simply helped it sprint across that finish line.

But therein lies the problem for Toyota. They are now the world's biggest car manufacturer, but the Prius, whilst a great success, makes up a hair-width slither of the company's overall vehicle sales. Toyota has dozens of combustion-based models, without even counting other owned brands such as Lexus. As of writing, only three of these models have the option of Hybrid engines, and the Prius is the only complete hybrid design.

In 2007, Toyota launched a strategy to increase US pick-up sales to 200,000 vehicles per year and position for the number one spot in the segment. The way into the market was the launch of the 14 miles-per-gallon Tundra pick-up. As they launched the Tundra they reportedly began intense lobbying against "clean car" standards in various US states and federal-mandated limits on "polluter vehicles" by 2020. You see the problem – brand stretch.

As if the point required illustration, Prius tagline phrases like "Free Energy Available" [when braking…] and "emits up to one tonne less CO_2 per year" [1 tonne of CO_2 less than an equivalent family vehicle with a diesel engine based upon 20,000 km a year], have put Toyota in hot water with advertising standards authorities in the UK, New Zealand and elsewhere. All this led to watchdog group Corporate Accountability International selecting Toyota for its 2008 "Corporate hall of Shame", stating:

"the company has hypocritically crafted an image as a corporate ally in the fight against climate change while working behind the scenes to stop greenhouse gas mandates from becoming law."

Toyota's reputation remains broadly intact, and it still enjoys the benefits of the Prius. But I would argue that that reputation is being stretched pretty tight and the walls are slowly starting to close in. This is the case for the entire automotive industry. Certainly in the USA, many have pointed to the collapse of the "Big 4" car makers as being as much about these groups producing the "wrong kind of vehicles" as the global credit crunch. Even if the industry stabilizes Toyota will eventually suffer what I call "the BP reality check". The scrutiny on their brand stretch will increase and increase the more they use the green fig leaf, and the bigger their market share grows. Then they will have a couple of high-profile slip-ups and – bang! There goes your reputation.

Beyond PR – The cardinal sin

I've already offered my disclaimer for being a pretty simple guy, so please excuse me rolling out one of the most cited case studies in how to build up and then destroy (or at least significantly damage) a reputation. In my opinion, no one has ever quite done it like BP.

When I joined Shell Renewables in 2002, Shell was generally viewed as the "most sustainable" of the oil majors, amongst both special publics (influencers and decision makers) and the general public. BP had already started making inroads into public perception, starting with the move "Beyond Petroleum".

Without any inside knowledge, let me say that I think Lord Browne was sincere with taking BP beyond petroleum. It was to be a very gradual shift beyond petroleum, however, and one that might have been his legacy only 30 or 40 years in the future. It was also a strategy that needed the entire organisation 100% behind it, and all doing the things required to get BP beyond petroleum.

Instead, it became a very loud and exposed brand positioning, with very little, or at least by far not enough, to stand behind it. Whilst in Shell Renewables, I felt we were doing a lot of real green projects, but probably not claiming enough reputational recognition for them. Meanwhile, I could see BP being very effective at positioning itself as "the green oil company", but not really seeing very much in the way of real initiatives. And when BP were launching projects, they appeared to fit much more in the "demonstration" space, than the "major infrastructure space". The brand stretch was palpable, but it was working – public perception was indeed that BP was doing the most in the green space.

And then it happened. First of all the terrible fire at BP's Texas City Refinery in 2005 that claimed 15 lives, injured hundreds and impacted thousands. The fire raised massive questions about BP's safety standards and procedures and reminded people that BP was still, after all, an oil company. Then, while the company was still dealing with the Texas fallout, the Alaska pipeline spill happened in early 2006. One million litres of crude oil spilled down the Prudhoe Bay slope in Alaska in an environmental disaster that has been compared to the Exxon Valdez spill.

After Prudhoe Bay, any illusions that BP was Beyond Petroleum and that it could continue to live up to being the UK's "Most Admired Energy Company" [FT 2005], were well and truly broken.

What followed was a word of pain in Russia, with BP effectively being forced to give up a large part of their investment to the Russian government (ironically the Russians used breach of environmental regulations as the lever against BP; a similar tactic they had employed against Shell on their Sakhalin Island project).

Lord Browne, whose retirement was already planned, took much of the blame for Texas City, Prudhoe Bay, and the Russian debacle. Many executives were thrown out of BP on the back of these events. Browne, however, who was eventually pushed out early on the basis of a personal "scandal", lost more than his position and reputation. He lost his legacy, and with it, BP lost Beyond Petroleum. If it ever was a real strategy, it will never come to pass in the way Lord Browne had spent much of his career planning.

Again, I actually think that's a shame. What tore down BP's reputation wasn't its lack of a real green business; it was its safety and maintenance procedures. But the greening of BP actually made the pain of that much worse. Again, it illustrates the risk of brand stretch.

The gap between what we say and what we do has always been critical in reputation management, but it's more important than ever.

It's not working

That's probably enough illustration. My point is that for all the millions being spent on advertising, and for all the companies stretching – coming out with more sustainability reports and green projects and initiatives – it's just not working.

It's not working for the following reasons:

- Delivery is traditional. These messages are being delivered largely through advertising, which we know is more expensive and less effective than ever. Beyond advertising it's those CSR reports no one reads, speeches, press releases… please!

- The tone is patronizing and the communication is one way. "Look at this great stuff we've been doing and reward us for it." "Don't ask questions about the other stuff we do, we can't/won't deal with that"

- The scale of the challenge for "polluter brands" is enormous. Without truly moving "beyond petroleum", it's insurmountable – the gap between "say" and "do" is simply too big

- Consumers – us – are more aware, and hence more cynical than ever

- "PR folk" have got an outdated set of skills to deal with issues via the same channels they are being attacked through

Not only is it failing to convince an already skeptical public that these are sincere messages or initiatives, it's actually creating reputational risk. And as we can see from the BP example, it might have nothing to do with the green positioning that brings down the house of cards.

"Don't panic"

In Douglas Adams' book, The Hitchhikers Guide to the Galaxy, the guide itself is a small handheld electronic encyclopedia. Any question about the Galaxy can be entered and an immediate graphical answer/explanation/Wiki appears as a response. Little did Douglas Adams know in 1978 that by 2008 we would all be carrying such guides around with us everywhere we go. It's called the Internet. More specifically, the mobile internet. With these devices we can look up any claim, statement, piece of data or sustainability report from a decade ago – with a few clicks.

Information is everywhere today, and immediately available. I'm regularly challenged during presentations, or conversations for that matter, on a comment or statement by someone who Googles my claim in the midst of the discussion. Thankfully I bookmark my sources on my iPhone so evidence can be entered by both sides! The point is, we need to communicate with this technology in mind – we need to understand the risk in being "loose".

OK, panic

As if the ability to instantly cross-check every statement didn't present a tough enough challenge, the information superhighway is now covered in roundabouts. As communications professionals, we used to manage our corporate reputations through Media Relations, Investor Relations, Internal Communications, and Marketing. How many of today's corporate PR departments have Wiki Managers, Blog Relations Managers, Viral Campaign Managers, Web Aggregator Coordinators, Twitter Managers, Social Network Correspondents, Engagement VPs etc. If you have any of these responsibilities covered in your teams, I can almost guarantee they're buried into a small part of "traditional" roles.

If you care about your organisations' reputation, these are the things you need to be looking at. Don't believe me? Do another unscientific test. Call the online editors of the five most important media outlets you deal with and ask them to list the top 3-5 sites they and their staff consult to decide what to write about, and as sources for those articles.

From Time magazine to the Times Online, you will hear minor variations on the following: Google (web search and news), Wikipedia, Digg, Reddit, and maybe YouTube, followed by their main competitors. Some will even tell you they use Digg/Reddit rankings to set the news agenda for their shift. Once you understand how important these sources are in deciding what the sites write about, and where they are getting information about your brand, then you have to realise how important it is to manage these channels, in the same way you try and manage information to traditional channels.

When I used to work for a major Dutch multinational, it used to surprise me how much more passionate our CEO would get about a negative article in the Dutch press (which might have been seen by 100,000 or so readers), than a positive mention in the Wall Street Journal (with a daily circulation of more than 2 million, including a major slice of the investment community).

I feel the same way today when I see the time and resources put into getting a citation in the Wall Street Journal, but ignoring the online buzz in blogs, Diggs etc. which can deliver recurrent mentions into the many millions. Once you make the connection between these millions of online users and how they influence the mainstream media – how they can start a movement to make and break a brand – then you see how incredible it is that most companies continue to do little or nothing to engage with them.

The 3 "Es"

If you're reading this chapter looking for revolutionary new thinking, then I'm sorry to disappoint. The simple guy I am, I just look around me and try and understand how new trends mesh with what we already know and understand. 99% of the time the answers are the same as they ever were. They just need to be made relevant with understanding of new channels or technologies.

Marketing blogger Vankatesh Rangachari, cuts through all the marketing babble best for me, when he summed up what great brands need to do today – basically the same as great brands have done in the past: Engage,

Educate, Entertain. I'm going to stay away from entertaining – that's less relevant for reputation management – and focus on the first two.

Engage

When we talk about Sustainable branding, and the most important thing to do is to Engage. Why?

- Today's stakeholders expect it. Even if they don't want to engage with you, they want to have the opportunity to do so. A bit like voting.

- It's simple to do it. The Internet has given a channel for brands to talk to 10 stakeholders or 10 million, all for a relatively inexpensive price tag, and for nothing compared to TV or other traditional media.

- It represents a huge opportunity. If you can use engagement to "activate" your audience you have the opportunity to create a loyal "tribe", more valuable to your reputation than any amount of investment.

- It becomes a table stake. Once you do it, you'll keep on doing it. It becomes easy.

   There are, of course, some rules of engagement. The "conversation" has to be honest, open, respectful and intelligent. Engage has to mean engage. It means listen, then respond. It doesn't mean "talk".

Educate

Once engagement is established, and once, and only once, you have earned the right to do so, you can educate the audience on you sustainable initiatives. Before a brand is ready to educate, you need to bear the following in mind:

- Green brands don't exist without green businesses;

- So identify the things you do well, and those you need to improve (gap analysis). Be ready to talk about both;

- Put your house in order as far as possible before you are ready to educate. Be proud of these initiatives, but choose a tone appropriate to your gap analysis;

- Stay true to who you are and what you do. If you're a bagel company, there's no point trying to convince people you're making bagels to save the planet;

- Understand that engagement is the vehicle for education.

Conversational marketing

In my view, this is all eventually leading to a new trend in reputation management: Conversational Marketing.

Federated Media is probably the first major publishing house to "get" this trend and begin to monetize it. The "Federated Media Guide to Conversational Marketing" is by far the best place to begin to understand the trend and its implications. In basic terms, its reputation management in a fully-engaged model.

As Federated Media put it, "Conversational Media is the evolution of formal, packaged goods media from mainstream media companies into more informal, author and consumer-driven products... [it] engages, rather than dictates, invites rather than demands, and listens as much as talks."

Federated Media has generated more than 50 million unique visitors to its channels so far, including blogs, social networks, and viral content. Brands including McDonald's, HP, BMW, Intel, P&G and others have signed up.

Managing reputation through engagement is not a new concept – I've already said that I don't do "new" concepts.

Royal Dutch Shell is a company that has been doing it to a greater or lesser extent for over fifteen years. The Brent Spar debacle, followed by the death of anti-Shell campaigner Ken Saro-Wiwa in Nigeria, forced the company to engage. Shell was one of the first companies to publish a Sustainability Report on the back of Brent Spar, and then the first to start online engagement through its TellShell website, including positive, and plenty of negative, comments. Shell never stopped engaging, but they did narrow their target audience to special publics. Following a couple of years of traditional corporate advertising, they appear to be moving back to engagement, and engaging met a broader public.

IBM has been running "Jams" for five years. These started as multi-day online engagements with their 50,000 strong workforce. By 2006 they had evolved into "InnovationJams" with 150,000 participants from 104 countries. This jam generated 46,000 ideas, IBM has committed US$100 million to the best 10. The rest have gone into shaping the company and their offerings to meeting the expectations of their engaged clients. IBM is now using the jams to effectively tap into the minds of their clients, together with hundreds of the best and brightest thinkers. Through the engagement, they get their ideas and then sell them back to them. And in doing so, they build a great reputation for engaging and listening.

In conclusion

I'm afraid my advice will get no more profound in my conclusion. I will tell you a few simple things I tell all my clients:

- Don't green your brand, green your business

- Do careful gap analysis, and make sure your company is joined-up – you can't build a sustainable reputation and then find out your marketing folks have signed a Formula 1 sponsorship deal

- Tell marketing to market your products and services, not your green credentials

- Remember the 3 Es. Engage around both your successes and fail-ings. Listen, learn, reflect, and then engage again. Only then educate. Be very careful in trying to entertain, especially if you're a bank….

- Reassess the organisation and skill sets of you communications team. Place an emphasis on online understanding, development and channel management

- Most brands have a long way to go before they get there and will burn a lot of money along the way

- Conversational marketing provides a roadmap and a relatively safe place to experiment

Do all the above (feel free to hire the author to help!), and together we will take the stain out of sustainability.

"Our reputation is at stake" – Corporate communications in the light of the global economic downturn

Dirk Popp

This global economic crisis is changing everything. Including communications. For there is an overlap between the crisis in classical media and the increasing need for crisis communications. A lot is at stake – including the future role of corporate communications within companies.

This crisis is especially vicious. Isn't it?

A preliminary remark: what follows is not intended as a refresher course on issues and risks, or on classical crisis communications and task forces. This article simply states what has changed and what has to be done differently.

The US National Bureau of Economic Research (NBER) defines recession as "a significant decline in economic activity spread across the economy, lasting more than a few months, normally visible in real GDP, real income, employment, industrial production, and wholesale-retail sales." The media use a rule of thumb: recession is when economic performance declines in two consecutive quarters. Looking at global economic data, one thing is certain: the collapse of Lehman Brothers in autumn 2008 triggered an economic crisis that transcends all previous categories.

For this crisis is profound, drastic and vicious. It is different because it has been extremely swift, affecting all countries almost simultaneously, because it has systemic causes and because none of the Keynesian or post-Keynesian formulas implemented in response has so far been effective.

The economic reputations of entire nations, the 'Masters of the Universe' of the financial sector, the automobile industry, the property sector – to name but a few – have suffered dramatic damage.

J. Klewes, R. Wreschniok (eds.), *Reputation Capital*, DOI 10.1007/978-3-642-01630-1_16,
© Springer-Verlag Berlin Heidelberg 2009

Even the idea of capitalism as the 'best economic system of all' is being questioned by Western governments though problematic protectionist and regulatory policies that, only a few months ago, would have been unthinkable. The social consequences cannot even begin to be foreseen. In the media and in public opinion in developed countries, a certain 'crisis desensitisation' is spreading.

As has been the case in the Islamic and Eastern world for many decades, the global recession is seeing the state take a new role in the Western industrial nations as well. If, as recently as 2007, nationalisation was still considered an idea of the Devil or of marginal communist parties, it has now become a commonplace in every responsible legislature.

Media in downturn – Crisis communication in upturn

Since the 1970s, the facts that affect a company's economic reputation have been increasingly scrutinised by NGOs, citizens and media.

We have become familiar with the idea that organisations and media operating independently of the state play an important role as watchdogs of our consumer democracy. And that regulatory, executive or legislative bodies trace these developments – perhaps with some lag, but ultimately clearly taking on board the concerns raised.

For companies that operate internationally, the trend in recent years has been towards a stronger role for reputation and a simultaneous increase in critical communication. The need for social reputation has forced global players to increasingly revise their business and supply models. One only needs to be reminded of campaigns about "brand-name sports shoes from Asian sweatshops" or "clean versus bloodstained diamonds".

NGOs have learnt their lesson from Brent Spar. What has remained is a campaign formula that focuses on a spectacular example rich in imagery, emotionalisation and trivialisation. But now, increasingly, entire sectors are coming under fire. The campaigns are designed more for the long-term and are focussing more heavily on business models. Sporadic 'unethical behaviour' is attacked in an exemplary way – but at the same time, it is embedded into a broader context, making it harder to dismiss.

And the David-versus-Goliath principle – that is, small and loud against big and self-assured – is being expanded in the age of Web 2.0 through concerted, sustained and networked campaigns that see many consumers unite against what they see as unacceptable state of affairs.

It is only at first glance that these trends appear to operate along familiar lines and in a way that is essentially no different to the general conditions that held in the second half of the twentieth century.

A fundamental shift in coordinates

The threat of crisis has – due to the permanent pressure for change on companies, and their increasing globalisation – become permanent. The wide range of risks that now need to be monitored is reflected in the fact that numerous "burning platforms" now no longer replace each other, but overlap – and in that it is necessary, due to different legal frameworks, to adjust communications specifically to particular regions or countries.

Managed corporate communications has thus become more complex, and is exposed to a wealth of external, dynamic and uncontrollable factors.

In addition, the 'old' media themselves are in crisis (economic pressure on TV and print media, layoffs), and with regard to the new media, most companies are seeking new ways to communicate appropriately at corporate level.

Web 2.0 is, both structurally and because of its speed, certainly the greatest future challenge as regards corporate communications in crisis situations.

In 2002, United Airlines filed for bankruptcy. In the online archive of the Sun Sentinel, this report is still available. However – and this was the first step towards a catastrophe – it bears no date. A user called up this article on Sunday, 6 September 2008, at 1 am – not a time at which many visitors are frolicking about the website. The result: the Sentinel website listed the story as one of its most read articles in the business section. The Google News crawler followed the link to the news, and since there was no date, Google supplied it with the current date, 6 September 2008. Until this point, everything happened automatically. It was in this way that the story reached Google News, and all Sunday long, it was read there by users, among them the employee of an investment service provider, who ran the story in a newsletter. Of course, he undertook no further research and blindly trusted this single source. It thus escaped his notice that United Airlines had been solvent again since 2006. But the news wrought havoc on the stock market. Share prices for United Airlines collapsed by 75% and trading in the shares had to be halted for several hours. A billion dollars was destroyed.

A similar thing happened with a report from 21 August 2008 about the emergency landing of a Condor aircraft in Mombasa which resurfaced in March 2009.

Due to organisational structures and approval processes in communications departments, companies are not set up to respond in Web 2.0. Propagation times of 3 minutes – as with the emergency landing of an Airbus on the Hudson River in New York in March 2009 – are characteristic for contemporary media practice. So, before corporate communications departments can swing into action, media users around the world have already formed their own picture of the event.

Unfortunately, it must be said that no convincing approaches have yet been found for solving this dilemma technically, or in terms of personnel or content. The technologies for quick, worldwide reactions and crisis communications are available: from Twitter and RSS through to many-to-one dialogue platforms. But internal company processes for opinion formation and approval are not yet developed to the point that an initial statement can be issued within a few minutes via Twitter. Or that individual customer enquires in the stakeholder group, and the most important ones, can be answered by the CEO.

What does this mean?

The wealth of overlapping risks leads to a range of issues lying dormant. Companies should assume crises are unavoidable, and that it is only a question of when they break out and how they can be prevented from becoming epic issues that cause long-term reputational damage.

Globalisation and new media act as accelerants

As regards economic reputation, it is essential that business models are changed so that the risk of crisis is reduced. Social reputation is crucially determined by the how of communication in the event of a crisis, and by the consistency with which a company changes itself.

The global economic crisis has both alleviating and exacerbating effects. With each report on the downturn in media and within organisations, there is desensitization towards the crisis. By now, it takes a fair bit to get on the front page or to trigger an extraordinary meeting of the supervisory board.

'Bad news' needs to be in the range of several tens of thousands of employees affected or a quarterly loss of tens of billions to garner national or international attention for more than a moment, or to achieve more than ten lines in national newspapers.

Of course, to this provisional rule there are exceptions that attract a lot of attention. These include B2C brands with a history – Märklin, Schiesser – or national institutions that possess emotional value for millions of people. In several recent cases, both emotional and economic value come together: for example, General Motors, Fannie Mae or Tata.

The exacerbating factor is that negative news is actually expected. 'Good news' comes with the proviso "depending how the economic situation develops". Of course, companies are obliged to check that their messages will hold for the middle term at least.

Some draw the conclusion that they must reduce their active external communications. Most companies, however, cannot escape their communicative duties and supply each statement with a caveat ("at present", "based on current information", "according to how the global economy develops") and refrain from making prognoses. Statements by the board and press releases become vague.

Also, the media are seeking confirmation for the unspoken thesis that "the whole economy is suffering". Nervous employees are rather inclined to leak internal news to the outside – on the one hand, to sustain the general tone in the media, and on the other hand, to increase pressure on the companies.

"Day-to-day business is eating up strategy"

The crisis is accelerating change in companies. This increases communicative speed and the pressure for success on corporate communications. The usual planning rituals are soon relegated to wishful thinking if they cannot keep up with the pace of events.

Many changes and measures for adjusting to economic conditions have to be communicated internally and externally. And in an ever shorter time. Here, the greatest danger is that messages and core statements are, in the short term, overtaken by events.

The solution is: corporate communications must at all times be ready to respond and be ready for action. It must also be tightly meshed with strategy development, HR and legal departments. All the processes and instruments of crisis communication are well-trained and implemented in the organisation.

Preparations must focus on the development of a story that is tenable in the mid-term – one that will not be made obsolete by eventualities in the coming months and that can serve as a basis for communicating trust and plans for the future both internally and externally.

In day-to-day business, internal processes that rob time and resources – from gathering information to approving it for release – must be reduced as much as possible, so the company can act quickly. This way, when crises overlap, there is no overload.

Experience certainly suggests there is little time for comprehensive, robust planning – something with an established place during the 'good times'. Of course, this presupposes a corporate culture that relies on the professionalism and integrity of the communicators and that – always within the framework of the strategic story – generally gives them wide latitude in implementing it on a day-to-day basis.

This approach only works in learning organisations that can, with ongoing communication, translate their experiences directly and 'on the fly' into changes in behaviour and content.

Crisis communications in practice: Proven instruments have to be deployed strategically

Even in times of crisis, there is no reason to fundamentally question proven instruments and processes for crisis communications.

The five basic escalation levels are obligatory for all companies: intelligent monitoring, handling critical issues, risk prevention, professional crisis response and consistency.

1. 360-degree monitoring for evaluating latent, critical issues in the relevant media must give management – ahead of time – a compact overview that is reduced to the essentials.

E-mailing a comprehensive, uncommented press review will not do. Today, the state of the art is to summarize, late in the evening, potential issues, the mood on the Internet, the political climate, the market situation and relevant media reports for the following day.

The intelligence required to draw the right conclusions from news and threads can only come from the communications team. They are familiar with both the issues and crisis communications, and have access to the board. The necessary updates, of course, are provided 24/7.

2. Issues management and risk mapping is a classical procedure for analysing and preparing for potential crises and issues, should they become public. The methods for identifying potential issues – categorised as information-related, physical, reputational, economic, HR-related, criminal and natural – rely on deep monitoring.

Prioritising and clustering potential latent or acute issues are also among the fundamental strategic techniques that communications professionals must master.

However, when both the pace of change in a company and the frequency of issue alerts significantly increases, there is little time for comprehensive research and cross checks.

So what has proved useful is scenario workshops? Experts in communications, strategy, HR, legal, business units, international business development and public affairs together identify potential issues and develop three basic scenarios, ranging from best case to worst case.

The advantages are obvious: the speed and most importantly the direct identification of issues that can result from overlaying various corporate plans. Deutsche Bank provides a classic example: the announcement, by CEO Josef Ackermann, of a 20% growth target came on the very day 6,500 jobs were cut. The simultaneity of the announcements itself created an additional issue, and a strong media response. Similar cases are now everyday media occurrences – whether it be bonus payments at AIG or GM management flying to Washington D.C. in a corporate jet. Events that are in themselves unsurprising together make for an explosive mixture: retention bonuses for investment bankers and US$200 bn in state aid here, a CEO trip by private jet here and a congressional hearing for state aid there.

It is the task of communications to link such issues mapping to monitoring in a simple, reasonable way, and to continually update it.

3. Risk prevention, through appropriate, organisational structures, crisis-response tools, simulations and training the employees, also is a classical instrument for corporate communications. In the coming months and years, it will be crucial for corporate communications departments and external consultants alike to accelerate this process or, as detailed above, to integrate it directly into the work of ongoing change / crisis communications.

For, there is not going to be the time for several months of risk-prevention work – at least in internationally active or listed companies. In addition, it is likely that corporate communications will be affected by budget cuts.

One practical solution is to activate or establish a permanent 'task force' with experts from various areas in the company. Here, change and issue communications can be bundled together. Involving those responsible for communications in these areas makes it possible to respond exceedingly quickly when these units perceive a need to communicate or when issues or crises in various units overlap. In such cases, at least, the task force must be able to set up independent 'sub-teams' that can act.

The advantage is strategic in nature, as this approach guarantees the consistency and the strategic fit of internal and external communications. From a tactical standpoint, this solution saves time and resources; that the management board and project groups are linked in via a fixed set of contact people makes it easy to implement.

4. The crisis response team is, sensibly enough, recruited from the issues management team. As far as the basic psychological requirements are concerned, important key points have already been named. See above for more on telling bad news and keeping morale high.

In past years – driven by the internationalisation of communication – virtual teams have become commonplace. Experience shows, however, that one cannot entirely avoid bringing people together to meet in one place.

It is recommended that companies make the experience of these teams beneficial for the whole organisation. For example, some employees might be trained 'on the job', or nearby evaluations and courses bundled together. This rule sounds simple – but too often it falls victim to day-to-day business. However, it saves important resources and above all time when the next issue presents itself.

5. It is only the consequences that a company takes during and after a crisis that douse the trouble spots for good and eradicate the source of the crisis. Anti-competitive behaviour will be eliminated in future, social and security standards increased, and so on. Nowadays, it is part of the business model that companies prove their capacity to learn and step up to their responsibilities.

The global economic crisis presents new opportunities that are vitally important for the future: worldwide, the recession and the extent of uncontrollable, unregulated risks in financial markets and the property sector have been taken as an occasion to ask fundamental questions about economic life and its relationship to politics. There is reason to doubt how earnestly this re-think of the global economy, high finance and free trade is being conducted.

But companies and organisations that out of critical developments derive specific, practicable and verifiable consequences for their business models will gain far more from the exercise than they would in 'normal' times. Corporations that today demonstrate their commitment towards a sustainable, social and climate-friendly market economy generate a positive response in the media and among stakeholders. They also benefit because it is precisely anxious clients and markets that are most open to optimism and encouragement.

For example, fair investment by external investors – that is, without exorbitant financial costs arising from this investment – or a flexible human resources policy, without a hire-and-fire mentality, are aspects that are central to success for many companies. Often, simply fostering – even in difficult times – a clear, open, transparent and, if need be, self-critical dialogue with media and clients would significantly bolster social reputation.

During the global economic crisis, it is true that the need for action is greater, but not fundamentally different. However, the current situation demonstrates that communication is a significant factor in guiding companies through the recession and preparing for the time after the recession (avoiding reputational damage, involving management and employees in difficult times, retaining key performers... many core tasks in the recession are crucially defined by communication).

As regards corporate communications, the maxim is still: "In good times like in bad times." Those who do not communicate now will have lost a great deal of credibility and interest vis-à-vis the media by the time the crisis is over. Those who continue openly and transparently to participate in dialogue with employees as well as media, management and clients will be able to register a significant boost in reputation after the crisis.

"Telling bad news and keeping morale high"

In times of crisis, the mode of internal and external communications becomes coarser. No one loves communicating layoffs, collapsing revenues or factory closures. But precisely this will be part of many everyday corporate communications for years to come.

The question of how corporate culture and the engagement of staff can be strengthened or saved through the crisis is outside the scope of this article. For corporate communications, what counts in the near future is more the question of how team motivation and communications morale can be sustained. For this, it is helpful for communicators, as well as for internal and external managers responsible for communications, to bear in mind some fundamental distinctions.

Every change communication can give rise to critical situations, with a seamless transition into crisis communications. There is nothing unusual in that. But preparing for planned, foreseeable issues – for example, protests in response to layoffs or difficult investor relations after a profit warning – is a different matter to the onset of an acute crisis.

A team can prepare for crises, withstand them, or try to find ways out of a crisis that has gone epic. The difference lies in whether the event, like a tsunami, begins with bad news and the end is foreseeable, or whether corporate communications simply has to assume it is dealing with a string of earthquakes.

In the current crisis, we need to understand clearly that we will probably more be dealing with a series of earthquakes. This gives rise, on the one hand, to the 'crisis desensitisation' already mentioned – many reports that in summer 2008 still would have made the front pages no longer pass the threshold of perception, because they must make way for other companies or states with bigger losses to report.

Now, communicators are gaining friends and supporters!

This insight, however, must not simply be limited to providing short-term reassurance. The dangers – even those that do not affect reputation– are bigger for corporate communications. Desensitisation can also set in for management, increasing internal resistance to active crisis communications. Above all, however, it becomes extremely difficult to preserve internal morale. And cynics only harm crisis communications.

If the critical situation in the company itself turns out to be bigger, another factor assumes importance: the board itself will need an orientation phase to adjust to the company's new and critical situation. It will respond differently and less predictably to unexpected, undesirable events than corporate communications is used to in normal times. For, the reorientation and decision phase suddenly calls for new patterns of thinking and behaviour. In this phase, communications can strengthen its own position: if it can come up with process knowledge and immediately available know-how in its internal and external response to the crisis. Note: immediately available and deployable. It still cannot strengthen its own position over night, but this engagement is a good long-term investment. If it can successfully avert damage to a company and confidently communicate critical situations internally and externally, corporate communications significantly relieves the burden on upper management. And thus shows the indispensability of its role for the weal and woe of the company.

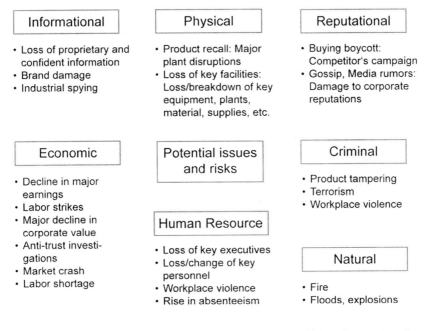

Informational	Physical	Reputational
• Loss of proprietary and confident information • Brand damage • Industrial spying	• Product recall: Major plant disruptions • Loss of key facilities: Loss/breakdown of key equipment, plants, material, supplies, etc.	• Buying boycott: Competitor's campaign • Gossip, Media rumors: Damage to corporate reputations

Economic	Potential issues and risks	Criminal
• Decline in major earnings • Labor strikes • Major decline in corporate value • Anti-trust investigations • Market crash • Labor shortage		• Product tampering • Terrorism • Workplace violence

	Human Resource	Natural
	• Loss of key executives • Loss/change of key personnel • Workplace violence • Rise in absenteeism	• Fire • Floods, explosions

Issues can be typified in forseeable or unpredictable, triggered internally or externally.

Fig. 1. Overview potential issues and risks

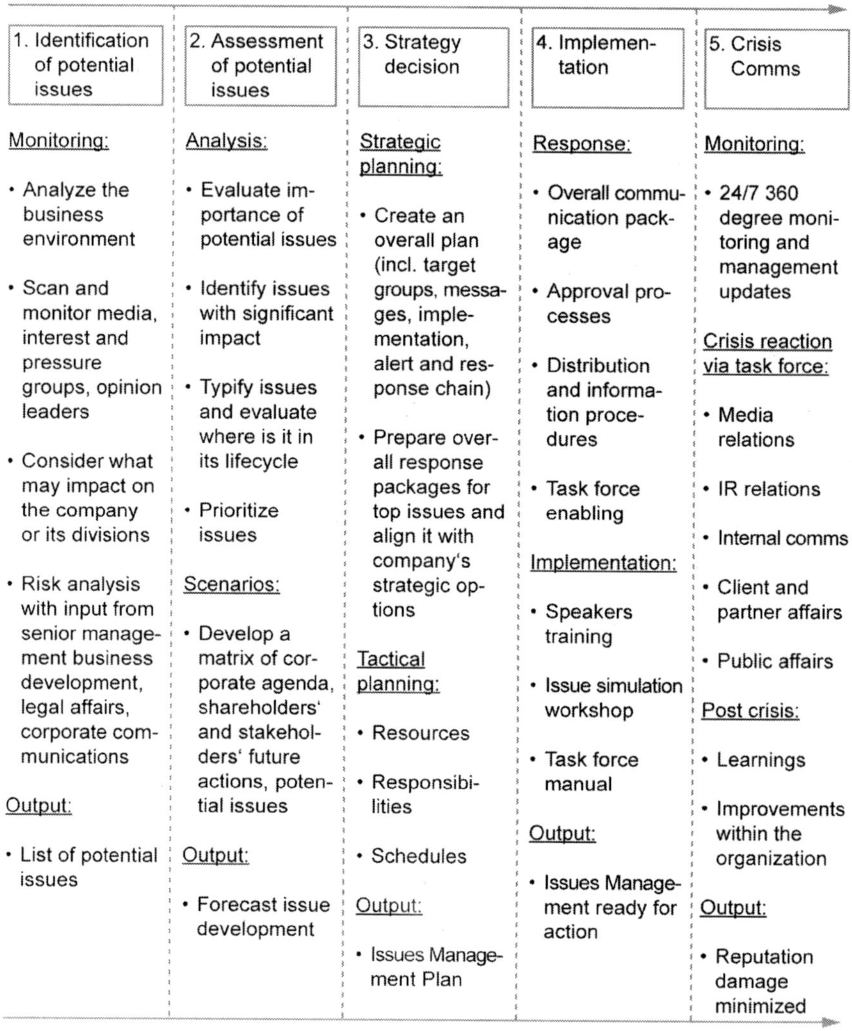

1. Identification of potential issues	2. Assessment of potential issues	3. Strategy decision	4. Implementation	5. Crisis Comms
Monitoring:	Analysis:	Strategic planning:	Response:	Monitoring:
• Analyze the business environment	• Evaluate importance of potential issues	• Create an overall plan (incl. target groups, messages, implementation, alert and response chain)	• Overall communication package	• 24/7 360 degree monitoring and management updates
• Scan and monitor media, interest and pressure groups, opinion leaders	• Identify issues with significant impact		• Approval processes	Crisis reaction via task force:
• Consider what may impact on the company or its divisions	• Typify issues and evaluate where is it in its lifecycle	• Prepare overall response packages for top issues and align it with company's strategic options	• Distribution and information procedures	• Media relations
• Risk analysis with input from senior management business development, legal affairs, corporate communications	• Prioritize issues		• Task force enabling	• IR relations
	Scenarios:	Tactical planning:	Implementation:	• Internal comms
	• Develop a matrix of corporate agenda, shareholders' and stakeholders' future actions, potential issues	• Resources	• Speakers training	• Client and partner affairs
		• Responsibilities	• Issue simulation workshop	• Public affairs
Output:		• Schedules	• Task force manual	Post crisis:
• List of potential issues	Output:	Output:	Output:	• Learnings
	• Forecast issue development	• Issues Management Plan	• Issues Management ready for action	• Improvements within the organization
				Output:
				• Reputation damage minimized

Fig. 2. Scheme for establishing crisis communications in companies

Part IV: New perspectives for reputation management in the 21st century

A good reputation is more valuable than money.

Publilius Syrus (1st century BC)

Community reputation communicates change to the world

Joachim Kuss

Like corporations, national states, regions and cities are in regional as well as international competition. In such highly complex social institutions, building a reputation that fosters growth basically follows the same rules as apply to corporate reputation. But complexity, diversity and the necessity of balancing a wide variety of conflicting interests make community reputation management – influencing public perceptions and actively shaping expectations – a particular challenge.

"Reputation is people's business"

In the midst of a harsh global economic crisis, the United States has elected Barack Obama as its 44th President. He is a candidate who has explicitly placed the moral renewal of the USA and comprehensive change at the centre of his politics. Whether his election is just a coincidence, or causal relationships exist, is outside the scope of this article.

But there are two surprising consequences of the Obama phenomenon. First, the astonishingly high voter mobilisation at a time when the number of non-voters is growing in all developed democracies. Second, the wave of hope, the euphoria, the expectations and the sympathy with the USA that gripped at least the occidental world with Obama's victory.

The high voter mobilisation, which favoured the young and, until recently, completely unknown Obama, cannot be explained by the USA's economic problems alone. Rather, it is also a moral crisis that has led to a loss of trust in the American government and in the claim to leadership of the oldest democracy in the world. The catchwords are familiar to all: Guantánamo, the torture scandal, Iraq, Afghanistan, the collapse of the Middle East initiatives, the dismantling of the authority of the UN and other world organisations.

J. Klewes, R. Wreschniok (eds.), *Reputation Capital*, DOI 10.1007/978-3-642-01630-1_17,
© Springer-Verlag Berlin Heidelberg 2009

Independently of the extent to which American politics is to blame for the economic crisis or the extent to which the above examples reflect how the USA actually 'lives out' its responsibility: in the eyes of the international media during George W. Bush's presidency at least, the USA failed to live up to its perceived role not only as the motor of the world economy, but also as the champion of human rights and democracy. The USA's clearly branded identity (frequently termed the 'American way of life' or the American Dream) only served to strengthen this impression. The apparent discrepancy between lofty claims and unfulfilled expectations allowed the media, pressure groups and stakeholders to paint a particularly grim picture of the country. A picture that, from the standpoint of community reputation management, becomes even more fascinating given that it was revised overnight with the inauguration of Barack Obama – despite the still-empty ministerial posts and incompleteness of the new administration's plans for structural changes. At that point, the hard facts – to which the media usually like to refer – had not changed at all. But the expectations of people in many parts of the world were re-oriented, giving the 44th President of the USA his first important transaction: the exchange of reputation capital for enormous reserves of trust.

This roughly-sketched example of America illustrates the characteristic tensions between the three dimensions along which reputation develops or emerges:

- Functional reputation requires competence in fulfilling the functional demands of a role. Clearly, Obama's team managed to position their candidate convincingly in the areas of expertise which were to prove decisive in the election.

- Social reputation requires adherence to social and moral demands (in terms of integrity). Obama embodied this by successfully distancing himself from what voters associated with 'Washington'.

- Finally, expressive reputation communicates the individual and emotional constants that make up identity. In this election campaign, it was impressively dramatised as calls for hope, change and a return to the American dream.

These are the three basic elements for establishing a reputation in today's media society. These shape the public perception and judgement of states, prominent individuals and corporations.

Once these driving forces for community reputation have been understood, two important lessons can be learned. First, reputations are changed by the *behaviour of an organisation*, independent of its extent and effect over time. Change cannot be achieved by communication alone. The Bush administration's communication reflected its fundamental denial of the importance of reputation. Had it understood the importance of reputation, it would have based its communication on an open and earnest dialogue with key international players. Self-correction and actual consequences would have had to follow on from an admission of errors, providing a chance to win back trust.

Second, expressive reputation is 'people's business'. Authentic, communicative personalities can work wonders at the expressive level, which change perceptions quickly and profoundly – even when the economic and social reputation remains unchanged. It is important to note, however, that words which are not followed by acts will just as quickly have the opposite effect.

"Community reputation is a phenomenon of globalisation"

Globalisation also conditions the reputation and perception of a city, region or nation. The majority of investors, students, highly skilled workers, congress organisers, employers and funding agencies are internationally orientated. This intensifies competition. Globalisation evens out differences: for example, in language, infrastructure, funding and credit conditions, trade policy – even management culture. As a result, the role of the reputational factors grows. Crucial differences are increasingly produced by communication.

But if, for example, a financial factor bucks the levelling trend – think of Europe's defeat in the semiconductor subsidy race – neither research clusters, infrastructure nor image will determine the competition for investment and highly skilled workers. Hard facts are created, and allegations of market foreclosure and the looming end of free world trade circulate.

Nevertheless, the communicative task of creating a reputation for cities and regions in the 21st century has become increasingly important in recent years.

Cities and regions that regularly use official external communications to improve their opportunities and image in international and regional competition are referred to here as 'public communities'. This requires that they dedicate a certain minimum of resources to external communications. The term also implies that a town or a region is seen as a single entity. From an external point of view, internal differences (which often change quickly) such as social strata, clusters, subcentres, movements and groups linked with companies and research are concealed behind the image of the public community, which usually is more durable. Community reputation management goes beyond the previous, traditional communications performed by public communities. Not only does it reflect political, economic and social relations – rather like an advertising message – but it actively enters into dialogue with the relevant protagonists.

The only new development in the light of the economic crisis is the shortage of money available to national states, institutions, regions and communities. This means that there is a lack of resources for fulfilling a key requirement of reputation management: namely, creating facts that positively stimulate social and economic reputation. It is difficult to cement a reputation as a nation of learning when the extra funding due to be invested in schools and universities is suddenly needed to support the financial system.

To the attentive observer, there are numerous examples of reputation management's growing worldwide influence and the most important contributing factors. Dubai is currently working hard to secure its future in the post-oil age. Reports about establishing a global metropolis in the deserts of the Middle East frequently deal with the image of the city and the formation of opinions that will come to be associated with Dubai in just a few decades – as a centre of culture, finance and tourism. However, the economic crisis is now spoiling not only construction work, but also the investment in reputation. The collapse of building investments has seen the image strategy falter.

In every debate about Berlin, there is talk of how to reach communicative target audiences. The question of reputation overshadowed sports activities in reportage and perceptions about the XXIX Olympic Games in China. After all, it was the declared goal of the Chinese government to actively alter the nation's reputation in the long term. Reputational goals invariably are part of stated policy objectives, which almost always attract criticism or approval from numerous voices in society, business and culture.

There are reports of community reputation management activities from Norilsk to Cape Town, Sao Paolo to St. Moritz and Boulder, Colorado, to Hoyerswerda, Germany. Some publish plans for structuring shrinking cities and discuss which hard and soft factors might positively influence regional development. Others struggle with the reputational risk of mega cities: from rampant violence via environmental destruction to poverty. Reputation management for communities and (federal) states, clusters and cities is seen as a panacea for declining populations and a lack of investors, political crises, a falloff in tourism or a lack of commitment on the part of citizens.

The real challenge is that a range of stakeholders define each nation, city or region. Residents, politicians, corporations, artists, journalists and many others take part actively, reactively, directly or indirectly in shaping a national or regional reputation. Wherever managing reputation is on the agenda, the first common denominator is a brand that is the expressive face of a complex and diverse community. In contrast to the largely centrally controlled branding of businesses and products, this type of brand communication is distinguished by the fact that it is ultimately uncontrollable and conditioned by a range of incidents and opinion-forming processes.

"If you concentrate too much on your image, you endanger your reputation"

There are an impressive number of studies on the importance of image for investor decisions. The *dernier cri* is the concept of a 'creative city', which builds on the fact that cities and regions with high proportions of visionaries, outsiders and mavericks develop more successfully than strongholds of conservatism and mediocrity. Previous studies and rankings about the impact of the complex factors that contribute to a community's expressive reputation have barely done justice to the complexity of the subject. On the other hand, the only way to achieve effective results in the media is to engage in simplifications bordering on the unacceptable, resulting in such exaggerations as "X is the most investor-friendly country in Europe", or "Y is the most attractive town in Germany".

The basis for a community's expressive reputation is the creation and communication of an attractive brand. This should appeal to target groups that are important for the future: for example, employers and investors, young families and students, scientists and artists.

Traditional marketing will not do. Neither will brand campaigns, or press and media relations. There is only one thing that really counts and pays off when it comes to community reputation management: recognising and decoding the expectations that result from the interplay between the people and events in a community, and working with these expectations on the basis of the community branding.

These expectations, significantly influenced by the troika of economy, politics and culture, are experienced and replicated by thousands on a daily basis. They attract tourists and are analysed by investors and students, and are the most important raw material of community branding and thus of the expressive reputation.

First and foremost, reputation management is about the facts. This tension between expectations and verifiable facts is, of course, also decisive for communities. The actual behaviour of protagonists in a community must also define its communication. Backing up reputation with actual marketing measures is a secondary issue – a city will gain a reputation with or without advertisement campaigns and trade fair appearances.

Metropolises such as New York or Berlin have been in the international spotlight for decades. However, they have lost none of their attractiveness through the multidimensional and contradictory expectations that they provoke – quite the opposite, in fact. And it is often artists or politicians, rather than marketing agencies, who express this multidimensionality most succinctly, using their keen sense for the city's genetic code. Frank Sinatra hits the nail on the head in his ode to New York: "If I can make it there, I can make it anywhere". This one sentence puts New York's raw, dog-eat-dog economic climate in a nutshell. Klaus Wowereit, the mayor of Berlin, achieved a similar feat when he described his city as "poor, but sexy". This became the international slogan for the new Berlin, a metropolis that is currently displaying its pulling power in the creative and artistic milieus especially.

As these examples suggest: every public community is sooner or later linked with talented communicators. It's people's business, after all! The Barack Obama phenomenon perfectly illustrates the fact that people need somebody to represent them, somebody who gives their community a face.

Community reputation management is known as one of the most challenging communication tasks for good reason. Only limited influence can be exerted over the structures and what is on offer. At the same time, it is important that the expectations of tourists, residents, businesses and students are met. If they are not, the reputation will not prove credible and will sooner or later become counterproductive. This means, however, that it is the task of community reputation management to make justified expectations visible and tangible, and to communicate strengths and advantages. Every statement and every message used in reputation communication must be anchored in fact. A campaign promoting a family-friendly city without expanding childcare services is as doomed to failure as shifting the image of a country without actual, serious political change. The

European Union candidate countries clearly demonstrate this. Their new claim to membership of one of the world's leading economic areas must be linked to concrete changes from the executive and legislature – and in all areas of social life, from business and culture to human rights and how they deal with their own history.

"Use and communicate the full range of events"

The examples above illustrate what makes community reputation management such an interesting task. It is diverse, extremely complex and cannot simply be taken one-to-one from another community. Events crucially determine public and media perception. Reputation feeds on facts and the opinion formation that reflects them. The opinions, on the other hand, are largely and self-referentially formed by the opinion makers themselves. This connection is well known and forms the basis of all professional public relations.

Compared to a corporate reputation, the multitude of protagonists who shape a community's reputation means a disproportionately high number of events, facts and opinion-forming processes. These events are rarely determined by communicative processes and are largely uncontrollable. A nation, region or city is not a product that develops and can be defined in its various facets. Professional community reputation management reflects this and purposefully incorporates damaging or negative developments. Factory closures are just as much part of an industrial region as is investment; marches and protests in a metropolis, or robust political conflict in a capital city are everyday occurrences. A communication strategy based on an ideal world will not work here – not even peaceful ski resorts have exclusively good news. Liberality and creativity, for example, can form the basis of a reputation strategy in a metropolis, even if the economic starting point is unfavourable. And in a metropolis, poverty, demonstrations – even by enemies of democracy – all are among the negative elements. A community that presents itself as a metropolis does not deny its unpleasant aspects, but speaks about them, perhaps by using irony. Nations have followed suit, preferring, for example, to discuss development potential rather than achievements and – freely following the maxim "the path is the goal" – incorporating public debates about shortcomings into their communications.

In reality, communities are often poor and hopefully at least somewhat sexy. The attempt to exclude bad news and raise target groups' expectations with false promises – which are inevitably disappointed – is as naïve as it is economically unwise.

"Community branding is the core of reputation management"

What does this mean for those in charge of communication? The perception of a community is shaped by the numerous activities, experiences and stories of its inhabitants. A community's reputation is lived on a daily basis and at the same time nourished by real life. This requires several basic elements. In order to influence a community's expressive reputation, identification platforms must be created that are readily and actively used by its protagonists. One such platform is usually community branding – the external representation of the city or region as a brand, fashioned by the protagonists. Branding offers numerous advantages, and the protagonists can use the brand to market facts and developments. Brand communication is professionally managed and designed with a long-term strategy in mind. At the same time, a close and direct connection to the expressive reputation is made.

Reputation processes are designed for the long-term, and evolve to be largely independent of political or civic special interests. The brand must be confidently positioned so that open dialogue with all stakeholders can be sustained, with a mixture of ironic self-mockery and self-confidence, in good and bad times. With a grasp of the political and economic contexts, the brand can drive reputational development by strategically communicating progress and future plans. The strategy here is quite conventional: a long-term plan with consistent messages. In practical terms: community branding must think beyond legislative periods and focus on selected, relevant target groups. Particularly in view of the number of protagonists, those in charge of branding need to find the courage to select themes and messages even if they overlook certain important members of the community. In strategic terms, too: the inhabitants are not the core target group of the brand. The reasons are simple. In short, they already live, work and invest in the community. Experience, or a glance in any newspaper, teaches us that major changes in a city's self-perception result first and foremost from external effects. The settlement of a new company after a rigorous selection process, rising student numbers or increased tourism boost a reputation far more than any campaign targeted at residents – provided the economic and infrastructure-related facts are in place. This is also evident in the Barack Obama phenomenon. Even during the election, before anything could change for the citizens of the United States, the internationally-held hopes of a new USA led to the American people actively doing their bit to help Obama to the White House, to "bring change to America".

Branding not only shapes a community's identity inwardly and outwardly. Above all, it creates a platform on which the political, corporate and social protagonists can agree on shared goals and messages. Just as the worlds of politics, economics, culture and science increasingly bring perceptions of themselves into the calculation, experts come on to the scene who bring a process-oriented approach to community communications. They are in a position to combine the most varied interests efficiently and effectively.

Brand communication is the appropriate platform for community reputation management. Branding for public communities builds on the experiences and methods of corporate and product branding. However, it also calls for attention to the peculiarities and challenges of community reputation management. Professional community branding links the uncertainty of public life to a clear, comprehensible strategy that primarily attempts to influence the expressive dimension. Unlike a corporate reputation, this kind of reputation has its roots in diverse, interconnected milieus. It is only authentic if it can deliver on its promises in a complex network of infrastructure, economy, politics, education, culture and population.

Practical rules for community reputation management

1. "Task forces spell early death for every strategy."

Of course, those responsible in a city or a country have to be involved. The initiative for sustainable reputation management must come from them. But this cannot hide the fact that the development of a strategy is not a matter for direct democracy.

2. "The citizens and electorate are not the core target audience of the communications strategy."

There is little to be gained from reinforcing the way the community sees itself. The members of a community perceive their home from a fundamentally different perspective than tourists and investors, students or employers. The balancing act between internal acceptance and international success can only be mastered if reputation strategy is based on real life and simultaneously delivers a visionary picture of the future.

3. "The hard facts must be correct."

Rankings are the hard currency. Be it the availability of childcare, unemployment rates, levels of education and literacy or infrastructure (the list goes on): everything is measured against international competition.

4. "The long-term development options must be understood."

A carefully considered public sector communication strategy is based on the decision-maker's agenda and communicates in a way that perfectly matches long-term perspectives. It anticipates future impulses that are relevant to economic or social reputation, whether it be policies that favour investment, families or the environment, plans for building and tourism, or social and cultural engagement by prominent individuals. In this way, the (strategically communicated) implementation of political, corporate, social and cultural master plans boosts the expectations raised by communications. Promises are delivered upon and made tangible.

5. "A community reputation must be insulated from the excitements of the day."

A long-term strategy is tied to the community's political-economic agenda. However, it is largely independent of the figures responsible for running day-to-day life. This applies especially in the public arena. Community reputation strategies must be far removed from the turbulence of political and economic affairs. Otherwise every change of government or main economic sponsor would lead to disruptions, U-turns and an undoing of previous work.

6. "The need for self-portrayal is an indispensable fuel."

Everybody likes to be part of a successful plan. And a community's public sector is shaped primarily by high-profile personalities. If the communication is successfully designed so that it is actively and frequently used by multipliers, an important tactical goal will have been achieved.

EU accession: Turkey's reputation on its journey towards EU membership

Interview with

Arzuhan Doğan Yalçındağ and Julia Schankin

"[...] in the old days one could win over an empire by marrying, today you can win over peoples by a leading article"[1]

The term "national public relations" appeared for the first time in 1978 in the context of the Israeli-Palestinian conflicts. But in the last 10 years, countries and regions have increasingly realised that reputation is just as important to them as it is to corporations. Countries also have come to realise that if reputation matters to them, it needs to be managed.

Reputation management has indeed become a burning issue for an increasing number of states and regions all over the world. This is due, firstly, to the increasing awareness that a good reputation attracts investors, tourists and 'high potentials' just as it eases access to capital and aids negotiations. Secondly, crises such as the tax scandal in Liechtenstein or the collapse of US investment banks have strikingly demonstrated how countries can be brought into disrepute by their political or economic subsystems. Against this background, governments are increasingly confronted with the fact that they must act as brand or reputation managers for their countries.

This is even truer when a country occupies a particularly prominent position on the international stage, as do the candidate countries for the European Union. Apart from having to meet basic standards with regard to their economic, financial and legal systems before they can join the EU, accession candidates are subject to intense public scrutiny in Europe. This presents great challenges, but also holds great potential,

---

[1] Kunczik M (1990) Images of nations and international public relations. The Media and Communication Department of the Friedrich Ebert Stiftung, Bonn

J. Klewes, R. Wreschniok (eds.), *Reputation Capital*, DOI 10.1007/978-3-642-01630-1_18,
© Springer-Verlag Berlin Heidelberg 2009

which can be harnessed for pinpointed, effective reputation management.

Turkey, whose candidature for the European Union has indeed catapulted the country into the centre of media attention, has managed particularly skilfully to use this unique situation to its advantage. Turkey's reputation management can therefore serve as a case study for examining the mechanisms and success factors of modern country reputation management.

The following discussion is between the editors and Arzuhan Doğan Yalçındağ, President of the Turkish Industrialists' and Businessmen's Association (TUSIAD) and Julia Schankin, specialist for reputation management at the European Centre for Reputation Studies (ECRS), and explores the notion of country reputation management. It gives insights into a campaign that bears all the hallmarks of successful reputation management, and that can thus be regarded as a yardstick for country reputation management.

Editors: First of all, how exactly does country reputation management work?

Julia Schankin (J.S.): As Mark Eisenegger has shown, reputation management in general is a question of three aspects, or dimensions, of reputation: the functional, the social and the expressive dimensions. And, as Eisenegger points out, this applies not only to companies and organisations, but also to individuals and states. This means: just like companies, countries must prove their qualifications and success – in other words, their functional reputation. For countries, this means demonstrating political power and economic success. You can see how a country's reputation can be damaged when these are neglected by looking at the position of the USA in recent years: the financial crisis has led to a worldwide critique of US capitalism, while George W. Bush's political decisions have substantially harmed America's political leadership in the world.

Editors: Can you give an example for the social dimension of a country's reputation: that is, its fulfilment of social and ethical expectations?

J.S.: You can also look to the USA to see the importance of the social dimension for a country's reputation: the scandals of Abu Ghraib and

Guantánamo discredited the United States as an incarnation of Western values such as liberty, democracy and human rights, and led to a loss of reputation compared to the Clinton era. Now, a country's reputation is also based on those parts of its identity that set it apart from other countries – or, the expressive dimension of reputation. Here, the countryside and the climatic conditions play as much of a role as the arts, traditions, cuisine, architecture and way of life of the country's people. Spain is often cited as an example for especially successful nation branding. It developed strong imagery around Joan Miró's sun symbol, and the campaign featured industrial facilities as well as cultural and popular facets of Spain, such as Pedro Almodóvar's films or Ibiza as a Mediterranean party island, in order to convey an attractive and unique image.

Editors: The example of Spain raises the question: how does country reputation management differ from pure image campaigning or nation branding?

J.S.: Country reputation management goes beyond pure image campaigning. Images are generally understood as simplified and typified conceptions of persons, organisations etc. that are mainly affective and emotional in nature. Reputation, however, consists of complex judgements that always have a normative component. Therefore, country reputation management isn't about generating ideal and to some extent random images. It is about demonstrating how the country manages to first fulfil and then shape the expectations of key stakeholder groups with respect to competence, integrity and attractiveness. Country reputation management – and this is its main challenge – must always be based on comprehensible and verifiable facts. Thus it massively depends on the actions of the state and the different actors within it.

Further, while country image campaigns seek to draw attention to the country's attractiveness, with reputation management, the focus is more on increasing trust and the intensity of relations. So, whereas image campaigning might be a sufficient short term strategy in the tourism sector, it certainly is not in political contexts such as the EU accession process. This is also why in a reputation management process, the demonstration of competence (functional reputation) and integrity (social reputation) must, as much as possible, come before attractiveness, as these are the main drivers for trust.[2]

---

[2] See Eisenegger (pp. 11-22 in this volume) for more details and a development of this point.

Editors: So, would you say that reputation management for countries and cities is functioning nearly the same way?

J.S.: There is one crucial difference between corporate and country reputation management: Unlike corporations, countries aren't organised hierarchically, but rather as a network structure. Therefore, it is impossible to align and control all messages circulating about a country. Once this is acknowledged, country reputation managers should rather focus on effectively organising communication between key actors, opinion leaders and stakeholders and involving them in a country reputation management process. Country reputation management needs a driving force and a strategic vision, but it just as well requires the support of key representatives of the political, economic, social and cultural spheres within the country.

Editors: After this introduction, could you, Mrs. Doğan Yalçındağ, please roughly describe your campaign and outline what objectives were set up to increase Turkey's reputation?

Arzuhan Doğan Yalçındağ (A.D.Y.): The starting point is Turkey of today: largest and fastest emerging market in and around Europe. A country with a developed industry that achieves 90% of its exports. A democracy that is in the process of accession to the EU. A rapidly developing information society. Countries at the crossroads of energy supply routes of Europe. A young, entrepreneurial and innovative society. In fact Turkey is determined to meet the criteria of membership to the EU. By then, as many European leaders, business organizations, NGO reports and academic research highlight, Turkey will be a great asset for Europe. Turkey will bring Europe the critical size and added value to better meet the challenges of the 21st century.

There is no doubt that in addition to the existing intergovernmental methods of diplomacy and technical process of membership negotiations, the dialogue between the citizens of the EU countries and Turkish people supported by comprehensive communication strategies play an essential role. In this respect the "reputation management" becomes a key factor, especially for a country on which the European public has so many misperceptions and significant deficit of information.

TÜSIAD, The Turkish Industry & Business Association aims to contribute on its side to the fulfillment of this deficit. We established in 2005 International Communication Committee with the support of our member companies. The committee agreed upon explaining the importance of Turkey's EU membership to both EU and Turkish public. Turkey's industrial, creative and innovative economy and society are the focal points of our action plans.

Editors: Did existing images, clichés and prejudices about Turkey play a role in defining these objectives?

A.D.Y.: Well, certainly, eliminating prejudices was a key objective for us. So, we wanted to focus on providing information instead of images or ideals. We wanted to demonstrate the 'modern' and 'European' aspects of Turkey and the Turkish people. For instance, in early 2006, we kicked off a DHL/Piyale Madra campaign. The goal of the campaign, implemented with DHL Express – which has played a leading role in the development of the transportation and logistics sector in Turkey – was to change the image of Turks in the minds of Europeans. In the course of the campaign, works by renowned Turkish caricaturist Piyale Madra were sent to over 300,000 foreigners across the globe on DHL Express packages. The reaction to this campaign was phenomenal. Turks in Europe are typically considered belligerent and opinionated. However, with this campaign, we managed to demonstrate to Europe that Turkish and European people in fact share a very similar sense of humour.

Editors: What role did the media play in your campaign?

A.D.Y.: Of course, we aimed for substantial coverage in the European media to spread the message and achieve positive visibility throughout Europe. Therefore, we did quite intensive media work. At the same time, from a reputation management perspective, the trustworthiness of the speaker is central, too. With this in mind, another of our objectives was to become an important contact point to which European media could turn on matters relating to Turkey. For this, the first pillar of our communications strategy between 2005 and 2007, various press trips were organised in France, Germany, and the wider EU, financed by our members' contributions. Opinion leaders, business people, and members of the press in these countries were invited to Turkey, meetings arranged with them in their home countries, and various activities organized to establish communication with the target audience in order to strengthen the perception of Turkey.

Editors: Speaking of opinion leaders – they are a necessary part of every reputation management campaign. How was this reflected in your campaign?

A.D.Y.: Well, we involved important opinion leaders, such as prominent politicians and business leaders, in different stages of the campaign. However, one important measure in relation to this was a brochure titled "Why Turkey belongs to Europe", which we distributed to key European media. The brochure features prominent representatives of leading German companies, such as Roland Berger, Dr. Arend Oetker and Prof. Dr. Norbert Walter, chief economist at Deutsche Bank, as well as German politicians with and without Turkish backgrounds. They are pictured in their professional environment, looking openly and directly at the reader. A quote appears next to each person, stressing different aspects of his or her relationship with Turkey and expressing a range of Turkey's strengths. This brochure combined several of our objectives: namely, conveying the message of Turkey's potential as a strong economic and political partner, countering prejudices and lending weight to our messages by having them voiced through influential people.

J.S.: I think this brochure illustrates well what a successful reputation management campaign can look like, and what factors should be considered. Not only does the content focus mainly on economic and political aspects, which are some of the main drivers for reputation, but it uses the prominence of the speakers to reinforce this proof of competence. As mentioned earlier, reputation is built – among other things – through stable relations with, and positive statements by, third parties. The more stable the relations are, the more trustworthy the third parties appear. And the better they are established as opinion leaders in their field, the stronger their value is for reputation-building processes. In fact, the more independent an opinion leader is or seems, the more authentic his or her message. By having the message spoken by widely respected business people and politicians from Germany – note: not Turkey –, such as Franz Müntefering, Günter Verheugen, Roland Berger and Dr. Oetker, TÜSIAD adds authority to its messages. In short, the readers trust Turkey, because they trust the judgment of these reputation bearers. The trustworthiness of their messages was further enhanced by distributing the brochure to key German media, such the Frankfurter Allgemeine Zeitung (FAZ), which in itself is a reputation bearer that inspires trust.

Editors: Mrs. Doğan Yalçındağ, stable relationships with key opinion leaders are essential for efficient reputation management as they convey and multiply the message in the relevant communication channels. Furthermore, they make it possible to check reputation management measures against concrete experiences. Can you expand on how you strengthened relationships with key opinion leaders in Europe?

A.D.Y.: Let me underline again that, as regards our communications strategy, the heart of our mission is reforming Turkey's negative image in European public opinion and, more importantly, establishing a more receptive climate for Turkey's accession to the EU in the lukewarm EU member states. We firmly believe that the message we convey to target groups should try to demonstrate the modern and industrial character of Turkey and the compatibility of Turks and European values, and increase Turkey's visibility in European countries where the perception of Turkey is negative. Hence, after the major success of the FAZ insert just mentioned in enhancing the perception of Turkey in Germany, we published another one-page advert in the FAZ in May 2008, promoting Turkish women's high participation in the work force. Similarly, in order to establish consistency and continuity in our campaigns and to be able to work efficiently in local media, we will be working closely with local PR agencies in Germany and in France in 2009.

Editors: Mrs. Doğan Yalçındağ, in our experience, it is advisable to first measure your reputation in relevant stakeholder groups and then work on the specific topics that have been identified as reputation drivers. This seems easier for a company, which in general knows its key stakeholder groups, than for a country. How did you approach this?

A.D.Y.: TÜSIAD conducted surveys with foreign businesspeople from Italy, England, France, Germany and Austria to determine the specific messages to be conveyed, such as modern life in Turkey, our closeness to European values. We then assessed the guidelines set out in the Turkey Promotion Council Report, compiled prior to our activities, together with other survey results. From there, we identified economics, politics, the EU membership process, and socio-cultural factors (that is, the human factor, women, art) as target aspects. Taking into account various perceptions of

Turkey in Europe, we agreed to adopt as the main message "Turkey is an industrial country that is growing stronger every day".

That said, one of the challenges in this whole process was indeed defining the target audiences. It was decided that France, Germany and Brussels, being at the centre of decision-making in the EU, would be focused on primarily for the accession process to the European Union. We focused mostly on the decision-making elite in these places. Between 2005 and 2007 we mostly targeted printed media with inserts and op-eds.

J.S.: The fact that TÜSIAD conducted interviews with key target groups before developing their messages certainly seems to me to be one of the key success factors in this campaign – precisely because reputation management is fundamentally about the management of stakeholder expectations. Therefore, an effective campaign needs dialogue and trustful relations with important stakeholders. That means: instead of developing messages in the ivory tower, we have to begin by listening to the expectations of key stakeholder groups. Based on these findings, in other words the reputation drivers, you can develop a strategy that reconciles the public expectations with the objectives of the company or institution.

Editors: Indeed, in international relations, dialogue is known to be the most important trust-building measure. In this sense, a solid reputation is always based on a relationship of trust. So, besides the initial survey, what role did dialogue play as a trust-building measure in your campaign?

A.D.Y.: Thank you for mentioning this – yes, from the beginning, dialogue has played a key role in our campaign. TÜSIAD Country Communication activities have been based on a concept that appears as the Third Pillar in the European Commission Recommendation of October 2004, calling for 'Civil Society Dialogue between the EU and Candidate Countries'. With this measure, the Commission wanted to avoid the problem that arose during the previous EU enlargement: that is, citizens being neither sufficiently informed nor prepared. So since 2005, various projects were undertaken in France, Germany, and Brussels that targeted precisely dialogue and transparency. Opinion leaders, business people, and members of the press in these countries were invited to Turkey, meetings arranged with them in their country, and various activities organized to establish communication with the target audience in order to change the perception of Turkey in a positive direction. We firmly believe that we were able through these conferences and seminars to establish our position as a valuable and accredited reference point to consult on matters relating to Turkey.

Editors: Can you give us some concrete examples of these dialogue measures?

A.D.Y.: In the second half of 2006, we participated in several seminars and conferences in Brussels, London and Paris, such as "Turkey and Europe: The Debate in the Public Opinions in France, Germany, and Turkey", a seminar with the French Institute of International Relations, "Political Situation in Turkey: Illusions and Real Issues", a seminar with the European House (La Maison de l'Europe), Chatham House Turkey Policy Group and "Turkey's Economic Outlook: Structural Changes, Perspectives in the Energy Sector", a seminar with the Centre d'Etudes Prospectives et d'Informations Internationales (CEPII), in order to explain thoroughly Turkey's economic, social and cultural assets. Our flagship measure, however, was "Turkey Week", which was organized to mark the first anniversary of the opening of accession negotiations with the EU, October 3-5, 2006 in Brussels, Paris, and Berlin respectively. The aim of this three-day event in three cities was to eliminate existing prejudices in public opinion in France, Germany and Brussels, which considerably influence Turkey's membership process for the European Union, and to present Turkey in Europe in the best possible way.

Editors: What role did opinion leaders and the media play in this event?

A.D.Y.: Certainly an important role! Turkey Week was accompanied by conferences, press conferences, exhibitions and concerts, press bulletins and various printed materials. Furthermore, we welcomed prominent political leaders of Turkey, top executives of the leading institutions in relevant countries and TÜSIAD members. Due to this extensive relational work, we managed to successfully put Turkey on the agenda in Brussels, Paris, and Berlin. It really represented a turning point in eliminating existing prejudices in French, German, and Belgian public opinion, which considerably influence Turkey's membership process for the European Union, and presenting Turkey in Europe in the best possible way. It was our key communications activity, with exhibitions, classic music concerts and a series of seminars on political and economic topics.

And let me highlight once more our focus on strong relations with opinion leaders: besides this flagship event, the TÜSIAD Country Communication Committee and TÜSIAD members held various meetings from 2005 to 2007 with government representatives, public administrators and EU officials in France and Germany. The aim here was to discuss with them the topics on the agenda, inform them on the developments in Turkey, and strengthen relations.

J.S.: Let me pick up on one aspect you mentioned before, namely prejudices and their impact on public opinion. This touches on an extremely important aspect of reputation management: issues monitoring. More and more corporations regularly screen the media for potentially critical or potentially positive issues that might subsequently impact on their reputation. In case of country reputation management, this is an ambitious task, since unlike corporate messages, the voices, opinions and events in a democratic country can (and should) never be controlled, nor are they readily predictable. However, knowledge about prejudices or critical public opinions in, let's say Austria regarding Turkey, is essential not only for developing targeted intercultural reputation management measures, but also for keeping track of changing expectations. Also, in my opinion, the messages of a reputation management campaign should constantly be checked – and adapted if needed – to take account of important political, economic and social events such as terrorist attacks, economic or political crises, upheavals etc.

A.D.Y.: Yes, we are absolutely aware of this and therefore our campaign was continuously accompanied by an issues monitoring process. Coverage on Turkey in the European press was monitored for five months before and nine months after we began our work in 2006. This not only showed us the results of our work, but also threw light on which issues impacted most on European countries regarding Turkey. Furthermore, given the relatively long monitoring period, we could observe topic careers. For example, in the June 2006 – March 2007 period, the issue of energy emerged as the second most mentioned issue in both France and Germany.

Among the countries examined, Germany was the one that covered Turkey most in the press, and the positive articles generally related to energy, economic growth, and Turkish businesses in Germany. The negative reports, on the other hand, mostly concentrated on the issues of EU membership, religion, Armenian genocide, legal matters, and reforms. From a quantitative point of view, EU membership was the most important issue in relation to Turkey. The Cyprus/Greece issue became considerably more prominent in the last nine months of the monitoring period, and the issue of religion maintained its place among the top four.

Interestingly, the issues didn't differ much between Germany and the other European countries. Examining just the general tone of the reports reveals that EU member states, and Austria especially, follow the same tendency as Germany, while the general tone of reports in United Kingdom and Spain was closer to those from France in their negativity.

J.S.: What is very interesting here is that all the issues that were mentioned positively relate to the functional dimension of reputation. The negative press coverage concentrated rather on issues to do with moral concepts and values, as shown by the issues of religion and the Armenian genocide. So there seems to be a strong need to discuss those normative concepts in the Western media. In my opinion, the negative press also suggests that dialogue and exchange between Turkey and EU member states on cultural and religious issues must by all means be continued. While these are issues that may go beyond the competence of TÜSIAD as a representative organisation for Turkish industry and businesses, the monitoring results might still be of great value for other Turkish authorities wishing to join the reputation management initiative with a stronger focus on social reputation. However, since you mentioned before that you have tackled prejudices and social developments in seminars and conferences, I would be interested to know to what extent you derived concrete measures from your issues monitoring.

A.D.Y.: After carefully analyzing the results of our previously organized conferences and seminars, we concluded that we needed a platform where each participant is free to express their opinion on critical matters concerning Turkey. Only in this way could we deal with sensitive issues in European countries where opinion polls show negative or poor judgments on Turkey. With this in mind, we laid the foundations for L'Institut du Bosphore in Paris, and the European Integration Institute in Berlin, to effectively and accurately promote our message of a modern and European Turkey to French and German intelligentsia as well as to the general public. A related PR campaign, to be run in parallel with the inauguration of the institutes, will be launched in national and regional media.

Editors: Finally, has news coverage given you insights as to the results of your campaign?

A.D.Y.: Our activities have given us access to a high number of media representatives, opinion leaders and business people and increased the country's visibility in the media. Indeed, during the last nine months of the campaign, that is from June 2006 to March 2007, we observed that coverage on Turkey increased more than threefold in France and Germany compared to the first five months. That in itself can be regarded as a success. As for qualitative analysis, we saw that the number of both positive and negative article headlines increased while the number of neutral headlines declined. The rate of increase in positive headings in the German press was higher, albeit slightly, than that of negative headings. The same effect was noticed in the other European countries. However, as we have seen before, the negative headings mainly dealt with questions of religion and moral/human rights issues. Issues relating to economic aspects were again seen in a positive light – which I consider a consequence of our activities. However, the fact that the issue of EU membership was mainly perceived in a negative way shows that there is still much to do, and the task here goes far beyond reputation management.

J.S.: This is in fact a crucial point, as it is more important how a country behaves than how it communicates. So, if reforms have not been adequately rolled out, you can't expect any positive press. The same is true for issues such as legal matters and even more so for such a big issue as EU membership. Country reputation management, unlike corporate reputation management, is always subject to a multitude of elements that can be neither controlled nor managed. If you're embarking on a country reputation management process, you're better off acknowledging these boundaries. I would even go further: if you want to see the future challenges for corporate reputation management, look now at country reputation management. You see, corporate reputation is becoming less and less controllable, too. What country reputation management can do, however, is to identify those areas in which the country is particularly successful. Based on that, key messages can be formulated, relevant audiences and stakeholders defined and measures to communicate these aspects to a wider public developed. And of course, as already stated, to involve and orchestrate multiple alliances and stakeholder groups to get the messages about the country across.

In my view, TÜSIAD's Country Communication Committee ran a campaign that joined forces with different opinion leaders, focused on the strengths of Turkey and addressed critical issues without claiming to do justice to every expectation in the European public sphere. And in this sense, TÜSIAD's efforts can be considered exemplary in the field of country reputation management.

A.D.Y.: Indeed, country image, with its many aspects, is a phenomenon too large to be managed by any single organisation alone. A country image can only be managed and benefits for all stakeholders only created when the state, private sector, non-governmental organisations and academic circles work together. And here, it is extremely important for successful country image management that the state assumes leadership, ensures the coordination of efforts that are underway and makes available the resources required.

Editors: In this case the taxpayer would have to pay for reputation management. How would you justify that?

A.D.Y.: As the world becomes more and more interconnected and interdependent, reputation becomes a key factor for countries to affirm their role and position within this web of relations. As mentioned earlier, a positive and stable reputation is required to attract investors, tourists, 'high potentials' etc. Therefore, reputation management is in the public interest. Besides, the media is an important battleground in the global competition for economic power, cultural attractiveness and scientific prominence. It would be fatal for a country not to invest in communications. That said, communications must of course be based on concrete action. Regarding the Turkish accession process, we all have to explain more clearly to the European public that Turkey will become a member only when two basic conditions are met. First, Turkey must be ready. It must create no additional problems for the EU, but bring significant benefits. Second, the EU must be ready. It must have completed its internal reform and have gained more public confidence due to better economic performance. In the end, the winners will be all European citizens – including the Turks.

Editors: Mrs. Doğan Yalçındağ and Mrs. Schankin – thank you very much for this discussion!

References

Christelis D (2006) Country reputation management. Identifying the drivers of South Africa's reputation in German media. University of Stellenbosch

Eisenegger M (2005) Reputation in der Mediengesellschaft – Konstitution, Issues Monitoring, Issues Management. VS Verlag für Sozialwissenschaften, Wiesbaden

Ermen, D (2004) A Framework for a Destination Reputation Management Process: a case study of three destinations <http://eprints.otago.ac.nz/561/1/David_Ermen.pdf>

Kunczik M (1990) Images of nations and international public relations. The Media and Communication Department of Friedrich Ebert Stiftung, Bonn

Pantelica (Serbanica), C (2008) Corporate Reputation in Romanian Socio-Economic Context. <http://steconomice.uoradea.ro/anale/en_volum-2008-economy-and-business-administration.html>

Risen C (2005) Re-branding America. Marketing Gurus think they can help reposition the United States – and save American foreign policy. <http://www.boston.com/news/globe/ideas/articles/2005/03/13/re_branding_america/> viewed on 04 January 2009

Further information on Turkey Week: Turkey@Europe_Week

Consistency: a proven reputation strategy. How companies can optimise their message

Joachim Klewes

Good news is not necessarily good for each group of stakeholders. And a company's reputation is a highly fragile phenomenon; one which can also be seen very differently depending on the stakeholder's perspective. The messages that a company's top management and communication teams send out, both internally and externally, therefore require a finely tuned balance. Some experts believe that a company should be able to adapt itself, chameleon-like, to a wide variety of expectations. However, this presents the risk of distancing the company too far from its own identity. The wide range of possible reactions to the same set of messages, depending on the stakeholder group, is demonstrated in an experiment the results of which are evaluated in this article.

Corporate Messaging – A challenge similar to herding cats?

A sunny day in late autumn in the communications department of a EURO-STOXX group. John Brown (as we shall call the Head of Communications) is holding in his hand a twenty page evaluation of media feedback for the current year. By the end of October, the company has sent out a total of 187 press releases – not including about 120 replies to queries from journalists and five exclusive interviews with the CEO. And not to mention contact between the press and the business units, or subsidiaries active in the individual markets, all of which completely bypassed Brown's team. Little wonder that the pie chart depicting the company's media image that he has in front of him shows more than twenty segments in every colour of the rainbow – that is how widely diverse and varied the company's messages come across in the media. It is also little wonder that CEO DelaFitte has reproached him once again for not having the company's reputation management under control…

J. Klewes, R. Wreschniok (eds.), *Reputation Capital*, DOI 10.1007/978-3-642-01630-1_19,
© Springer-Verlag Berlin Heidelberg 2009

As in our – only slightly fictionalised – example, the challenges facing "messaging", that is, the systematic shaping and positioning of a company's messages, are daunting. This is particularly true for large corporate groups active in various business areas. Whenever it comes to focussing clear messages for specific company stakeholders, we have to reckon with alienating other stakeholders, or at least confusing them. An example from Europe's industrial heartland, Germany, is provided by the diffuse messages put out in the run-up to Commerzbank's acquisition of Dresdner Bank in late August 2008:

One and the same message that not only Commerzbank but also the China Development Bank was showing an interest in the suffering Allianz insurance group's bank affiliate was received in completely different ways by their four main stakeholder markets:

- Financial market: fantasies about a bidding contest;

- (Private) customer market: possible uncertainty about the future of the bank's branches;

- Employee market: relief about the possibility that mass dismissals could now be avoided;

- Opinion leader market (politics, NGOs, etc.): uncertainty about the possible takeover of a major German bank by a foreign investor (and interestingly finally a national solution materialised).

With this type of ongoing message dynamic, every head of communications is faced almost daily with the challenge of balancing the timing and content of various rumours, expectations and queries.

Reputation – A complex concept

More fundamental than this, however, is the dilemma that a company's reputation is almost always interpreted differently by its individual stakeholder markets. "Good reputation" as a core, intangible company resource has been the subject of numerous research projects and investigations by management consultants for at least a decade; but the problem is that reputation is not a homogeneous object.

There has been no shortage of attempts to differentiate the concept of reputation. Gary Davies, professor at the Manchester Business School, heads a qualified academic team specialising in reputation research. He uses the metaphor of a company personality[1] in order to distinguish between the various reputation-forming "character traits" of an organisation.

In his reputation monitor, Manfred Schwaiger, professor at the LMU in Munich and board member of the non-profit European Center for Reputation Studies, has been using what is probably the most differentiated model[2] for numerous large European companies for many years: Extracting from more than twenty reputation factors, he isolates three specific items each as key indicators for "sympathy" and "expertise", the bipolar components of a company's reputation. This allows him to act in a far more precise manner than early protagonists in reputation measurement, such as Fombrun or the studies by Fortune magazine.

Largely independently of the Anglo-Saxon mainstream of reputation research (whilst simultaneously maintaining precision), the authors Gaillard, Louisot and Rayner present reputation as a construct, consisting of the organisation, the message to stakeholders and the expectations of the stakeholders. These elements are perpetually in alternating reciprocal relationships with one another in a delicate balance that reacts easily to shocks and which therefore has to be controlled with the greatest of care.[3]

The approach put forward by Carola Hillenbrand and Kevin Money at the Henley Business School in the UK a mere three years ago provides a useful conceptual integration of a variety of individual reputation concepts. They differentiate between a strategic and a personal level of reputation. On each of these levels, we can distinguish between *reputation-forming activities*, the *actual reputation* (understood as an asset), and the *effects of reputation* – a useful matrix with six fields, in which numerous individual phenomena, and measuring and management approaches can be classified.

---

[1] See also the article by Davies G, Chun R (2009) The Leader's Role in Managing Reputation in this book, pp. 311-323.

[2] See also the article by Schwaiger M, Raithel S and Schloderer M (2009) How Reputation Influences Stakeholder Behavior in this book, pp. 39-55.

[3] See also the article by Gaultier-Gaillard, Louisot JP, Rayner J (2009) Managing Reputational Risk – A Cindynic Approach in this book, pp. 115-141.

Table 1. Reputation matrix

Level	Value-generating (reputation-forming) activities	Intangible company values (reputation facets)	Effect of reputation (market-related values)
Strategic level: concepts such as "company identity" or "reputation quotient"	e.g. confidence building measures in personnel development in the employee market	e.g. corporate culture	e.g. brand loyalty
Individual (identity) level	e.g. observation, experience, reception	e.g. knowledge, attitudes to the company	e.g. purchasing or patronage behaviour

Source: Money and Hillenbrand 2006

Observing the reputation building process – The Reputation Experiment

It is possible to specify a useful stakeholder differentiation in all of these fields. A good example of this would be a reputation experiment carried out by the author at the Freie Universität in Berlin. This experiment used the operationalisation of reputation developed by Schütz and Schwaiger (Schütz and Schwaiger 2007) and focussed on the financial market's stakeholder perspective.

The investigation centred on three leading energy suppliers in Germany. E.ON, RWE, Vattenfall[4] – almost all every Germans purchase their household energy either directly or indirectly from these companies. Out of a large, incentivised online sample,[5] two groups were identified with comparable structures and 100 test subjects each, all of whom specified a strong degree of familiarity with the subject of stocks and shares and who were all aware of the companies in question (preselection).[5] In April 2008, the two groups were initially asked to provide their assessment of the three companies' reputations.

In light of trends in media reporting at that point in time, the rather negative overall assessment of the three companies' reputations was hardly surprising. The public's critical view of the three energy giants was also

---

[4] None of these companies commissioned the study.

[5] The subjects received payment for each interview from the institute commissioned to carry out the study.

confirmed by data from the Brand Index,[6] which is representative of the German population at large and was used for control purposes. However, the participants were not only asked about the reputation of the individual companies: Each participant had to distribute a fictional investment of €10,000 across the three companies; in other words, they had to act in the stakeholder role of investor. Almost two weeks later, the investigation was repeated.[7] This time, however, half of those questioned (the "experimental group") were presented with news reports that were expected to have a positive or negative (or neutral) effect on investment decisions.[8] In this way, different messages from the company were simulated, which then in fact resulted in different changes to the replies from the experimental group. As expected, these changes did not occur in the control group, who were not exposed to the "reputation stimulus".

So what was the effect of the various messages? First of all, it is very interesting that negative messages showed a significant influence on the assessment of reputation – incidentally, far more markedly for women than for men. "Negative messages" here refers to news reports that would tend to produce unfavourable effects from the point of view of the capital market. The simulated (!) bad news, such as reports concerning failed investments or demonstrations against the company, led directly to a collapse of good reputation. In contrast to this, neither explicitly positive (top marks from the capital market perspective) news reports, nor more neutral news led to any noticeable change. This confirmed both the findings of many experienced reputation experts, which show that building up a good reputation is *not only* achieved by PR-induced messages (as opposed to the company's actual behaviour) and certainly not with one-off actions (as opposed to years of work), and the popular perception that a reputation can be ruined in moments.

Surprisingly, "good news" had a far greater (and significant) effect on the subjects' simulated investment behaviour. This demonstrated that not only negatively formulated messages and news (from a financial market perspective) had a significant effect (sale of stock/collapse in stock price), but that the reverse was also true (purchasing stock/price advances). When it comes to a person's own interests, a company's good reputation is possibly of secondary importance – which might contradict the information that the same people would provide if asked explicitly.

---

[6] For a good overview, see http://www.brandindex.de/ (Accessed 19.09.2008)

[7] External factors that could modify the participants' behaviour, such as the company's actual share price trend and developments on the DAX index, were taken into account.

[8] A later section of the questionnaire checked that the test subjects in fact understood that this was the intention of the stimulus.

The study was not confined to simulating the investor's stakeholder perspective. A further segment of the questionnaire dealt with the participants' willingness to switch energy suppliers – an option that has been discussed extensively in European media and which more than three quarters of those questioned had seriously considered. Each participant in the study had the option of deciding whether he or she would switch to one of the three companies in the event of unchanged or cheaper energy rates.

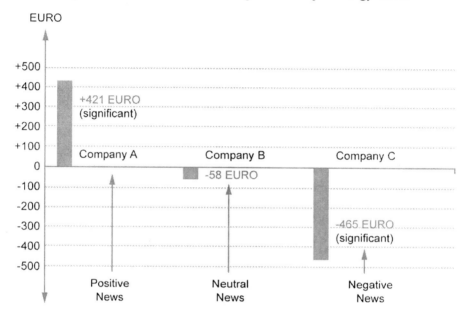

Average change in investment behaviour in consequence of different news reports (Experimental group, N = 96, April 2008)

Fig. 1. Change on average

Once again, the set of messages to which the experimental group was exposed had significant effects – albeit in unexpected ways. Neither the positively (from the capital market perspective) nor the negatively phrased messages increased the willingness of participants to change companies – in stark contrast to the neutral, seemingly harmless messages. These messages obviously accentuated the dimensions that could make a switch attractive from the customers' stakeholder perspective, such as a certain "proximity".

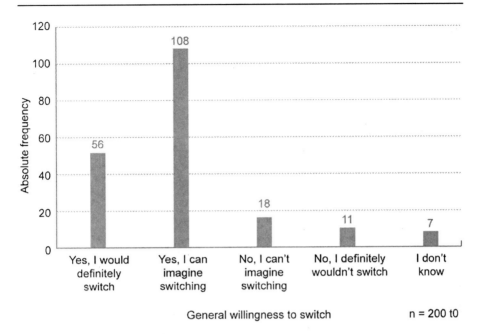

Fig. 2. Willingness for change

The results are clear: when the study began, about three quarters of the respondents could at least imagine switching energy providers. In the second stage of the experiment, however, there was a clear change in the experimental group. Compared to the control group, willingness to switch had increased significantly, particularly in the case where participants were exposed to messages that were neutral from a capital market perspective but which accentuated "proximity". Female participants in the online experiment showed a more marked willingness to change energy suppliers.

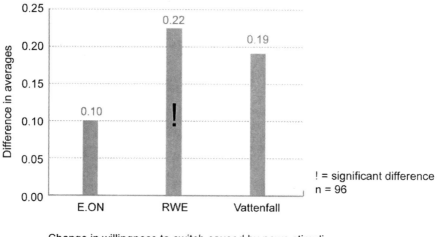

Change in willingness to switch caused by news stimuli
in the experimental group (t1-t0)

Fig. 3. Change of willingness

The experiment therefore provides clear indications of how different messages with a reputational effect incentive are received by a stakeholder group – bearing in mind that a single person can, of course, have various stakeholder expectations simultaneously.

Strategies for successful corporate messaging

But which strategies can a company use in order to balance its messages to the extent that the positive effects on one of the stakeholder groups do not have a disproportionately damaging effect on its reputation with other stakeholders? As an example, let us take a look at Porsche, the automobile manufacturer with outstanding international success. In recent years, they have managed to balance out the positive messages about exorbitantly high profits and good share prices in such a way that customers do not consider the fast sports cars to be excessively overpriced and switch over to competitor products.

In theory, it should be possible – in line with the classic method taught in business management – to translate the various effects on reputation in the different stakeholder groups into a standardised "currency". The effects could, for example, be expressed as a financial parameter which also has to be projected onto a common timepoint. However: the necessary procedures are not yet available for this. Besides, under the real circumstances facing a company it is not about maximising a particular individual value, instead, it is almost always about achieving a balance – related to force – between various internal and external interests; that is, "negotiating" between various organisational units and their protagonists, as well as external forces.

In practical business situations, at least six pragmatic strategies have emerged for solving the "chameleon problem", in other words, ideally adapting to differing stakeholder expectations in a company's reputation management. Some of these strategies are used independently, some in combination.

Strategy 1: Integration using umbrella messages

In this strategy, the messages that are relevant to the various stakeholders are presented unsaid beneath a guiding theme with which they are all equally compatible. The international automobile company mentioned above, Porsche, has provided prime examples of this in recent years. Here, umbrella metaphors such as "performance", "success" or "flexibility" can be found beneath the concrete messages for the capital market, sports car customers and employees.

Strategy 2: Focussing on the CEO

A variant of the umbrella message strategy is to strongly focus messages on a single, strong personality who speaks for the company – and who embodies all the fundamental facets of the umbrella message. In his article, Gary Davies[9] examines the pros and cons of this type of reputation management, which is typically expressed through the company's CEO. A prime example of this is the charismatic head of the British-based Virgin Group, Richard Branson.

Strategy 3: Differentiating the timing of messages

Another tried and tested strategy is to decouple the timing of messages that may diverge. Listed companies often try to separate their publications concerning CSR topics – which may accentuate the company's long-term obligations – from the mandatory publication times for the capital market (such as publishing quarterly figures).

---

[9] See Davies G and Chun R on pp. 311-323 in this volume.

Strategy 4: Differentiating media

Another way is to clearly separate the channels of communication according to target groups and messages. One example of this is the international logistics group Deutsche Post World Net / DHL: Information that is relevant to the financial markets is focussed strictly – and generally using digital communication – on the corresponding specialised journalistic target groups. Where a specific customer group is concerned – an extreme example would be collectors of special edition postage stamps – the company focuses in the media on a journalistic sphere that is specialised in a particular topic, with a large proportion of freelance journalists and specialist publications.

Strategy 5: Differentiating interfaces

Today, large companies almost always provide the various stakeholders with specific contact persons. In this way, interested parties, depending on their expectations, can contact a respondent who is particularly proficient in their needs, who "speaks their language" and, ideally, is constantly available concerning various issues. Major chemical companies, for example, differentiate between spokespersons for a wide variety of media departments (business, finances, technology/innovation, etc.) and media formats (general print media, specialist journals, radio, television, online), as well as for specific subject areas (local, CSR, etc.).

Strategy 6: Organisational or sender differentiation

One of the most effective strategies for solving the chameleon problem is to differentiate senders: This strategy can always be observed where companies differentiate themselves organisationally to the extent that specific organisational units primarily deal with specific subjects and stakeholders. The subsidiaries of the branded article giant Procter & Gamble, for example, almost never express anything about higher-level strategic questions or financial performance. Conversely, almost all corporate headquarters directly forward queries from consumers or the media regarding specific regional subjects to the channels of distribution in question or to regional offices. In this way, the individual senders of company messages can develop a clear profile and more easily avoid conflicts between divergent stakeholder expectations.

By combining these strategies, large and diversified companies in particular can optimise their reputation management and ease the "chameleon problem" of conflicting reputation messages.

However: neither the established message strategies nor a combination thereof, not even strictly formulated one voice policy rules, can entirely remove the chameleon problem. The core of this problem is that every company has to act within a network of widely differing relationships. The option of not communicating with the various stakeholders at all is not one that is available. All experienced communication managers know their Watzlawick and are aware that companies are also sending out clear messages to individual stakeholders if – and particularly when – there is "radio silence".

There is a clear difference between the colour-changing reptiles and companies: in the natural world, it may well be possible to adjust perfectly to your surroundings. In the reality of business, however, company message strategies are only successful if they focus proactively on core aspects of a strategy in line with the corporate identity. Successful messages require one thing in particular from top management: a commitment to a clear course.

Autistic companies believe they can focus on one segment of this world of interrelations – on the parts that relates to financial exchange. This is not the route to lasting success. Incidentally, this lesson has been learnt the hard way by even the traditionally most silent in that normally reserved and guarded sector: retail. Even Lidl and Tengelmann, to name but two Central European retail empires, can no longer afford to keep up "zero messaging".

As always, the answer to an effective solution of the chameleon problem is apparently simple. It does not involve adjusting the company's messages to the (varied or even contradictory) stakeholder expectations. Instead, it consists of the company rediscovering its own compass for directing its messages, or developing a new one. To run with the metaphor: All companies do, of course, have something like a magnetic field, a strategy on which the managers' actions are based – ideally, this is a well thought out system with clear statements about the company's vision, mission and values. However, what these basic attitudes (some call it identity) mean for messaging in practice, is something that has to be translated into clear positions for reputation management: This means developing a compass of clear language rules for a variety of issues and stakeholders, coordinating these rules internally, implementing them and writing them down. And, if necessary, changing the company's behaviour, if there is no other way of ensuring consistent messages.

This type of message compass has one overriding advantage: it makes it possible to keep on a steady course amidst the confusion of differing expectations bombarding those at the top of the company from both inside and out. Even if the company has to keep treading on the toes of individual groups with its messages, its behaviour will be easier to predict both internally and externally. And the credibility gained makes it possible to apply its messages "more quietly", in regulated doses and – with luck – using fewer means.

References

Davies G, Chun R (2009) The Leader's Role in Managing Reputation. In: this book, pp 311-323

Gaultier-Gaillard S, Louisot JP, Rayner J (2009) Managing Reputational Risk – A Cindynic Approach. In: this book, pp 115-141

Money K, Hillenbrand C (2006) Using Reputation measurement to create value: An analysis and integration of existing measures. Journal of General Management, Vol 32 No1

Schütz T, Schwaiger M (2007) Der Einfluss der Unternehmensreputation auf Entscheidungen privater Anleger. In: Kredit & Kapital, Vol 40 pp 189-223

Schwaiger M, Raithel S, Schloderer M (2009) How Reputation Influences Stakeholder Behavior. In: this book, pp 39-55

The Agora of the 21st century: On the invention of many-to-one communication

Robert Wreschniok

One-to-many communication, in which the sender addresses a number of target groups, has become a central feature of public communication in business, politics and society. However, although this form of 'one-way communication' clearly dominates the way the communication with broad audiences is organised, it does not always contribute to effective reputation management. On the contrary, it can actually hinder it. With reference to the Agora, the public-assembly space in the ancient city-state of Athens, one can outline a completely new communications model that only apparently is diametrically opposed to the conventional system: many-to-one dialogue. This new style of mass communication allows the concerns of millions of people to be efficiently bundled together and prioritised. This structured form of dialogue – metaphorically speaking, the Agora of the 21st century – makes it economically attractive to engage directly with large interest groups. Wherever many concerns are addressed to a single addressee, many-to-one dialogue delivers information that makes the management of (corporate) reputation easier and more efficient.

In ancient Greece, the Agora was a vast square in the centre of the city-state (or *polis*) that free citizens could use for military, judicial and political assemblies. It developed from the fifth century BC to become the most important centre of the *polis* community. Even today, it is seen as having been a central feature of the Greek city-state, and as a significant step in the development of Athenian democracy. Its open architectural design alone, with its characteristic *stoai* (or roofed colonnades), allowed citizens to converse with each other directly on a wide range of topics, and created a visual opposition between the Agora and the archaic fortress complex of the Acropolis, the established centre of power in ancient Athens.

Beneath the arcades and between the columns of the Agora, not only politics and business but also philosophy was publicly debated – that is, at-

J. Klewes, R. Wreschniok (eds.), *Reputation Capital*, DOI 10.1007/978-3-642-01630-1_20,
© Springer-Verlag Berlin Heidelberg 2009

tempts at understanding the world and humanity. There, the freedom of thought unfolded in a peaceful debate (or *agon*) characterised by an open exchange of views and arguments. Probably one of the best known visitors to the ancient Agora was Socrates. There, he developed a philosophical method of structured dialogue termed maieutics.

Through systematic questioning, Socrates pointed up logical inconsistencies in the arguments of his interlocutors, in order to lead them to knowledge. His most famous student was Plato, who practised his version of the Socratic method in dialogues at the antique Agora. Raphael's famous fresco in the Vatican, "The School of Athens" of 1510, gives us an impressive illustration of this.

Fig. 1. Raphael, The School of Athens (1510)

In the fourth century AD, this form of public and democratic exchange met its final demise (Camp 1989). With the dawn of the Middle Ages, a new system of Christian feudal states superseded the political and cultural dominance of a Mediterranean shaped by the Graeco-Roman tradition. From 500 AD on, feudal societies emerged. There was no longer any provision for 'free citizens' in the new social order and hierarchy. Nor was there any space for reviving the Agora. Rather, the opposite was true: the feudal state culminated in absolutism, a form of government in which a ruler's authority rested on a divine right to absolute power ("L'État c'est moi"), and was not subject to the political influence of other estates or their institutions.

With the historical epoch of the Enlightenment, an "aristocracy of education" gradually began to supplant the "aristocracy of birth" (Eisenegger 2003). The closed, feudal society of estates, in which birth determined the rank and reputation of its members, was replaced by today's pluralistic and open media society. In principle, modern society offers all individuals an opportunity to make a good name for themselves and to secure a reputable position in society, business or politics. This new, undreamt-of openness, however, also has seen society become increasingly complex and opaque. In view of this, a return to the Agora has been inconceivable.

During the Enlightenment, particularly in the seventeenth century in coffee houses and literary salons, there developed perhaps the ideal type of what Habermas has termed the "bourgeois public sphere" Habermas 1991), in which free citizens debated topics of general, public interest. But this form of functioning public discourse, as the pre-condition for functioning democracy, was politically unwelcome. In fact, the ruling regimes regarded them as too dangerous. Even from a technical perspective, open dialogue at this time could not reach such a wide public that all free citizens would in fact be able to participate. Instead, there was a process, which Habermas describes as a "refeudalisation of the public sphere" (Habermas 2001): a system of mass media, or one-to-many communication, was established, which again subjected public communications to particular interests. Independent debate among politically mature citizens was no longer possible.

"Onwards comrades, we have to go back"

Indeed, it seems naive, wishful thinking to desire a return to an intimate dialogue between politicians and voters, companies and customers, advisers and those who seek advice, between the famous and powerful and those who made them famous and powerful, under the arcades and between the columns of the Agora. And quixotic – mainly because the signs of the times are pointing in the opposite direction. What began in the Middle Ages with the royal town crier – who, under fanfare, announced the King's new laws, taxes, duties and pacts – has been perfected in the past 100 years: one-to-many communication shapes our image of public communications as a one-way street running from politicians to citizens, from business to consumers, but also from academia and culture to its target groups.

One-to-many communication has, through the invention of mass media, triumphed. Progressing from the printing press to the radio to today's global network of newspapers and TV broadcasters, and the omnipresence of advertising, it has become characteristic for our modern media society. Just as, around 2 500 years ago, open and direct dialogue in the Agora was characteristic in the classical *polis* for Athenian democracy.

But it is precisely the perfection of one-to-many communications that now makes it no longer part of the solution but, as will be explained below, part of the problem. It has made the reputation of companies, institutions or people one of the most fragile commodities of our time (Eisenegger/Imhof 2004).

Reputation opportunities and risks in the media society

The reputation of people in leading positions, be it in business, politics or academia, but also the reputation of companies or institutions, is produced communicatively and is therefore constantly under suspicion of being staged (Eisenegger 2003). This suspicion is reinforced millions of times each day by classical one-way communications. Whether it be billboard advertising, television spots, Internet offers or advertorials: never before has there been such a diverse and differentiated range of communications tools available for external and internal target groups. Today, there are few repositionings, product launches, corporate or political changes that are not escorted by a sophisticated communications campaign. At no point in history has more energy, money and personnel been invested in advertising, public relations, sponsoring or public affairs. Never were expectations higher regarding the effectiveness of communications for enhancing reputation or its return on investment.

But: the effectiveness of communications activities has in many cases lagged behind expectations. Never before have the employees and executives of a company felt so poorly informed. Never before have so many executive boards been forced to admit it is becoming harder and harder to communicate corporate strategies to stakeholders.

The Harvard Business Manager put the dilemma in a nutshell, citing internal communications as an example:

"Employees don't get too much, but not enough information. They are overwhelmed by the flood of e-mails, newsletters, fax newsletters and many more. What really interests people is never there anyway." (Harvard Business Manager 9/2008)

And even from the media and the public itself, the calls for more open and more transparent communications have never been louder. Wherever you look, classical one-way communications has degenerated to a kind of background noise – one that passes the real needs of target groups by.

There are three main factors responsible for this situation, illustrated here using corporate communications as an example:

1. Conventional mass media are suited to only a limited extent to transmitting corporate messages in an authentic and undistorted way. It is becoming increasingly difficult to influence directly or indirectly the choice and presentation of news (for example, by professional media relations). Given the increasing tabloidisation of the mass media, caused by pressure on publishing houses for greater circulation and commercial success, it is often not the (from the company's perspective) most important strategic message that gets the headlines, but the part of the message with the most potential for conflict or scandal.

2. There are many signs that even the influence of paid one-to-many communications – that is, buying advertising space to transmit corporate messages – is waning. People no longer want just to believe; they want to understand. Advertising does not satisfy this need, in particular because it must quickly attract attention. Also, there is a credibility problem with paid communications.

3. In the one-to-many communications model, there is also no efficient feedback loop that can record and appropriately take account of the actual needs of the addressees, whether they be clients, employees or managers. Until now, companies had to determine how the public perceives their company using market research, focus groups, or classical – and thus selective – suggestions and complaints management. Or, a company uses a cost- and personnel-intensive call centre to give the semblance of being open to dialogue. Even the time-consuming monitoring of social media, such as blogs, Internet forums and social networks yields only an imprecise and weakly structured reflection of public opinion. And even if companies start to listen: the question

remains of how to deal with the unstructured and widely spread opinions and critics out there.

More and more companies are coming to see that the Internet represents a new sphere of influence, wielding enormous influence over their company's reputation. At the same time, the means of communication currently available to companies seem inadequate. Now, a global search is underway for ways to actively manage the unstructured and uncontrolled torrent of questions, ideas and concerns issuing from the thousands of people who are speaking up online and exchanging ideas. The aim of such a process is to enable companies to identify, weight and sort the questions and concerns that really matter to stakeholders. The goal is to reshape the process of opinion formation to make it more efficient from a company's perspective.

The Agora of the 21st century

As mentioned above, at the classical Agora, the administrative centre of the *polis*, the opinions formed were mainly political. Given that, it is perhaps not really all that surprising that the first to exploit the newest means of opinion formation in the Internet are also politicians. On 3 October 2006, German Unity Day, Chancellor Angela Merkel became the first to adopt a completely new form of direct dialogue with interested citizens. With the online platform www.direktzurkanzlerin.de ("direkt zur Kanzlerin" means "straight to the Chancellor"), she can bundle and answer the questions that matter most to people in Germany. This new form of communication can also be classified as a many-to-one dialogue. The principle: the many different representatives of various interests exchange their ideas with one central contact person or with one organisation. In the case of the www.direktzurkanzlerin.de portal, any citizen can pose their questions to Angela Merkel online. The system groups the submissions by topic and, using a new process, filters out duplicate questions.

Citizens can vote on the remaining queries using the same platform. The questions or issues that are most important to them obtain a higher ranking. At the end of each week, the three top-ranking questions are answered by the Federal Press Office on behalf of the Chancellor. In this sense, the Agora of the 21st century went into operation on 3 October 2006.

Fig. 2. Homepage of www.direktzurkanzlerin.de

The democratisation of communications

Since its inception, this new form of many-to-one communication has been used more than 35 million times in Germany alone. The whole dialogue takes places publicly and can be viewed by anyone. One unique feature of the system: like in the classical age, the Agora of the 21st century only needs a moderator to steer the dialogue – and this, however, is an important difference – with any number of people. In this way, it becomes possible for the first time for individuals like Angela Merkel, but also for organisations and companies, to enter into an open dialogue with a large number of people at a reasonable cost. A feedback loop now exists for opinions, ideas, questions and concerns. An orderly system that automatically identifies, weighs and sorts issues that matter to any number of people, and thus makes active opinion formation considerably more efficient.

The rapid spread of the first many-to-one medium underscores its relevance: now, the new Agora is used not only by leading German politicians. During the primaries for the American presidential election in 2008, too, Barack Obama asked their voters for direct feedback, and so was able to give his campaigns crucial definition. Many-to-one portals have found their way into business at Deutsche Telekom or Metro Group, to organise internal communications with more then 120.000 employees or international top-executive talk in more then 48 markets.

The many-to-one principle enables a dialogue that transcends hierarchies. In this way, a CEO, for example, can make contact with the entire staff and is no longer dependent on the information of a few. The often silent majority of employees can be heard even if they limit their participation to voting on a dialogue kicked off by fellow employees. This makes it possible to identify challenges or areas that may need optimising ahead of time and pass these on to those responsible, so that changes actually can be made. It ensures that the ideas of all employees are listened to by the boss – in person, and in an orderly and structured way. The Agora of the 21st century helps, to turns 'those affected' into 'those involved' and significantly increases the speed of innovation cycles.

For classical campaigning, whether seeking votes as a political party, fundraising as an NGO, promoting a product as a company or generating motivation in internal change programmes, significant savings have been observed: only four weeks after launching many-to-one dialogue in a large international company, 278 questions had been asked and around 72,000 votes submitted. Employees read questions and answers published on the many-to-one dialogue platform more then 380,000 times – a number that can be compared with the circulation of a leading German newspaper like the *Süddeutsche Zeitung*.

Whereas previously, a large part of the investment needed to be set aside for mobilising a target group, many-to-one campaigns begin at a point where mobilisation has already begun. The 'target groups' emerge from their roles as the pure receivers of messages, becoming messengers themselves. They develop into a new, central functional group that can create economic value.

And last but not least, this form of controlled mass communication opens a new channel for dialogue with stakeholders. It enables a form of communication between senders and stakeholders that is unfiltered by the media, and that is open even in times of acute crisis. Rumour-mongering and agitation in the Internet, as it is witnessed thousands of times daily on an immeasurable number of Internet forums, blogs and discussion groups on Facebook or Youtube, gain a new outlet. The new form of dialogue will not prevent opinions from being formed on the Internet, but it will ensure that all issues relevant to opinion formation can be addressed (and actively shaped by the company itself) in a context over which the company has control. This gives communications managers an opportunity to deal with the incorrect, the half-true and the misleading. Control is achieved not by containment but with controlled anticipations. Scandals or waves of complaints can in this way be identified or even addressed and measures taken to stem the tide.

Are companies ready for many-to-one dialogue?

A brave new and fascinating world appears to have emerged here at the beginning of the 21st century. But is there the threat of a certain 'agoraphobia' gripping communications managers – a fear, that is, of the new wide, open public spaces? A fear of the democratisation of communications, of open and transparent dialogue with internal and external audiences? Is this really a dream, or is it more a nightmare for those in charge of communications for a company, a party, a ministry, an association, or some other institution? The first answer to this justified and indeed central question is already given by the classical Agora, which in about 500 BC used border stones, called *horoi*, to provide a effective – and legally binding – limit to the forum's purpose. Upon the *horoi*, which were placed at the entranceways to the Agora, was written: "I am the boundary of the Agora". These border stones were intended to prevent uncontrolled behaviour. Criminals, conscientious objectors, and other undesirables were excluded.

And it is only with such clearly marked 'border stones' that dialogue within the Agora of the 21st century, too, becomes controllable and truly justifiable: the new form of dialogue is protected from uncoordinated, inappropriate and anarchic communications. Like the ancient *horoi*, special rules and software functions set limits that enable structured communications. They ensure that the addressee remains in control of the dialogue, and can actively steer the issues and discussions – and that unwelcome contributions do not find their way into the Agora of the 21st century. A periodic reporting system alerts the addressee ahead of time to issues that could present a crisis or opportunity. She can define the time frame over which each issue is voted on, giving her enough time to involve, as is customary, experts from various specialist departments or executive staff when responding. The most important difference: the time which one can now take to write a well-founded answer, does not lead, as in the past, to frustration and annoyance on the part of the sender. ("I have awaited an answer for more than three weeks – my question has clearly landed right near the bottom of the pile.") Quite the opposite: if the issue resonates with other participants in the dialogue, the sender of the question feels validated. A circumstance that – as experience has shown with the Chancellor's dialogue portal since it went live in October 2006 – has not led to a single complaint, but obviously is understood as part of accepting the rules of the democratic game. Apart from that, each participant in the dialogue is still free to use conventional means of contact, either additionally or alternatively.

People seek dialogue

In the medium term, many-to-one dialogue will play an increasingly significant role and establish itself as an equally important technique alongside other forms of classical communication. It works democratically and, for once, meets calls from the media and public for more transparent and open communication. In this sense, it makes a valuable contribution as a trust-building measure in the corporate communications portfolio. It helps alleviate the structural inadequacies of classical one-to-many communications and disarm reputation crises.

A new channel for dialogue has arisen that, thanks to its directness, is superior to classical mass media. Its reciprocal flavour places it a cut above the usual one-way forms of communication such as TV spots, advertisements, billboards and press relations. In future, it will be more and more self-evident for interest groups and individuals to address those responsible directly on all issues. In doing so, they step out of their role as target groups and become a new, central functional group capable of generating economic value. And by letting this happen, companies in return recover a shade more control over the management of their reputations.

References

Camp JM (1989) Die Agora von Athen. Mainz

Eisenegger M (2003) Reputationskonstitution in der Mediengesellschaft. In: Jarren O, Imhof K, Blum T (eds.), Mediengesellschaft, Opladen 2003

Eisenegger M, Imhof K (2004) Reputationsrisiken moderner Organisationen. In: Röttger U (ed.), Theorien der Public Relations, pp 235-256

Fombrun C, Wiedmann K (2004) Unternehmensreputation auf dem Prüfstand. Welche Unternehmen haben die beste Reputation in Deutschland. In: Planung & Analyse, Vol 28 No 4 pp 60-64

Habermas J (1962) Strukturwandel der Öffentlichkeit. Untersuchungen zu einer Kategorie der bürgerlichen Gesellschaft (accept. habil. Univ. Frankfurt/Main), Neuwied, (new ed. Frankfurt a.M. 1990)

Imhof K, Gaetano R (1996) Die Diskontinuität der Moderne. Zur Theorie des sozialen Wandels, Frankfurt/New York, pp 68-129

Pleon Kohtes Klewes (ed.) (2004) Im Geheimer Mission. Deutsche Unternehmen im Dialog mit kritischen Stakeholdern. Eine Umfrage unter den 150 Größten Unternehmen, Bonn/Berlin.

Schwaiger M (2004) Components and parameters of corporate reputation – an empirical study. In: Schmalenbach Business Review, Vol 56 pp 46-71

Sottong H (2008) Interne Kommunikation – Fehlende Glaubwürdigkeit. In: Harvard Business Manager, No 9

The leader's role in managing reputation

Gary Davies and Rosa Chun

The leader of an organisation has a central role in managing reputation. Leaders can personify their company to many different stakeholders. Their personality will influence that of the organisation they lead. In a crisis internal and external stakeholders may insist that the leader accepts a prominent role. Research indicates that while the reputation of the leader and organisation are distinct from one another, they are strongly associated. Where the leader adopts the role of company spokesperson nearly half of corporate reputation may emanate from his or her own image. Other senior managers, for example the manager of a local branch, should also recognise their role in managing reputation among employees and among the local customer base and community. Our research shows that the external reputation of a service business is heavily influenced by the employees' views of their employer's reputation. Employees develop their view from their experience at work, something which is influenced by company culture, created in turn by the style of its leaders.

The potential role

The leader is a significant symbol for any organisation and what the leader says and does can be more important symbolically than operationally when it comes to managing reputation. For example at a time of crisis the way the leader responds can have a major impact on reputation (Vidaver-Cohen, 2004). The leader also acts as a major source of information about the organisation, both internally to employees and externally, not only to financial markets, but also to the media, local and national government and increasingly so to the public and to the company's customers and potential customers. The source credibility literature suggests that the effectiveness of any source of information depends upon how trustworthy that source is perceived to be (McCracken 1989). It follows that how trustworthy a

J. Klewes, R. Wreschniok (eds.), *Reputation Capital*, DOI 10.1007/978-3-642-01630-1_21,
© Springer-Verlag Berlin Heidelberg 2009

leader appears to be will influence our views of how much we can trust what is said, and by implication whether we can trust the organisation itself.

Our focal issue in this chapter is then the relationship between leader reputation and organisation reputation, one that is more claimed than tested (Gaines-Ross 2003, Laurance 2004). The second area we examine is the leadership role that any manager may have in their organisation. Most studies of the influence of leadership reputation rely on media content analysis or opinion surveys rather than on research among stakeholders and so we lack objective evidence of the links between the reputation of the leader and that of the led with the public. What limited evidence we have also tends to ignore the role of middle management in managing and projecting a positive reputation. First then the CEO role, one that should embrace an overall responsibility for reputation, even to the point of being akin to being the "corporate brand manager". Many also argue that because the reputation of any organisation involves many line function areas, that only at this most senior level do these sometimes disparate aspects of reputation management come under one authority (Davies *et al* 2003). That said how much responsibility should there be for reputation issues at the CEO level? The role is complex enough without having yet another responsibility added to it.

The spill-over from leader to corporate reputation

Commercial research into practitioners' opinion of the contribution of leader reputation to corporate reputation suggests a very high interaction, with nearly half of the latter believed to emanate from the former. Our own work in the field of political imagery tends to support this figure. Politics offers an excellent laboratory to study the interaction between the leader's reputation and that of the organisation. Unlike in business, political leaders *have* to seek media attention and the "customer", in this context the voter, will also be relatively aware of the identity of the competing leaders and of their parties.

Our approach to measuring reputation is to use the personification metaphor, to ask respondents to our research to imagine that an organisation has come to life as a human being and to give him/her a personality test. The test, what we call the Corporate Character Scale has various dimensions, just like its human equivalent, Table 1. We can use the same scale when assessing the leader's reputation.

Table 1. The Corporate Character Scale: Dimensions and Items

Dimension	Items
Agreeableness	Friendly, pleasant, open, straightforward, concerned, reassuring, supportive, agreeable, honest, sincere, trustworthy, socially responsible
Enterprise	Cool, trendy, young, imaginative, up-to-date, exciting, innovative, extrovert, daring
Competence	Reliable, secure, hardworking, ambitious, achievement oriented, leading, technical, corporate
Chic	Charming, stylish, elegant, prestigious, exclusive, refined, snobby, elitist
Ruthlessness	Arrogant, aggressive, selfish, inward-looking, authoritarian, controlling
Informality	Casual, simple, easy-going
Machismo	Masculine, tough, rugged

In 2001 and 2005 just prior to general elections in the UK the reputation of the three main parties and that of their leaders was measured (Davies and Mian 2010) and compared. Figure 1 shows the data for 2001 for the two main parties, Labour, headed by Tony Blair, and the Conservatives (the party of Margaret Thatcher), led by William Hague. The third party, the Liberal Democrats, was led by Charles Kennedy. The figure shows the average scores from 876 voters and compares the reputation of leader and party. These are clearly similar in profile. But while the scores given by voters correlate strongly and positively, the average scores for the two are still statistically distinct. We tested the directionality of the spillover between leader and party imagery and found that the notion of a leader's reputation shaping that of the party was more convincing than *vice versa*. In other words, there is a stronger spillover from leader to corporate reputation.

By 2005 Tony Blair's reputation had been damaged by Britain's involvement in the second Gulf war. In particular his ratings for agreeableness, the dimension including trust, had declined, particularly among voters for other parties. The ratings for the Labour party from Labour voters were relatively unaffected but amongst those loyal to other parties ratings had declined. On average 45% of the variance in the reputation of the party could be explained by that of the leader, confirming the data from opinion surveys, but as most commercial sectors would not have media prominent CEO's heading all businesses, we would expect the spillover effects in the commercial sector to be somewhat lower. Nevertheless, using your CEO could appeal as a very cost effective way to manage corporate reputation.

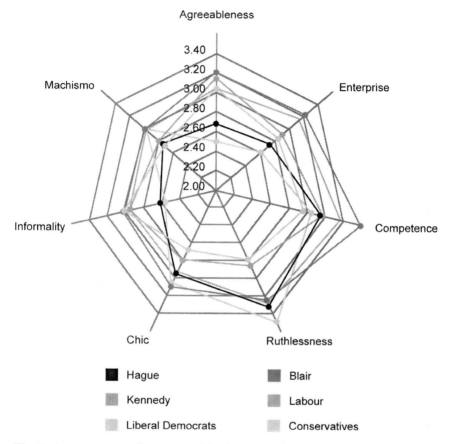

Fig. 1. Average scores for party and leader reputation 2001

By 2006 the Labour party realized that Tony Blair had become an electoral liability for the next general election as his influence over their party's reputation would become increasingly negative. Historians may wonder in 100 years time why the most successful leader of the Labour party was dumped almost immediately after winning a third consecutive election and overseeing a period of almost unprecedented economic growth in Britain. The answer is one word, "reputation". It had nothing to do with his actual ability in the role as prime minister.

The curse of the charismatic CEO

Having just read our first two sections, our reader should not jump to the conclusion that leader reputation is a panacea for corporate reputation management. The link between CEO and corporate reputation can be a double-edged sword, first if the leader's image falters, revenue may suffer before the leader can be replaced (Khurana 2002). The fortunes of the world's largest jewellery retailer did not survive the ill-judged jokes of its CEO, Gerald Ratner, who in a speech to a business audience explained that his low prices were due to his products being 'crap'. The joke went well but was publicised by two tabloid newspapers to a very different audience the following morning, his customers, to whom any jewellery was a significant purchase and often a present to a loved one. Customers of Martha Stewart's business empire, after she had been found guilty of lying to government investigators looking into her well-timed personal stock sale in late 2001, would also have been influenced by the changing image of the founder in their attitude and behaviour towards the company she led. This time the company survived the negative associations of its leader but it was certainly damaged by them.

Many companies carry the name of their founders or are associated with them; examples would include Disney, Sainsbury, Gucci and Laura Ashley. Many CEOs also choose to play the role with external stakeholders of being the company spokesperson, by being presented to the media as a personality or even by appearing in consumer advertising (Park and Berger 2004). A frequently quoted example of both is that of Richard Branson and the Virgin Group where the Virgin brand image is associated with the image of Branson the person. The Virgin-Branson reputation is full of anomalies. He himself has made a career out of playing David to the other guy's Goliath, attacking British Airways dominance of the North Atlantic as monopolistic, taking on Coca-Cola, the world's number one brand and launching his own brand of Cola at a cheaper price. Yet not all Virgin products represent value for money and not all Virgin businesses have been successful. Despite this Branson is trusted over other business leaders and the Virgin brand represents a marketing franchise second to few others. He has had his critics but the mud from any business crises never seems to stick to him.

One view of him is that of a master publicist, someone with a sure touch when it comes to the media. A Virgin train derailed in the North of England. A passenger died and many were injured. The accident followed a number of similar events and the media were quick to look to where they should allocate blame, to the train company or to the owners of the track, Network Rail? Fortunately for Branson the head of Network Rail quickly acknowledged that the problem lay at his company's door. But Branson had already moved on, almost ignoring the accident itself and instead praising his employees (and in particular the engine driver) for their bravery. The media descended on the local hospital to interview a bandaged and bemused looking driver, protesting that he was no hero (which made it even more attractive to see him as one). A tragedy had been turned into positive media coverage. The problems will come for Virgin should Branson lose his touch or the media turn on him as they have on many before.

How to replace a charismatic leader once he retires is another issue as the Bernard Matthews company found to their cost. The turkey meat company was founded in 1950 under its owner's name. By the 1980s it was big enough to advertise on national television and the ads were fronted by Matthews himself. He and his catchphrase (he described his products as "bootiful" in a strong rural accent) were synonymous with the company. His ageless picture was used on much product packaging. In 2007 an outbreak of avian flu turned people away from the product almost overnight. The public could not understand why Matthews had not come forward to front for his company, not realising that he was now in his late 70s, underlining the need to plan the succession of any media-prominent CEO whose persona is inextricably associated with that of the business.

A change of leadership will often be accompanied by a decline in share price while the replacement of leaders thought to be past their sell by date can see prices rise. In 1996, the value of shares in Sunbeam increased by half when it was announced that Al Dunlap had been hired as CEO. The following year $3.8 billion was added to AT&T's market capitalisation on the day that C. Michael Armstrong was named the new CEO. In 2002 Tyco International shares jumped 46% the day after it was announced that respected Motorola executive Ed Breen was the new leader of the troubled conglomerate.

The leader is a significant symbol of the organisation, the mere presence of a Ford or a Disney in the company hierarchy is something that attracts media comment for better or for worse. How such individuals behave influences our opinion of their corporate brand. Think for a second about the personality of Paris Hilton, not in charge of the hotel business that her family gave their name to, and in reality far more associated with her own branding activities in perfume and jewellery, but ask yourself how much spillover is there from her persona to the hotel chain's imagery? Does her rather spicy lifestyle add a certain cachet to an otherwise undifferentiated brand? If the Ford on the car company's board had similar racy associations, would it have been easier to obtain a premium price for Ford cars?

The personality of the leader

To many stakeholders, particularly employees, the leader can personify the organisation (Grunig 1993). We believe too that leader personality can influence the culture of the organisation. Culture is that tricky word that can mean a whole host of things to different people but which fundamentally stands in our opinion for 'how we do things around here'. The cumulative experience of an employee will define their view of the employer's reputation, this perspective increasingly being referred to as the employee brand. Our work shows clear links between the employee view of reputation and that of the customer, particularly in a service organisation where there is direct contact between employees and customers. So organisational culture influenced by the leader can be a potent force to influence customers. After all it is the actual experience that customers receive, rather than what they are told it will be, that determines how the customer will see the business.

However the personality of the CEO can also have a negative impact on corporate culture. This infusion process can be divided into two parts. First there is their recruitment strategy. Recruiting and keeping the people who fit the organisational culture is particularly important for organisations with strong leadership. Larry Ellison the co-founder and CEO of the Oracle Corporation, (listed 14th on Forbes's list of the world's richest (Forbes 2008)) reportedly valued intelligence more than maturity and experience when recruiting employees. But one analyst commented "I don't know if they got the smartest people but they definitely got the most arrogant" (Parthasarathy 2003). Despite his charismatic leadership and success with Oracle, Larry Ellison is criticized for being arrogant and ruthless, and for shaping Oracle's aggressive culture and identity (Sto 2002). He appeared to hire similar people, who in their turn recruited others cast in the same mould, producing a distinctive culture but one which had its darker side.

The second aspect of the same process by which the CEO's style can have a negative influence is through setting systems for reward and sanction. Many leaders believe that the most appropriate way to treat their key employees is by offering large bonuses and stock options. The effect this can have on an organisation's culture and ultimately on reputation is all too obvious in the recent banking crisis where the enormous financial incentives paid to employees appear to be at the heart of an industry that lost sight of the traditional values associated with banking – conservatism and prudence. CEOs set the tone for their organisations. They can be ruthless in sacking people who do not perform up to expectation or do not fit the organisational culture, even though they might be reasonably successful. At Enron employees were appraised twice a year in a process known as 'rank and yank' (Gladwell, 2002). Employees had to obtain a rating or ranking from their peers on a three-point scale. Those who fell into category B or C, instead of A, faced the strong possibility of being 'yanked' within the next year (Swartz and Watkins, 2003). This ruthless process created an internal culture that spilt over into how Enron treated its customers.

Charismatic leaders are often risk taking, insecure and narcissist (House and Howell, 1992). Many appear to be intolerant of any challenge to their authority and the elimination of dissent helps their accumulation of power at the centre. To survive members replace their pre-existing beliefs and values with those of the organisation and its leaders.

In summary, the infusion of the positive aspects of CEO personality into organisation culture (visionary, honest, and competent) helps achieve a positive reputation and consequently growth, member identification and affinity, while the infusion of negative aspects of personality (dominance, narcissism, ruthlessness) driven by personal ambition and the pursuit of short term profitability, can be destructive to the organisation's reputation and future success.

The leader's role in a crisis

Earlier we described how one CEO Richard Branson, handled a crisis involving an accident which led to the death of one of his customers. In any similar situation the media and the public will look to see and hear the reaction of the company's head. Many CEOs are media shy or feel they lack the skills to deal with aggressive questioning and delegate the burden of facing the cameras and journalists. But most recognize the need for the leader to represent the organisation at a time of crisis. How leaders deal with such circumstances appears to us to differ widely, not only within a single culture but also across cultures. Within Western society there appear to be two options when the media and the authorities are looking for someone to blame: Option 1 express concern but don't apologise or admit guilt as this implies an acceptance of legal liability; Option 2 express remorse, or even admit guilt as the reputational damage in the longer term from rejecting responsibility and deflecting blame can be far greater than any compensation claims. Two examples then to illustrate the disbenefits of such denial.

In 2002 a high-speed train derailed just outside of Potters Bar station in the south of England. Seven died and others were injured, some very seriously. The cause of the incident was quickly discovered to be a set of faulty points. Responsibility for track maintenance lay with Jarvis, a diversified engineering and construction company. Jarvis' reaction was to imply that sabotage was the likely explanation. However in 2003 a government investigation decided that the principal cause of the accident was poor maintenance of the points. In 2004 Jarvis finally admitted liability and offered compensation, but by then the reputational damage had been done. The media had already decided who was to blame and a typical story about another Jarvis company would have started with a reminder to the reader, "Jarvis, the company that was responsible for Potters Bar...", even though that particular subsidiary had nothing to do with railway maintenance.

In 2006 confectionery manufacturer Cadbury withdrew large amounts of products from the market following concern over salmonella contamination. The company had taken some months to report the problem and when the news broke it denied that there was any risk to health, a claim that was challenged by an independent medical expert. Subsequent press releases from Cadbury expressed concern but fell short of accepting responsibility for the hospitalisation of scores of consumers. While it is difficult to prove whether food poisoning has been caused by any particular source, the circumstantial evidence here was strong, with the same strain of virus being involved and many of those hospitalised recalling consumption of a Cadbury product prior to falling ill. The incident cost the company more in the short term in recall costs while long term effects on sales appear to be negligible. But can one be sure? Probably no: for example a relatively minor incident in 2007 over incorrect product labelling made the pages of the newspapers whereas normally this would have been ignored.

In both cases the same point emerges. Journalists are human beings who have good memories. If they feel that they have been mislead by a corporate's denial of liability, they are likely to change their attitude towards that firm. Trust is a central issue in reputation. Trust stems from experience, and if the organisation appears to be bending the truth then trust evaporates.

We are fascinated by the differences between the expectations of society following a crisis in Eastern societies. In 2000 up to 15,000 people in Japan fell ill after consuming milk products from Snow Brand, a leading

Japanese dairy foods company. The cause of the problem was poor hygiene in one factory. The company tried to downplay the event, very much as would be the norm in the West, but even appeared reluctant to recall the suspect product. Sales fell and eventually the President and other senior executives resigned in atonement for what had happened. The new CEO made clear statements of regret. He acknowledged the mistakes of the past and showed a determination to move forward by implementing significant change. One essential feature of showing contrition in Japan is for senior managers to appear in public and for them to bow low to demonstrate their sorrow. How low they bow is used by the public apparently to assess the genuineness of their contrition.

While we are certainly not advocating identical behaviour in the West, the use of apology by the CEO would appear to us to be something worthy of consideration. There appears to us to be a battle between two sources of advice at a time of crisis. The legal department, with cause for concern about liability and breach of insurance conditions. will advocate reticence in accepting blame. However the reputation function might well offer the competing view that an apology will defuse the situation and allow the company to move on with limited short and long term damage to reputation. As reputation is worth typically the equivalent of half a year's turnover, losing that can be far more damaging commercially than most compensation claims.

The role of other leaders

The CEO is not the only leader who can influence a company's reputation. Other senior executives may well be better placed or better able to deal with the media. The Finance director will have a special role with the markets and the financial media. However in our work we have found many examples of how far more junior managers in large organisations have a key leadership role to play in managing reputation.

We have worked with a number of retail organisations. While each store in a chain may look very similar to the others, business performance can differ markedly. Retailers commonly put this down to local differences and to the "manager effect", the belief that some managers are inherently better at gaining sales than others. Now this is odd, as managers have limited discretion in modern retailing. They do not negotiate with suppliers nor influence which products are stocked or how they are priced. In sectors such as grocery they cannot even decide upon how products are displayed. Strict budgeting makes it difficult to influence staffing levels. So how can managers have such a marked effect? In our work with service companies we generally measure the reputation among staff and customers for a number of branches. We find small but significant differences in the views these two stakeholders hold of the different retail outlets, and these differences often explain large differences in financial performance, particularly in sales growth.

Take for example one fashion retailer. The sales in one store were declining while in others they were growing. There were significant differences in one aspect of reputation, the one we label as informality (casual, simple and easy-going). The core customer is a young mum with children who she takes shopping with her. Such clientele value the laid back approach of staff who do not appear phased by children and their tendency to behave inappropriately at times. After all the employees themselves are often young mums too, working part time and on a work pattern that is also quite casual. Loud pop music is often the norm. We hated the places but then we were not the core customer. But our dislike gave us the clue as to why another branch was doing badly. The new manager, like ourselves, was uncomfortable with the laid back culture. Her previous job had been with another chain store but one where the culture was more regimented and orderly. She had been trying to change the behaviour of her staff to align more with what she had been trained to expect at her previous employer, with a negative effect first on her staff and then on her customers.

We worked with a food retailer for some years, helping to train their managers to be 'local brand managers' for their company. We emphasised how the attitude and behaviour of their staff would influence customers almost at a subliminal level. A new director for stores took a more aggressive approach in line with a change in company policy. Costs were to be cut. We started to see a rise in the scores we were recording for ruthlessness (arrogant, aggressive, selfish, inward-looking, authoritarian, and controlling). Managers reported an increase in pressure and many admitted that they were passing this on to their teams. Simultaneously suppliers had been complaining in the media about price pressures, for example farmers claiming that the price they received for milk was now below their cost of production. The increasing reputation for ruthlessness had a negative impact on sales, while one for agreeableness (pleasant, open, straightforward, concerned, reassuring, supportive, honest, trustworthy) which correlated positively was if anything decreasing. Worse, managers' satisfaction often correlated positively with their perceptions of how ruthless the organisation was: it certainly didn't for employees and customers. We worked on ways whereby managers could absorb the ruthlessness that they were experiencing and focus instead on passing on more agreeableness to their employees.

In summary, a company's reputation is fundamentally a function of the way it treats people, mainly its staff and its customers. The leader plays a special role in signalling how this is to be through policy but also through his/her own behaviour. Managements have a special role in transmitting this to their own staff. In turn the micro-behaviours of staff transmit the same policy and culture to customers.

References

Davies G, Chun R, Vinhas daSilva R and Roper S (2003) Corporate reputation and competitiveness. Routledge, London

Davies G, Mian T (2010) The Reputation of the Party Leader and of the Party being Led. European Journal of Marketing, forthcoming

Forbes (May 3, 2008) The World's Billionaires. Special Report

Gaines-Ross L (2003) CEO Capital: A Guide to Building CEO reputation and Company Success. Wiley, Hoboken NJ

Gladwell M (20 August 2002) The talent myth. The Times (T2), pp 2-4

Grunig JE (1993) Image and substance: from symbolic to behavioural relationships. Public Relations Review, Vol 19 pp 121-139

House RJ, Howell JM (1992) Personality and charismatic leadership. Leadership Quarterly, Vol 3 No 2 pp 81-108

Khurana R (September 2002) The Curse of the Superstar. Harvard Business Review, pp 60- 66

Laurence A (2004) So what really changed after Enron? Corporate Reputation Review 7, pp 55-63

McCracken G (1989) Who is the Celebrity Endorser? Cultural Foundations of the Endorsement Process. The Journal of Consumer Research 16, pp 310-321

Parthasarathy MC (2003) Larry Ellison – The Source of Oracle's 'Wisdon'. ECCH case collection 803-017-1

Park DJ, Berger BK (2004) The presentation of CEO's in the press 1990-2000, increasing salience, positive valence and a focus on competency, and personal dimensions of image. Journal of Public Relations Research Vol 16 pp 93-125

Sto FM (2002) Oracle of Oracle: The Story of Volatile CEO Larry Ellison and the Strategies behind his company's phenomenal success. Amacom

Swartz M, Watkins S (2003) Power Failure: The rise and fall of Enron. Aurum Press, London

Vidaver-Cohen D (2004) Management, meaning and a meeting of the minds: How symbolic power preserves reputation in times of corporate crisis. 8th International Conference on Corporate Reputation, Image, Identity and Competitiveness. Fort Lauderdale, Florida

Coca-Cola Hellenic reputation case study

Jens Rupp

A company's success with customers, consumers, suppliers, authorities and all relevant stakeholders depends on its reputation. In Europe, public trust in companies has eroded over the past 20 years. Reversing this trend since its creation in 2000, Coca-Cola Hellenic has succeeded in establishing long-lasting, trusting relationships with many of its stakeholders across its 28 diverse countries of operation. This chapter shows how the company is developing mutually beneficial partnerships within its four CSR action areas of marketplace, workplace, environment and community.

Coca-Cola Hellenic's actions are transparently described in its annual CSR report along international reporting guidelines. The verifiable achievements are recognized by stakeholders and increase the company's reputation and, consequently, its performance, competitiveness and long-term value for shareholders.

Reputation is, without doubt, the most important asset in the business world.

It helps to distinguish a company in the marketplace, with governments, with NGOs and with the media. It consolidates a company's success and safeguards its future.

Almost by definition, a good reputation is something which evolves over time. It is built, little by little, slowly and deliberately with countless actions and deeds. This distinguishes "reputation" from "image", or "brand", both of which can be built in a relatively short time through high levels of marketing spend.

Reputation is how a company lives its values. It's what an individual or enterprise *does*, not how it perceives itself. It comprises the words spoken when the door is closed after an individual has left the room, not what is said to him when he is present.

J. Klewes, R. Wreschniok (eds.), *Reputation Capital*, DOI 10.1007/978-3-642-01630-1_22,
© Springer-Verlag Berlin Heidelberg 2009

Building a solid reputation is essential for the long-term existence of a company. Maintaining that reputation is an essential part of the ongoing work in any company: ensuring that the components of its business model, operational philosophy and behaviour are fully understood and implemented by all employees, and communicating company policies and positions on social, environmental, or whatever the challenges are of the moment that face society, whether it be the consumer, customer, government, NGO or other special interest group or stakeholder.

The Athens based Coca-Cola Hellenic Bottling Company S.A. (Coca-Cola Hellenic) is the authorised producer and distributor of products of The Coca-Cola Company in 28 countries and territories. All but one, Nigeria, are on the continent of Europe including the whole of Russia, Central Europe, South-East Europe and Western European countries such as Ireland, Switzerland and Italy.

Following a merger in 2000, almost overnight Coca-Cola Hellenic went from being a modestly sized group to one of the largest in the global Coca-Cola system and the biggest bottler of non-alcoholic beverages in Europe, serving a population of about 550 million people.

Activities stretched from Ireland in the West to Russia in the East; a vast territory that encompasses markets that are well established as well as those that are developing and emerging. A dizzying range of cultures and traditions is found across the company's new network, along with a mix of business practices, codes of behaviour and legislative requirements.

The initial priority for the new management team was to meld the disparate business units into a cohesive entity, with all participants understanding, appreciating, and pursuing the same objectives. This was addressed by putting in place relevant and proven management and structural mechanisms, fine-tuning them and directing their effective implementation.

At the same time, steps were taken to convey to stakeholders information about what this recently created Coca-Cola Hellenic was all about: its mission, its philosophies, its attributes, its aspirations. For Coca-Cola Hellenic, the definition of "stakeholders" was all-encompassing: it included everyone who was in any way touched by the Company and its operations – employees, business associates, customers, consumers, governments, NGOs, industry monitoring groups, community organisations, the media, shareholders, and even competitors and antagonists.

Considering the comprehensiveness of such an audience, it was necessary for the outreach approach to be equally broad-reaching. Young as the Company was, it understood that it needed to begin establishing, growing and strenuously protecting a strong, positive reputation for the Company itself and the brands it produces. In order to do so, it needed to be perceived as a credible partner, internally and externally; one that adds value, communicates in an open, transparent manner, builds trust and effectively manages its four key areas of operational connectivity: environment, workplace, marketplace and community. The primary objective was to create long-term value for all stakeholders.

This would result in a number of benefits arising from constructive relationships with stakeholders, and would create a climate in which the business could thrive.

Among the key benefits identified were:

- A desire by consumers to do business with the company.

- A willingness of pressure groups and NGOs to work with the company.

- An increased level of pride among employees and higher levels of retention.

- A heightened confidence among investors, and a greater willingness to contribute financing.

- A greater inclination by legislators to assist operations and help remove obstacles hindering them.

- A disposition by members of the media to report positively or at least avoid writing negatively about the company.

- An interest among suppliers to work together with the company and in doing so, expand opportunities.

In order to achieve these ends Coca-Cola Hellenic management evaluated the essence of the Company's operations and the ways in which it was viewed. This involved an assessment of strengths the Company possessed materially or intrinsically.

Clearly, the highest profile aspect of the Company was its brand. Its name includes that of the world's best-known and most successful soft drink, Coca-Cola, a beverage that has enjoyed huge popularity for more than 120 years[1] and is regarded by experts[2] as the most valuable consumer

---

[1] The carbonated soft drink Coca-Cola was created in 1885.

[2] Interbrand, a leading international brand consultancy. On 21 September 2008 it reported The Coca-Cola Company's image to be the most valuable in the world for the eighth consecutive year, based on the amount of the company's revenue attributable to its brand.

brand in the world. Through this association, stakeholders immediately conjure up an impression of the Company.

The brand differentiates the Company from its competition. Through marketing activities, advertising and publicity, and in the use of the brand name on products and business units across the Company's territories, there is a high level of awareness.

Closely associated with the brand was the Company's image. This was seen as being inextricably linked to the Company's reputation but limited to beliefs in, and personal evaluation of the products only. If brand image is positive in people's minds, reputation may also be positive, however, the connection is fragile.

The brand relates to what the company creates; what it does as a business. The image of the Company, underpinned by the brand, gives people a preferred impression about the Company; not what it actually is, what it stands for, or where it is headed. That is the job of reputation.

Reputation and trust

Neither brand nor image alone is capable of inspiring trust in a Company. This is especially true in today's world where businesses are coming under greater scrutiny. In an increasingly interconnected world, where events in one country are almost instantly transmitted globally through the news media, and where facts are shared with the click of a computer mouse, there is a compelling need to go beyond passively relying on people's admiration for a company well-run, producing products that are appreciated.

Today, there is a need for a new basis of trust.

A telling survey (Ipsos Mori Reputation Summer 2006) showing the shift in public opinion over the past three decades shows the extent to which attitudes about the role corporations play in communities are regarded. Respondents were asked to consider the statement "The profits of large companies help make things better for everyone who uses their products and services." In 1976 fully 56% endorsed the view while only 31% felt that this was untrue. In the early 1980s a major change in thinking occurred, with the number of those believing that "big business" was a force for good plunging to just 40%, with those holding the opposite view rose to almost 50%. The trend continued, with only slight fluctuations up to 2006 when it was found that that over the 30 year period a complete reversal had occurred; by that time 53% did not view large companies in terms of improving lives, and no more than 21% did.

Another, more comprehensive study (Edelman Annual Reputation Survey) that surveyed people in the world's three key economic regions found an equal level of scepticism about the trustworthiness of businesses in Europe specifically. When asked "How much do you trust each institution to do what is right?" in rankings of NGOs, Business and Government, Europeans placed NGOs at the top of the list with 57% approval, Business second with 42% and Government last with 33%. In the United States, similar attitudes prevailed, with NGOs on top with 54%, Business slightly behind with 49% and Government a long way back at 38%.

While the results for NGOs and Government in different regions could be the subject of interesting debates, the main outcome is very revealing. Across the regions where the biggest businesses have their bases and conduct the majority of their operations, people's trust in companies in Europe is less than 50%.

Such research can be regarded as something of a wake up call for companies. However, for those who have been paying attention, alarms about the trustworthiness of businesses have been sounding increasingly in recent years as consumer organisations, community groups and activist associations have raised their voices and drawn attention to concerns where they feel corporations have betrayed consumer trust. Criticisms range from use of child labour in production and causing environmental degradation to producing unsafe or harmful products.

Clearly, more and more people are watching the producers of their goods and services more closely, and there is growing demand for businesses to mean what they say, and to do the "right" thing.

Evidence of this can be found in the General Public Corporate Image Survey conducted by Ipsos Mori in the United Kingdom. In 1984 respondents stated that the quality of products/service was the most important fact they took into account when making a judgement about a company. Customer care came second and honesty was their lowest concern. Eighteen years later, at the beginning of the 21st century, honesty had become the primary consideration, with product/service quality being pushed into second place, slightly ahead of customer care.

Other matters are also on the minds of communities when they view the actions of today's businesses. Given a list of "issues" related to corporate operations in a 2006 survey (Ipsos Mori Reputation Summer 2006), people overwhelmingly chose "Concern for the Environment" as something companies should pay particular attention to. "Caring for Employees" came second and "Conserving Energy" a close third. Other matters, including providing more jobs, investing for the future, keeping prices reasonable, caring for customers, providing good quality products and services, training the workforce, safety for the workforce and providing equal opportunities were highlighted in descending order.

Other research (Ipsos Mori Reputation Summer 2006) in developed countries in 2005 concluded that among the key drivers of opinion for favourability the integrity of a company had the greatest impact for all "Special Publics"[3]. This was followed by environmental responsibility, standing up for human rights, possessing a long-term perspective, setting standards and, lastly, communications.

The evidence indicated that reputation equated with trust, and that trust involved an active, credible engagement in the areas of life that was of greatest concern for stakeholders. To build that trust would require a leader with a deep and wide experience of life and people. Someone, who could interface easily with the ordinary consumer and the extra-ordinary politician. Producing quality products was a plus, but it did not much matter if there was no or little evidence of good, responsible behaviour. A positive image was no match for positive action, especially in regard to the issues that people locally, regionally and internationally believed really mattered.

Building reputation responsibility

Going beyond reporting to, and communicating with stakeholders about the Company and its activities, Coca-Cola Hellenic determined to enter into "partnerships", initiating actions and genuine, productive engagement with each of them in structured, defined and meaningful ways.

Briefly, the people targeted, and the engagement with them, involved the following:

- Consumers (550 million people) – Consumer hotlines, surveys, research, focus groups, plant tours, websites;

- Customers (1.4 million retailers) – Account management teams, newsletters, events, surveys;

- Employees (41,000 staff) – Engagement surveys, management briefings, meetings, negotiations with representatives, grievance procedures;

---

[3] Definition: Special Publics – Government leaders, NGOs and Key Influencers.

- Communities (local, national and international) – Plant visits, public policy debates, community meetings, partnerships, sponsorships, lectures at universities;

- Governments (local, national and European) – Public policy debates, discussions, trade associations, industry groups, advisory councils, local chambers of commerce;

- Investors (institutional and individual) – Annual shareholders' meeting, quarterly briefings and roadshows, webcasts with investor participation, dialogue with analysts and financial media;

- Suppliers (of ingredients, packaging, equipment, services) – Recycling organisations, packaging associations, joint projects, meetings;

- Civil society (NGOs and other bodies) – Memberships, dialogue, partnerships;

The Coca-Cola Company (partner, shareholder, supplier) – Senior management forum, Top-to-Top Council, Coca-Cola Environment Council, Global Quality Standards Board, Corporate Responsibility Core Team, joint projects, daily interaction.

Corporate social responsibility

In order to provide a genuine basis for it actions, and to demonstrate its commitment to positive engagement, Coca-Cola Hellenic entered into a social contract with all of its publics by embracing the principles of Corporate Social Responsibility (CSR) and sustainable development. By open, transparent public reporting, the company intended to directly address the concerns and questions of its stakeholders. Sensitive to scepticism in some quarters that CSR would involve authentic actions and was in fact little more than empty promotional exercises to counter criticism and provide a surface gloss of seeming accountability, the Company ensured that its efforts would be carefully monitored, independently assessed, benchmarked and publicly reported under internationally set guidelines.

Coca-Cola Hellenic made the decision to guide its efforts under the Brundtland[4] definition of sustainable development: "Meeting the needs of the present without compromising the ability of future generations to meet their own needs". The Company's priorities and targets are initiated by the

---

[4] The **Brundtland** Commission (26 Oct 2008), formally the World Commission on Environment and Development (WCED), is known by the name of its Chair Gro Harlem Brundtland.

Group CSR Council which comprises function heads from across the business, and operates under the supervision of the board-level Social Responsibility Committee. Country operations translate initiatives into programmes that meet local needs and senior managers are held accountable, and rewarded, for performance. In addition to submitting itself to independent verification measurements, the company publishes annual CSR reports on its activities in line with global reporting standards. Production of this report is a cross functional task managed by the Social Responsibility Council, and overseen by a sub-committee of the board of directors.

Within this framework, Coca-Cola Hellenic began enacting rules and standards for its engagement at all levels of its operations, internally and externally, with its CSR commitment, transparency and honesty embedded into the fabric of its business through all aspects of planning, development and execution by being officially integrated into its Business Plan.

The CSR initiatives were targeted in the Company's four core impact areas: Environment, Workplace, Marketplace and Community. In all instances, efforts included internal programmes and others linked to outsiders ranging from governments and NGOs to educational institutions, industry associations, business partners and communities.

Under Environment, the Company implemented ISO 14001, the international specification for environmental management systems (EMS), and identified three key areas of engagement:

1. Water Use and Conservation

2. Energy and Emissions Reduction

3. Solid Waste Management, Recovery and Reuse

Examples of water programmes and activities include:

- Ensuring the treatment of all used water.

- Implementation of a Water Savers programme to minimise water use.

- Membership of the "Green Danube Partnership" with the International Commission for the Protection of the Danube River (ICPDR), developing public awareness programmes.

- Protection of endangered wetlands and restoration of waterways.

- Assistance for farmers in protecting watersheds.

- Founding signatory of the CEO Water Mandate of the UN Global Compact, committing Coca-Cola Hellenic to addressing sustainability issues in its own operations and in communities.
- Partnerships in all territories of operation with NGOs to protect and preserve water resources.

Examples of energy reduction programmes and initiatives:

- Signatory of the UN Global Compact Caring for Climate statement and the Bali Communiqué.
- Development of 16 Combined Heat and Power (CHP) generation plants (by 2010) that will reduce CO_2 emissions by 20% across all operations.
- Development of beverage coolers that are 20% more energy efficient.
- Installation of the energy control devices that reduce electricity use by up to an additional 35%.
- Building awareness and implementing programmes to conserve energy in all operations.
- Testing and adopting energy-efficient vehicles wherever practicable.

Examples of solid waste management and reduction programmes and initiatives:

- Reduction of packaging weight in all three main packages; PET plastic, metal (aluminium and steel), and glass.
- Increase in the use of recycled material, particularly in PET bottles.
- Investment in packaging management systems that collect, recover and recycle post-consumer packaging.
- Building packaging management systems in emerging and developing markets together with other industries.
- Reducing plant waste and increasing the amount of recycled waste.

In the workplace, Coca-Cola Hellenic seeks to provide an inclusive, safe and healthy place in which employees will be encouraged to realise their full potential and be rewarded.

Examples of workplace programmes and initiatives:

- Adoption of Occupational Health and Safety (OHSAS) 18001 standards across all bottling plants.

- Stringent implementation of a Code of Business Conduct Policy that offers "whistleblowers" protection.

- Provision of at least 18 hours of training for every one of its 47,000 employees each year

- Signatory to the UN Global Compact on international standards for working environments, including non-discrimination and employee communication.

- Compliance with World Business Council for Sustainable Development (WBCSD) and Global Reporting Initiative (GRI) guidelines on detailing workplace policies and practices.

- Development of a Leadership Pipeline scheme for leadership development and succession planning across all countries of operation.

The marketplace activities of Coca-Cola Hellenic are directed at assisting customers and suppliers through "best practice" education and adherence to international operating requirements, and acting responsibly in respecting consumer choices.

Examples of marketplace programmes and initiatives:

- Introduction of ISO 9000/22000 quality standards in bottling plants

- Founding signatory to the European Beverage Industry (UNESDA) Commitment to support the EU Platform on Diet, Physical Activity and Health

- Implementation and audit of Supplier Guidance Principles of ethics and environmental performance

- Guide customers in the fragmented trade sector with effective business development through sustainable practices.

Across communities, Coca-Cola Hellenic takes an active role in contributing to and supporting development, as well as protecting the interests of the inhabitants.

Examples of community programmes and initiatives:

- Membership of the respected London Benchmarking Group (LBG) which measures a company's community involvement (which shows Coca-Cola contributed more than €10 million annually, equal to 1.5% of pre-tax profit.

- Marketing responsibly under the beverage industry organisation guidelines that restrict activities in primary schools and targeting youngsters under the age of 12 years.

- Conducting post-consumer waste management schemes in every country to reduce litter and develop recycling practices.

- Investment in Europe's first industry-owned and operated PET bottle-to-bottle recycling plant in Austria.

- Introduction and marketing of an increasing number of "wellness" and "nutrition" products, expanding consumer choices including low and no calorie drinks such as Coke Zero.

- Contribution to emergency relief efforts when natural and man-made disasters occur.

- Conducting and supporting a vast range of healthy lifestyle activities, especially those involving sports events.

Since 2003 Coca-Cola Hellenic has informed stakeholders of the action it takes in sustainable development, and the progress made towards reaching goals by publishing an annual printed and Internet version of its Social Responsibility Report.

Each successive report has shown steady improvements in almost all parts of the business, with specific examples given of particular actions by individual country operations, through initiatives by employees themselves or in association, with external bodies and groups.

This has led to working together with other industry members to establish responsible marketing policies, to become a founding signatory of the CEO Water Mandate and Caring for Climate project under the United Nations Global Compact, uniting with educational institutions and governments to create and distribute water conservation teaching kits in schools of the Danube River watershed, and many others.

In all, Coca-Cola Hellenic works with more than 200 organisations at local, national and international levels in pursuing sustainability goals.

Through its efforts, the Company has achieved acceptance and recognition from numerous quarters. Since its beginning, the Company was listed on the FTSE4Good Index which measures the performance of companies meeting globally recognised corporate responsibility standards, and in September 2008 it was included for the first time in both the Dow Jones Sustainability World Index and the Dow Jones STOXX Sustainability Index.

Increasingly, as Coca-Cola Hellenic's commitment is seen as going far beyond rhetoric to achieve authentic, verifiable results, acknowledgements of its contributions encouragement and gratitude have been expressed.

The UN Secretary General commended Coca-Cola Hellenic as a "Leader", and it has been named a UNGC "Notable Reporter". The Company's Community Water Partnerships have garnered global awards, such as the Thiess Riverprize "Best River Basin Partnership", as well as a €1.5 million award from the EU for a joint project with WWF Hungary and a €2.5 million grant from the UNDP for the Vatra Dorna Conservation Project in Romania.

When Coca-Cola Hellenic announced a pioneering plan to construct 15 Combined Heat and Power (CHP) plants in order to make significant reductions in CO_2 emissions, European Union Vice President, Commissioner Gunter Verheugen stated at the project launch in Brussels during the 2008 Energy Week stated: "This initiative shows that CSR is not about words but about changing reality. It demonstrates that environment and economic goals can be pursued in unison. It also demonstrates how innovation is not just a driver of economic competitiveness, but can also underpin business contribution to wider societal goals, such as the fight against climate change."

Coca-Cola Hellenic invested in Europe's first industry-owned bottle-to-bottle PET recycling plant in Austria, and the country's Minister of the Environment, Josef Pröll, said at the official inauguration: "This demonstrates perfectly what a successful environmental policy should look like. It is the perfect solution for the environment, economy and consumer."

Speaking of the voluntary measures introduced to ensure responsible marketing, EU Commissioner Markos Kyprianou, said: "I have particularly noted the commitments... on marketing, advertising and commercial communications... accompanied by proposals for a range of key performance indicators."

Director General, DG Sanco, European Commission Robert Madelin added: "The commitments are at the extreme end of best practice."

Watching reputation grow

As Coca-Cola Hellenic made CSR an integral part of its planning, embedded the principles into operational practices, and reached out into the communities it serves, the Company noted additional benefits in its own

business capabilities, heightening performance that adds to its competitiveness, and increasing long-term value for investors.

The results have been shown in many cases through unsolicited awards
and external recognition. In Poland, the local business unit was judged
"Partner of the Year" in the Drinks, Juice and Waters category in a survey
conducted by Restaurateur magazine, and the soft drink Kropla Beskidu
was named "Brand of the Year" by Media and Marketing. In Hungary,
Coca-Cola was awarded the title of the country's "Most Trusted Brand".
Belarus cited the beverage "Brand of the Year" in 2006.

Coca-Cola Hellenic's reputation as a good employer has been consolidated. Polish students pronounced the Company as being the "best employer". Students in Ireland regarded it as the "most desirable workplace."
In Serbia, a study by the Selectio Group found it to be the "Best Employer", and in Italy, operations have achieved tremendous success by being voted in the top three best companies to work in the country, and in the
top 100 in Europe by the Great Place to Work Trust Index[®].

As reputation has grown, so too has performance. Coca-Cola Hellenic
has been rewarded with steadily improving growth throughout each successive year since its founding. In 2007 it reach a noteworthy milestone in
its operations: unit case sales of two billion within a single year. EBITDA[5]
rose from €496 in 2001 to more than one billion euros. Net profit went
from a €19 million deficit to a positive €472 million. Return on Invested
Capital went up from 3.9% to 12.2%.

These impressive results can be considered even more so when compared with the Company's peers. Between 2006 and 2007 the change in
revenue, EBIT and EPS was 7% above the nearest competitor in each instance. The change in Gross Margin bps was 100, which was lower than
the leader but some 60% above the next closest group.

In 2007 Coca-Cola Hellenic's stock appreciated by 50% for the year and
outperformed the major stock indices (S&P 500, FTSEurofirst 300) as well
as that of its peer group. At 20 February 2007 market capitalisation stood
at US$16 billion, versus US$12 billion for Coca-Cola Enterprises, the next
highest. The growth made the Company one of the best performing global
FMGC stocks over the period, giving it a third place ranking overall. At
the same time, it made Coca-Cola Hellenic the No. 1 global beverage stock
(including alcoholic as well as non-alcoholic beverages).

---

[5] Earnings before interest, taxes, depreciation and amortisation (EBITDA)

In the view of Coca-Cola Hellenic, the commitment made to CSR had made a difference. The engagement in CSR and sustainability programmes comprising marketplace initiatives, community activities, environmental leadership, workplace and human rights practices, and reporting standards had inculcated best practices in its operations.

Through the setting of clear guidelines and targets, establishing systems for monitoring and accountability, and reporting progress transparently to allow independent judgement, the Company had provided fertile ground in which its reputation could flourish – and provide a strong basis for continued, sustainable operational success.

The global economic difficulties being experienced at the time of writing certainly present a major challenge for maintaining the Company's impressive growth during its first seven years of operation. To address these, prudent cost-control measures, vigorous and creative leadership activities, and a recommitment to long-term strategic planning are being added to the armoury of "weapons" to help Coca-Cola Hellenic weather the economic storm and drive it forward.

The question may be asked whether building reputation will contribute to a company's ability to rise like a phoenix when the financial markets stabilise.

Coca-Cola Hellenic is cautiously confident. The gains observed through reputation-building by a dedication to CSR are considered to be genuine and verifiable, they are too valuable to be undermined by downgrading or decreasing efforts.

As Socrates (469 BCE – 399 BCE) said of reputation, "…it is like fire; once you have kindled it you may easily preserve it, but if you extinguish it, you will find it an arduous task to rekindle…"

Never underestimate the importance of details

Interview with

Tomaso Galli

By some estimates, the luxury goods industry generates roughly 175 bil-lion Euros turnover each year, with products ranging from yachts, to cars, jewellery, watches, leather goods and apparel. Companies that want to flourish in this business need to offer more than cutting edge products and exceptional quality to justify the price tag that is often associated with luxury items. This is one of the reasons, why brand reputation is so well-guarded. In the interview, Tomaso Galli, who has 25 years experi-ence working in communications, 10 years of which in the luxury indus-try, offers insights into how iconic brand status may be achieved and re-tained through communications.

Editors: Mr. Galli, if I wanted to build a reputation in luxury today, what would your advice be?

Tomaso Galli (T.G.): Let's focus on ready-to-wear and accessories, as these are the luxury segments that I know best. The first thing is to clearly understand which is your core product category. All luxury brands, from Louis Vuitton to Prada, from Gucci to Hermès, Chanel, Yves Saint Laurent to name just a few, started with one category in which they made a name for themselves, be it leather goods, travel luggage or ready-to-wear. So the first and most important thing is to focus and develop a precise point of view. Then you start gaining credibility, you establish a reputation and build the brand.

J. Klewes, R. Wreschniok (eds.), *Reputation Capital*, DOI 10.1007/978-3-642-01630-1_23,
© Springer-Verlag Berlin Heidelberg 2009

Editors: What role does communication play in this early phase?

T.G.: What you do is as important as what you say. What is your product strategy, in terms of quality, design, price positioning? And, what is your distribution strategy? You clearly articulate these and then you communicate your point of view in an effective, coherent way. In fashion, everything starts with the fashion show. This is the key moment. It is the designer's statement about his or her vision. So, obviously, you have to be able to put together a great show, presenting something new and involving the audience. It has to be a combination of substance and presentation, there is nothing you can do with communications only.

Editors: Assuming I have the substance...

T.G.: From a communications perspective, you have to ensure that the event is executed flawlessly. All the details have to come into place. From the design of the invitation card to the music, from the timing and pace to the lights, the press in attendance and the seating, the assistance before and after the show... In the following days, you invite key magazines to re-see the show pieces, so that they can study the collection in detail. And then you start making decisions on which outfits go to which publications first, which could be worth a cover, etc. There are a number of strategic decisions to be made to ensure the best coverage in the fashion press.

Editors: Should I only focus on the fashion press?

T.G.: Not exclusively, but the fashion press is paramount in this early stage. You want to establish and maintain strong, positive and strategic relationships with the key players. I am not referring only to daily newspapers and magazines that can be very influential when it comes to sales. You need to reach the core fashionistas, and it's essential to be present in trendy, niche magazines that sell few copies, but are very influential in fashion circles. Establishing a relationship with these titles is crucial for your positioning in fashion.

Editors: Do personal relationships with the journalists count more in fashion than in other industries?

T.G.: No, there are a lot of parallels to building the brand in other industries. I believe that strong relationships are extremely important but you cannot build and maintain a successful brand unless you have some substance.

Editors: Are there any other assets that are critical for my brand reputation?

T.G.: For luxury brands, it is essential to have directly operated stores. There you have a formidable communications tool. You control the presentation of your product and you have a direct relationship with the clients. This is one of the reasons why creating a brand from scratch is so difficult. The investments you need to make are very high. You have to be present worldwide, in all the important cities. The store must be impeccable, and in the appropriate location, which is almost always the most expensive street in any given town. Also critical is distribution in luxury department stores, such as Nieman, Saks, Bergdorf, Harrods, Galeries Lafayette, KaDeWe. This allows you to attract customers who would not otherwise enter into your stores. There, you are directly confronted with the competition and you can see how you stand vis-à-vis the other brands.

Editors: What about advertising?

T.G.: Advertising is fundamental in any brand-building exercise. Not only the creativity defines your positioning and communicates your point of view. The media planning has to be quite sophisticated, balancing the global direction of the brand with an effective local approach. You have to also reconcile brand building and commercial objectives. It is interesting to look at two brands that have been launched successfully in the past few years. One is Stella McCartney, who adopted the approach discussed earlier, starting with the fashion show and then press office, advertising, celebrities, etc.. Tom Ford chose a totally different, unexpected strategy. Instead of a fashion show to present ready-to-wear, he started with licensing deals for eyewear and fragrances and got the licensees to invest in strong advertising campaigns. But Tom Ford is a unique case, because he was already a superstar in fashion (and beyond) as the creative director of Gucci, together with CEO Domenico De Sole the mastermind of a spectacular turnaround.

Editors: If we look at the more established companies: What is their reputation strategy?

T.G.: They might seem all the same to an outsider, but every brand has a different strategy. You have to be specific and thoroughly understand your positioning as a brand, your DNA so to speak. What is your point of view? What do you want to be? How do you want to be perceived? To maintain that perception, you have to be very disciplined and coherent in all forms of communications: the fashion shows, events, marketing materials, celebrity endorsement, advertising campaigns. Everything has to be very consistent. Always. A concrete example? Look at a brand that wants to appeal to a wide audience, and you will probably find million dollars events and endorsement from celebrities such as tabloid newspapers' favorites: footballers wives and blockbuster movie protagonists. For a trend-setting brand, a more discreet approach would maybe include more intimate events and the endorsement from a good, though lesser known actress or a cerebral movie director.

Editors: Apart from celebrities, what other relations are important?

T.G.: As in any other industry, relationships are an asset in a broad spectrum. In terms of business, you need strong relations with the luxury department stores, with media groups, strategic suppliers, creative talent inside and outside of fashion. As this is not a highly regulated industry, political decision-makers are not as relevant as, say, in the telecommunications or energy business. From a brand/product perspective, it is crucial to establish strong relationships with the trendsetters. These do not necessarily have to be seen in the media all the time, but they are the ones who are regarded in their respective circles (art, architecture, business, high society, politics, entertainment...) as role models. All of these relationships are useless if you do not cater to your customers first...

Editors: What about non-governmental organisations?

T.G.: Typically, there is not much constructive dialogue between NGOs and fashion companies. For the moment, it seems to me that NGOs are just too aggressive and that the aim on the corporate front is mainly to avoid confrontation. I think there is room for improvement and more positive interaction in the future.

Editors: Most established companies have expanded their focus to other categories, such as fragrances or eyewear, in order to gain larger revenue. Are they putting their reputation at risk?

T.G.: I don't think so. It always depends on how you expand your focus. For example, Chanel has a huge fragrance business but nobody would question its positioning as a high-end luxury brand. It's true that when you have Marilyn Monroe saying that all she wears in bed are a few drops of Chanel n°5 that can't be bad for your reputation... But on top of this, Chanel does a great work in the stores, in communications, fashion shows, etc. It's the execution that matters. The quality of the product and the way you communicate are the key. Again, and I can't stress this point enough, you have to be very disciplined in everything you do to achieve your target.

Editors: How would you rate attempts by established consumer brands, for example from sports, that try to enter the luxury business?

T.G.: More than luxury, I would use the word cool. In sports, look at Puma. In cars look at BMW – with the Mini – or Fiat – with the 500. Being cool allows these brands to reach audiences that wouldn't normally consider them. And it probably allows to go for higher prices and higher margins. It is not an easy thing to do, and there is no winning formula. But when it makes sense and it's done properly, it does pay dividends.

Editors: A lot of luxury brands are borne in Europe. Do they have to adapt their strategies to other markets, such as Asia?

T.G.: When most brands entered the Asian markets in the 1980s they replicated the exact same thing they had done in Europe. Products, store design, display, PR and advertising were exactly the same for every country in the world. In the last decade, certain things have started to change and you now have products which are tailored for the Asian market and local execution which can be adapted to different realities. But, in general, the brand strategies don't change dramatically.

Editors: One of the reasons for this might be that your target group – the elite population with a sizable disposable income – does not differ that much in its demographics.

T.G.: In a way, that is true. Most of the people we target are frequent travelers, well educated and attentive to trends in an increasingly globally connected world. If you want to build a strong brand you have to be global and you have to be true to yourself wherever you operate. In addition, the Internet has influenced the way everybody around the world gets information about brands and even buys fashion. But still, there are enormous differences across countries, languages, economies. And that is reflected in the publications people read, the products they buy, how quickly they adopt new trends or get bored of the old ones, etc.

Editors: It seems that luxury businesses direct a lot of attention to their brand, and less to corporate communication. Is this a valid interpretation?

T.G.: Yes. I have to agree with this.

Editors: Does corporate communication play a role at all?

T.G.: We have to make a distinction between brands that are part of big conglomerates like PPR, Richemont and LVMH, and brands that are family owned businesses. The publicly traded companies manage their corporate brands and have dedicated functions for IR, corporate communications, corporate social responsibility (CSR). In these companies, corporate communications tends to be very separate from brand management, but it plays a very important role. For family-owned companies, it's obviously less relevant to nurture a corporate brand.

Editors: Are customers, opinion leaders and key media not asking for more information?

T.G.: There are countries, such as Great Britain and Germany, where in fact consumers are starting to ask more questions. Most frequently, people want to be reassured that the products they buy are produced by legitimate factories, with fair compensation for the workers, no child labour involved, no harm to the environment and no endangered animals killed.

Editors: Still, some luxury goods companies seem to be especially secretive towards the media...

T.G.: I wouldn't say secretive. Although sometimes too concerned about control. Which means that press offices are required to send their photos to selected media only, to use quotes of the creative director for specific occasions only, to be very discerning in lending outfits for photo shoots, etc. But when your image is such an important asset for you, it is understandable that you do not want the tabloid newspapers to manage it for you.

Editors: Unlike most industries, fashion is shaped by strong and enigmatic personalities. How are they involved in communications?

T.G.: Strong personalities for sure. I don't know about enigmatic. It is clear that the Creative Director of the brand has the ultimate say on the creativity of the advertising campaign, the mood and tone of an event, the design of a product catalogue, the editorial strategies, and so on. As the reputation of a company is not determined by one or two things only, but by a thousand different factors, you need to take a lot of decisions, and this requires strong leadership. The worst thing that can happen is when you have too many people arguing and a decision is made late or not at all. So decision makers are very important.

Editors: Is there anything that other industries can learn from the luxury business?

T.G.: This is a very complex business. Margins can be very high, but you have to do a lot of things right in a short period of time. You also need to continuously look into the future and anticipate trends. Probably the ability to create and maintain a certain degree of coolness is what characterizes the best brands in addition to an obsessive attention to the little things when it comes to presentation and execution.

Editors: Are there other industries that focus on details to the same extent?

T.G.: At the end of the day, attention to detail in the execution is what differentiate successful from non successful businesses in every industry. It's just that the specifics are different.

Editors: Most companies can benefit from their reputation when faced with difficult economic times. Is this true for luxury businesses as well?

T.G.: When consumer confidence is down, a strong brand image is definitely helpful. Consumers who spend less money on luxury items, want to focus on products that have good quality/price ratio and offer a sense of security. Successfully navigating through a crisis and leading a brand to a stronger position at the start of a new cycle is one of the most exciting propositions for any communications/ brand management professional. We shall see next year who the winners are...

Editors: Mr. Tomaso Galli – thank you very much for this discussion!

Is there no prescription? Reputation in the pharmaceutical industry

Andrea Fischer

The reputation of the pharmaceutical industry is at best contradictory. Despite the undeniable benefits it brings by developing new medicines, its profit orientation and relatively high profit margins are viewed with mistrust. This is underscored by sporadic reports about sometimes dubious practices with risky consequences for patients and real health improvements. The industry can only confront this with a long-term strategy built on more openness and a greater readiness to face public debate. This readiness must be demonstrated by both a visible corporate strategy – that must be implemented right through to the lowest level of staff – and in the way the industry deals with increasing calls from the public for greater transparency.

"How in the hell do we have such a bad reputation?"

The pharmaceutical industry helps millions of people worldwide. Its medicines have meant – in conjunction with improvements of living conditions and hygiene in general – a significant increase in life expectancy. They also help the sick lead decent lives, despite their illness.

Investors regard the pharmaceutical industry as a good investment because it offers secure and competitive returns even in times of crisis. Researchers and other highly qualified people seek work in the industry. But the public (including the potential end users of these industrial products – the patients) sees the industry in a bad, or at best ambivalent, light.

These are the remarkably consistent results of surveys conducted over many years in practically every industrialised country. In 2007, Pfizer's vice president, responsible for communications worldwide, posed the question at a conference hosted by the Business Development Institute: "How in the hell do we have such a bad reputation?" Even those who themselves have benefited from medicines are receptive to negative news

J. Klewes, R. Wreschniok (eds.), *Reputation Capital*, DOI 10.1007/978-3-642-01630-1_24,
© Springer-Verlag Berlin Heidelberg 2009

about questionable practices in the industry, stories that illustrate its ostensibly evil character.

For example, reports claiming companies were carrying out unsupervised experiments on children in Africa or Asia. Or that information on undesirable side-effects was being suppressed and patients thus endangered. Such reports fuel suspicions that the industry is boosting its profits at the expense of human lives; the claim it is greatly benefiting health is seen only as a tired justification of unscrupulous behaviour.

Given this, it is hardly surprising that the industry's alleged rogue practices are made the subject of crime films and books (for example, the film The Fugitive with Harrison Ford or the book The King of Torts by John Grisham).

With respect to both its image in pop culture and the way its practices are presented in investigative reports, the pharmaceutical industry is viewed as one that makes profit on the backs of people in need. This image persists all over the world. There are indeed differences between individual countries: in the USA, the issue of price is important, because those without, and even many with, health insurance find medicines unaffordable. This aspect is less emphasised in countries with comprehensive insurance schemes, such as in Europe. But generally, the industry's reputation is not positive.

Even if people generally accept that companies are allowed to make a profit, when it comes to health large corporations' activities are viewed with considerable suspicion. Here, the fundamental ethical principles that most people believe should hold in capitalist economies are particularly called for. Also, people are especially sensitive about receiving good and truly beneficial treatment, so that reports about the unintended side-effects of medicines, or a bad doctor or even his willingness to accept payment for positive articles about a new medicine or favourable test results, receive a high level of attention.

Of course, many people and organisations earn their money with healthcare, but the large size of pharmaceutical companies and the high number of reports about their questionable practices has led to a fundamental mistrust of the industry. At the same time, there have only been half-hearted attempts by the industry to counter this negative image – either because they do not see the need, or because they fear that any attempt to broach the topic will first and foremost reinforce the negative image. There is even less readiness to discuss why profit orientation is necessary to ensure the industry's success – or even to support it by establishing ethical rules that prescribe how exactly companies should behave.

But: if the pharmaceutical industry does not present itself in an active and self-confident way, it cannot expect the situation to improve. For, apart from itself, it has no other advocates.

All just a question of communication?

The pharmaceutical industry cannot be content with its portrayal in public debate. To make matters worse, each year it becomes even more counter-productive when it comes to co-determining the ground rules that govern its activities in public dialogue. It responds by strongly emphasising its responsibility, by broadcasting its achievements, with active lobbying and self-portrayals to match in brochures or on the Internet. But the industry adheres to the same business model, adapts to current challenges with mergers and internal change processes, reacts to political changes in market conditions – and continues to make substantial profits all the while.

Still, it attempts in all countries to underscore its commitment to society, so that people recognise it as making a valuable contribution to the welfare of society as a whole. In the USA, the pharmaceutical industry led the way through its Partnership for Prescription Assistance (PPA) and showed how people without health insurance can get expensive medicines (largely through foundations linked to the individual member companies of PhRM, the American industry association).

In Europe, the industry mainly points to its commitment to research. In Germany, it has done so for years with a publicity campaign. This campaign put the pharmaceutical industry on the offensive, allowing it to rightly point out the advances made possible by modern medicine. The motto "Research is the best medicine" ("Forschung ist die beste Medizin") is illustrated by testimonials from people who have overcome an illness with the help of medication. To complement this, individual researchers working for the industry are shown together with their achievements. The campaign was circulated widely with classical advertising methods, but despite its successes, it was not able to fundamentally change the industry's ailing image.

However sensible these efforts may appear, they will always be up against reports about the industry's actual or alleged misconduct – reports about people that were not adequately informed about the possible side effects of medicines, about the over-pricing of innovative medicines or about the industry's alleged refusal to ensure that people in developing countries have access to medication.

The industry rightly points out that one or two bad apples cannot be taken as representative. However, even if there are journalists who insist on savaging the pharmaceutical industry, that is no reason for executives to erect protective walls around the industry. After all, not all negative reports are poorly researched, and after all, the industry is from time to time caught engaging in actually dubious practices.

More than anything, however, a purely reactive response to accusations by the industry is not suited to creating a sustainable and deeply embedded positive image. The situation is exacerbated by the industry's traditionally restrained communications policy, which all too often gives, as it were, the 'bad apples' and scandals a chance to dominate the public agenda.

Unfortunately, this is where positive campaigns like that of the German industry and the American PPA) initiative for reimbursing medicine costs to the needy most often come unstuck. On their own, they will not be able to repair (or: restore?) the pharmaceutical industry's reputation.

For, when it is a whole industry that is at issue, reputation is not only a question of good public relations or praiseworthy CSR projects. Rather, it is crucially determined by everyday practice, something that must withstand critical scrutiny from journalists (and, increasingly, doctors and patients, too). The success story of the chemical industry's reputation makeover could point the way here. Not until there was a visible and verifiable improvement in the environmental consequences of its production processes did the chemical industry lose its image as a dangerous environmental miscreant.

A long way: Approaches to improving reputation

The accusations are manifold, but when summarised boil down to the following points: unethical marketing practices, safety of the products, lack of responsibility towards people in poor countries. These points – which conceal a range of detailed allegations – are the most important areas in which pharmaceutical companies must work on their reputation.

This path will be one that the industry must follow for many years. It must undertake a long-term and conspicuous review of its practices, and then make lasting changes. And it will have to ensure that individual companies do not stray in the process. Only then can negative reports be avoided in future – or, if they do arise, be legitimately dismissed. In such an event, the industry will be able to point to a number of efforts, made over several years, aimed at improving industry practice. In this sense, it must be ready to take many more far-reaching steps in order to permanently dispose of prejudices against it.

We market our products according to strict rules

Even those who accept that a pharmaceutical company must make profits in order to sustainably finance its business model often are uneasy at the industry's paying doctors for their favourable opinions. The question of whether doctors are being encouraged by remuneration or particularly attractive professional development opportunities to see the merits of a product (and publish accordingly), and whether they are in this way influencing guidelines – irrespective of actual study results, is repeatedly raised.

Numerous guidelines have now appeared from the industry, describing the proper way to interact with important opinion leaders. The German industry – similar initiatives exist in other countries, for example the French CEMIP – has instituted a "Voluntary Self-Control for the Pharmaceutical Industry" ("Freiwillige Selbstkontrolle für die Arzneimittelindustrie") and has done valuable work towards the implementation of these guidelines. Based on national and European codes of conduct for co-operation with specialists (that is, doctors) and with patient organisations, it acts as a complaints body to which anyone can turn if they believe a company has broken the rules.

To date, it is mainly companies in the pharmaceutical industry that have used this instrument of reciprocal monitoring. The work of such an institution would surely be more effective and have more clout if it were made transparent through the involvement of other stakeholders. That would make it more prominent and would do much more to improve the industry's standing.

As regards the safety of the products, there are no indications in Western Europe or in the USA that people believe state authorities to be working unreliably and that the problem thus lies in their approval processes. But when those products are used, they are eyed with scepticism, for example because using them for extended periods can have side-effects that are not discovered in the limited context of pre-approval clinical trials. However, problems can also arise if the medication is taken in too high doses or even incorrectly administered to the body.

To remove any suspicions in this regard, it would be worthwhile to intensify health services research, which investigates the long-term use of products within therapy and under everyday conditions. The institutes for reviewing medication, which operate in all industrialised countries (including IQWIG, HAS, NICE), and issue recommendations on which medications should be covered by health insurance, have called for such research.

In reality, the idea falters because health services research is underdeveloped, and often, there are few or insufficient resources available. Financial support for such research (perhaps via a foundation), and especially the manifest support for such research that providing funding would demonstrate, would increase pressure on governments to assign state funding to the purpose. The pharmaceutical industry could contribute in this way to the establishment of such research, research initiated by independent committees and monitored jointly with various groups in society. Only thus would the research results have an authority capable of removing suspicions and of clarifying the debate about the effectiveness of medicines.

Equally, public relations for medicines is viewed critically. In the USA, advertising for prescription-only medicines is permitted, but even there there are constant discussions about what companies are, and what they should not be, allowed to do. In Europe, by contrast, the situation is clear, since advertising is not permitted in any EU member state. Violations of the law are punished swiftly, and quickly attract critical public attention.

Not without justification, the industry has long complained that this strict law prevents it from using its expertise as a manufacturer and developer to inform end users about its products. The European Commission recently responded with a guideline proposal, which would in future allow the industry, within certain strict limits, to publish information about – but not advertise! – its products. Patient organisations, however, have considerable misgivings about the proposal.

At present, it does not look as if this moderate proposal by the EU Commission will find a majority, even if new research (for example, Prognos's 2008 survey on patient information) certainly does show that patients desire more information from the industry (and believe they can distinguish it from advertising). But the resistance from patient associations is too strong. The industry would have had to seek an open discussion with all stakeholders, and jointly develop a model for providing more patient information. Instead, all parties to the debate have returned to their entrenched positions.

For example, in Sweden, the industry has long used a strictly controlled model, FASS, to deliver the information doctors receive to a wider public. FASS is accepted by all parties, and could have served as a blueprint for a new European approach.

We produce safe products

One of the prejudices circulating about the pharmaceutical industry is the alleged riskiness of its products. Of course, a pharmaceutical product is always risky for the person using it, precisely because of its potency. For exactly this reason, all industrialised countries have in past decades established functioning approval agencies, which demand that producers comprehensively test their products before any approval can be issued.

Despite this, when medicines are taken for long periods in the real world, the risk of an unexpected reaction remains, a risk that even the most sophisticated tests cannot foresee. The most effective way for the industry to respond to this is with the health services research mentioned above, the whole point of which is to investigate the long-term effects of medicines under everyday conditions.

Also, the comprehensive tests often mean that a medicine, despite years of developmental research and having passed the first stages of testing, must be withdrawn shortly before it is due to appear on the market. The industry repeatedly points out the high risk it is taking and uses this argument to explain that it needs high profitability because of this risk. Here, a more open policy, focused on explaining the protracted development cycle and the sometimes late awareness of adverse effects or risks, would surely help.

Alongside this, most European states have now set up additional agencies that – in order to decide whether health insurers should cover certain medicines – investigate the effects of medicines both comparatively and under real conditions. (These include the German IQWIG, the French HAS and the UK's NICE.) The USA has recently decided to introduce such tests.

The agencies do not carry out their own studies but check the results of existing studies and compare them. In this way, they hope to establish whether a medicine actually has the claimed healing effect, or whether other medicines could achieve the same result. These agencies – which differ from country to country – are always the subject of controversial discussions about their methods, their criteria and their decisions. Above all, their decisions trigger heated debates when they recommend withdrawing cover for certain medicines.

An important agent in these debates is the pharmaceutical industry itself, which on the one hand provides many of the studies used in the evaluation process, but which also criticises the agencies' approach. Even though many of these discussions are about the actual methods applied when evaluating the products, in the public mind they further blacken the image of the industry, since it is seen as not wanting to have its products monitored.

A prominent, public and positive stance by the industry towards a critical examination of its work could help counter this impression. This does not mean always approving the agencies' approach in every detail – some points here are surely contestable. But a fundamentally positive attitude – which could be evinced by actively promoting and working towards the creation of a uniform, pan-European watchdog – would help prevent the industry from being seen as thwarting stricter controls of pharmaceutical products and their use.

The industry is afraid of over-strict standards and the use of invalid criteria for evaluating its products. It is afraid that its keenest critics now also have, as it were, state-endorsed means at their disposal. In fact, however, its refusal only further fuels suspicions it is forestalling a closer assessment of its practices because it fears for its profits.

But pharmaceutical research is shifting towards a more precise delineation of target groups for individual products anyway ('personalised medicine'), meaning that the 'blockbuster' model (huge medicine sales for large target groups) will no longer apply in future. Also, promoting a European agency would serve the industry's own interests, since a multitude of different authorities in individual member states can only stand in the way of a European common market for pharmaceutical products.

In this context, a corporate strategy that measures the performance of employees by the revenue they generate falls short. Instead, companies will have to make the quality of their marketing strategies a performance indicator per se. This will also entail adopting a positive and constructive approach to criticism from without. Part of this is also seeking active communication with stakeholders, including specialist critics – a way of communicating that understands their criticisms not only as obstructiveness or as criticism at the end of the rollout process, but as a resource that can help improve the product. Such a shift requires reorienting the business ethos, so that all employees are involved and it is made clear that there are new rules and a new approach for dealing with criticism from without.

We care about others

The pharmaceutical industry devotes the largest portion of its resources to researching illnesses that affect people in wealthier parts of the globe. Most of its marketing efforts, too, are concentrated there. This has led to a perception that the industry does not care the least bit for the poor. It does not research how to fight their diseases, and if medicines do exist, it makes them so expensive that they cannot be used in poorer countries.

This assessment of the distribution of resources corresponds with reality – pharmaceutical companies, like all businesses, make products for the people who can buy them. At the same time, however, the industry has in recent years gone to considerable lengths to develop products for poorer countries or to distribute them – once they exist – to people there. Apart from the efforts of individual companies, the industry as a whole has gifted considerable sums to the Global Fund to Fight AIDS, Malaria and Tuberculosis, and to the International AIDS Vaccine Initiative (IAVI).

But these efforts are still almost unnoticeable and not widely known. One reason is that each company wishes to advertise its commitment under its own name only. This prevents the industry as a whole from attracting attention to its efforts. Another reason is that the industry always doubts that its efforts will be appropriately rewarded – and wonders whether each new project will, in fact, only stir up new debates about whether it could be doing more.

As much as one can understand these concerns, this restraint has tended to consolidate the impression that the pharmaceutical industry as a whole is indifferent to the substantial health problems facing the developing world. It is repeatedly criticised for this, one example being criticism of the industry's patent policy from health NGOs like "Doctors Without Borders".

For this reason, the first and most important step would be for the pharmaceutical industry to become noticeable and visible with regard to its engagement in poor countries. The International Federation of Pharmaceutical Manufacturers and Associations (IFPMA) has taken a crucial step with a page on its website titled "Health partnerships – developing world", but it is still too low-key.

And it is much more than just a question of information. It is also important that the industry be prepared to have its projects examined – and, if need be, criticised – by organisations that are committed to providing medical services in poor countries. Most projects from the industry are already in conjunction with NGOs, however, meaning a further examination and publication of those activities would not necessarily expose the industry to more criticism.

Rather, active public relations offer the industry a chance to fashion a picture in which it is no longer the one at fault. For an overview of individual activities would also make clear that many problems have to do with state-organised – or even not at all organised – health services in poor countries, meaning that supplying medicines in itself will not alleviate the problem. The industry's involvement therefore should not and cannot be restricted to providing medicines alone. It also must concentrate some of its activities on the basic conditions of health policy.

Further, there is now a global public sphere, where negative incidents spread rapidly – much quicker than 'good news'. And so, international pharmaceutical companies must also deal with this public. When one branch of a company or a supplier in a certain country actually engages in unethical experiments with poor people, this must be shut down immediately and conspicuously (and any chance of a repeat ruled out). Here it becomes obvious how important it is for a company to have the greatest possible transparency in its internal operations, since this makes it possible to realise in good time when something is out of order, and presents a chance to take timely action to fix it. This is also helpful for errors that are made in marketing products in industrialised countries and that must be avoided. Certainly then, this is an important strategic element for modernising a company.

But alongside an active response to shortcomings, the pharmaceutical industry must turn from being the object of reports to being an actively engaged agent, so that it becomes clear how many factors actually are involved in improving the health of people in poor regions, and, more importantly, that the pharmaceutical industry is ready to, and will, do its part.

Increasing the visibility of the industry's activities would facilitate a wider-ranging discussion about fundamentally improving the health of the poor and about what the real obstacles are. In this way, the recurring discussion about patent law can be confronted with strong arguments that make clear that ownership of knowledge about medicines does not hinder, but in fact enables, progress – and that the companies that exploit (mandatory) patents to produce apparently cheap medicines also do this to maximise profits and are in no way simply acting as Samaritans.

The pharmaceutical industry must become an important voice in international debates about health. That would undoubtedly do the discussion as a whole some good – but this requires that the industry should first gain credibility. Only then can it counteract and help shape discussions that make unrealistic calls for the virtually free provision of medicines to the developing world – instead of leaving them entirely to the critical NGOs.

We can work better

Even with this strategy, the industry will not be able to repair its image overnight – but it can take visible and palpable steps. For a bad reputation that has built up over many years cannot be easily mended, no matter how determined the effort.

The changes that have long been made in actual company practice have not been communicated or verified actively enough. The strategy therefore must be different from the one before: speaking confidently about the quality of the industry's work, openly admitting any mistakes and promptly taking steps to effect change, and convincingly presenting its involvement in poor countries, which has been insufficient to date. In this way, the industry can appear as one that plainly cares for the concerns of its employees and patients, and that also takes seriously the needs of people in poor parts of the world – even though it is not able to fully satisfy them (but one can expect neither from industrial corporations).

An important instrument for such an active strategy will be to involve patients even more than before in the work of the pharmaceutical industry. Individual companies certainly have had good experiences with patient advisory councils when carrying out studies (as supervisors and consultants). This should encourage further openness in dealing with studies and their results.

Such an approach does not require disclosing actual product formulas, but rather a readiness to take the future consumers of a product seriously. Why not publish short versions of the studies, given that they will be presented to an approval agency anyway for a final check? But such openness also involves citing previous studies that have demonstrated the un-workability of other approaches. Certainly, companies have many reasons for not doing this. On the other hand, only by being open in this way can they allay suspicions that negative material is somehow being suppressed.

More public access to research that has already been conducted requires a new platform for the purpose. For, although the regulatory agencies (the German BfArm or the European EMEA) publish a great deal, they do so in a form that is useful only to specialists. It would certainly make a good impression if the European pharmaceutical industry were to work together with approval agencies to make the studies accessible to a wider public. This would quite clearly prove the industry's serious commitment to keeping the public well informed about its activities.

In addition, the industry can use the growing interest for patient involvement and arrange patient forums, where information is always asked for and given. Here, it is not just about providing information on new medicines, but about actively involving patients in studies as advisors. It is about providing comprehensive information on the global state of research, information on how medicines can be sensibly used and on the necessary compliance aspects. To take one example: Pfizer in Germany has had good experience redesigning patient information leaflets with a joint working group that includes patients.

It is worth looking for ways to increase patient involvement on every level. This will be difficult at first and will perhaps even prolong processes – but it is an important condition for gaining trust. Patient involvement will become a global standard for evaluating and discussing medical and socio-political processes, and if the pharmaceutical industry took the lead here, it would send a clear message that goes beyond the actual cases themselves. Specialist medical groups, too, the preferred contact and co-operation partners of the pharmaceutical industry, are becoming more critical and thus more stubborn regarding offers of co-operation. That is why for this stakeholder segment, too, only a significantly changed and improved business policy (and thus reputation), will be able to ensure fruitful co-operation in the long term.

Such an active strategy for the pharmaceutical industry is not only advisable because it no longer wants to live with its bad reputation. If such efforts are not undertaken, and the reputation of the pharmaceutical industry remains dubious, it will become more attractive for politicians to demand special sacrifices from the industry when it comes to financing healthcare.

In this sense, a strategy aimed at improving reputation is also a strategy for securing the business model. Being content with the notion that patients who have been helped are grateful while everyone else remains receptive to fundamental criticisms of the industry will no longer do. The role of patients and with it that of the critically interested public, is already growing, both due to the necessary involvement of stakeholders in internal consultations and because social media are generating publicity of their own.

The response to this must be a comprehensive strategy that touches the entire business concept, one that makes the industry's achievements visible – and verifiable. For the pharmaceutical industry has done much to improve the world's health. It should no longer allow that fact to be obscured by actual or alleged mistakes.

Part V: Reputation strategies for the 21st century

*Associate yourself with men of good quality if you esteem your own
reputation for 'tis better to be alone than in bad company.*

George Washington (1732-1799)

Who wants to be a millionaire? Investment strategies for reputation management in the 21st century

Robert Wreschniok and Joachim Klewes

Consulting experience has shown that there are four basic approaches to managing corporate reputation. These resemble the four classic strategies for investing on the stock market. But none of these investment philosophies will suit every company in every situation. Seeking maximum reputational return, without heeding the risks, can lead to empty pockets – and a ruined name. But simply 'playing it safe' with reputation ignores the specific challenges of the 21st century. Anyone nowadays seeking to become a reputation millionaire must follow ten golden rules.

There are essentially two approaches when it comes to competition between companies. Either you play for time and hope that, in the long run, the principle of evolution will take care of things, and the fittest will survive. Or, as is more common, you trust in the power of strategy: "Strategy has an impact on the effect of competition and the pace of change. In this sense, it produces an important effect: it accelerates time" (Oetinger 1993, translated from German). So, those managing companies need to ask two central questions. First: in order to more quickly reach the goals we have set, which resources should we deploy, and how? And second: in so doing, how can we strike the balance between effectiveness and efficiency?

These questions must also be answered by those who wish to be the first choice for potential clients in their line of business. Strategic reputation management can help foster an excellent reputation that, as it were, goes before the company.[1] Such companies become the first port of call for 'high potentials', who will put themselves through an arduous assessment centre ordeal for a chance to work there.[2] Banks and investors extend a 'credit of trust' when it comes to negotiating an increase in capital.[3] Politi-

---

[1] See Vonwil/Wreschniok on pp. 83-99 in this volume.
[2] See Thompson on pp. 73-81 in this volume.
[3] See Schwaiger on pp. 39-55 in this volume.

J. Klewes, R. Wreschniok (eds.), *Reputation Capital*, DOI 10.1007/978-3-642-01630-1_25,
© Springer-Verlag Berlin Heidelberg 2009

cians ask for advice when debating important legislation because they value the company's integrity, expertise, experience and specialist knowledge.[4] No more than a wild fantasy?

In fact, there are companies like this in most sectors – they are often admired, sometimes marvelled at, always watched. Those trying to catch up suspect they can close the gap by investing wisely in reputation. Because delivering functional and social expectations of the public on the one hand and manage to build a unique identity on the other hand[5] creates trust[6] and this trust builds the informal framework of a company. This framework provides „return in cooperation" and produces Reputation Capital. The higher the Reputation Capital, the less the costs for supervising and exercising control. In this sense reputation – whether understood directly as a company's "social capital" (Bourdieu 1983) or indirectly as a catalyst that magnifies a company's social capital[7] – makes it possible to create value through social relationships that produce an asymmetric exchange.[8] Reputation is a corporate asset that can be managed, accumulated and traded in for

- trust,[9]

- legitimisation of a position of power and social recognition,[10]

- a premium price for goods and services offered,

- a stronger willingness among shareholders to hold on to shares in times of crisis,[11]

- or a stronger readiness to invest in the company's stock.[12]

---

[4] See Lochbihler on pp. 101-111 in this volume.

[5] See Eisenegger on pp. 11-22 in this volume.

[6] It is this unique approach which differentiate the thoughts in this article from other methods in this filed of interest as e.g. Jackson (2004).

[7] See Silberstein-Loeb on pp. 23-36 in this volume.

[8] It would appear many stakeholders tend to go for companies that are economically and socially better positioned rather than those that are worse placed. They tend to structure their relationships to companies in a hierarchical way. At the top are the companies that have accumulated the most social and cultural capital. To paraphrase Bourdieu, social capital is what companies with the right relationships enjoy; or, those that make the reliable impression that they have the right relationships (Bourdieu 1983). Cultural capital is what attaches to companies that 'call the shots' in their sector. In business practice, one speaks of opinion leaders or 'best-in-class companies'.

[9] See especially von der Crone on pp. 179-195 in this volume.

[10] See Eisenegger, pp. 11-22 and Rupp, pp. 325-338 in this volume, as well as Eisenegger (2005) and Eisenegger (2008).

[11] See Schütz (2007) and Schwaiger M, Raithel S, Schloderer M on pp. 39-55 in this volume.

[12] See Klewes on pp. 287-298 in this volume.

Particularly in times of economic crisis, the importance of this special kind of capital becomes clear. And, as is so often the case, the true value of an asset is only recognised after it is lost. When the public first became aware of the property and financial market crisis in early 2008, one refrain was rehearsed repeatedly by business journalists in the opinions published in major international media outlets. In essence, it was: "When the New Economy bubble burst at the start of the twenty-first century, a lot of money went up in flames. What distinguishes the property and financial market crisis is that it is not money, but mostly trust that is going up in flames." Somehow, many readers took this message to be reassuring, perhaps reasoning: "As long as it's only trust, and not money, it can't be so bad." But the rude awakening came in October 2008 when the investment bank Lehman Brothers went bankrupt. Hardly anyone could conceive of the collapse of such a renowned bank. But when just that happened, confidence evaporated – and not just in this one bank, but in the banking system as a whole. Massive write-downs in confidence, or reputation capital, led to the biggest economic crisis since 1929 and subsequently to a huge loss of value on stock markets.

At several points in this book, it is shown that a corporate reputation that inspires trust feeds on factors that relate to economic competence. In other words: it relies on an intact functional reputation.[13] So, it is not surprising that economic crises often evolve into crises of confidence and that crises of confidence, in turn, mean an increasingly bigger risk for the economic performance of a company.

Reputation as a strategic investment

An interesting result emerges from analysing several clients Pleon has advised in recent years. Namely: successfully accumulating reputation capital follows a similar logic to the classic investment strategies of the finance markets. Whether one is building up financial or reputation capital, the basic approaches are similar. Examining these strategies can help one become aware of, calculate and manage the risks.

---

[13] See Schwaiger, Eisenegger, Vonwil/Wreschniok, Silberstein-Loeb in this volume.

According to our observation of the market,[14] four investment philosophies can be distinguished:

1. Hedge strategy,

2. Growth strategy,

3. Value strategy,

4. Total return strategy.

These are used in practice by companies (and other organisations) to increase valuable reputation capital and to safeguard it against loss. In the following, they are presented as 'ideal types'.

The hedge strategy

Hedge strategies are extremely speculative since they rely on complex bets about the future development and use leverage in an attempt to increase profits. The greater the potential return, however, the greater the risk.

Applying this to reputation management, the strategy essentially relies on placing the communicative focus on one topic or one person as a reputation driver. This resulting leverage produces an effect for a certain time, independently of the company's real position. The company is betting, as it were, that it will be able to fulfil the promises made at some later point.

Hedge strategies are therefore closely coupled with corporate strategy. Indeed, the two almost fuse. And it is here that the actual 'hedge' takes place:[15] if the business strategy is successful (for example, if the sales targets strived for are reached, or the desired market penetration or market leadership achieved), you can cash in on the expectations fired up by the communications strategy. There is the prospect of tidy reputational returns.

Companies or politicians use hedge strategies to build up the image of a charismatic leader, for example, or to occupy major issues on the public agenda. They hope to yield positive short-term returns on their reputation. They systematically network with institutional reputation bearers or opinion leaders to secure their 'licence to operate' – in other words, the social and cultural capital they need to achieve the goals they pursue.

---

[14] A range of benchmarking studies and expert surveys conducted by Pleon with clients from 1998 to 2008 (unpublished).

[15] Something that hedge funds, in fact, seldom still do today.

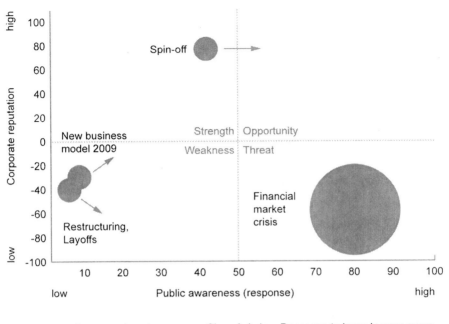

Fig. 1. The chart shows which corporate issues enhance or diminish reputation and how much coverage these issues were given in the media. A reputation index (vertical axis) is used to measure how reputation is affected by an issue, and is calculated on the basis of three factors: (1) diffusion (how widespread media coverage of an issue was), (2) intensity (average number of reputation-related issues as a proportion of all articles), and (3) persistence (the time period over which an issue was reported on). The higher the reputation-index value is, the more positive the impact of the issue on reputation. The level of media coverage of an issue is measured by calculating the proportion of articles about the company in selected major media (horizontal axis).
Source: ECRS/Pleon

Figure 1 shows an extract from the communication strategy of a company that is following a hedge strategy. The chart shows the situation at the beginning of a particularly dynamic phase of communications activity. The company is preparing for a spin-off (that is, part of the company will be spun off as an independent company). Excellent reputation values (about +82 points on a scale from -100 to 100 points) are achieved in media reporting. In fact, the spun-off company is even opinion leader within its field. The next step is to use the right levers to achieve – in less than eight weeks – higher public awareness while maintaining the already high reputation values. The company hopes this would mean a favourable start for the spin-off on the stock market.

Hedge strategies are found not only in connection with IPOs, spin-offs or mergers and acquisitions. They are also used for political campaigns or start-up companies that hope to conquer market niches or that have opened up "blue oceans" with new business ideas (Kim/Mauborgne, 2005). Examples include: entrepreneurs who revolutionise internet searches or make social networking dead easy; those who have realised the market is ripe for cosmetic products produced under fair conditions; a hick-town producer of sports shoes that has achieved enormous success by presenting its products as embodying a global lifestyle.

The growth strategy

On the stock market, a growth strategy tries to identify markets with future growth ahead of time. Investors thus select companies that have the highest growth potential for their portfolios. They are less concerned with individual companies, but rather entire sectors of the economy.

A similar approach is adopted by companies trying to understand how specific sector-related issues affect their reputation and that of their competitors. In order to reach their mid-term goals, they assume a controlled reputational risk, which they limit through careful analysis. Companies adopting a growth strategy perform a business calculation using reputation driver analyses. This identifies the areas in which reputation management activities will in fact improve their competitive position. To determine these reputation drivers, they tend to conduct stakeholder analyses of various kinds. Their definition of stakeholders depends on the task at hand, and might be restricted to specific opinion leaders (politicians, investors, journalists etc.) or extend to the wider public.[16] Depending on the method used, several reputation drivers may be measured using stakeholder surveys, including the credibility of a company, the quality of its products or services, its market position, its sense of responsibility or the management's leadership.

---

[16] See Schwaiger M, Raithel S, Schloderer M on pp. 39-55 in this volume.

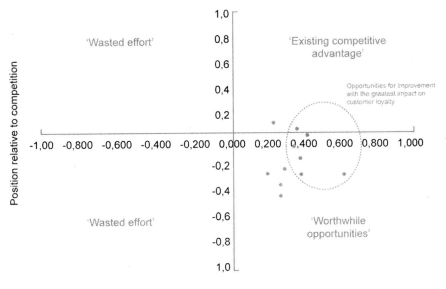

Fig. 2. The chart shows an extract from an efficiency analysis of individual positioning factors, based on a reputation driver analysis. The vertical axis maps the company's reputation drivers position relative to the competition. The horizontal axis maps the extent to which reputation drivers affect customer loyalty. The reputation drivers in the circle represent those with the greatest potential for improving customer loyalty. By enhancing these reputation drivers, a company can either close the gap on its rivals or build on an existing advantage. Data source: results of a representative stakeholder survey. Calculation of reputation driver model by the Institut für Marktorientierte Unternehmensführung at the Ludwig-Maximilians-Universität, Munich.
Source: ECRS/IMM.

In Figure 2, the quadrant marked 'Worthwhile opportunities' contains the reputation drivers with the most potential for improving the company's competitive position. The quadrant 'Existing competitive advantage' contains the reputation drivers for which the company was already clearly ahead of the competition in public opinion at the time of the survey. The two quadrants marked 'Wasted effort' contain the reputation drivers that either do not play an important role for the company's reputation, or that are already so strongly dominated by the competition that the investment required outweighs any potential gain. An efficiency analysis like this identifies a set of two to four reputation drivers that should form the core of the reputation strategy. Investing here will have the greatest positive impact – in this example, with regard to *customer loyalty*.

More generally though, a reputation driver analysis can of course be carried out for any corporate goal: from attracting new business or improving employee motivation through to improving supplier relations. The aim will always be to identify ahead of time where one is ahead of or behind the competition, and to get the best return on a particular investment. With a growth strategy, the effect of communications on reputation drivers is enhanced by what we termed 'agenda alignment': that is, aligning communications with specific issues that relate to the company's sector. Such issues have a significant impact on the public perception of reputation (see also Figure 1). Their interpretation by the media and the public follows particular patterns.[17]

Examples for companies adopting a growth strategy include: global players whose business is so complex that they no longer can afford to be number one in absolutely every area; companies operating in sectors and competitive constellations that require all the hard factors to be optimised to the full, and who fall back on intangible assets to find new competitive advantages and USPs.

The value strategy

Unlike the growth approach, the value strategy relies on assessing companies individually. The focus is on identifying undervalued listed companies that have a good market position, high returns and steady profits. Ideally, the portfolio will, over the long term, increase in value reliably and continuously.

As it applies to communications, too, the value strategy tolerates only moderate risk in the accumulation of reputation capital. The main focus is on a circumspect and sustainable corporate policy. Further, it attempts to achieve goals both for and over the long term. Compared to the investment strategies already mentioned, this reputation strategy is much more inwardly focused. Thus, the primary target groups are the company's own employees, followed by business partners and clients. Traditionally, these companies feel a duty to uphold the highest ethical and social standards in dealing with their stakeholders. As Robert Bosch once said: "It is better to

---

[17] See the 'Ten golden rules for reputation management in the twenty-first century', in this article below.

lose money than it is to lose trust". In relation to external parties, the value strategy centres around sober, objective corporate communications that serve to strengthen perceptions of the company's functional competence (functional reputation) and economic performance.

But here, the focus of reputation management is minimising internal risks to social reputation. The company will not tolerate internal structures and processes that could lead to public concerns focusing on matters of integrity or social or environmental issues (social reputation), rather than economic performance. In this sense, a value strategy relies on putting structures in place to neutralise potentially scandalous developments or even negative media coverage before they happen.

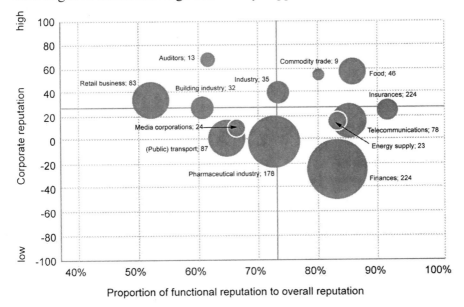

Fig. 3. This chart shows the proportion of functional reputation to overall reputation (horizontal axis), and the (aggregated) overall reputation (vertical axis) for various business sectors in Switzerland for the second half of 2007. The size of the circles shows the intensity of coverage for each sector in major media. For an explanation of the reputation scale, which ranges from -100 to 100, see Figure 1 in this article.
Source: ECRS/fög.

Figure 3 clearly shows the relationship between economic and social reputation in various business sectors – a relationship that is significant for the makeup of overall reputation. The study examined companies in each sector that adopted a value approach. The two lines that cross on the chart indicate average values for each axis. The horizontal line shows the average reputation value for all sectors (+25). The vertical line shows the average share of functional judgements (that is, judgements relating to competence and economic performance) in overall reputation (functional reputation as a proportion of overall reputation averages at about 76%). Typical examples for companies successfully pursuing a value strategy can be found in industry, raw materials trade and food production (not retail), where functional reputation as a proportion of overall reputation is between 80% and 93%.

The value strategy is often used by family-owned SMEs that have a good reputation among specialists and specialised industries. Sometimes they are 'hidden champions': global leaders in their field that, outside their home region, are known only to experts.

The total return strategy

The investment strategy known as 'total return' has only one overarching goal: to yield a positive absolute return where possible. At the very least, the capital invested must be preserved, regardless of surrounding developments on the stock market.

Total return strategies *in communications*, too, are regarded as particularly secure and promising. The low risk, however, comes at the cost of low reputational yield. Compared to the other investment strategies, both internal and external communications activities here are the least intense by far. Strictly speaking, total return is less a self-contained, forward-looking strategy in its own right, and more a case of simply sticking with the tried and true.

There is another important difference to the value approach: those who adopt total return strategies see no need to invest in internal communications. The following statements are typical for companies that follow a total return strategy:

- "We have no need for reputation management or for active communications, internally or externally. This approach has served us very well in the past 150 years and it will continue to do so in future."

- "We invest in the quality of our products. That is our guarantee for high customer satisfaction, and that's all that matters to us."

- "You know, last year we had our public and media image analysed for the first time. We found out that we are practically invisible – and we're doing very well as things stand."

But these convictions are now colliding with the specific communicative conditions of the twenty-first century. The media system has become ever more differentiated. It operates according to market principles and its own system-internal logic, and in recent decades it has become increasingly anchored in society.

This process is strikingly illustrated by the rapid increase in the quality and quantity of media reporting. A constantly expanding range of media forms and formats delivers more comprehensive information faster, generating more attention and penetrating more and more sectors of society.

This increased penetration is complemented and intensified by the emergence of new spaces of influence on the internet. Today, anyone with an internet connection can potentially form their opinion without recourse to conventional information channels or major media outlets. The problem with this double structural shift in the media system – that is, increased media penetration in society[18] and increased informational autonomy due to the internet – is that cycles of scandal have taken on a fiercer dynamic in recent years. The resulting losses in reputation mainly affect business associations and institutions. Often, it is those following total return strategies who suffer. The reason: the neo-liberal model of the 1990s sought to delegate the solution of fundamental social problems almost exclusively to the economic system (Eisenegger 2005: 79). In a globalised world, the state was, until recently, regarded as unfit to provide solutions. The search for those responsible for current economic woes has suddenly trained the spotlight on companies that had successfully kept themselves out of the media for decades. And this without a deterioration in their product quality[19] or any other structural company processes.

Often, this affects companies worst that have not succeeded in establishing a clear, recognisable profile among the stakeholder groups that matter in times of crisis. Such companies become the football of media interests and internet opinion forums. Questions about good governance, the social

---

[18] Media impact is strengthened by an almost collective orientation toward the anticipated preferences of audiences or readers. This makes political conflicts in the publications of different media outlets rather uncommon. Instead, there is a strong convergence across all media in the opinions regarded as being worthy of publication.

[19] At the same time, products are less and less likely to be assessed independently of their supplier. Especially in a B2B context, questions like "Who is the most reliable partner?" or "Who am I still going to be able to work with in ten years' time?" often determine purchase decisions. And it is a supplier's reputation that often crucially determines the answers to these questions.

quality and integrity of behaviour towards employees or external interest groups are hotly debated in the media and on social networks – independently of whether the company affected plays an active role in this or not.

Silberstein-Loeb sums this development up in the following way: "Seen this way, the most important question facing any company that seeks to profit by its reputation is: how imperfect is the market? If the market is highly imperfect and information moves slowly or ineffectively, then a company may safely profit from an unreliable good reputation. If the market is an effective source of information, however, then firms should be wary about pursuing such strategies." (Silberstein-Loeb 2009: 31). This is surely the crucial reason why more and more companies in B2B today – who for a long time saw no need to establish their reputation profile among a wider public beyond their target group of customers – are now examining reputational risks and returns.

Total return strategies are occasionally found in industry: in particular, the chemical industry until the late 1980s or the pharmaceutical industry today. Other examples are SMEs, or companies whose clients are mainly businesses. But generally, this strategy is no longer well adapted to the realities of today's media society.

Table 1. Comparison of the four investment strategies for reputation and capital

	Hedge	Growth	Value	Total return
Main characteristic	Monothematic, aggressive, target-group-oriented communications	Focused profile based on careful analysis of reputation drivers and sector-related issues	Consciously inward-looking reputation management that focuses on structures	Focus on products or services without any attempt at communicative support
Communications investment	High expenditure on external communications	Balanced investment between internal measures (including analysis) and external communications	Considerably higher investment in internal process optimisation and a carefully dosed investment in external communications	Kept to a minimum
Opportunities	Quick establishment of a distinctive reputation	Well secured reputation profile, well-grounded and resting on several pillars	High multiplier effect among employees and specialists	Low attention and publicity, as long as companies are not in public crisis
Risks	Words not followed by action; public criticism. Disappointed expectations	Low degree of profiling compared to more aggressive players	Reputation profile not supported by widespread recognition	Descent into crisis – no buffer of trust; Internally: lack of orientation and support by company policy
Especially suitable for	Companies that are starting up or turning themselves around	Companies in oligopolistic markets	B2B, 'Hidden champions', larger SMEs	Unsuitable today
Time scale	Short-term	Mid-term	Long-term	Long-term
Typical examples	Apple (iPod), Google (until about 2006), McDonald's (I'm loving it), Oracle, Body Shop, Starbucks	EADS; Siemens. Deutsche Telekom, Nokia, Vodafone, SAP	Bosch, Faber Castel, Webasto, JM Family Enterprises, Stew Leonard's, S.C. Johnson & Son	Aldi (until about 2000), Grünenthal, G&D until 2008, Munich Re (until 2007), Coca Cola (until the 1990s), Nestlé (until about 1980), Dow Chemical (until about 1988)

Source: Authors

Return versus risk

So, which strategy is best for my company? When answering this question, one should take into account not only specific reputational risks and opportunities, but also the general conditions that apply in society and the media in the twenty-first century. Reputational risks mostly arise from the attention patterns of the mass media[20] or, increasingly, from the logic governing publishing on online social networks. Both factors significantly determine recipients' perceptions and define what can constitute a reputational risk.

Settling on a reputation strategy involves weighing up the risk-return ratio in each case – in other words, the reputational opportunities and risks. This makes transparent the relationships governing the communicative production of reputation in our modern media society. In terms of practical consultancy, a method based on Markowitz (2007) provides a good basis for establishing a reputation management strategy. It enables one to determine a risk-return ratio for possible reputation management strategies. It also shows how greater returns can be achieved at low risk by diversifying the set of communications instruments used. We now look at some concrete examples to illustrate the process for determining the risk-return ratio.

Reputation is produced communicatively

Given the choice between placing an advertisement or featuring in a positive 'top story' about the company published by a major media outlet whose audience or readership matches the desired target group, management will mostly opt for the journalistic report. This is because they anticipate it will yield a higher reputational return. This very simple example illustrates the first factor in weighing up risk and return for a reputation strategy. Opting for paid, direct communication in the form of advertising usually gives you almost complete control over the message, the placement and timing. Relational communications, on the other hand (that is, communications mediated via third parties using unpaid channels) carries maximum risk: low control over the message, low control over placement, low control over timing. But if the result turns out well, the reputational return is exceptionally high.

---

[20] See Herkenhoff on pp. 197-213 in this volume.

This is due to a variety of reasons, some of which are in apparent conflict with each other:

1. A top story usually feeds on real corporate substance and positive experiences. In other words, it is not an advertising promise; rather, it confirms specific public expectations.

2. Risk can be further minimised by using professional media relations. This approach benefits from the substantially better credibility of independent media reporting over paid advertising.

3. One can achieve opinion leadership in a particular subject area even when public expectations are at odds with the material presented.

This example illustrates the most important rule of risk control: reputation is produced communicatively and is thus under permanent suspicion of being staged.[21]

Reputation management means management of expectations

Society's increasing awareness that reputation is constituted through communication produces risks. And this is especially key because twenty-first century markets are characterised by a high degree of media penetration into all social and economic relations. Active reputation management (in the sense of systematically minimising risk) therefore begins well before stakeholders begin to form their perceptions about a company or a person. It starts by objectively analysing the processes and developments in the company's environment that currently affect perceptions and expectations both within and outside the company. These are identified and prioritised (and possibly adjusted or discarded) in an issues mapping process. In this way, risks can be identified continuously and neutralised actively – that is to say, communicatively. Retail companies, for example, now need to continuously monitor the conditions under which their goods are produced in emerging nations – for example, to rule out the use of child labour.

Continuously attending to reputational risks is also important because increasingly, facts are refracted through the prism of the zeitgeist: business behaviour that just a few years ago would have been regarded as completely innocuous is suddenly considered morally reprehensible and worthy of scandal. Questions about environmental protection, diversity, equal-

---

[21] See Eisenegger on pp. 11-22 and Vonwil/Wreschniok, pp. 83-99 in this volume.

ity, the use of taxpayer funds or even executive remuneration (an issue now being ferociously debated worldwide) flare up and then subside.

This also impinges on corporate activities. It is for example a surprising but empirically proven fact: CSR-related communications often turns out to be counterproductive.[22] A series of empirical studies conducted since 1998 has shown, for example, that reputational perceptions about a company are determined as much as 80% by their economic performance.[23] Whether or not a company stands out in the area of corporate social responsibility is not irrelevant – but it has considerably less impact on its reputation. By contrast, corporate communications that is objective, reputable and reliable is often the best thing a company can do for its reputation.

One-to-many communication reaches its limits

Companies also should be careful about the way itself they do communication naturally every day. One-to-many communication, in which the sender addresses a number of target groups, has become a central feature of public communication in business, politics and society. However, although this form of 'one-way communication' clearly dominates the way the communication with a broad audience gets organised, it does not always contribute to effective reputation management. On the contrary, it can actually hinder it. Unidirectional forms of communication no longer measure up to the realities of communication in the twenty-first century, especially given the new communicative behaviours engaged in by many stakeholders (for example, online social media) and the resulting expectations of a company's communications policy[24].

This new communicative behaviour has lead, among other things, to increased market transparency and to faster cycles of scandal. While these are impossible to control, they can be counteracted with controlled preemption.[25] Examples include working through a company's historical role in the Third Reich or its co-operation with the former apartheid regime in South Africa.

---

[22] See Vonwil/Wreschniok on pp. 83-99 in this volume.
[23] See Eisenegger and Vonwil/Wreschniok in this volume.
[24] See Wreschniok on pp. 299-309 in this volume.
[25] ibidem.

The role of the CEO is changing

These forces have led to a re-evaluation of the role of the CEO in forming the reputation of a company. The media still vigorously participate in publicly and theatrically exalting CEOs to almost superhuman status, only to hail their later downfall with equal verve. Companies run the risk of falling into this 'personalisation trap'. Experience has clearly shown, both in the current economic crisis and after the collapse of the New Economy: "Too much CEO" means extreme risks for a company's reputation. The formula 'CEO capital equals reputation capital' no longer holds true.[26]

Control over messages becomes harder

The question of how to manage corporate messaging processes goes hand in hand with that of positioning the CEO. How do I deal with information that will be understood, interpreted and morally judged in completely different ways by different target groups?[27] Who should say what to whom, and when? The best example is communicating restructurings. Lay-offs might be good news to investors and push up stock prices, but at the same time destroy reputation capital among other stakeholder groups.

Perceptions are shifting from hard to soft business factors

But market conditions themselves have changed, too. The perceived importance of hard and soft business factors has shifted in favour of intangible assets.[28] This leads to a heightened reputational risk, one that has become especially glaring in the economic crisis. Listed companies are being 'reputationally devalued', with some of the stocks of global players trading at just half their actual book value. Also, increasingly fierce competition is itself leading to a deadlock. Today, there is not much difference in the hard factors relating to company operations or production. In any given sector, the number of companies that are able to deliver comparable products of good quality and at a reasonable price is increasing rapidly.

---

[26] The exception is the necessary deployment of the CEO in the hedge strategy (see this article above). See also Davies and Chun on pp. 311-323 in this volume.

[27] See Klewes on pp. 287-298 in this volume.

[28] See Schwaiger M, Raithel S, Schloderer M on pp. 39-55 in this volume.

And still, bad company should be avoid

Last but not least, any assessment of reputational risk should always include a company's closest circle of contacts. Or, as George Washington
succinctly put it: "Associate yourself with men of good quality if you esteem your own reputation, for 'tis better to be alone than in bad company"
(Washington 1985).

Table 2. Ten golden rules for reputation management in the twenty-first century

10 Golden rules for reputations management in the twenty-first century.

1. Be authentic: Reputation is always under suspicion of being staged.
   Playing it straight is the only way to ensure you don't get found out.

2. Keep the proportions right: Remember the 80:20 rule. Roughly 80%
   functional reputation to 20% social reputation is a good ratio. The right
   tool to boost reputation is not CSR activities, but reputable corporate
   communications.

3. Demonstrate depth: Concentrating exclusively on your image puts
   your reputation at risk. Superficial one-to-many communications is one
   reason for the crisis of confidence afflicting the 21st century.

4. Get the perspective right: Don't ask what the message should be.
   Instead, look for the structures that will shape public perception and
   determine the space in which your messages will appear.

5. Fulfill expectations: The only way to deal with rumours, criticism and
   moral outrage on the internet is controlled preemption –
   not containment.

6. Move with the zeitgeist: Know the agenda. It's always changing,
   so reputational risks always need to be reassessed.

7. Know which currency you're trading in: CEO capital is not the same as
   reputation capital. The personalisation trap inherent in the media
   system means: too much CEO harms reputation.

8. Be a chameleon: Stay true to yourself, but adapt to the expectations of
   your environment. The world has become much too complex to simply
   stick with the 'short and simple' principle in communications.

9. Keep intangible value in mind: A company's book value no longer
   provides much guidance. Watch for the gulf between reputational
   out-performance and reputational devaluation.

10. Avoid bad company: There is a high risk that their negative behaviour
    will rub off.

The ten rules in Table 2 should be followed when systematically measuring, weighing up and planning how to deal with reputational risks and potential returns as part of a reputational risk-return analysis. At the same time, they are the foundation for developing a reputation strategy that helps a company to reduce complexity and re-orient itself in nowadays unpredictable, complicated markets.

One man, one company, two sectors: The first reputation millionaires of the 21st century

Who is going to win the collective struggle for recognition in the twenty-first century? And which of the reputation strategies promises most success? The first ten years of the twenty-first century provide several different answers.

Take Barack Obama, 44th President of the United States. Many commentators have described his election campaign as the longest and most fiercely fought in American history. But it also represents one of the most efficient reputation-building processes of all time. Obama and his team clearly opted for a hedge strategy, focused the spotlight on one person and one issue – and won. In an incredibly short time, Obama managed to accumulate an incredible amount of reputation capital. On taking office, he was able to cash that in for large reserves of global trust. As described above, however, the main risk of a hedge strategy lies in sustaining and meeting the enormous expectations that must be built up.

German firm Siemens provides another impressive example of successfully acquiring fresh reputation capital. After a catastrophic run of reputation losses, Siemens finally managed under its own steam to overcome the biggest crisis of confidence in its history – thanks to a resolute value strategy. Siemens set its sights on changing the structures and behaviour within the company that had led to the crisis of confidence. First, there was a phase of inner cleansing, which more than anything involved the company's employees, and was accompanied by internal audits and programmes for renewing corporate culture and values. Only since mid-2008 has the company gradually shifted towards a growth strategy. The first cautious steps in this direction were taken with the "Siemens Answer Programme". Here, Siemens is actively positioning itself on pre-defined global megatrends such as demographic change, urbanisation and climate change, using its in-house expertise. It is able to answer pressing questions, link these issues to its own business model, and thus build up its opinion leadership.

The pharmaceutical industry has not come quite as far as Siemens, but it is well on the way. Even traditional proponents of the total return approach are now switching to value or growth strategies. There is every indication that the sector is now where the chemical industry was at the end of the 1980s. At that time, it was recognised that a fundamental rethink was required, especially in the matter of environmental protection, so that the industry could maintain its licence to operate in the face of an increasingly critical public. The substantial improvement in the chemical industry's reputation points to the determination with which this path was followed – and more importantly, can be followed.

Last of all, there is the finance sector, which is something of a problem child in these days. Will this sector ever earn reputation capital again? To be fair, one should note that the public's relationship to the finance sector was strained well before the current crisis broke out. In reputation measurements made by Pleon, the industry only managed to generate positive average reputation values in just on three out of the past ten years. In any case, the finance sector is due for a value phase aimed at consolidation – in other words, a period of self-reflection and re-orientation. Only after this is completed can one even begin to contemplate systematically expanding and developing issues of potential opportunity, as part of a growth strategy. The only danger is the prospect of a return to the autism of the total return strategy after this period of self-reflection. As explained above, the specific and new conditions of the twenty-first century mean this strategy promises more reputational risk than return.

References

Bourdieu P (1983) Ökonomisches Kapital – Kulturelles Kapital – Soziales Kapital. In: Kreckel, R (Ed.): Soziale Ungleichheiten, Göttingen, pp 183-198

Chan KW, Mauborgne R (2005) Blue Ocean Strategy: How to Create Uncontested Market Space and Make Competition Irrelevant. Harvard

Eisenegger M (2005) Reputation in der Mediengesellschaft – Konstitution, Issues Monitoring, Issues Management. VS Verlag für Sozialwissenschaften, Wiesbaden

Eisenegger M, Imhof K (2008) The True, The Good and the Beautiful: Reputation Management in the Media Society. In: Zerfass A, Ruler van B, Sriramesh K (eds.) Public Relations Research. European and International Perspectives and Innovations. VS Verlag für Sozialwissenschaften, Wiesbaden, pp 125-146

Jackson K (2004) Building Reputational Capital: Strategies for Integrity and Fair Play that Improve the Bottom Line. Oxford Univesity Press, New York

Markowitz HM (2007) Portfolio Selection – Die Grundlagen der optimalen Portfolio-Auswahl. FinanzBuch Verlag, München

Oetinger Bv (1993) Vom Wesen der Strategie. In: Das Boston Consulting Group Strategie Buch. Berlin

Schütz T, Schwaiger M (2007) Der Einfluss der Unternehmensreputation auf Entscheidungen privater Anleger. Kredit und Kapital, Vol 40 No 2 pp 189-223

Washington G (1985) George Washington's Rules of Civility & Decent Behavior in Company and Conversation. Carlisle

Part VI: Appendix

About the authors

Prof. Rosa Chun is Professor of Business Ethics and Corporate Social Responsibility at Manchester Business School, England. She has taught internationally at Rotterdam School of Management, Netherlands, Bocconi University, Italy, and Otaru University in Japan. Her work on corporate reputation and virtue ethics has appeared in the Harvard Business Review, Journal of the Academy of Marketing Science, Journal of Business Ethics, Corporate Reputation Review and International Journal of Management Reviews. She has held major research grants, and has consulting experience with Tesco, House of Fraser and Checkpoint Meto.

Jeremy Cohen is the founder and CEO of the We. Consulting Group, Soapbox TV, thebridge.com, and co-founder and President of Smart Girls LLC. Following more than 10 years in senior corporate brand and communications roles in companies including Shell and Philips, he is a respected thinker and trend watcher in the areas of new media, the environment and technology.

Prof. Dr. Hans Caspar von der Crone is a Professor of Private, Commercial and Corporate Law at the University of Zurich (Ordinarius). He is senior partner with von der Crone Rechtsanwälte in Zurich; his legal practice focuses on corporate and commercial law as well as capital market and securities law. His work includes counselling and litigation for clients, as well as international arbitration. Academic publications of Hans Caspar von der Crone focus on commercial and corporate law, with a main focus on issues regarding listed companies.

Prof. Gary Davies is Professor of Corporate Reputation at Manchester Business School where he heads the Reputation, Brand and Competitiveness Research Group. He has published in the leading marketing and advertising trade press and authored 13 books and over 200 articles in the academic and business press. At MBS he teaches strategy, reputation and competitiveness, crisis management, corporate communication and reputation management. He works as a freelance consultant in market strategy and reputation, most recently for the British police, the city of Moscow and mail order company JD Williams.

Dr. Mark Eisenegger is co-head of the Research Institute for the Public Sphere and Society (fög) of the University of Zurich, associate lecturer at the Universities of Zurich, Lugano, and Fribourg and member of the ECRS Board. Dr. Mark Eisenegger has specialised in organisational and corporate communication as well as reputation research and media transformation.

Andrea Fischer was the former German Federal Health Minister from 1998 to 2001 and a member of parliament from 1994 to 2002. Before entering politics she was research assistant at the Science Centre in Berlin and at the German Federal Pension Fund, holding a masters degree in economics. She has consulting experience in public affairs on a national and international level, strategic planning, and campaigning for companies in the healthcare field like pharmaceuticals, medical devices, hospitals, sickness funds. Throughout her career she has published in a variety of papers.

Tomaso Galli has a degree in political sciences from Genoa University, he lives in London and advises global brands on a vast array of brand management issues. From 2005 to 2009, Galli was Director of Communications and External Relations for the PRADA Group, overseeing all aspects of corporate and brand communications for all the Group's brands. From 1999 to 2004 he was in charge of Corporate Communications at the Gucci Group and prior to this he worked 9 years for Ketchum in London and Milan. Tomaso started his career at PR agency Barabino & Partners in Genoa, Italy, in 1984.

Prof. Dr. Sophie Gaultier-Gaillard is Associate Professor at Paris 1 Panthéon-Sorbonne University and Director of the professional master's degree in Global Risk & Crisis Management.

Dr. Frank Herkenhoff is heading the Media Relations department at Deutsche Börse AG. Previously he was a consultant at Pleon focussing on the financial business sector. He is also a lecturer at Leipzig University in the field of public relations. Herkenhoff holds a Masters and a PhD degree in mass communication.

Alex Hindson is head of group risk at Amlin. Before this, he led the Enterprise Risk Management (ERM) practice of Aon Global Risk Consulting, providing consulting services to a wide range of corporate clients across Europe. He has extensive practical experience of implementing ERM within large corporates in a variety of sectors and geographies. Prior to this, Alex worked in the chemical and pharmaceutical industry for 17 years, initially for ICI and AstraZeneca. Originally a chemical engineer,

Alex led the implementation of ERM and business continuity. He is a director and fellow of the Institute of Risk Management.

Prof. Dr. Joachim Klewes is Senior Partner of Pleon and co-founder of the public relations consulting firm Kohtes Klewes. His expertise of more than 25 years includes major assignments in the fields of organisational consulting, corporate change and crisis as well as corporate communications. Outside of Pleon, he has held managerial positions on a national and international level. He is an associate professor at the Freie Universität Berlin, founding partner of the opinion research institute com.X and a frequent writer, publisher and speaker.

Joachim Kuss born 1970 in Dresden, has been with Pleon since 2000 especially engaged in change and transformation communications. His focus is on technology companies and public sector clients. Prior to Pleon, he worked as conceptioner in an advertising agency and an online editor for a German broadcasting network. He holds a university degree in theology and a diploma in marketing communications.

Peter Lochbihler has been active in EU public affairs since 2001. Through his work he has been a close and enthusiastic observer of the European Union. As general manager of Pleon Brussels, Peter supervises international accounts and develops and implements public affairs strategies for clients from various business sectors. Leading the European public affairs practice, the coordination of pan-European campaigns is another feature of his work. Peter did European Studies in Osnabrück, London and Paris and at the College of Europe in Bruges.

Prof. Jean-Paul Louisot, MBA, ARM is a Professor of Risk Management at Paris 1 Panthéon-Sorbonne University, Dean of Curriculum at the CARM Institute and Senior Director of Knowledge Resources, Insurance Institute of America.

Dirk Popp is Managing Partner at Pleon Gemany and European Practice Leader for Crisis Management. He has been working in the field of communications for more than 15 years. Before joining Pleon in 1996 he was working for a PR agency completing a traineeship with a focus on journalism. He is mainly engaged in crisis and change communication on a national and international level. In this context he develops strategies for internal and external communications, advises top executives and acts as interim spokesperson if required. Dirk Popp has a teaching assignment at the Technische Universität Dresden's department of communication science and is also author of a large number of publications.

Jonathan Silberstein-Loeb is a research fellow at the Oxford University Centre for Corporate Reputation. He received his PhD from the University of Cambridge.

Jenny Rayner is Director of Abbey Consulting in the UK which provides training and consultancy services in risk management, corporate governance and internal audit. Jenny is the author of Managing Reputational Risk: curbing threats, leveraging opportunities, published by John Wiley in 2003.

Sascha Raithel is a graduate research assistant and Ph.D. student at the Institute for Market-based Management (IMM) at the Ludwig-Maximilians-University of Munich (LMU). His scientific work is focused on the subjects of corporate reputation and marketing performance measurement. Since 2004 he is working as analytics consultant for an international marketing and communications agency on numerous projects.

Dr. Jens Rupp is Sustainability Manager at Coca-Cola Hellenic Bottling Company SA. He has been with Coca-Cola Hellenic since 2001. Jens Rupp started as a local environment manager, led the first bottling operations to ISO14001 certification and produced the first environmental report. He has been corporate Sustainability Manager since 2005, coordinating environmental activities in 28 countries. He is a member of the company's Corporate Social Responsibility council and manages CSR reporting and stakeholder relations. Previously, Jens worked with an energy consultancy, where he pioneered energy saving and energy awareness programmes for state and national governments. Jens holds a doctorate in ecology from the University of Oxford and a European Master in Environmental Engineering and Management from the Swiss Polytechnic School.

Julia Schankin has been with Pleon since 2007 and is specialised in reputation management and crisis communications. She is also in charge of external relations at the European Centre for Reputation Studies, and specialising in country reputation management. Julia holds an MA in communication studies and spent several years abroad in Paris and Brighton. Throughout her studies she was sponsored by a grant from the Studienstiftung des Deutschen Volkes.

Matthias Schloderer is teaching and research assistant at IMM. He studied business administration with focus on empirical research and corporate planning, marketing, and market psychology at Munich School of Management. His research focus at the IMM is corporate reputation and structural equation modelling (SEM) techniques (PLS) as well as psychological aspects of marketing.

Prof. Dr. Manfred Schwaiger is full professor of business administration at the Ludwig-Maximilians-Universität of Munich (LMU), head of the Institute of Market-Based Management (IMM) at LMU and member of the ECRS Board. Besides his scientific work, Professor Schwaiger has carried out numerous consulting projects for large German companies (on the subject of corporate reputation, customer retention, employee motivation, corporate communications, and market strategy).

Dr. Reimer Stobbe has been head of the work group for communications controlling at the International Controller Association since 2006. From 2004 until May 2008, he was responsible for planning and controlling in Corporate Communications at Münchner Rückversicherung. Subsequently, he began work at the Marketing Department of the Munich Re Group's Communications. Between 1999 and 2004, he participated in building and developing the communications infrastructure at Munich Re and held different leadership positions in internal and marketing communications. From 1996, he was head of corporate communications at the Sparkasse Wetterau.

Ansgar Thießen is currently working as a research assistant at the institute of media and communication science at Fribourg University, Switzerland. During his research projects he specialized in crisis communication and corporate reputation management and was also member of the international network crisis communication at Ilmenau University, Germany. His practical experiences come from strategic communication consulting (corporate and crisis communication) as well as business consulting.

Kelvin Thompson is founder and Managing Partner of Rosemont Executive Search and MontaRosa. Previously he was Global Head of Private Equity & Alternative Financing at Heidrick & Struggles. His clients include Fortune 500 companies, investment banks, hedge funds and private equity firms, consumer and technology clients. His experience spans Europe, Asia and the United States. Earlier, he was at Norman Broadbent International as President of US operations and Chairman of Global New Media, Entertainment & Technology. Kelvin is a regular speaker and panel leader at international conferences and has written numerous papers and articles.

Lic. Phil. Matthias Vonwil was born 1974 and studied sociology, business administration and political science at the University of Zurich. Since 2009 he has been head of the qualitative market research at GfK Switzerland and responsible for the GfK BusinessReflector. He has published various articles on reputation, media coverage of economic organisations and organisational communication. Contact: matthias.vonwil@gfk.com

MLaw Johannes Vetsch studied law at the University of Fribourg, Switzerland. He is Research Assistant to Prof. von der Crone at the University of Zurich.

Robert Wreschniok is a senior consultant at Pleon and is responsible for reputation management and stakeholder dialogue. After completing his MA in International Relations he received a certification for Strategic Foundation Management from the University of Basel. He is a board member of the European Centre for Reputation Studies and spokesman for the Private Institute of Foundation Law.

Arzuhan Doğan Yalçındağ is the acting head of the Turkish Industrialists' and Businessmen's Association (TUSIAD). She began her professional career in 1990 at MILPA, Co., where she established and managed the mail order company with the German Quelle Company. Between 1993 and 1995 she worked on the establishment of Alternatif Bank, where she later served as a Board Member. From 1995 to 1996 she was appointed to the management team of Milliyet Magazine Group. In 1999 Mrs. Yalcindag initiated a project between CNN International and Dogan Broadcasting Holding, together with Time Warner partnership, resulted in the news channel CNN TURK. She is currently CEO of Dogan Broadcasting.

Index

Breinigsville, PA USA
20 April 2010
236475BV00003B/20/P